THE HANDBOOK OF
CAPITAL INVESTING

THE HANDBOOK OF CAPITAL INVESTING

Analyses and Strategies for Investment in Capital Assets

Anthony F. Herbst
University of Texas at El Paso

HarperBusiness
A Division of HarperCollins*Publishers*

International Standard Book Number: 0-88730-449-4

Library of Congress Catalog Card Number: 90-4569

Printed in the United States of America

Library of Congress Cataloging-in-Publication Data
Herbst, Anthony F., 1941–
    The handbook of capital investing : analyses & strategies for
investment in capital assets / Anthony F. Herbst.
        p.   cm.
    Includes bibliographical references and index.
    ISBN 0-88730-449-4
    1. Capital investments.   I. Title.
HG4028.C4H453   1990   90-4569
658.15'2—dc20   CIP

90 91 92 93 CC/HC 9 8 7 6 5 4 3 2 1

Contents

Preface

The aim of this book is to tie together the theory, quantitative methods, and applications of capital budgeting. Consequently, its coverage omits few, if any, topics important to capital investment. My intention is to effect a harmonious blend of the old, such as the MAPI method of capital investment appraisal, with the new, such as the Capital Asset Pricing Model (CAPM). I have tried to provide a balanced treatment of the different approaches to capital project evaluation and have explored both the strengths and weaknesses of various project selection methods.

A work on this subject necessarily uses mathematics, but the level of mathematical sophistication required here is generally not above basic algebra. Although I have favored clarity and readability over mathematical pyrotechnics, the book's level of mathematical rigor should be sufficiently high to satisfy most users.

The book's treatment of risk is deliberately deferred to later chapters. The decision to do this, rather than treating risk earlier, was based on my belief that readers new to the subject are less overwhelmed by the added complexities of risk considerations—and better able to comprehend them—after they have become thoroughly familiar with capital budgeting in an environment assumed to be risk-free.

In Chapter 21 I try to present a balanced treatment of the CAPM, including some of the important criticisms of its use in capital budgeting. I know that some readers might prefer an earlier introduction of the CAPM, as well as its subsequent use as a unifying theme. I chose not to employ that structure for three reasons.

First, although the CAPM may be adaptable to capital budgeting decisions involving major projects (e.g., the acquisition of a new company division), serious questions exist concerning its applicability to more typical projects for which estimation of expected returns alone is difficult, to say nothing of also estimating the project's beta. Second, company managers increasingly appear to be placing primary emphasis on the survival of the firm rather than on consideration of systematic risk in their capital investment decisions, thereby diluting the implications of the CAPM. In other words, top management does indeed care about unsystematic (or company) risk, to which portfolio diversification may, in some cases, give little importance. To the management of a company, such risk may not always be reduced easily, and, if neglected, may imperil the company.

Third, the CAPM is concerned with risk. For the reasons stated earlier, I felt that the book would better serve its audience if it examined capital investment under assumed uncertainty first, without the added complexities that a simultaneous treatment of risk would entail.

For those who may wish to obtain them I have developed a computer program and spreadsheet templates for several applications illustrated in the book. Also, for those who might want to use the book for instructional purposes, I have end-of-chapter questions and problems and a solutions manual. All of these are available, at extra cost, directly from me. Please write for further information.

I again want to thank those reviewers and others who helped to improve the book through their constructive criticism and suggestions. The list includes Don Panton, James B. Henry, G. David Quirin, J. Daniel Williams, Ron Rizzuto, Wayne Perg, Phil Horvath, Doyle Kupper, and James B. Weaver. For any remaining errors or omissions I alone must bear responsibility. I would appreciate hearing from users of the book concerning suggestions for improvement.

Finally, I want to thank once more my wife, Betty, who typed the original manuscript at least three times and took care of details relating to correspondence and permissions.

A. F. H.

Department of Economics & Finance/CBA
The University of Texas at El Paso
El Paso, Texas 79968-0543

THE HANDBOOK OF
CAPITAL INVESTING

I

The Basic Framework

1

Introduction

Once we consciously think about the nature of capital investment decisions, we realize that such decisions have been made for
millenia, since humans first awakened to the idea that capital[1]
accumulation could improve life. The earliest investment decisions involved what today would be considered very primitive.
But to the early nomadic hunter-forager the first capital investment decisions were quite significant. To the extent that time and
energy had to be diverted from the immediate quest for food and
for security from enemies, to the production of tools for the hunt
and to defense installations, food storage facilities, and so on,
capital investments were made. Such primitive capital creation
required time and effort. And the benefits that could have been
expected to result were uncertain; it took foresight to build capital.

As society evolved, the benefits of capital accumulation gradually became more indirect and complex, involving specialization
and cooperation not previously envisioned, and the associated
commitment of resources more permanent. Additionally, social
norms and institutions had to be developed to facilitate the evolution. For example, the changeover from nomadic to agrarian life
required a great increase in capital: in the form of land clearing,
construction of granaries, mills, irrigation canals, tools, and fortifications. The fortifications were a necessary adjunct to deter
those who would, by force, seize the benefits achieved. The
changeover required a commitment that, at least in the short run,
tended to be irreversible. And it became more and more irreversible, for the change caused social and economic institutions to be

[1]The word *capital* is used in several senses. It may refer to physical plant and equipment
(economic capital) or to the ownership claims on the tangible capital (financial capital).
In this book, unless otherwise indicated in a specific instance, the word shall refer to
physical or economic capital.

3

developed to support it and coordinate the various requisite activities.[2]

MAGNITUDE OF CAPITAL INVESTMENT

In the United States in 1989, business capital expenditure on new plant and equipment amounted to $472.08 billion out of a gross national product (GNP) of $5,203.8 billion, using annualized data for the second quarter of 1989. This meant that 9.1 percent of measured national economic activity was used for business capital investment. If government expenditure on capital goods (plant and equipment) was reported separately from total government expenditure on goods and services, the total of business and government capital expenditure would exceed 10 percent of GNP. Inclusion of expenditures on owner-occupied dwellings would raise the total still higher.[3] Figure 1-1 displays the trend in business investment since 1979, in contrast to government spending over the same period. Figure 1-2 illustrates business spending on plant and equipment alongside corporate profits and taxes. It is readily apparent that capital investment is an important component of economic activity, both absolutely and relatively.

GENERAL PERSPECTIVE ON CAPITAL INVESTMENT

Because resources are scarce (as economists have long maintained) and because capital investment figures prominently in the economy, decisions on capital budgets ought to be made on as sound and rational a basis as possible. The general irreversibility of capital investments, and their legacy for future costs as well as benefits, make such decisions of great importance both from the standpoint of the individual firm and at the level of national policy.

Economic theory recognizes that for any given level of technology, the factors of production (land, labor, and capital) *together* in

---

[2]C. Northcote Parkinson writes of such differences between agricultural and nomadic societies in his book *East and West* (New York: New American Library, 1963).

[3]"Gross private domestic investment" as a percentage of GNP in the United States was slightly above 16 percent for 1979. In the second quarter of 1989 it was at an annual rate of 12.98 percent.

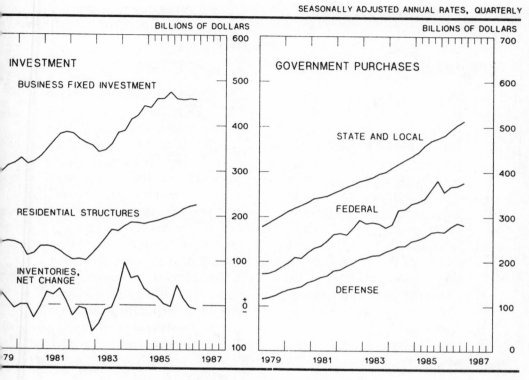

Figure 1-1. Selected Components of GNP

combination are required to produce goods and services. Production of any good or service, then, is a function of combined
factors, with the function corresponding to the state of known
technology.

At the national policy level the dual goals of high employment
(low unemployment) and increasing standard of living are normally accorded primary importance. These goals require that for
given levels of technology the stock of capital increases apace
with growth in the labor supply or, if technological growth is
toward the more capital-intensive side, to exceed it. As long as
the goals are the same, this will hold for every type of government because political philosophy cannot change the feasible mix
of land, labor, and capital for a given technology.

Few in business and industry would dispute the view that the
press and media generally tend to emphasize labor's employment
problems while generally ignoring the problems of underemploy-

SEASONALLY ADJUSTED ANNUAL RATES, QUARTERLY

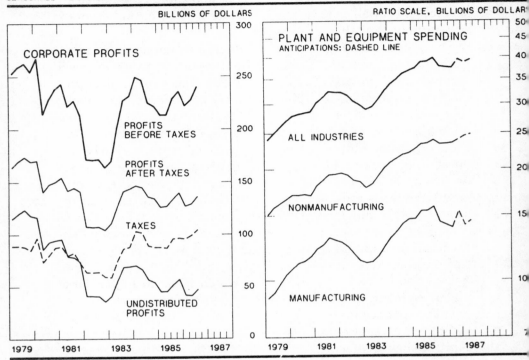

Figure 1-2.   Corporate Profits; Plant and Equipment Spending

ment of capital, reduced or negative capital accumulation, and return on investment. Such imbalanced editorial policy, however, is understandable to the extent it exists because much of the public identifies their interests with labor rather than with capital. However, it reinforces popular notions that, although not clearly incorrect, are at least suspect and thus tend to contribute further to problems faced by labor and capital alike. The notion that the interests of labor and capital are mutually exclusive may be useful to left-wing rhetoricians, but it fails to address the problems of underemployment and sagging productivity in societies in which labor and capital are undichotomized. In the industrial nations of North America, Europe, and Asia, for example, it is common for workers to own shares in their own employer or other corporations either directly or through their pension fund. Worker representation on corporate boards has been accepted in some European nations for many years and the practice seems to be growing. Thus the interests of labor and capital are not easily separable, if at all, because so many are neither entirely worker nor entirely capitalist.

The proper mix of factors of production is necessary to minimize unemployment of labor without resorting to government "make work" projects. But it depends on wages that reflect productivity and value product. Adoption of government policies that ignore capital in order to aim at direct treatment of labor unemployment, or low minimum wages, is bound to failure in a broader sense. Still, we see such policies being publicly advocated, whereas capital investment necessary to create a real expansion in jobs is ignored. Return on capital investment in the United States is today generally less than can be earned on the same funds if put into government bonds, after taking capital consumption into account. This has the effect of dampening enthusiasm for capital investment and consequently moving funds to nonproductive uses. Since capital must complement labor, fewer productive jobs are created, which leads to higher labor unemployment, more public policies to treat the symptoms, and still more disincentive to capital investment. In fact, recent studies at the University of Chicago indicate that in the United States, capital is being consumed at a faster rate than it is being created; industry is paying liquidating dividends. This has serious implications for the economic policies of government.

Concern that capital will replace labor may be legitimate in the short run, if myopic. If the relative costs of labor and capital should favor a capital-intensive production mix of factors, this should present no problem provided the distribution of benefits is equitable. In other words, replacement of some labor by capital may increase the quality of life for labor provided that the benefits are shared by labor. The laying-off of some workers while others are put on extended overtime or continue to work a normal 40-hour week does not further equitable distribution. But a reduction in the standard work week to fewer than 40 hours may. If it were not for capital accumulation and improved technology yielding increased productivity, workers would not have a 40-hour standard week but one of 60 hours or so, as was once the standard not so many decades ago.[4]

---

[4]Determination of what is equitable and what is not is a matter that must be decided outside the scope of this book.

Most of the developing nations are capital poor, but have abundant labor that is not highly skilled or educated. For them it makes sense to adopt labor-intensive methods of production, gradually shifting to capital-intensive technologies as their capital stock is increased and the quality of labor increases. In the developed, relatively capital rich nations it is not sensible to adopt labor-intensive methods of production, for this wastes productive capacity. It is very ironical that although developing nations strive to accumulate capital, developed nations often follow policies that discourage capital growth and may cause the capital stock to shrink relatively if not absolutely. One may well wonder if it would not be more honest and efficient simply to donate capital to the developing nations to raise their capital intensity while lowering that of the donor nation.

Capital investment decisions have repercussions that may extend far beyond the immediate time frame, because they involve long-term commitments that are not readily undone. The decision *not* to invest is a capital investment decision also. And future repercussions may be compounded by the often very long planning periods for capital goods and the fact that it takes capital and labor together to produce more capital goods. The "production process" to create "human capital"—skilled labor—is a lengthy one, and the more sophisticated the capital goods to be produced generally the higher the quality of human capital required.

CAPITAL BUDGETING

In the private sector, capital investment and the analysis surrounding it are generally referred to as *capital budgeting.* Capital budgeting focuses on alternative measures of project acceptability. Tangible factors are emphasized, although, to the extent that their effects can be weighed, intangibles must be considered. Capital investment in the private sector has perhaps tended to pay less attention to intangibles than its public sector counterpart, *cost-benefit analysis.* This may well be due to the inherently more qualitative nature of social and political goals and constraints.

In private enterprise, profitability provides the principal criterion for the acceptability of particular prospective investment projects through its effect on the market value of the enterprise. Capital budgeting centers on an objective function that the management seeks to maximize, subject to various constraints. Often the primary constraint is imposed by the funds available for investment. When this constraint is binding, it is referred to as *capital rationing.* In the public sector, a reasonable alternative is provided by minimizing a cost function, constrained by specifying minimum levels of services to be provided. The aggregate effect of private and public support for capital investment is to raise a nation's standard of living, both in tangible benefits and in terms of intangible benefits such as greater security and less social stress. To the extent that the benefits accrue to a few rather than to the many, it is the social and political institutions that are responsible.[5]

Emphasis throughout this book is on private sector capital budgeting. Yet, some of the methods covered are applicable without modification to public sector investment, and others are applicable with modification.

The following sections set forth some principles that will be used throughout the remainder of the book.

CASH FLOWS

Emphasis will be on *net, after-tax cash flows. Pretax net cash flow* is defined as total cash inflow associated with the capital investment less its net cash outflow. After removing the portion that will be paid out for income taxes, at the enterprise's marginal rate, we are left with net, after-tax cash flow for the time period over which we have measured or estimated the flows. Cash flows will be estimated for *each* division of a capital investment's life, although some may well be zero. Normally the divisions will be annual, but they can be quarterly, semiannual, or for some other time period if desired. The major focus in this book will be on what is to be done with the cash flow estimates once they are obtained, rather than on how to make cash flow estimates, although Chapter 3 does address the subject.

Cash flow estimates in practice will normally be as much, or more, the result of experienced judgment by persons in such diverse functional areas as production engineering, marketing,

[5]For a lucid presentation of a rationale for aggressive national policy encouraging capital formation, see E. A. G. Robinson, *The Structure of Competitive Industry* (Chicago: University of Chicago Press, 1958).

and accounting than the result of objective measurement. We can estimate future results a priori, but measure them only after they occur. The management charged with responsibility for capital budgeting must insure that adequately accurate estimates are obtained and, where possible, objective forecasts used. It may be necessary to stress to those participating in the process through which estimates are obtained that it is cash flows that are sought, not accrued profits or cost savings. It is cash that may be used to pay dividends, employee wages, and vendor bills and it is cash that may be invested in new plant and equipment.

It is vitally important that all relevant cash flows attributable to a capital project be included. An early survey suggested that many firms, even some fairly large ones, failed to include all associated cash flows in their analysis. Today we may expect that fewer firms would be making the errors found in this survey. However, such omissions as do occur can seriously bias the measures of project acceptability and destroy the usefulness of whatever technique is employed.

COST OF CAPITAL

The organization's cost of capital, expressed as a decimal or percentage, is used in two basic ways in capital budgeting: as a minimum profitability rate that prospective project returns are required to exceed and as a discount rate applied to cash flows.

The literature dealing with cost of capital is voluminous; yet the concept and the measurement of cost of capital are still unsettled. For our purposes cost of capital will be assumed to be independently derived, along the lines suggested in Chapters 4 and 21, except where it is explicitly stated otherwise. The reader is referred to those chapters for works dealing in depth with this topic. The importance of cost of capital should not be minimized: An adequate estimate is *crucial* to proper application of capital-budgeting techniques, because all but the crudest techniques incorporate it in one way or another.

In the author's experience the importance of obtaining good estimates of the firm's cost of capital is often overlooked. The result is that capital budgeting may, in practice, become somewhat a burlesque: sophisticated techniques yielding accept/reject decisions based on crude and incorrect data. One of the largest firms in the United States in the 1970s was using 8 percent as its overall, marginal cost of capital. At the time, by generally accepted measure, the firm had a cost of capital above 10 percent. In capital investment methods that employ discounted cash flows, and these methods are all conceptually better, this was a serious error. Paradoxically, the same firm went to considerable effort to obtain finely detailed project cash flow data from its marketing, engineering, production, and accounting staffs at the same time. As a result, projects were undoubtedly undertaken that, had an adequate cost of capital been used, would have been rejected. The stock market performance of this firm during the 1970s, vis-à-vis comparable firms in its industry, tends to support this view.

RISK AND UNCERTAINTY

For better or worse we live in a world of probabilities, with little more than the proverbial death and taxes certain. In general, capital-budgeting projects are no exception, although some specific classes of capital investment, such as in leasing, may approach certainty sufficiently to be treated as if they were risk free.

Risk

Risk is usually defined to prevail in situations in which, although exact outcomes cannot be known in advance, the probability distributions governing the outcomes are either known or may be satisfactorily estimated. In a risky environment, probabilities may be associated with the various results that may occur. Life insurance companies, for example, can predict within close tolerance how many policyholders in any age grouping will survive to age 65, even though they cannot predict accurately which individuals within the group will reach that age. Those poker players who are successful in the sense of being net winners over the long run understand risk. Winning card combinations have associated probabilities, and successful players must take these into account, at least intuitively, to win on balance. In gambling games probabilities can generally be determined with precision, whether the players know the odds explicitly or through a sense gained by experience in playing.

In games of chance the thrill of risk-bearing itself may be more important than the prospect of gain. And in capital investment the taking on of risk for the sake of doing so may hold appeal to some individuals in management. However, if management is to serve the interests of the organization's owners and creditors, it must manage risk, not be managed by it. Managers may undertake risky investments (later we show that this can be actually beneficial to the enterprise), but they must strive to commit funds to investments that in the aggregate promise a greater probability of gain than loss. This is not to say that individual projects offering a small probability of great gain in return for a great probability of small loss must never be undertaken. For example, often such probabilities can be altered by managerial action. Such projects, however, will constitute a relatively small proportion of the firm's total capital budget. Managers could do worse than be guided by the Machiavellianlike principle that a single loss on a clearly high risk project may do more harm to their reputation than a string of gains on other projects. When portfolio effects are taken into account, this is an unhappy state of affairs, but one those making capital investment decisions must be aware of.

Later we treat in detail the topic of portfolio risk—risk of the total of the enterprise's investments. Although it is both informative and a necessary beginning to examine individual investment projects by themselves, it is important to recognize such interrelationships of investments as may exist and to analyze the effect on the total enterprise that acceptance of any particular project would likely cause.

Uncertainty

The generally accepted distinction in the literature between risk and uncertainty is that in the case of uncertainty we know the possible outcomes are random variables, *but* we do not know the probability distribution that governs the outcomes, or its parameters, and cannot estimate them a priori. Because capital-budgeting decisions are one of a kind, there is insufficient prior experience with similar situations for indicating the probabilities associated with the possible outcomes. Because they are unique, such capital investments are not amenable to Bayesian revision; they will not be repeated. In the more extreme cases even the entire range of outcomes that could reasonably be expected to occur may be unknown.

In the following chapters we shall first consider project analysis in a certainty environment for all project parameters. This has the advantage of allowing us to concentrate on basic principles and gain a firm understanding of them before complicating matters. Later the assumption of certainty is relaxed in order to deal with risk in individual projects and risk relationships between capital investment projects and the enterprise. Uncertainty considerations will be mentioned where appropriate as a complicating factor requiring attention and planning for unforeseen contingencies.

2

Objective of Capital Budgeting

Unless one restricts attention to the very general social goal of accumulating capital in order to increase national welfare, it is difficult to define only *one* objective for capital budgeting to achieve. The classical economics assumption of profit-maximizing entrepreneurs may not be considered appropriate for government or nonprofit, private institutions. Furthermore, that assumption is not operationally feasible, and doubts have been expressed as to whether it represents the true motivation of managers in either private enterprise or in government.

Alternatives to the classical assumption of profit maximizing behavior have been proposed. Among these, the more prominent include the concepts of "satisficing" and organizational decision-making. Satisficing owes much of its development to Herbert Simon, who observed that "Administrative theory is peculiarly the theory of intended and bounded rationality—of the behavior of human beings who *satisfice* because they have not the wits to *maximize.*"[1] This view is supported by the observation that managers make decisions without the complete information classical economic theory assumes they possess. Managers may intuitively take into account the classical concepts of rationality, including marginal analysis and game theory. However, there is no evidence to support the notion that managers attempt to perform the complex calculations demanded by classical economic theory in other than rare individual instances. Even if they wished to do so, managers usually do not have the detailed and exhaustive data that classical theory would require.

Other, behaviorally oriented theories of management decision-making have been developed, including those of Cyert and

[1]Herbert A. Simon, *Administrative Behavior*, 2nd ed. (New York: Macmillan, 1957), p. xxiv.

March,[2] which expand and supplement the satisficing concept, and Galbraith,[3] who views managements of large, widely held corporations as serving their own interests above those of the owners, and in some cases above those of the nation. Because of the diversity of human behavior and the evolution of attitudes and institutions, it is likely that additional behavioral theories will be developed that attempt to elaborate or offer alternatives to those proposed to date.

The behavioral theories, although realistically portraying management in human rather than mechanistic terms by incorporating a wider spectrum of behavioral assumptions than profit maximization, have contributed to better understanding of organizations. Like the classical model of profit maximization, however, they are not operational. Although profit maximization provides a normative model of management behavior, the behavioral models are descriptive. They describe what management *does* rather than what management *should* do or, more specifically, they fail to specify what objective criteria that management should use in reaching decisions that best serve those who employ them. Also, although profit maximization provides a nomothetic model, the behavioral models to date are ideographic, or nonuniversal.

Our intent is to develop capital budgeting as much as possible within a normative framework. Therefore, we shall leave the behavioral models at this point and proceed to define a normative model that can be operationalized. The model that is adopted can be applied to both private and public enterprise.

A NORMATIVE MODEL FOR CAPITAL BUDGETING

A serious deficiency of the classical economics principle of profit maximization, which prevents its adoption as operating policy, is that it does not indicate whether long-run or short-run profits are to be maximized. A firm's management, for example, might maximize short-run profits by formulating a policy that would simultaneously alienate customers, employees, and creditors over a period of a few months. It might attempt charging the highest

---

[2]Richard M. Cyert and James G. March, *A Behavioral Theory of the Firm* (Englewood Cliffs, N.J.: Prentice-Hall, 1963).

[3]John K. Galbraith, *The New Industrial State* (Boston: Houghton Mifflin, 1967).

prices the market will bear while lowering quality, paying minimum wages, letting the firm's financial structure, plant, and equipment deteriorate, and so on. Such behavior would surely injure the firm's chances to survive beyond the short run. Once owners of a firm have decided to liquidate it, they might adopt such an irresponsible mode of operation, but they could not thus operate and expect the firm to survive for long.

A less extreme manifestation of short-run profit syndrome is not uncommon. It has taken root in firms that neglect proper maintenance of plant and equipment and steadfastly refuse to abandon worn or technologically obsolete equipment until a new replacement can "pay for itself" in one or two years. This thinking blossoms into the specious yet appealing notion that plant and equipment, although seriously worn and obsolete, should not be abandoned because they have been "paid for" years ago. In other words, such assets are considered "free" resources to the firm because they were fully depreciated in the past. In truth, the firm pays increasingly more in high scrap rates, in higher than necessary labor content, and in machine repair and tooling costs as time goes on. The assets were paid for when acquired, *not* when depreciated. Depreciation merely enabled the firm to recover the cost of the investments through tax remission over the years of their useful or economic lives.

The opposite of this obsession with short-run profits is preoccupation with the prospect of profits in the long-run future. This, in the extreme, is a much less common pathological condition than short-run profit obsession. Probably this is, at least in part, due to the fact that firms that seriously neglect short-run profits cannot survive for long. A firm may be able to neglect long-run profits and yet survive as an economic cripple; a firm that neglects short-run profits is likely to be an early fatality.

A tendency toward overly great emphasis on long-term profits may be observed in firms that, although showing poor current performance, spend lavishly on public relations, landscaping and lawn care around factory and office facilities, excessive employee benefits, research and development, and so on. The key word here is "lavishly." All firms are expected to spend reasonable amounts on such indirectly beneficial things that make the world more pleasant and that may not be strictly defensible in terms of expected tangible benefits. It is ultimately for the owners and creditors of the enterprise to determine what is reasonable, although in reality management may to a considerable extent be protected by the shield of ignorance surrounding the enterprise's operations. It is uncommonly difficult for ordinary stockholders to obtain the detailed information necessary to challenge successfully the mishandling and largess by management.

It would appear that management is caught between the horns of a dilemma. Short- and long-run profit maximizations seem to be contradictory. Is there any way to resolve the conflict, the ambiguity? Yes, there is, if we recognize that money, our economic *numeraire*, has time-value.

BASIC VALUATION MODEL

The model of managerial behavior we adopt is that of modern financial management, which is not part of classical economics although it might be considered a direct descendant:

$$\text{Maximize Wealth, or Value, } V = \sum_{t=0}^{\infty} \frac{R_t}{(1 + k)^t} \qquad (2.1)$$

subject to governmental, economic, and managerial constraints. The terms of this basic valuation model are:

t is Time Index
R_t is Net Cash Flow in Period t
k is The Enterprise Cost of Capital

This model resolves the ambiguity over whether it is long- or short-run profits that should be maximized. It is the *total discounted value* of all cash flows that is to be maximized. The theoretical *value of the enterprise is defined in terms of its profitability over time.* One may, of course, adopt the continuous analog of this discrete-time model, although traditionally this has not been common or especially useful.

The nature of this model is such that its maximization may be powerfully facilitated by an effective financial management that can raise adequate funds at minimum cost. This becomes clear if one considers that denominator terms containing k are raised to progressively higher powers. And it underscores the need for good estimates of the enterprise cost of capital.

Contemporary literature recognizes that there is interaction between the cost of capital k and the risk characteristics of the cash flow stream R_t over time. In other words, if the firm undergoes changes that alter the variability of its overall cash flows over time, this will have an effect on its cost of capital. The theory behind this notion has not yet become operational, and, although we shall deal with it in Chapter 21, for now it will suffice to adopt the principle that the cost of capital will not be increased if the enterprise invests its funds in capital projects of similar risk to the existing assets of the firm. If projects are accepted that are *less* risky than the existing asset base of the firm, a tendency will be for the cost of capital to decrease. This principle will be useful for a certain time; however, it ignores portfolio effects that imply that certain investments that are *more* risky than the existing asset base may actually serve to reduce the enterprise's risk and thus its cost of capital. Portfolio effects are considered in detail later.

Operational Adaptation

We adopt the simple convention of accepting prospective investments that add to the value of the enterprise. In an environment in which there is no *capital rationing*—that is, where funds are sufficient to accept all projects contributing to the value of the enterprise—we accept all profitable projects. In the more common situation in which funds are scarce compared to the investment cost of the array of acceptable investments, we should try to accept those projects that contribute the maximum amount to the value of the firm. Nothing in this contradicts the behavioral theories of management. Other motivations may deter achievement of *maximum* value increase. But even satisficing management, or management merely interested in remaining in control, should still try to attempt to increase the value of the enterprise, even if not to the fullest possible extent. Management that habitually does otherwise does so at its peril because the owners may replace the existing management.

The Cash Flows

For individual projects that consist of only one of many items of capital equipment it is difficult, if not impossible, to associate net cash flows or even accounting revenues directly. In these cases it may sometimes be possible to treat a package of such individual items of plant and equipment as a single, large capital-budgeting proposal. This is likely to be the most useful when the package alone will support a new product line, or when replacing an entire production facility is contemplated.

Alternatively, the cash flows associated with the individual capital equipment components may result from cost reduction. Cost reduction may be considered a positive cash flow because it represents the elimination of an opportunity cost. Such costs are defined as those attributable to inaction or the result of adopting some alternative to the best available action.

CASH FLOWS AND THE PUBLIC SECTOR

Because the equivalent of positive cash flows may be obtained from a reduction in costs, the basic valuation model can be useful in public sector cost benefit-analysis. Cost reduction frees resources that would otherwise be wasted, so that they may satisfy other public demands. Also, maximization of the value of public enterprise may be considered beneficial, because such institutions are owned by all citizens of the community, state, or nation. Maximization of their value therefore serves to maximize the public wealth of society. Value in such cases is drawn from the tangible and intangible benefits provided to the citizens and not in the funds accumulated by the institution, which should be minimal. In other words, the money accumulated by public enterprise should be distributed as it is accumulated in the form of social dividends, paid through reduction in required external funding by taxes or government borrowing, or by increase in desired services provided. Unfortunately, the performance of some government institutions may lead one to believe that this, in fact, is not done, perhaps because the bureaucrats managing them are not answerable to the citizens nor held accountable by elected officials.

3

Estimating Project Characteristics

In order to apply any systematic method of capital-budgeting evaluation and project selection it is necessary to first obtain estimates of relevant project characteristics or parameters. The methodologically superior methods of evaluation also require an estimate of the firm's cost of capital, which is the subject of the next chapter. This present chapter focuses on those characteristics of a particular project or aggregation of projects that become manifest in cash flows attributable to the project.

PROJECT TYPES

Let us define those capital investment projects as *major* projects, that in themselves generate net cash inflows, and as *component* projects those that do not in themselves directly generate net cash flows. Examples will serve to clarify the distinction. Investment in plant and equipment to produce a new product line that will generate sales revenues as well as production, marketing, and other costs would be classified as a major project. Investment in a new toolroom lathe would be classified as a component project. It will be used to service other capital equipment in the plant or produce prototype parts. The lathe then will not produce directly attributable cash inflows, but will necessitate directly attributable cash outflows for operator wages and fringe benefits, electric power, and so on. A new spline rolling machine that will replace several milling machines in a plant producing transmissions would also be considered a component project. The spline rolling machine in such a production facility would not produce a product that is sold without other machining and assembly operations being performed on it. Thus, product revenue cannot be directly associated with this machine except through rather tenuous cost accounting procedures that may not properly reflect its revenue contributions.

Major projects have *both* cash inflows *and* cash outflows directly associated with themselves. Component projects ordinarily do not. Therefore, although attention to value maximization may be appropriate for major projects, cost minimization will generally be more suitable an approach to component projects. For instance, a cost reduction brought about by replacing an older (component project) machine by a newer and more efficient machine contributes to net cash inflow as much as an increase in revenue with costs held constant. In this case the net cash flow is attributable to eliminating opportunity cost that is associated with less than the most efficient production equipment for the particular operation.

To further clarify the distinction between project types, assume that for a given cost of capital and risk level we want to maximize net cash flows by holding costs constant while increasing cash revenues. For major projects this may be appropriate. On the other hand, for component projects we may more easily achieve the same result by minimizing costs for a given level of cash revenue. An analogy may be made with the terminology of mathematical programming, with the major project considered the *dual* problem of cost minimization. Generally, we may expect an equivalence between maximizing some objective function subject to cost constraints and that of minimizing cost subject to some performance constraints.[1]

Most capital-budgeting techniques have been oriented to selecting projects that will contribute toward maximization of some measure of project returns. However, the MAPI method proposed by George Terborgh departs from these by selecting projects that contribute to minimization of costs. The MAPI method is treated in detail in a subsequent chapter.

PROJECT CHARACTERISTICS

The quantitative parameters of an investment that are relevant to the decision to accept or reject the project are:

[1]See for example A. O. Converse, *Optimization* (New York: Holt, Rinehart and Winston, 1970), p. 5.

Initial Cost
Project Useful Life
Net Cash Flows in Each Time Period
Salvage Value at End of Each Time Period

These parameters, together with the enterprise's cost of capital, provide information on which a rational decision may be based according to objective criteria. In addition to the above quantitative parameters, sometimes qualitative considerations will also affect the investment decision. For example, one production facility may use a collection of custom-designed machinery, whereas another employs more or less standard production machines. If the specialized machinery cannot practicably be converted to producing other machined products, and if the probability that the particular products for which this specialized machinery is acquired will be abandoned prematurely is high, then the decision to adopt standard production machinery may be superior even though it may promise somewhat lower benefits if things go well for the product line.

Qualitative considerations may be crucial, especially in the area of contingency planning. In answering the "what if" question of what alternative use may be made of capital investment projects if things do not go as well as expected, management may prefer the array of projects that offers flexibility over the somewhat more efficient, but highly specialized, alternative. For example, a firm that produced automobile fabric convertible tops and decided in 1970 to acquire new automated equipment to stitch the seams, predicated on a 15-year useful machine life, would have found in 1976 that original equipment market sales were vanishing. In 1976, Cadillac, the last of the United States automakers to produce fabric-covered convertibles, announced it was phasing out such models. Unless the replacement market would continue to provide sufficient sales into the mid-1980s, the firm would need to find alternative products suitable for production on the specialized equipment. Perhaps fabric camper-trailer tops or similar items could be produced as profitably on the specialized machinery. If not, the firm would find that its decision in 1970 was, with benefit of hindsight, the wrong decision.

No general rules or procedures have been developed for contingency planning in capital budgeting. Each case has its own unique attributes that prevent uniform application of rigorous principles. It is in such aspects of decision-making that there is no reasonable alternative to the judgment of management. For instance, how should a firm that produces barrel tubes for shotguns incorporate in its decisions the possibility that a Congress will be elected that is disposed to outlaw private firearms ownership or restrict ownership drastically? Given that such a Congress is elected, what is the contingent probability that it will find time to act? Will a later change in congressional composition reverse such legislation? If so, would consumer demand return to its former level? Such a firm must incorporate factors such as these into its capital-budgeting decisions in order to ensure flexibility in using its physical capital in case the environment in which it operates suddenly changes. And is there any firm not subject to environmental changes?

INITIAL COST

Capital-budgeting projects will generally require some initial cash outlay for acquiring the project. Such cost may arise from construction outlays, purchase cost or initial lease payment, legal fees, transportation, and installation, and possibly from tax liability on a project that is being replaced by the new one or from penalty costs associated with breaking a lease on the replaced project. Cash costs attributable to the decision to accept a capital project should be included in the initial project cost. Costs that would be incurred regardless of whether or not the project were accepted—"sunk costs"—should not be allocated to the project cost. With some projects, especially large ones involving design and construction over several years, initial costs should be considered as the negative net cash flows incurred in each period prior to the one in which net cash flow becomes positive.

Sunk Cost

Unrecoverable costs associated with previous decisions should not be allocated to a new project under consideration. For instance, assume that a firm purchased a $400,000 machine 5 years ago, which had at the time an estimated useful life of 20 years, and that $228,571 has still to be claimed as depreciation against taxes on income at a rate, which yields a tax reduction of $118,857 spread over the next 15 years. Assume now that a technologically improved machine is available to replace it. Should the unrecovered tax reduction be added to the other costs of the new machine? The answer is "no," in this case. However, the unrecovered tax reductions may be included as costs in the years in which they would have been realized. Now, what if the $400,000 machine suddenly breaks down and cannot be repaired? In this event the unrecovered tax reductions from depreciation should not be charged to a replacement machine, either in the initial cost or in the cash flows over the remaining depreciable life of the broken machine. For tax purposes the broken machine's remaining value will be charged to the firm's operations as a loss which will have no effect on the replacement decision. Similarly, equipment that is discarded because of a change in the firm's operations should not have any of its cost charged to new equipment that is subsequently acquired.

The problem of what costs to include and what costs to exclude from a particular capital investment project will be resolved by focusing on cash flows and ignoring accounting costs. Does acceptance of the candidate project increase or decrease cash flow in years zero through the end of its anticipated economic life? If acceptance of the project precipitates changes in cash flows, then these must be taken into account in evaluating the project. Noncash items, and items such as sunk costs, must *not* be included in project evaluation, even though specific dollar figures are associated with them.

What if costly preliminary engineering studies have been completed and research and development costs incurred? Should these be included in the cost of the project for capital-budgeting evaluation? No, they should not, for they represent sunk costs— water over the dam—and subsequent acceptance or rejection of the project will not affect them. The handling of such sunk costs in the accounting framework may be a different matter; for tax or control reasons they may be associated with the project. Since in this book our concern is capital budgeting and not accounting, such matters will be ignored. They are irrelevant to the decision of whether or not to accept a project, except to the extent that they affect *cash flows.*

Components of Initial Cost

In addition to the obvious component of initial cost, namely, the basic price of the capital project in question, some less obvious costs must be included. Among them are:

Transportation and Insurance Charges
Installation Costs, including special machine foundations, movement of other equipment to get the new project to its location in the plant, installation of service facilities such as electric, hydraulic and pneumatic lines, and so on.
License or Royalty Cost
Required Additional Working Capital Investment
Operator Training Costs

Transportation and insurance costs may be included in the vendor's price. In many instances, however, delivery will be F.O.B. the vendor's plant. In these cases failure to include the proper transportation and insurance costs will understate the project's initial cost, perhaps seriously so when heavy equipment is difficult and expensive to ship.

Installation costs may include the full expense of project installation. With industrial machinery that will be placed in an existing plant, it may be necessary to move intervening equipment to allow room for the new equipment. In some instances the plant structure itself may have to be temporarily or permanently modified or the disassembled equipment moved in pieces to its site in the plant. Worker safety may require installation of sound-dampening materials, special ventilation equipment, dust collectors, fire extinguisher systems, and so on. Heavy machines usually require a concrete "anchor" to be poured prior to installation, with the foundation sometimes being several feet thick and as large or larger than the machine attached to it. Machinery often requires foundations to be built so that vibrations created are not communicated through the plant floor. Adequate vibration dampening can increase installation cost considerably, but it is required in environments in which precision may be affected by this type of unwanted disturbance.

License or royalty cost for use of patented equipment or processes may require an initial payment as well as the customary periodic payments as production gets underway. These should be included in the project cost.

Required additional working capital investment is an item that is easy to overlook. Usually, this will not be a significant factor with component projects, but will be important for most major projects as defined earlier in this chapter. Additional net working capital required to support accounts receivable, inventory, or other current asset increases (net of current liability increases) are included in project cost. Recovery of such net working capital requirements at project termination may be incorporated in salvage value or the last period's cash flow, which are equivalent means of handling this factor.

Operator training costs, if not included by the vendor in the basic equipment cost, must be added to the project cost by the purchaser. Such training is to be expected with capital equipment employing a new technology or capital equipment whose operation by nature is complex. For instance, it is generally required when large-scale computer systems are acquired, that operators and support personnel be trained properly in correct use of the equipment. This is true even though the new machine replaced an older model of the same vendor, or a smaller machine of the same series with a different operating system or fewer options than the new one.

In addition to these initial cost items, others may be found in particular cases. The rule to follow in determining whether a cost item should be included in the initial cost of a capital investment project is to answer the two following questions. If the answer to both is in the affirmative, the cost should be included in the initial cost of the project.

1. Is the cost incurred only if the capital project is undertaken, that is, accepted?
2. Is the cost represented by a cash outflow?

If the answer to both is "yes," then only the cash outflow associated with the cost should be included in the initial cost of the project. Noncash costs should be excluded. For this purpose we assume net working capital increases to be cash flows, although "internal" to the firm. Increased working capital requirements must be funded, and the money committed will generally not be released until the end of the project's useful life.

USEFUL LIFE

The investment merit of a project will depend on its useful economic life. Useful economic life of capital equipment may end long before it becomes physically deteriorated to the point of inoperability. Economic life, and decline in the value of capital equipment over the economic life, may mean that project abandonment prior to the end of the originally anticipated *project* life will be of greater benefit to the firm than holding the project to the end. This topic is taken up in detail later.

Terborgh defined the cumulative effects on decline in capital serviceability over the period the equipment is held as *operating inferiority*.[2] This is a meaningful concept, and it will be adopted here. Operating inferiority is determined by two components: physical deterioration and technological obsolescence. Physical deterioration is what is normally considered to be the determinant of project life. However, technological obsolescence will be far more important in determining the economic life of some projects.

Consider an accounting firm that purchased a large number of mechanical calculating machines in 1970, assuming an economic life of ten years. If the machines were to be kept in service over the full ten years, they could be expected to undergo steady physical deterioration. As time went on, more frequent and more serious breakdowns would be expected, and expenditures for repairs would increase accordingly.

Some rotary, mechanical calculators cost $1000 or more in 1970. At about the same point in time, due to advances in technology, a variety of electronic calculators came on the market. Not only was the cost substantially less, as little as one-fourth the cost of their mechanical predecessors for some of them, but they were superior in several respects. The electronic models were substantially faster, immensely quieter, less subject to mechanical problems because of the dearth of moving parts, and provided number displays that were larger (sometimes), illuminated, and generally easy to read. Thus it was that the mechanical calculator fell victim to technological obsolescence. They simply were inferior in most respects to their modern descendants, even if still quite serviceable.

---

[2]George Terborgh, *Dynamic Equipment Policy* (Washington: Machinery and Allied Products Institute, 1949), pp. 61–62.

In firms whose employees devote a large portion of their working time to calculation, by 1975 few mechanical calculators were in use. Why? Because replacement with the best technology allowed less wasted time waiting for results, a quieter atmosphere more conducive to productive work, and reduced repair costs. If an employee spent half of each day working with a calculator, and the new calculator was 25 percent faster, the same employee could do the equivalent of one hour additional work in the same four hours. Such efficiency gains are easily translated into money terms. An office employing four such people, by equipping each with the new technology, could avoid hiring the fifth person when the workload expanded by as much as 25 percent.

Physical Deterioration

For many types of capital, experience with similar facilities in the past may provide useful guidelines. For instance, we would expect that the physical life of a punch press purchased today would, on the average, be similar to that of a new punch press of 20 years ago.

With capital that employs new technology, or a new application of existing technology, managers and engineers experienced with production equipment may provide useful estimates. However, capital goods produced by a firm not likely to stay in the business and maintain a supply of replacement parts may negate an otherwise good estimate of useful life. Unavailability of a crucial part from a supplier will mean either producing the part in the toolroom, contracting to have it custom made, modifying the machine to take a similar standard part, or abandoning the machine. This last alternative obviously ends the useful life.

Physical deterioration of major projects, as defined earlier, may well be concerned with that of plant and equipment components. It is not meaningful to speak of *the* physical deterioration of a major project unless this is taken to be synonymous with deterioration of the buildings housing the operation, or unless the major project is indeed one major item of capital equipment that dominates all others. If our major project is a division of the firm composed of one or more buildings, each housing 100 or more items of capital equipment, what meaning can we attach to physical deterioration of the project? The answer is none; at least this is true if component projects are added and replaced as time goes on. On the other hand, if our division is based on operation of one dominating item of capital, such as a toll bridge or a carwash, it may well be meaningful to refer to physical deterioration of the major project.

Technological Obsolescence

Although we may often be able to obtain workable estimates of physical life for capital equipment and corresponding physical deterioration over time, it is a very different matter for technological obsolescence. Technological innovations that contribute to the obsolescence of existing capital tend to occur randomly and unevenly over time. Sometimes technological changes are implemented rapidly during relatively short intervals of time: The technological advances in computer equipment since the 1950s have been profound, and in the 1990s may not only continue but may continue at a rapid pace for some time yet. Theoretical developments, such as holographic, laser-directed computer memories, once the engineering obstacles have been overcome, and artificial intelligence software promise yet further waves of innovation in the industry.

Terborgh's approach to incorporating technological obsolescence into the operating inferiority of capital equipment is difficult to improve upon. His recommendation, basically, is to assume, in the absence of information to the contrary, that technological obsolescence of existing capital will accumulate at a constant rate as time goes on.[3] In the absence of information to the contrary, such extrapolation from the past into the future is reasonable. However, should information be available that implies more rapid or less rapid technological change, this information should be employed, even if only qualitatively.

Should the firm delay an investment when technological changes are expected in the near future? The answer to this question may be found in evaluating the merit of investing today with replacement when the technologically improved capital becomes available, and evaluating the merit of the alternative— that of postponing investment until the improved capital is available. Comparison of the merits of the alternatives will serve to determine the better course of action. Methods for performing

[3]Ibid., p. 65.

such analysis, once the net cash flows are determined, are covered in later chapters.

The subject of technological obsolescence in capital budgeting is not limited to the firm's physical capital; it may apply also to the human capital of the enterprise, and certainly does apply to the product lines on which the cash flows of investment projects are predicated. For example, the replacement of vacuum tubes with transistors and integrated circuits, and later with miniaturized circuits made possible by large-scale integration, caused televisions incorporating vacuum tubes to be obsolete. A firm that based its capital investment decisions on continued demand for sets with vacuum tubes found that later it had still serviceable equipment for a product no longer in demand. Similar examples are to be found in mechanical versus electronic calculators, automatic versus manual automobile transmissions, and piston versus jet propulsion aircraft engines, to name just a few of the more obvious.

CASH FLOWS

In capital budgeting we must base our analysis on the net cash flows of the project under consideration, not on accounting profits. Only cash can be reinvested. Only cash can be used to pay dividends and interest and to repay debt. Only cash can be used to pay suppliers, workers and management, and tax authorities.

Over the long run, both total firm cash flow and total accounting profits provide measures of management performance. However, in the short run the two will generally not be highly correlated. The firm, for example, may have had a very profitable year as measured by "generally accepted accounting principles" and yet have no cash to meet its obligations since the "profits" are not yet realized but are tied up in accounts receivable that may or may not be eventually collected.

Determination of net cash flows involves consideration of two basic factors: (1) those that contribute to cash inflows or cash receipts and (2) those that contribute to cash outflows or cash costs. Major projects, as defined earlier, will have both these factors affecting them throughout their economic lives. Component projects, after the initial outlay, will be directly involved with cash outflows, but only *indirectly* with cash inflows.

Estimation of cash inflows for major projects generally requires the joint efforts of specialists in marketing research, marketing management, and design engineering, and perhaps staff economists and others as well. If the firm does not have the required expertise itself, it may hire the services of appropriate consultants.

For cash outflow estimation, joint contributions of design, production, and industrial engineering, production management, and cost accounting are required for major projects. Additionally, staff economists and labor relations personnel may contribute information relevant to probable cost increases as time goes on.

Financial management will be responsible to top management for analyzing the effects on the firm's financial strength if the project is undertaken and for obtaining the funds necessary to finance the undertaking. Finance personnel will undoubtedly be involved in recommending which major projects should be accepted and which rejected based on their analysis of the project, its interactions with the existing assets of the firm, and consequently its profitability in cash terms. Accounting staff will be concerned with the project's effect on reported profits and tax liabilities and all the attendant details.

Cash inflows for a major project will be determined by (1) price at which each unit of output is sold; (2) the number of units of output sold; and (3) the collection of accounts receivable on credit sales. Estimation of these items is not easy, especially for a product dissimilar to product lines with which the firm may already have had experience. Proper estimation, as mentioned earlier, involves persons from different functional areas within the firm, and possibly external to it.

For component projects we will be concerned with cash outflows. If a given task must be performed by capital equipment, then we shall seek to obtain capital that will do so at lowest cost. Thus, on initial selection of mutually exclusive candidate projects, we will select the project that minimizes cost or, alternatively and equivalently, the project for which the saving in cash opportunity cost is maximized. Of course, we must assume that all component projects admitted to candidate status are capable of performing the tasks that must be done within the environment of a major project. Projects that cannot should not be treated as candidates.

Cash Inflows (Cash Receipts)

Assume that we are examining a *combination of several* machines that will produce a single product our new firm plans to sell. The principals of our firm are experienced in sales and engineering of such a product; both worked for years for a larger company that produced similar products. Some preliminary orders have already been obtained from firms that will purchase the product we will produce. It is estimated that at a price of $17.38 per unit, our firm can reasonably expect sales of 100,000 units per year.

If we assume that sales and cash receipts on sales will be uniform throughout each year, and that unit price and sales volume will be constant from year to year, the task of cash inflow estimation is trivial. If we have no uncollectable accounts receivable, our cash inflows each year will be unit price times number of units, that is, $1,738,000.

Life is usually not so simple as this, however. Sales probably will not be uniform throughout the year, but there will be seasonal variations. Sales from year to year will seldom be even nearly constant. Possibly sales will grow from year to year along a trend of several years' duration, or decline for several years. Such variations are very difficult to predict in advance, and are aggravated by unforeseen developments in competition, the national economy, and other factors.

In the final analysis, estimation of cash inflows will depend on managerial judgment, conditioned by the economic environment and knowledge of the firm's competition and trends in product design and improvement. Also, in many industries revenues may be influenced by advertising expenditures, so that firms may, in fact, individually and collectively, influence the level of demand for their products. Seldom will a firm be in the position of having a mathematical model that provides reliable demand and revenue forecasts, especially for periods beyond one year. There are too many qualitative, vague, and intangible factors at work that cannot be quantified given the current state of the art in mathematical modeling. Proper incorporation of these factors requires human judgment, and perhaps not a little luck.

It will often be useful to prepare several forecasts, including a "worst case" forecast in which it is assumed that whatever can go wrong for the firm's sales will go wrong. Of course, unanticipated factors and events may make actual events still worse, but we would assume that for a proper "worst case" forecast, actual experience would be no worse, say, 95 times out of 100. In other words, a good "worst case" forecast should have a *small* probability associated with it that actual events will turn out worse. "Best case" and "most likely" forecasts may similarly be made. The population projections of the United States Bureau of the Census, in fact, have been prepared on the basis of high, low, and most likely. Because we can never expect an exact forecast, it is extremely useful to be able to bracket the actual outcome, so that we may say that the probability is *p* percent that the actual outcome will fall between the best case and worst case estimates, where *p* is a number close to 1.0. For this approach to be useful, the best case and worst case forecasts cannot be so far apart as to make them meaningless.

Let us now go back to our example. If $17.38 per unit and 100,000 units are taken to be our most likely forecast for the coming year, we may determine that $14.67 and 40,000 units is the worst that is likely and $23.00 and 200,000 the best that is likely to happen. If we can attach a (albeit subjective) probability of .05 or 5 percent that the actual revenue will fall short of the worst case, we have useful information. The chances of sales revenues being less than the worst case are then only five in 100.

Cash Outflows

To some extent estimates of cash outflows may be made with more confidence than those for cash inflows. For example, the initial investment outlay is made at the beginning of the project's life, and may often be estimated precisely. In fact, the supplier may provide a firm price for the cost of the investment. However, other cost components may prove to be almost as difficult to forecast as factors affecting cash receipts.

What specific items do we consider as cash outflows? Anything requiring cash to be paid out of the firm or to be made unavailable for other uses. Suppose that the machines we are considering for purchase are to be treated as one project. Assume that the project costs $3 million for purchase and installation. For simplicity, assume also that we plan to run production on a constant level, so that labor, electricity, and materials will be constant for at least two years. In addition, cash will be tied up in raw materials and finished goods inventory and in accounts receivable. Setting aside the notion of worst and best case forecasts for now, let us deal with the most likely production and cost forecast, and the most likely annual cash revenue forecast. We obtain the following:

Year 0	Cash Outflow	Cash Inflow
Initial Investment	$3,000,000	
Wages	100,000	
Fringe Benefits	50,000	
F.I.C.A., etc.	20,000	
Raw Materials Inventory	200,000	
Finished Goods Inventory	500,000	
Accounts Receivable Investment	400,000	
Electric and Other Direct Variable Costs	10,000	
	$4,280,000	
Cash Receipts on Sales, Net of Discounts, and Bad Debt Losses		$1,738,000
Net Cash Flow	($2,542,000)	

Note that no overhead or sunk cost items have been included in the cash flows. In the second year of operations, if no new investment in inventories or accounts receivable is required, and the same amounts of labor, electricity, and so on, at the same rates are employed, we obtain:

Year 1	Cash Outflow	Cash Inflow
Wages	$100,000	
Fringe Benefits	50,000	
F.I.C.A., etc.	20,000	
Electric and Other Direct Variable Costs	10,000	
	$180,000	
Cash Receipts on Sales, Net of Discounts, and Bad Debt Losses		$1,738,000
Net Cash Flow	$1,558,000	

Wages and fringe benefits include those of direct labor plus the portion of indirect labor that services the machinery: machine set-up, materials handling, and so on.

Ordinarily, in expositions of the various capital-budgeting techniques, we assume for simplicity of explanation that cash flows occur only at the end of a period (usually a year) and not over that period. Period zero in such treatment includes only the installed cost of the capital equipment. Subsequent periods include net cash flows arising from cash receipts minus cash disbursements, the latter including whatever additional investment that may be required in capital equipment, inventories, and so on.

Interest expenses are specifically excluded from cash costs because methods of project evaluation that employ discounting already incorporate the interest costs implicitly—they are imbedded in the discount rate and not in the cash flows.

TAXES AND DEPRECIATION

Since firms generally pay income taxes on earnings and depreciation is deductible as an expense, there is an effect on cash flow. Cash that does not have to be paid as tax to the government serves to increase net cash flow because it is a reduction in cash outflow.

The rationale behind allowing depreciation to be tax deductible is that it represents recovery of investment rather than profit. And since the benefits of capital investment occur over the economic life of the project, it is deemed appropriate to spread recognition of the investment outlays, as expenses, over the same period. Various accounting conventions and tax authority rulings on how the depreciation charges may be calculated, and what depreciation lifetimes may be used for various asset types, have complicated a basically simple concept. Profitable disposal of capital equipment may subject the firm to additional taxes on residual salvage value. Such details are covered in texts in accounting and in financial management. Here we are concerned only with basic concepts and the effect of depreciation on cash flow, not on the details of tax rules. Tax laws change from time to time, not only for various theoretical reasons, but as part of the economic "fine-tuning" of the federal government to encourage or discourage new investment, as the situation of the national economy may indicate.

Several methods of calculating depreciation for each year of a capital investment's life have been devised. Because cash may be invested, it is generally better to charge as much depreciation as possible in the early years of a project's life, thus deferring taxes to later years and simultaneously retaining more cash in the early years. This is especially true during times of rapid inflation. Unless the firm has tax losses larger than it can use to offset taxable income, it will charge the maximum allowable depreciation in the early years of a capital investments' life. Given that money has time value, to do otherwise would not be in the best interests of the owners of the enterprise. The more rapid the rate of price inflation, the more incumbent it is to charge the maximum depreciation in the early years for tax purposes. However, for management control purposes the firm may use the depreciation schedule that is considered to match most closely the actual economic deterioration in the capital project from year to year. Yet, with high rates of price inflation in capital goods, the depreciation charged against the original cost if unadjusted may be of little usefulness. Such adjustment, however, is beyond the scope of this book.

Depreciation

Until 1981 there were two depreciation frameworks in the United States: (1) the General Guidelines and (2) the class life asset depreciation range (ADR) system. The latter could be considered a precursor to the current accelerated cost recovery system (ACRS).

The General Guidelines could be used for any depreciable asset. The ADR system was authorized by the Revenue Act of 1971. Examination of these and the fundamental methods of depreciation will help in understanding ACRS depreciation. And, given the propensity of Congress to change the tax laws, we have not seen the end of changes in allowable methods of depreciation. By understanding the basic methods one can easily grasp what is involved in new procedures.

A firm could select the ADR system in preference to the General Guidelines for any depreciable asset acquired after 1970 until ACRS came into being in 1981.. A firm elected each year either to use or to not use the ADR system for those depreciable assets acquired during the fiscal year.

Under the ADR system, assets corresponded to various classes. For example, one class was 00.241—light general purpose trucks. The range for that class was three years at the lower limit, four years "guideline," and five years upper limit. The firm could choose the lower limit to achieve the most rapid depreciation. What the change to ACRS depreciation did was tantamount to mandating that all firms would use ADR depreciation with the lower limit.

It will be helpful to understanding if we now review the fundamental methods of depreciation. Then we shall examine the General Guidelines and ADR system before considering ACRS, which derives from ADR.

Straight-Line Depreciation

The notion behind the straight-line depreciation is that the investment's residual value declines by a *constant dollar amount* from year to year uniformly over the useful life. Therefore, the initial investment is divided by the number of years of useful life, and the result used as the annual depreciation charge. This is the least useful method for deferring taxes to the later years of the project's life.

Double-Declining-Balance Depreciation

With declining-balance depreciation it is assumed that the residual value of the investment at the end of any year is a *fixed percentage* of the residual value at the end of the previous year. Alternatively, we take as declining-balance depreciation a constant *percentage* of the residual value at the end of the previous period. In United States practice, the method used is that of *double-*declining balance (DDB), in which the percentage value of decline is multiplied by a factor of two. This results in accelerating the depreciation charges and deferring larger amounts of taxes to later years. Salvage value is excluded from the calculations in this method.

Sum-of-the-Years' Digits Depreciation

The method of sum-of-the-years' digits (SYD) depreciation is implemented by writing the years in the asset's lifetime in reverse order, and then dividing each by the sum of the years in the useful life. Depreciation for each year is then determined by multiplying the original asset cost by the factor corresponding to each year. A project lasting five years will therefore have 5/15 (or 1/3) of the original value charged to depreciation in the first year and 1/15 charged in the fifth and last year. This method, like that of double-declining balance, provides for accelerated asset depreciation.

Comparison of the Basic Depreciation Methods

Assume we have an asset that cost the firm C and has a depreciable lifetime[4] of N years. Then the annual depreciation charges with the three methods for $0 < t \leq N$ are:

Straight Line $\quad$ C/N

Double-Declining $\quad$ $C(1 - 2P)^{t-1}2P$ where $P = 1/N$
   Balance

Sum-of-Years' $\quad$ $C(N - t + 1)/[N(N + 1)/2]$ since
   Digits

$$\sum_{t=1}^{N} t = \frac{N(N + 1)}{2}$$

EXAMPLE 3-1

For illustration, let us take a project with $C = \$100,000$, $N = 10$, and calculate depreciation at the end of each year with each method. We assume zero salvage value.

The *total* depreciation charged with each method is equal to the cost of the project. Total depreciation cannot, of course, exceed the investment acquisition cost. Note that with double-declining-balance depreciation, the final year's depreciation charge is the sum of the double-declining-balance amount plus the undepreciated balance.

In practice, firms will usually switch from one method of depreciation to another when it is advantageous to do so, and when the tax authorities will allow the change. For instance, under GG a firm may switch from double-declining-balance depreciation to straight-line depreciation. Of course, the straight-line depreciation charge will not be based on the original cost and lifetime, but on the *undepreciated balance* and remaining depreciable life at the time of the switch.

In this example the firm could, under the GG, switch to

---

[4]The depreciable lifetime of an asset will often be different from the useful economic life. This happens because tax authority rulings concerning the lifetime that may be used for depreciation may not properly reflect the useful economic life of such asset in any particular firm.

Table 3-1. Comparison of Depreciation Methods Under General
Guidelines, With Zero Salvage

Year	Straight Line	Double-Declining Balance	Sum-of-Years' Digits
1	$ 10,000	$ 20,000	$ 18,182
2	10,000	16,000	16,364
3	10,000	12,800	14,545
4	10,000	10,240	12,727
5	10,000	8,192	10,909
6	10,000	6,554	9,090
7	10,000	5,243	7,273
8	10,000	4,194	5,455
9	10,000	3,355	3,636
10	10,000	13,422[a]	1,819
	$100,000	$100,000	$100,000

[a]$2684 plus remaining $10,738 undepreciated balance.

straight-line depreciation in year six. In this year straight-line
depreciation of the remaining balance yields the same dollar depreciation as the double-declining-balance method. However, in
years seven, eight, and nine the amount charged to depreciation
is larger with straight line.

In no case may the firm depreciate more than 100 percent of an
asset. This means that if an asset costs C, and is expected to have
a salvage value of $S, no more than $(C − S)$ may be depreciated.
Let us now consider an example in which salvage value must be
taken into account. *Note that DDB depreciation ignores salvage*, although no more than $(C − S)$ may be charged.

EXAMPLE 3-2

Let us take a project with C = $130,000, N = 10, and S =
$10,000. We shall assume the firm will switch to straight-line
from DDB depreciation, as allowed by the GG, as soon as this is
advantageous.

EXAMPLE 3-3

*With ADR system, salvage is treated the same way as with DDB under the
GG; that is, it is ignored.* As always, however, no more than 100
percent of the asset value may be depreciated. The following
example shows the results of using ADR with the same asset just

Table 3-2.   Comparison of Depreciation Methods under General
Guidelines, with Salvage

Year	Straight Line	Double-Declining Balance	Sum-of-Years' Digits
1	$ 12,000	$ 26,000	$ 21,818
2	12,000	20,800	19,636
3	12,000	16,640	17,455
4	12,000	13,312	15,273
5	12,000	10,650	13,091
6	12,000	8,520	10,909
7	12,000	6,816	8,727
8	12,000	5,754[a]	6,545
9	12,000	5,754	4,634
10	12,000	5,754	2,181
	$120,000	$120,000	$120,000

[a]Straight-line depreciation in years 8, 9, and 10 on the remaining balance. No more
than 100 percent of the asset may be depreciated. Salvage is expected to be $10,000
and $102,738 has been charged by the end of year seven. The straight-line amount is
obtained by dividing $(120,000 − 102,738) by 3. This yields $5,754, which is larger
than the DDB charge of $5,453 would be, so the switch is advantageous.

considered. *In practice, because ADR allows a choice of depreciable asset life,
we should not expect that the asset life will remain ten years.* If a shorter life
is allowed, the firm will take it to maximize accelerated write-off.

General Guidelines allows the firm to switch from DDB to
straight line only; *ADR allows the firm to switch to SYD from DDB.* This
allows for the greatest amount of depreciation in the early years.
Switching from DDB to SYD will always be advantageous in the
second year of the project's life. Applying this to Example 3-2
yields the following results: Actual depreciation in the second
year will be the same; SYD will yield greater depreciation in the
subsequent years.

ACRS Depreciation

As a part of the Economic Recovery Tax Act of 1981, new manda-
tory depreciation rules were promulgated. The new rules were
termed *accelerated cost recovery system* (ACRS). The purpose in the
new depreciation rules was to stimulate investment.

Under ACRS depreciation, assets belong to one of several asset
life classes. ACRS depreciation is based on the assumption that

all assets are placed into service at the midpoint of their first year (the half-year assumption) regardless of when during the year they are acquired.

After 1985 the ACRS schedule was to have been based on double-declining-balance depreciation in the first year of service, with a switch to sum-of-the-year's digits depreciation in the second year. However, since the law was first enacted there have been several changes, and doubtless there will be more modifications to the law. Despite the tendency to tinker with the law every year or two, an understanding of the fundamental depreciation methods will enable one to adapt that knowledge to subsequent changes in the law.

The Tax Reform Act of 1986 changed the system to the Modified ACRS and established six asset classes in place of the four that had existed. Except for real estate, all depreciable assets fall within one of the six classes. The law also changed by requiring a switch from double-declining balance to straight line in the year for which the straight line amount exceeds the DDB amount. And, after the change in the law three-year class assets are depreciated, reason for this change is that the half-year convention was made to apply to the last year of service as well as the first by the 1986 act.

Table 3-3 contains the ACRS schedule current under the 1986 Tax Reform Act. If history is any guide, by the time you read this the schedule will have changed again, and possibly more than once.

Canadian Depreciation

Depreciation is generally called "capital consumption allowance" in Canada, or "capital cost allowance." Because the *Income Tax Act* was changed in 1949, only the declining-balance method has been generally allowed. This is not a double-declining balance as discussed earlier, but a declining balance based on assigned, fixed rates. The rate is applied to the undepreciated book balance of the asset, and the firm need not charge depreciation in years when it has losses.

All assets acquired within a tax year qualify for a full year's depreciation. There are 25 asset classes, each assigned a fixed capital cost allowance rate. All assets of a class are pooled together. Total capital consumption is calculated by multiplying

Table 3-3.   Depreciation Rates for ACRS Property Other Than Real Property*

Recovery Year	3-Year (200% DB)	5-Year (200% DB)	7-Year (200% DB)	10-Year (200% DB)	15-Year (150% DB)	20-Year (150% DB)
1	33.33%	20.00%	14.29%	10.00%	5.00%	3.75%
2	44.44	32.00	24.49	18.00	9.50	7.22
3	14.82	19.20	17.49	14.40	8.55	6.68
4	7.41	11.52**	12.49	11.52	7.70	6.18
5		11.52	8.93**	9.21	6.93	5.71
6		5.76	8.93	7.37	6.23	5.28
7			8.93	6.56**	5.90**	4.89
8			4.45	6.56	5.90	4.52
9				6.56	5.90	4.46**
10				6.56	5.90	4.46
11				3.26	5.90	4.46
12					5.90	4.46
13					5.90	4.46
14					5.90	4.46
15					5.90	4.46
16					2.99	4.46
17						4.46
18						4.46
19						4.46
20						4.46
21						2.25

*Assumes the half-year convention applies. Accuracy to two decimal places only.
**Switchover to straight-line depreciation over the remaining useful life.

Table 3-4.   Comparison of Depreciation Methods under ADR System, with Salvage

Year	Straight Line	Double-Declining Balance	Sum-of-Years' Digits
1	$ 13,000	$ 26,000	$ 23,636
2	13,000	20,000	21,273
3	13,000	16,640	18,909
4	13,000	13,312	16,545
5	13,000	10,650	14,182
6	13,000	8,520	11,818
7	13,000	6,814	9,455
8	13,000	5,423	4,182
9	13,000	4,362	0
10	3,000	3,487	0
	$120,000	$120,000	$120,000

Table 3-5. Comparison of Optimum Depreciation to DDB and SYD, with Salvage

Year	Optimum Depreciation	Method Used	Double-Declining Balance	Sum-of-Years' Digits
1	$ 26,000	DDB	$ 26,000	$ 23,636
2	20,800	SYD	20,800	21,273
3	18,489	SYD	16,640	18,909
4	16,178	SYD	13,312	16,545
5	13,867	SYD	10,650	14,182
6	11,556	SYD	8,520	11,818
7	9,245	SYD	6,814	9,455
8	3,865	SYD	5,423	4,182
9	0	SYD	4,362	0
10	0	SYD	3,487	0
	$120,000		$120,000	$120,000

the book balance of each pool by its corresponding capital cost allowance rate and adding the products together.

Capital gains and losses result only when a given asset pool, not an individual asset, is sold. Capital cost allowances due to a specific asset can remain in effect indefinitely if the given asset expires without salvage value, if there are other assets in the same asset pool, and if the firm generates income from which the capital cost allowance can be deducted.

Summary on Depreciation
1. Under the general guidelines, the only switch that can be made is from DDB to straight-line depreciation.
2. Under the general guidelines, only the DDB method ignores salvage value.
3. With ADR system the depreciable life is chosen from an IRS guideline range for the type of asset to be depreciated.
4. In the ADR system, salvage value is ignored (as it is with DDB under the general guidelines) in calculating depreciation with SYD and straight line as well as DDB.
5. Under the ADR system, it is permitted to switch from DDB to SYD when this becomes advantageous to the firm. The switch will be made in the second year in order to maximize the early write-off of an asset.
6. Although salvage is ignored under ADR (and DDB with the general guidelines), the maximum that may be depreciated

is the difference between the asset cost and its salvage value.

It can be shown that under the ADR system, maximization of the tax deferral in the project's early years will always be achieved by using double-declining-balance depreciation in the first year, and sum-of-the-years' digits depreciation in the second and subsequent years.

Because depreciation rules change from time to time, it is wise to consult the current tax code.

Investment Tax Credit

From time to time the federal government has provided special tax credit on new asset purchases in order to encourage aggregate investment in the economy. In recent years the credit has been increased from 7 percent to 10 percent (more in certain special cases) on new investment. The effect on cash flow is much the same as that of depreciation: It facilitates cash recovery during the first year of the asset's life. Because the rules governing application of the investment tax credit contain some complications, and may change from year to year, the current tax code should be checked when estimating the cash flows for an investment project that may qualify for the investment tax credit. At the time of this writing the investment tax credit is affected by the useful life of the asset. If the asset life is less than three years, no credit may be claimed. The credit applies to one-third the asset cost if the asset has an economic life of three years but less than five; and two-thirds if the asset cost is five years but less than seven. The credit applies to assets described as "qualified investment" under Section 38 of the Tax Code. It is equal to the amount allowed on new assets under Section 38 plus as much as $100,000 of the cost of newly acquired used assets qualified under Section 38. In no case may the investment tax credit exceed the firm's total tax liability for the year.

Unused portions of the investment tax credit are treated in the manner of capital losses: They may be carried back three years and forward five. The firm is restricted in applying the tax credit. If its tax liability is above $25,000, the credit claimed for the year may not exceed $25,000 plus 50 percent of the tax liability exceeding $25,000. If an asset is abandoned prior to the end of its estimated life, a portion of the tax credit claimed may have to be added to the firm's tax bill in the year. The amount will equal the difference between the credit actually claimed and the amount that would have been used had the actual asset life been used originally to calculate the credit.

Inflation

Over a span of time when price levels are fairly constant, depreciation rules and practices may be reasonably equitable in allowing the cost of the project to be recovered. A capital investment costing, for example, $150,000 will provide recovery of $150,000, which may be used to purchase a successor project at the end of its useful life. However, if capital equipment prices were to increase at 12 percent per annum, at the end of only ten years it would cost $465,870 just to replace the worn machine with an identical new one. Existing depreciation rules do not take this into account, and therefore capital recovery is inadequate to provide for replacement investment when required. This is one of the many matters that will be treated in some detail later, because of its significant effect on investment.

4

Cost of Capital

The cost of capital is a complex and still unsettled subject. It is discussed in finance texts in detail far beyond what we can devote to it in this text. In this chapter, intended primarily as a review, some of the more important considerations from the theory on cost of capital will be discussed, and some operational principles illustrated. Cost of capital is treated further in Chapter 21, within the context of the capital asset pricing model.

INTRODUCTION

Stated succinctly, the traditional view has been that the firm's cost of capital is the combined cost of the debt and equity funds required for acquisition of fixed, or permanent, assets used by the firm. Under this definition, even such things as permanent, non-seasonal working capital requirements are acquired with capital funds. Short-term financing with trade credit and bank lines of credit is generally excluded from cost of capital considerations. "Short term" is understood to include periods of one year or less, in which such balance sheet items as accounts payable and line-of-credit financing would be expected to be turned over at least once, or eliminated. Alternatively, the firm's cost of capital is the rate of return it must earn on an investment so that the value of the firm is neither reduced nor increased.

In terms of the firm's balance sheet, cost of capital relates to the long-term liabilities and capital section, to the firm's capital structure.

Although the specific account titles to be found for the various components of capital structure may differ, depending on the nature of the firm's business, the preferences of its accountants, and tradition within the industry, certain communalities exist. There will usually be long-term debts in the form of bond issues outstanding or long-term loans from banks or insurance companies. There will always be equity: For corporations this means common stock, retained earnings, and perhaps "surplus"; for proprietorships and partnerships it may be just an "equity" account. Because, for a variety of reasons, the corporate form of organization is dominant, and because the principles for dealing with corporate organization may be straightforwardly applied to proprietorships and partnerships, we will concentrate on corporate organization.

Each component item in the firm's capital structure has its own specific cost associated with it.

COST OF CAPITAL COMPONENTS

Debt

An important characteristic of debt is that interest payments are tax deductible,[1] whereas dividend payments are not. Thus the after-tax cost of debt is $(1 - \tau)$ times the pretax cost, where τ is the firm's marginal tax rate.

If a firm borrows $1 million for 20 years at annual interest of 9 percent, its before-tax cost is $90,000 annually, and if the firm's marginal income tax rate is 48 percent, the after-tax cost is $46,800, or 4.68 percent. The cost of debt is defined as the rate of return that must be earned on investments financed solely with debt,[2] in order that returns available to the owners be kept unchanged. In our example, investment of the $1 million would need to generate 9 percent return pretax, or 4.68 percent after tax, to leave the common stockholders' earnings unaffected.

For purposes of calculating the component cost of an item of debt, it is not important whether the particular debt component is a long-term loan from a bank or insurance company, or whether it is a mortgage bond or debenture, or whether sold publicly or privately placed. There is one important exception, however—that of convertible debentures. Such bonds are convertible at the option of the purchaser into shares of common

---

[1]Although interest payments are tax deductible, principal repayments are *not*. This is a point often overlooked, although not a conceptually difficult one to understand.

[2]Note that this view ignores risk and the interactions between cost of capital components. In practice, the firm should evaluate potential investments in terms of its overall cost of capital whether or not the actual financing will be carried out by debt, equity, or some combination.

stock in the firm. Because of this feature, they are hybrid securities, not strictly classifiable as either debt or equity. It is beyond the scope of this book to treat such issues, and the reader is referred to standard managerial finance textbooks as a starting point in the analysis.

Preferred Stock

Preferred stock fills an intermediate position between debt and common stock. Ordinary preferred stock has little to distinguish it from debt, except that preferred dividends, in contrast to interest payments on debt, are not tax deductible. And the firm is under no legally binding agreement to pay preferred dividends. However, such dividends must be paid before any dividends to common shareholders may be paid, and unpaid preferred dividends are usually cumulative. If they are not paid in any period, they are carried forward (without interest) until paid.

The cost of preferred stock may be defined similarly to that of debt. It is the rate of return that investments financed solely with preferred stock must yield in order that returns available to the owners (common stockholders) are kept unchanged. Since preferred issues generally have no stated maturity, they may be treated as perpetuities,[3] as may securities issues with exceptionally long maturities.[4] Therefore, the component cost of a preferred stock that pays a dividend D_p and can be sold for a net price to the firm of P_p is given by:

$$k_p = \frac{D_p}{P_p} \tag{4.1}$$

There are many variations of preferred stock, including callable issues, participating, voting, and convertible stocks. Convertible preferreds, like convertible bonds, present problems of classification that are beyond the scope of this book. Principles estab-

[3]A perpetuity is a security that has a perpetual life, such as the British consols issued to finance the Napoleonic Wars and, more recently, a bond issue of the Canadian Pacific Railroad.

[4]The noncallable 4 percent bonds issued by the West Shore Railroad in 1886 and not redeemable before the year 2361 (475 year maturity) could be considered perpetuities. Unfortunately for the bond owners, many firms do not have perpetual life, and thus there is risk that the firm will fail and the bonds will be rendered worthless.

lished for treating convertible bonds are also applicable to convertible preferreds.

Common Stock and Retained Earnings

We will consider equity to exclude preferred stock and to include only common stock and retained earnings. In other words, we take equity to mean only the financial interest of the residual owners of the firm's assets: Those that have a claim (proportionate to the shares held) of assets remaining after claims of creditors and preferred shareholders are satisfied in the event of liquidation.

The cost of equity has two basic components: (1) the cost of retained earnings and (2) the cost of new shares issued. In general terms, the cost of equity can be defined as the minimum rate of return that an entirely equity-financed investment must yield to keep unchanged the returns available to the common stockholders, and thus the value of existing common shares.

There are two different but theoretically equivalent approaches to measuring the firm's cost of equity capital. The first is a model premised on the notion that the value of a share of common stock is the present value of all expected cash dividends it will yield out to an infinite time horizon. We shall refer to this as the *dividend capitalization model.*[5] It is derived under the assumption that the cash dividend is expected to grow at a constant rate g from period to period. The model is:

$$k_{re} = \frac{D}{P} + g \tag{4.2}$$

where D is the expected annual dividend for the forthcoming year, P is the current price per share, and g is the annual growth rate in earnings per share.[6]

Unfortunately, estimation of the cost of equity capital is not as

[5]For detailed development of this and related models, see James C. T. Mao, *Quantitative Analysis of Financial Decisions* (New York: Macmillan, 1969), chap. 10.

[6]The cost of new shares is found similarly, except that the share price must be adjusted for flotation costs. Thus, if we denote flotation costs, as a proportion of the share price, by f, the cost of new equity is given by:

$$k_e = \frac{D}{P(1-f)} + g$$

simple and objective as Eq. (4.2) suggests. Dividends may be quite constant for some firms, but price per share is subject to substantial volatility, even from day to day. This may require that one obtain an average, or normalized price. For corporations whose shares are not actively traded there may be no recent market price quotation. Growth is affected not only by the individual firm's performance, but also by the condition of the economy. Therefore, estimation of the firm's cost of equity capital is not simply employing a formula, but also a substantial amount of human judgment. More complex formulations than Eq. (4.2) have been devised, but still no means for bypassing the need for exercising judgment have been seriously proposed. The more complex formulas suffer from the same problems as Eq. (4.2).

The second approach to estimating the firm's cost of equity capital is with what has come to be known as the capital asset pricing model, or CAPM. Although the dividend capitalization model could be characterized as inductive, the CAPM might be better characterized as deductive. The CAPM yields the following equation:

$$k_e = R_F + \beta(R_M - R_F) \tag{4.3}$$

where R_F is the rate of return on a risk-free security, usually meaning a short-term United States government security[7] such as treasury bills, and R_M is the rate of return on the market portfolio—an efficient portfolio in the sense that a higher return cannot be obtained without also accepting higher risk. The beta coefficient relates the return on the firm's stock to the return on the market portfolio. It is obtained by fitting a least-squares regression of the historical returns on the firm's stock to the historical returns on the market portfolio; it is the slope coefficient of the regression. Beta measures the risk of a company's shares that cannot be diversified away, and provides an index that indicates the responsiveness of returns on a particular firm's shares to returns on the market portfolio.[8]

---

[7]Even U.S. government bonds are not entirely risk free because of risk of change in their value caused by change in the market rate of interest. With short-term securities, however, such risk is slight, at least for magnitudes of market changes usually seen.

[8]In the development of β, capital appreciation is taken into account explicitly in addition to dividends.

The CAPM thus provides us with a means for estimating the firm's cost of capital with market data and the β coefficient, which relates the firm to the market. The dividend capitalization model, in contrast, requires only the current market price of our firm's common shares. Because of this, the CAPM data requirements are greater. Furthermore, the question of stability of the betas over time has not been resolved.

EXAMPLE 4-1

If we assume that we have obtained the beta for our firm, which is 1.80, that the risk-free interest rate is 6 percent and the return on market portfolio is 9 percent, we obtain as our estimate:

$$k_e = 6\% + 1.80(9\% - 6\%) = 11.4\%$$

The CAPM deals with risk *explicitly* through the firm's β coefficient. The dividend capitalization model, on the other hand, implicitly assumes risk is fully reflected in the market price of the firm's shares.

OVERALL COST OF CAPITAL

The overall cost of capital is obtained by calculating an average of the individual components, weighted according to the proportion of each in the total. Suppose a firm has the following capital structure:

Debt (Debentures Maturing 1998)	$30,000,000
Preferred Stock	20,000,000
Common Stock	15,000,000
Retained Earnings	35,000,000
Total	$100,000,000

Assume further that the after-tax costs of the components have been estimated as shown in Table 4-1. Calculation of the weighted average cost of capital is performed as shown.

Note that this average cost of capital is based on historical, balance sheet proportions, and on debt and preferred stock costs that were determined at time of issue of these securi-

Table 4-1.   Calculation of Weighted Average Cost of Capital

	(1) $ Amount (Millions)	(2) Proportion of Total	(3) % Cost	(4) (2) × (3)
Debt	30	.30	4.16	1.25%
Preferred	20	.20	9.00	1.80
Common	15	.15	15.00	2.25
Retained Earnings	35	.35	14.00	4.90
		Weighted average cost of capital		10.20%

Table 4-2.   Calculation of Marginal Cost of Capital

	(1) $ Amount (Millions)	(2) Proportion of Total	(3) % Cost	(4) (2) × (3)
Debt	3	.30	4.68	1.40%
Preferred	2	.20	12.00	2.40
Common	1.5	.15	17.00	2.55
Retained Earnings	3.5	.35	15.00	5.25
		Marginal cost of capital		11.60%

ties.[9] In capital investment project analysis, we are not concerned with average cost of capital. We are interested in the *marginal* cost, for that is the cost of funds that will be raised to undertake prospective capital investments. We cannot raise money at average historical cost, but at today's marginal rate.

Now, what if the firm must raise an additional $10 million? If the capital structure is judged to be optimal (more about optimal structure later), funds should be raised in proportion to the existing capital structure. If its profits are adequate, the firm may utilize retained earnings rather than float new common shares, providing that dividend policy will not be seriously affected. Assume that the $10 million will be raised in amounts and at costs illustrated in Table 4-2.

This 11.60 percent *marginal cost of capital* suggests that market conditions have changed, and that investors require higher yields

[9]Once a bond or preferred stock issue is sold the firm is committed to paying a fixed, periodic return per security. Even though capital market conditions may subsequently dictate higher or lower yields for similar securities of comparable risk if they are to be sold now, the interest and dividend payments on such securities sold in the past do not change.

than formerly. The result of raising additional funds at a marginal cost higher than the average historical cost will be to raise the new average cost figure somewhat. The new average cost is given by:

$$10.33\% = (100 \times 10.20\% + 10 \times 11.60\%) \div 110$$

One may be tempted to ask why the entire $10 million should not be raised with debt, thus at the lowest attainable marginal cost. This question arises naturally, but ignores the interrelated nature of financing decisions. Investors and creditors have notions about the proper mix of debt and equity for firms. Therefore, although today the firm might raise the entire $10 million with debt, at a later date it could find it has no reserve borrowing capacity, and also cannot borrow on favorable terms or at acceptable cost. In such a situation the firm may find that to raise funds it must float a new issue of common stock at a time when required yields are higher than normal, in a depressed stock market. This, however, would be a disservice to the current stockholders. The cost of any one capital component alone cannot be considered the true cost of capital for yet another reason. The cost of capital associated with any particular component is for that component to be a part of the whole firm, within the context of the firm. Bond purchasers are not merely buying bonds, they are buying bonds of a firm with a balanced financial structure. Because the overall results of the firm are what matters to the suppliers of funds, and because funds are not segregated by their origin, it would be inappropriate to use the cost of a component as a substitute for the overall cost.

Analysts have observed that stock and bond prices often move in opposite directions. Therefore, the financial manager has some flexibility in establishing the appropriate financing mix over the short run. Indeed, it is expected that financial management will use its best judgment in such matters. Sometimes it is better to raise funds with bonds, at other times with common stock. However, future price and yield trends must be anticipated; investors and creditors will not willingly tolerate marked deviation in capital structure from established norms over long periods. And the indenture agreements of prior bond issues or loans may well restrict the firm's latitude in using more leverage.

OPTIMAL CAPITAL STRUCTURE

In the early 1960s considerable controversy erupted over the theory proposed by Modigliani and Miller that the firm's cost of capital is invariant with respect to its capital structure,[10] depending only on the risk class to which the firm belonged. The original M and M theory did not take taxes into account, particularly the tax deductibility of interest payments on debt.[11] Subsequent modification of the M and M theory to include tax effects weakened their original conclusions. Since business income taxes are a reality in most nations, and interest payments for businesses a tax deductible expense, most authorities today agree that there is an optimal capital structure or range of optimal structures for any particular firm. The theory of M and M is elegantly developed and well worth reading. But it will not be discussed here because we cannot take up the required space. Instead, we shall examine the implications of optimal capital structure.

Existence of an optimal capital structure for any given firm suggests that financial management should try to obtain the optimal. Examination of the basic valuation model introduced in Chapter 2 reveals why this is desirable. Attainment of the lowest overall cost of capital will do proportionately more to increase the value of the firm than will an increase in the net cash flows, because of the compounding of terms containing k, the cost of capital.

We must recognize, however, that the world does not remain stationary. The quest for optimal capital structure requires that one follow a moving target, adjusting and readjusting sights as capital market conditions and investor and creditor attitudes change. Optimal capital structure, in practice, is not a once and for all time achievement. Rather, it involves periodic review and adjustment. Within a range of leverage, the firm may at times choose to finance more heavily with debt than with equity. Such a process, however, cannot continue indefinitely or the firm's leverage will become excessive, and with this the risk of insolvency, so that the cost of debt increases and onerous indenture

---

[10]F. Modigliani and M. H. Miller, "The Cost of Capital, Corporation Finance, and the Theory of Investment," *American Economic Review* (June 1958), pp. 361–397.

[11]Modigliani and Miller also assumed perfect capital markets, with investors able to borrow and lend at the same interest rate and zero transactions costs. This created arbitrage opportunities not found in the real world.

conditions are imposed, not to mention the financial leverage effects on variability in common stockholder returns.

At other times the firm may finance more heavily with equity, or employ preferred shares. An analogy may be drawn to a driver who must use accelerator and brakes to adjust to a speed that is optimal for road conditions—a speed that is safe and yet gets the driver to one's destination in minimum time or with minimum fuel consumption. The driver may use the brakes several times in sequence before using the accelerator, or the accelerator for some time without braking. (Unlike debt and equity, however, we may surmise that brake and accelerator will never be used simultaneously.)

The following example assumes constant capital market conditions and investor attitudes for purposes of illustration. Figure 4-1 illustrates the cost of capital schedule for a hypothetical firm. For simplicity, it is assumed that debt and equity may be raised in arbitrarily small increments, although this abstracts from real world considerations that militate against small issues of either debt or equity.

Note that the cost of equity capital, k_e, rises continuously as leverage increases. This reflects the increasing risk to the common shareholders as financial leverage increases: Shareholders require a greater return as variability in earnings allocated to them increases. The cost of debt, in contrast, begins at 4.68 percent [9

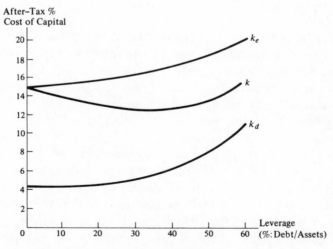

Figure 4-1.   Cost of Capital Schedule for a Firm.

percent pretax $\times$ (1 — 48 percent marginal tax rate)] and does not rise until leverage goes beyond 20 percent. Beyond this amount creditors become increasingly sensitive to the risk of firm insolvency as earnings become less and less a multiple of the interest that must be paid.

Lowest overall cost of capital is reached at 40 percent leverage, even though at this leverage the component costs of equity and debt are not at their lowest levels. Beyond 40 percent leverage the overall cost of capital rises for additional leverage at a faster rate than it declined prior to the optimum, thereby reflecting the rapidly rising debt and equity schedules.

If one could find an industry in which the firms were similar except for leverage, a schedule like that in Figure 4-1 could be produced. Each set of observations for a given leverage would correspond to one firm, or the average of several if multiple observations at the same leverage were obtained. However, it is difficult to find an industry in which the firms are really similar, because most firms today are in varying degree diversified in their operations, and are normally classified on the basis of their major activity. Furthermore, size disparity between firms would present problems to the extent that there may be differences in access to capital markets, industry dominance, product brand differentiation, and so on.

INTERACTION OF FINANCING AND INVESTMENT

The foregoing discussion of the firm's cost of capital assumed that cost of capital was independent of the firm's capital investment decisions. In practice this view may be unrealistic.

If the firm consistently follows the practice of investing in capital projects that yield a return equal to or greater than its existing cost of capital, and do not affect the riskiness of overall returns to the firm on its investments, *then* we may assume independence of cost of capital and investment. However, if the firm adopts a policy of adopting investments that alter its overall profitability or variability in earnings, we must recognize that there are likely to be resultant changes in the cost of capital components and thus the firm's overall cost of capital.

Changes in the firm's cost of capital through pursuit of investment policy that alters the characteristics of risk (that is, variability in return and probability of insolvency) are not necessarily adverse. The firm may reduce its cost of capital by reducing risk.[12] On the other hand, the firm may increase its cost of capital if it consistently adopts investments that, although offering high expected returns, at the same time contain commensurately high risk. This will not necessarily be so, but discussion of this point is deferred to Chapter 21, after portfolio effects have been considered. Depending upon the correlation between project returns on new investments and the existing capital assets of the firm, risk may actually be reduced *overall* by adopting a very risky new investment.

A simple example with an intuitive interpretation will serve to illustrate this point. Assume that the firm undertakes a very risky capital investment project, but has returns that are expected to be highly negatively correlated with the firm's existing assets. Acceptance of the project will reduce the overall riskiness of the firm. If, in a particular year, the existing assets provide high cash returns, the new investment will provide low returns. However, if the cash returns on existing assets were low, then the new investment would provide high returns. The overall result will be to smooth out variability in earnings and thus reduce risk.

[12]Some portfolio-approach advocates would argue that, since investors can diversify their portfolios to reduce risk, it is unnecessary, and perhaps even detrimental to stockholder interests, for the firm to diversify its investments.

II

Traditional Methods of
Project Evaluation

5

Traditional Methods That Ignore Time-Value of Money

PAYBACK AND NAIVE RATE OF RETURN

Payback

The payback period criterion has consistently been demonstrated to be the single most popular measure of project merit used in practice. Possibly, the payback criterion is the oldest of capital budgeting measures as well.

The payback method is extremely simple to employ and intuitively appealing. To apply the method to a project costing amount C with uniform cash flows of amount R each period, one need only take the ratio of C to R:

$$\text{Payback} \equiv \frac{C}{R} \qquad (5.1)$$

when R is uniform each period. In cases in which cash flows are not expected to be uniform, the method is somewhat more complicated.

$$\text{Payback} \equiv P + \frac{C - \sum_{t=1}^{P} R_t}{R_{t+1}} \qquad (5.2)$$

where

$$C - \sum_{t=1}^{P} R_t > 0 \text{ and } C - \sum_{t=1}^{P+1} R_t \leq 0$$

Two illustrations will serve to make the procedure clear. We consider first a project designated as project A. This investment requires an outlay today (at $t = 0$) of $5000, and will yield uniform net cash flows of $2500 each year over its economic, or useful life, of ten years.

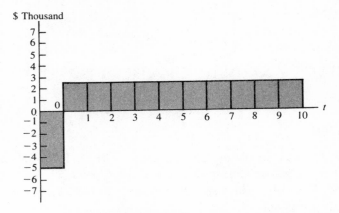

Figure 5-1.   Project A.

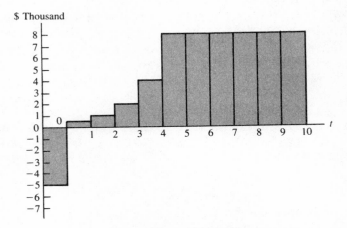

Figure 5-2.   Project B.

Applying formula (5.1), since the cash flows are uniform, we obtain a payback for project A of:

$$P(A) = \frac{C}{R} = \frac{5000}{2500} = 2.0 \text{ years}$$

The parenthetical A with P serves to distinguish this from the payback on other projects.

Next let us consider project B, which, although requiring the same initial outlay in year $t = 0$ of $5000, has a nonuniform net cash flow sequence. Cash flows for B in years $t = 1$ through $t = 4$ are $500, $1000, $2000, and $4000, respectively. In years $t = 5$ through $t = 10$, the cash flows are uniformly $8000. Since project B has nonuniform cash flows, formula (5.1) is not applicable. We must instead use (5.2). To do this we proceed as follows, taking the absolute value of C, and successively subtracting the net cash flows:

$$
\begin{array}{rl}
C & = \$5000 \\
-R(1) = & 500 \\
\hline
& 4500 \quad P = 1 \\
-R(2) = & 1000 \\
\hline
& 3500 \quad P = 2 \\
-R(3) = & 2000 \\
\hline
& 1500 \quad P = 3
\end{array}
$$

The remaining $1500 is less than the cash flow in year four. It represents the unrecovered portion of the initial outlay. The question now is how far into year four we must go to recover this remaining amount. Implicit *in the payback method is the assumption that cash flows are uniform over a particular period* even if nonuniform from period to period. Therefore, we must go into year four:

$$\frac{\$1500}{R(4)} = \frac{\$1500}{\$4000} = \frac{3}{8} \text{ or } .375$$

Combining results, we obtain the payback period for project B of:

$$P(B) = P + .375 = 3.375$$

This procedure for calculating payback is in the form of an *algorithm.* An algorithm is a systematic, multiple step procedure for obtaining a solution to a problem. Other, more complicated algorithms will be introduced in later chapters. Many may be converted into computer programs in order to reduce human effort and with it the chance of calculation errors.

The Naive Rate of Return

When a manager who relies on the payback criterion speaks of rate of return, this normally refers to something other than time-adjusted return on investment. For example, a project that promises a two-year payback will be said to offer a 50 percent per year rate of return. This we refer to as *naive* rate of return (NROR), since it ignores the effects of cash flows beyond the payback period as well as the effects of compounding from period to period.

$$\text{NROR} \equiv 1/\text{Payback (in years)} \qquad (5.3)$$

The criticisms of payback are thus equally applicable to naive rate of return.

Strong Points of Payback

1. It is easily understood.
2. It favors projects that offer large immediate cash flows.
3. It offers a means of coping with risk due to increasing unreliability of forecasted cash flows as the time horizon increases.
4. It provides a powerful tool for capital rationing when the organization has a critical need to do so.
5. Because it is so simple to understand, it provides a means for decentralizing capital budgeting decisions by having nonspecialists screen proposals at lower levels in the organization.

Weak Points of Payback

1. It ignores all cash flows beyond payback period.
2. It ignores the time value of funds.

3. It does not distinguish between projects of different size in terms of investment required.
4. It can be made shorter by postponing replacement of worn and deteriorating capital until a later period.
5. It emphasizes short-run profitability to the exclusion of long-run profitability.

To illustrate, let us consider along with projects A and B another project, C. This project also requires an investment of $5000, and yields net cash flows of $5000, $1000, and $500 in years one, two, and three, respectively. It offers no cash returns beyond year three. Payback for project C is easily seen to be 1.0 year.

If we rank the three projects now in terms of payback, we obtain:

Project	Payback	Ranking
C	1.0	1
A	2.0	2
B	3.375	3

If we assume that A, B, and C are mutually exclusive, the reliance on payback alone implies that project C will be selected as the best project because it has the shortest payback of the three. In the absence of project C, A would be selected as preferable to B. But which project would management prefer to have at the end of four years? Clearly, project B is preferable at that point, if there is any reliability in the estimates of project characteristics, and if we can assume reasonable certainty of these estimates.

Let us next consider the effects of a large negative salvage value for project C in year four. Has the payback measure for this project been changed? No, it has not, because cash flows beyond payback are ignored.

Terborgh[1] has provided perhaps the most clever and effective statement of the way payback favors delaying replacement of an already deteriorated capital project until it has deteriorated still further. Payback treats relief from losses *caused* by undue delay in

---

[1]G. Terborgh, *Dynamic Equipment Policy* (Washington: Machinery and Allied Products Institute, 1949) p. 207.

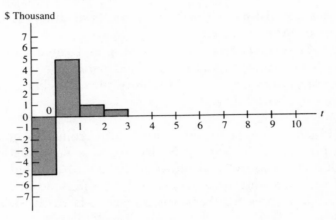

Figure 5-3.   Project C.

replacements as return on the new investment. Consider Ter-borgh's analogy:

> A corporation has a president 70 years of age who in the judgment of the directors can be retired and replaced at a net annual advantage to the company of $10,000. Someone points out, however, that if he is kept to age 75, and if he suffers in the interval the increasing decrepitude normally to be expected, the gain from replacing him at that time will be $50,000 a year, while it should be substantially higher still, say $100,000 at the age of 80. It is urged, therefore, that his retirement should be deferred. The genius advancing this proposal is recognized at once as a candidate for the booby hatch, yet it is not different in principle from the rate-of-return requirement.
>
> No one can deny that the advantage of $100,000 a year (if such it is) from retiring the president at 80 is a real advantage, given the situation then prevailing. The question is whether this situation should be deliberately created for the sake of reaping this gain. Similarly, the question is whether a machine should be retained beyond its proper service life in order to get a larger benefit from its replacement. The answer in both cases is obvious. The executive who knowingly and wilfully follows this practice should sleep on a spike bed to enjoy the relief of getting up in the morning.

Considering the strong and weak points of payback all together, is there any merit on balance in using this method? Absolutely not, *unless* payback is not the sole criterion employed. As a single criterion, payback may be worse than useless because its implicit assumptions disregard important information about events beyond payback. As a tie-breaker to supplement other methods, payback has considerable merit if we assume that, *other things being equal,* rapid cash flow in the early years of an investment is preferable to the later years. This view is reinforced if one considers that the further from the present we attempt to estimate anything, the less reliable our estimates become. In other words, once we introduce risk into our considerations, we will *ceteris paribus* prefer early return of our investment to later recovery of it.

Unrecovered Investment

A concept related to payback, but taking the time-value of money into account, is *unrecovered investment.* [2] Again taking C to be the cost or investment committed (at $t = 0$) to a capital project, and taking rate k as the firm's per period opportunity cost of the funds tied up in the project, unrecovered investment is defined by

$$U(k, t) = C(1 + k)^t - \sum_{i=1}^{t} R_i(1 + k)^{t-i} \tag{5.4}$$

Note that if we set $k = 0$ for values of $U \geq 0$, and $k = \infty$ for $U < 0$, we find that $U = 0$ defines payback as in the previous section.

If for all periods we take k as the firm's cost of capital, then it follows that the value of t for which $U = 0$ provides us with a time-adjusted payback period. The value of t for which this is true will not necessarily be an integer. The t value thus obtained suggests how long it will take for the firm to recover its investment in the project plus the cost of the funds committed to the project. If k is in fact a precise measure of the enterprise's opportunity cost, then the t for which $U(k, t) = 0$ corresponds to the time at which the firm will be no worse off than if it had never undertaken the project. Since we assume cash flows occur at the end of each period, this relationship will be approximate but nevertheless useful.

The subject of unrecovered investment is treated further in Chapter 14. The concept of time-adjusted payback is used

[2]David Durand, "Time as a Dimension of Investment," *Proceedings of the Eastern Finance Association* (April 1973), pp. 187–192.

in the method of analysis discussed in the appendix to Chapter 11.

ACCOUNTING METHOD: ALIAS AVERAGE RETURN ON AVERAGE INVESTMENT

The accounting method[3] involves calculation of an average net cash return on the average investment committed to a project. It is not as popular a method of capital-budgeting project analysis as payback, but it is nonetheless still frequently encountered today. It is easy to apply: It requires only that one:

1. Calculate average *accounting profit*[4] by $\frac{1}{N} \sum_{t=1}^{N} A_t$.
2. Calculate average investment by $(C + S)/2$.
3. Divide average return by average investment, and express as a percentage.

Thus the average return on average investment (ARAI) is defined as:

$$\text{ARAI} \equiv \frac{\sum_{t=1}^{N} \frac{A_t}{N}}{(C + S)/2} \neq \frac{\sum_{t=1}^{N} \frac{R_t}{N}}{(C + S)/2} \tag{5.5}$$

Note that if A were uniform, with straight-line depreciation and $S = 0$, ARAI would be similar to the naive rate of return (NROR). This is because the A_t terms include depreciation, whereas the R_t terms include the cash flow dollars shielded from taxes by depreciation.

Strong Points of Accounting Method

1. It is easily understood.
2. It does not ignore any periods in the project life.
3. It is, in a sense, more conservative than payback and naive rate of return.

[3]National Association of Accountants, *Financial Analysis to Guide Capital Expenditure Decisions*, Research Report 43, 1967.

[4]Note that this is at odds with our stated use only of net, after-tax cash flows in capital investment project analysis.

4. It explicitly recognizes salvage value.
5. Because it is easy to understand, it (like payback) may provide a means for decentralizing the process of preliminary screening of proposals.

Weak Points of Accounting Method

1. Like payback, it ignores the time-value of funds.
2. It assumes that capital recovery is linear over time.
3. It does not distinguish between projects of different sizes in terms of the investment required.
4. It conveys the impression of greater precision than payback since it requires more calculation effort, while suffering from faults as serious as that method.
5. It does not favor early returns over later returns.
6. The method violates the criterion that we consider only net cash flows. We can only pay out dividends in cash and reinvest cash; not book profits.

COMPREHENSIVE EXAMPLE

Consider the following two projects. They have net, after-tax cash flows and depreciation charges as shown. It is assumed that the class life asset depreciation range system is used, with a switch from double-declining balance to sum-of-the-years' digits method in year two. Project D has zero salvage, E has salvage of $20,000. The depreciable lifetime for D is five years, for E it is eight years. Note that project D's economic life is a year longer than the depreciation life used.

	Project D	Project E
Initial Outlay	$100,000	$100,000
Cash Flow/Depreciation for Year:		
1	$25,000/$40,000	$40,000/$25,000
2	35,000/24,000	30,000/18,750
3	40,000/18,000	20,000/16,071
4	40,000/12,000	20,000/13,393
5	40,000/6,000	20,000/6,786
6	40,000/0	20,000/0
7	0	20,000/0
8	0	20,000/0

Payback periods are calculated as follows:

Project D

$ 100,000	
−25,000	
75,000	$P = 1$
−35,000	
40,000	$P = 2$
−40,000	
0	$P = 3$

The payback for project D is exactly 3 years.

Project E

$ 100,000	
−40,000	
60,000	$P = 1$
−30,000	
30,000	$P = 2$
−20,000	
10,000	$P = 3$

and $10,000/20,000 = 1/2$

So the payback for project E is $3\frac{1}{2}$ years.

We calculate ARAI on the basis of accounting profits, not cash flows. If we assume that the timing of accounting profits and cash flows is approximately the same, the accounting profit in any year t, A_t, will be equal to the net, after-tax cash flow, R_t, less the depreciation charged in that year: $A_t = R_t - D_t$.

Then ARAI for the investment projects is:

Project D

$$\frac{1}{6} \quad (\$25,000 - \$40,000 +$$
$$35,000 - 24,000 +$$
$$40,000 - 18,000 +$$
$$40,000 - 12,000 +$$
$$40,000 - 6,000 +$$
$$40,000 - 0)$$
$$\div$$
$$\frac{1}{2} (\$100,000 + 0)$$

$$= \frac{\$20,000}{\$50,000}$$
$$= 40\%$$

Project E

$$\frac{1}{8}$$

$$
\begin{aligned}
(\$40{,}000 &- \$25{,}000 + \\
30{,}000 &- 18{,}750 + \\
20{,}000 &- 16{,}071 + \\
20{,}000 &- 13{,}393 + \\
20{,}000 &- 6{,}786 + \\
20{,}000 &- 0 + \\
20{,}000 &- 0 + \\
20{,}000 &- 0)
\end{aligned}
$$

$$\div$$

$$\frac{1}{2} (\$100{,}000 + \$20{,}000)$$

$$= \frac{\$13{,}750}{\$60{,}000}$$

$$= 22.92\%$$

If we assume the firm has a 10 percent annual cost of capital, the unrecovered investment at the end of year three for each project is:

Project D

$$\$100{,}000 (1.10)^3 \qquad \begin{aligned} &- \$25{,}000 (1.10)^2 \\ &- 35{,}000 (1.10)^1 \\ &- 40{,}000 (1.10)^0 \end{aligned}$$

$$= \$133{,}100 - \$108{,}750$$

$$= \$24{,}350$$

Project E

$$\$100{,}000 (1.10)^3 \qquad \begin{aligned} &- \$40{,}000 (1.10)^2 \\ &- 30{,}000 (1.10)^1 \\ &- 20{,}000 (1.10)^0 \end{aligned}$$

$$= \$133{,}100 - \$101{,}400$$

$$= \$31{,}700$$

6

Traditional Methods That Recognize Time-Value of Money: The Net Present Value

The internal rate of return considered in the next chapter involves finding the unique real root to a polynomial equation with real coefficients. At best this is a tedious calculation when performed manually, particularly for projects with unequal cash flows for many periods. The net present value (NPV), which is considered here, involves the much simpler task of evaluating that polynomial equation with real coefficients for a given discount rate, which usually will *not* be a root to the polynomial. The NPV is defined in the equation:

$$\text{NPV} \equiv C + \sum_{t=1}^{N} \frac{R_t}{(1 + k)^t} \quad \text{or} \quad \sum_{t=0}^{N} \frac{R_t}{(1 + k)^t} \tag{6.1}$$

if we let $C = R_0$, or in the more compact form:

$$\text{NPV} \equiv \sum_{t=0}^{N} R_t(1 + k)^{-t} \tag{6.2}$$

This equation appears to be identical to the basic valuation model in Chapter 2. There is a subtle difference, however, that the notation does not reflect. In the basic valuation model the R_t are the total or aggregated net, after-tax cash flows in each period. In Eq. (6.1), on the other hand, the R_t are the net, after-tax cash flows of the project under analysis. Although the same symbol is used in each, the meaning is somewhat different.

72

The NPV of a particular project provides a measure that is compatible with the valuation model of the firm. This much is perhaps obvious because of the mathematical form of the equations. Since we take as given the management goal of maximization of the enterprise's value, we recognize that acceptance of individual projects with a positive NPV will contribute to the increase in that value. In the absence of capital rationing, in other words, if there is no shortage of money to accept all projects with positive NPVs, the enterprise should do so.

In reference to the calculation of NPV, the conventional approach has been to calculate first the *gross* present value, which is the present value of all the net, after-tax cash *inflows,* and then subtract the initial outlay that is assumed to be at present value since it is incurred at $t = 0$. For projects requiring net outlays beyond the initial period, the outlays are brought to present value in the same manner as the cash receipts.

In the calculation of NPV we take the discount rate, k, as *given.* The rate used is generally[1] the organization's cost of capital; more particularly, it is the *marginal* cost of capital. If an investment yields a discounted return greater than its discounted cost, it will have NPV > 0. Conversely, if the discounted cost exceeds the discounted returns, it will have NPV < 0. Therefore the rule for project adoption under the NPV criterion is:

$$\text{If NPV} \leq 0, \text{reject}$$
$$> 0, \text{accept}$$

The discounting process employed simply allows cash flows to be compared after they have been adjusted for the time value of money. The time reference we use is immaterial: We could just as easily have used net *future* value by adjusting the cash flows to their compounded (rather than discounted) value at $t = N$ rather than at $t = 0$. However, it is a traditional convention that NPV rather than net future value be used.

The NPV method may be further clarified by means of an example. Let us assume that k, the discount rate, is 15 percent per annum and find the NPV for project A, considered in the previous

[1]In the case of risky projects, which we are not considering in this section of the text, a "risk-adjusted discount rate" or "hurdle rate" is sometimes used as an alternative to other methods for dealing with risk.

Table 6-1.   The NPV Calculations for Project A

Year	Present Worth Factor	×	Cash Flow	=	Present Value
1	.86957		$2,500		$2,173.92
2	.75614		2,500		1,890.35
3	.65752		2,500		1,643.80
4	.57175		2,500		1,429.38
5	.49718		2,500		1,242.95
6	.43233		2,500		1,080.82
7	.37594		2,500		939.85
8	.32690		2,500		817.25
9	.28426		2,500		710.65
10	.24718		2,500		617.95
	5.01877				$12,546.92

chapter. This project requires an initial outlay of $5000 and returns $2500 each year over a ten-year useful life, net after taxes. Table 6-1 illustrates the NPV calculations. Notice that because the cash flows for this project are a uniform $2500, we could have summed the present worth factors and then multiplied the sum once by $2500 to get the NPV. However, this summation has already been done: The results are listed in the table in the appendix for annuity present worth factors.[2]

Now, to obtain *net* present value, we need remove only the $5000 project cost that, since it occurs at $t = 0$, is already at present value. (That is, the present value factor for $t = 0$ is 1.00000.)

Therefore the NPV for project A is:

$$\$7546.92 = \$12,546.92 - \$5000$$

at $k = 15$ percent. Since NPV > 0, the project is acceptable for investment.

Next, let us find the NPV for project B (also considered in a previous chapter). The calculations are shown in Table 6-2.

Note that since cash flow in years five through ten is a uni-

[2]Alternatively, if we have a modern calculator, we can find the present worth of annuity factor for N periods and rate k from the relationship

$$a_{\overline{N}|k} = \frac{1 - (1 + k)^{-N}}{k}$$

Table 6-2. The NPV Calculations for Project B

Year	Present Worth Factor	×	Cash Flow	=	Present Value
1	.86957		$ 500		$ 434.78
2	.75614		1,000		756.14
3	.65752		2,000		1,315.04
4	.57175		4,000		2,287.00
	−2.85498				$4,792.96
5	.49718		8,000		$3,977.44
6	.43233		8,000		3,458.64
7	.37594		8,000		3,007.52
8	.32690		8,000		2,615.20
9	.28426		8,000		2,274.08
10	.24718		8,000		1,977.44
	5.01877				
	2.16379	×	8,000	=	17,310.32
				Gross PV	$22,103.28
			Less C at $t = 0$		−5,000.00
				NPV	$17,103.28

form $8000, the present value of these flows can be obtained by multiplying by the present worth of annuity factor for ten years *less* the present worth of annuity factor for four years: $8000(5.01877 − 2.85498).

If we were considering A and B as mutually exclusive projects, B would clearly be preferred since its NPV of $17,103.28 is more than 2½ times larger, *and* the required $5000 investment is the same for both projects.

The internal rate of return (IRR), which the next chapter covers, is a special case of NPV. The IRR is that discount rate for which the NPV is equal to zero. In other words, the IRR is that rate of discount for which the present value of net cash inflows equals the present value of net cash outflows.

Figure 6-1 illustrates the NPV functions for projects A and B for various discount rates. Negative rates are for purposes of illustration only, not because of any economically meaningful interpretation of such rates as cost of capital. Note that the IRR of each project is at that rate of discount where the NPV of that project intersects the horizontal axis, and that NPV = 0 at these points. It can be shown that for all investments with $R_0 = C <$

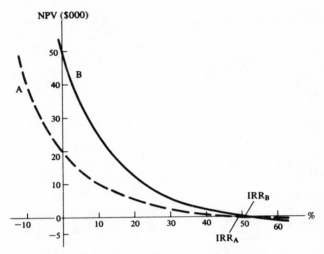

Figure 6-1.   NPV Functions for Projects A and B.

0, and $R_t \geq 0$ for all $0 < t \leq N$, that the NPV function is concave from above. For projects having *some* $R_t \geq 0$ for $0 < t \leq N$ this will not necessarily be true.

Let us consider an investment project that has some negative cash flows after $t = 0$. We will call this project AA. The cash flows over a four-year economic life are:

R_0	R_1	R_2	R_3	R_4
-1000	1200	600	300	-1000

This project has two "IRRs": -8.14 percent and $+42.27$ percent. Quotation marks are placed on the IRR because, as we shall see in Chapter 10, neither rate is internal to the project and neither measures the return on investment for this project. Figure 6-2 contains the graph of the NPV function for this project. Note that NPV is positive until the discount rate reaches 42.27 percent, but that the NPV is concave from *below* up to this point.

We shall consider such projects in later chapters in more detail. For now it will be useful to make a mental note that they are neither purely investments nor purely financing projects (loans to the enterprise) but a mixture of these. Because many projects are

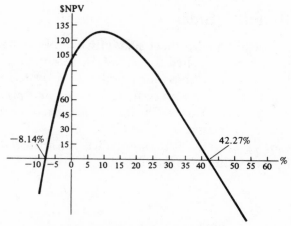

Figure 6-2. NPV Curve for Project AA.

of this nature, it is important that we have means for their proper analysis, although we shall defer this until later.

UNEQUAL PROJECT SIZE

A difficulty that arises with NPV is that marginally valuable projects may show a higher NPV than more desirable projects simply because they are larger. For example, consider projects D and E.

	Project D	Project E
Cost $= R_0$	$100,000	$10,000
Cash Flows, R_1 through R_{10}	30,000	10,000
R_{11}	0	0

Again using $k = 15$ percent, we see that the NPV for project D is $50,570, whereas that for project E is only $40,190. Therefore, D would seem preferable to E. However, D costs *ten times* as much as E. The extra NPV is only 11.5 percent of the additional $90,000 required investment—an amount less than the 15 percent cost of capital.

This problem is a serious one, especially when capital is limited and consequently there is capital rationing within the organization. Fortunately, this problem is easily corrected.

The Profitability Index

The problem of unequal project size with the NPV is easily corrected by using what is called the *profitability index* (PI). The PI may be defined in two ways; these are identical except for a constant of 1.0. The more common way is by the ratio of *gross* present value to project cost. Under this definition an acceptable project, one with NPV > 0, will have a PI > 1.0.

This author's preference is to define PI as the ratio of *net* present value to present value of project cost:

$$PI \equiv \frac{NPV}{C} \quad \text{or} \quad \frac{NPV}{R_0} \tag{6.3}$$

Thus, if NPV > 0, PI > 0. On the other hand, if NPV ≤ 0, PI ≤ 0. It is immaterial which definition is used, provided that it is used consistently. They are identical except that definition (6.3) yields a PI that is 1.0 less than that obtained under the alternative definition.

Let us look again at projects D and E in terms of their PI.

$$PI \quad \frac{D}{.5057} \quad \frac{E}{4.019}$$

The results obtained favor project E, because the return on the investment is much better proportionately than that on project D.

UNEQUAL PROJECT LIVES

Another problem exists with the NPV and the derivative PI. This is due to the effect of unequal project lives. For example, let us assume that a given operation is expected to be required for an indefinite time, and that two mutually exclusive projects, F and G, both have acceptable NPVs and IRRs. However, project F will last for ten years and project G will last for only five, after which it will have to be replaced. Can we determine which should be accepted on the basis of PI as defined earlier? No. We must take into account the effect of the difference in project lives. As an aid in defining how this should be done, let us consider specific projects F and G.

Net Cash Flows

Year	Project F	Project G
0	$100,000	$100,000
1	30,000	40,000
2	—	40,000
3	—	40,000
4	—	40,000
5	—	40,000
6	—	0
7	—	—
8	—	—
9	—	—
10	30,000	0

Letting $k = 15$ percent, we obtain for the projects:

	F	G
NPV	$50,563	$34,086
PI	.506	.341

Since project G will have to be replaced at the end of year five, we need to take this into account systematically. (We assume it can be replaced for $100,000 at that time, ignoring the effects of inflation.) One way is to assume that if it is adopted, project G will be replaced by an identical project at the end of year five and then treat the cash flows over the entire ten-year period explicitly. In other words, we calculate NPV and PI for project G that now has cash flows:

Net Cash Flows

Time	First Project G	Replacement	Combined
0	$-100,000		$-100,000
1	40,000		40,000
2	40,000		40,000
3	40,000		40,000
4	40,000		40,000
5	40,000	$-100,000	-60,000
6		40,000	40,000
7		40,000	40,000
8		40,000	40,000
9		40,000	40,000
10		40,000	40,000

The values obtained now for project G are:

$$NPV = \$51,033$$
$$PI = .510$$

so that, contrary to the unadjusted results previously obtained, project G is preferable. The method illustrated for adjusting for unequal lives can be tedious to apply, since it requires us to calculate NPV over the least common denominator number of years of the project lives. In this example project F lasted exactly twice as long as project G, so this presented no problem. However, what if we had one project lasting 11 years and another lasting 13 years (both prime numbers)? In this case we would have to evaluate 143 cash flows for each project!

Level Annuities

A much easier equivalent method is to calculate the time-adjusted annual average (level annuity) for each project. This is done by multiplying the unadjusted NPV by the capital recovery factor (also called annuity with present value of 1.0) for the number of years of useful life in the project. The capital recovery factor (CRF) is the reciprocal of the present value of annuity factor.[3]

For projects F and G, the time-adjusted annual averages are:

Project F $50,563 × .19925 (10-year CRF) = $10,075
Project G $34,086 × .29832 (5-year CRF) = $10,169

It is apparent that project G offers a higher NPV on an annual basis than does F. Now, to convert these results to adjusted NPVs for the projects over the longer-lived project, in this case ten years, we need only multiply by the present value of annuity factor corresponding to this number of years. Thus, we obtain adjusted NPVs of:[4]

Project F $10,075 × 5.0188 = $50,564
Project G $10,169 × 5.0188 = $51,036

[3]The CRF is defined by the equation $k/[1 - (1 + k)^{-N}]$ for rate k and N periods. The CRF enables us to spread out any given present value over a specified number of years as well as providing a means for finding a time-value-adjusted average present value.
[4]Minor rounding errors make the calculated result different by a small amount.

And the corresponding profitability indexes are .506 and .510.

SUMMARY AND CONCLUSION

Now that we have seen how two difficulties with NPV may be surmounted with the profitability index and uniform annual equivalents, what can we say in summary about NPV?

Strong Points of NPV

1. It is conceptually superior to payback and accounting methods.
2. It does not ignore any periods in the project life nor any cash flows.
3. It takes into account the time value of funds.
4. It is consistent with the basic valuation model expressed in Chapter 2.
5. It is easier to apply than internal rate of return since it involves evaluating a polynomial rather than finding a root.
6. It favors early cash flows over later ones.

Weak Points of NPV

1. It, like IRR, requires that we have an estimate of the organization's cost of capital, k. Also, the given k is embedded in the NPV, whereas with IRR the internal rate can be judged by management. Management will determine whether it is reasonable that the IRR is greater or less than k when k is not known with confidence.
2. It is more difficult to apply than payback or accounting method, and thus less suitable for use by lower levels in the organization without proper training in its application. That may not be feasible.
3. Unless modified by conversion to uniform annual equivalents and converted to profitability index, NPV will give distorted comparison between projects of unequal size and/or unequal economic lives.

7

Traditional Methods That Recognize Time-Value of Money: Internal Rate of Return

DEFINITION OF THE IRR

The internal rate of return (IRR) is defined as the rate of interest compounded from period to period, which exactly equates all net cash flows to the required outlay. Alternatively, the IRR is the rate for which the net present value (NPV) of the cash flows is equal to zero. Thus IRR is the rate of discount r, which satisfies the relationship:

$$C = \frac{R_1}{(1 + r)^1} + \frac{R_2}{(1 + r)^2} + \frac{R_3}{(1 + r)^3} + \cdots + \frac{R_N}{(1 + r)^N} \quad (7.1)$$

If we rename C to R_0, this can be restated as:

$$0 = \frac{R_0}{(1 + r)^0} + \frac{R_1}{(1 + r)^1} + \frac{R_2}{(1 + r)^2} + \cdots + \frac{R_N}{(1 + r)^N} \quad (7.2)$$

or in the more compact equivalent forms:

$$0 = \sum_{t=0}^{N} \frac{R_t}{(1 + r)^t} = \sum_{t=0}^{N} R_t(1 + r)^{-t} \quad (7.3)$$

Equations (7.1), (7.2), and (7.3) define a polynomial equation with real coefficients $R_0, R_1, \ldots, R_n$. The IRR is thus the root of a polynomial. Unfortunately, under some circumstances there may be two or more real roots, or an economically misleading root, and this creates some significant problems. The general case of multiple roots will be dealt with later. For now we consider

82

only investment projects that have only one sign change in the coefficients, which we are assured by Descartes' rule of signs can have but one real, positive root. Cost C, or as we will normally call it from now on, R_0, we assume to be negative, and R_1, R_2, R_3, . . . , R_N to be positive. In later chapters this assumption may be relaxed.

In general, finding the IRR can be a troublesome task when the cash flows after R_0 are nonuniform. We shall therefore deal first with a project with uniform cash flows. To illustrate the calculation of IRR when cash flows are uniform, let us consider project A from Chapter 5 again, and use Eq. (7.1):

$$\$5000 = \frac{\$2500}{1 + r} + \frac{\$2500}{(1 + r)^2} + \cdots + \frac{\$2500}{(1 + r)^{10}} \qquad (7.4)$$

which, since the R_t are uniform, can be rewritten:

$$\$5000 = \$2500 \sum_{t=1}^{10} \frac{1}{(1 + r)^t} = \$2500 \sum_{t=1}^{10} (1 + r)^{-t} \qquad (7.5)$$

so that we have:

$$2.0 = \frac{\$5000}{\$2500} = \sum_{t=1}^{10} (1 + r)^{-t} = \frac{1 - (1 + r)^{-10}}{r} \equiv a_{\overline{10}|r} \qquad (7.6)$$

Since the last term on the right here is the summation representing the present value of an annuity of one for ten periods at r percent,[1] we look in appendix Table A-4.[2] Moving across the row

---

[1]The term is derived from the formula for the summation of a geometric progression, which is:

$$\text{Sum} = a\frac{\rho^N - 1}{\rho - 1}$$

where ρ is the common ratio (in the case above, $\rho = (1 + r)^{-1}$), a the first term in the progression, and N the number of periods. For an ordinary annuity this becomes:

$$(1 + r)^{-1}\frac{(1 + r)^{-N} - 1}{(1 + r)^{-1} - 1} = (1 + r)^{-1}\frac{(1 + r)^{-N} - 1}{-r(1 + r)^{-1}}$$
$$= \frac{1 - (1 + r)^{-N}}{r} \equiv a_{N\,r}$$

[2]Modern hand-held calculators provide a better approach: Calculate the factor for a trial r, and revise the estimate until the result is satisfactorily close. If a table is readily available, it provides a good first guess, of course. Many reasonably priced calculators are available with circuitry preprogrammed to provide very precise solutions for r.

that corresponds to the ten periods, we find the factor 2.003 under 49 percent. Since this is very close to 2.0, we might conclude that the IRR for project A is essentially 49 percent (the actual rate is 49.1 percent to the nearest one-tenth percent).

Now let us see what must be done when cash flows are not uniform for all periods beyond $t = 0$. Finding the IRR for project B is not so easy, because the cash flows are not uniform. To find r we use the appendix tables for single-amount present worth and for annuity present worth.

First, let us estimate that r is 60 percent. We then proceed as follows:

Year	Present Worth Factor	×	Cash Flow	=	Present Value
1	.62500		$ 500		$ 312.50
2	.39063		1000		390.63
3	.24414		2000		488.28
4	.15259		4000		610.36
5					
6					
7	.2391		8000		1912.80
8	(1.6515 − 1.4124)				
9					
10					
		Project present value at 60%	=		$3714.57

Since the cash flows in years five through eight are a uniform $8000, we need multiply this amount only once by the present worth of annuity factor for ten years at 60 percent *less* the present worth of annuity factor for four years at 60 percent. Notice that the latter is equal to the sum of the single-amount present worth factors for years one through four. The project present value at 60 percent is $3714.57, which is less than the $5000 investment outlay. Therefore we know that 60 percent is too high a discount rate, and that IRR is less than this. Let us next try 50 percent.

Year	Present Worth Factor	×	Cash Flow	+	Present Value
1	.66667		$ 500		$ 333.33
2	.44444		1000		444.44
3	.29630		2000		592.60
4	.19753		4000		790.12

5			
6			
7	.3604	8000	2883.20
8	(1.9653 − 1.6049		
9			
10			

$$\text{Project present value at 50\%} \quad = \quad \$5043.69$$

This is just slightly above the $5000 investment cost. We have bracketed the IRR, and now know that it is very close to 50 percent. We can now refine our result by interpolation.

$$\frac{\begin{bmatrix} 60\% \\ r \\ 50\% \end{bmatrix}}{50 - r} = \frac{\begin{bmatrix} 3714.57 \\ 5000 \\ 5043.69 \end{bmatrix}}{43.69}$$

$$r \quad = 50 + \frac{436.90}{1329.12} = 50.329\% \text{ or } 50.3\%$$

This interpolation assumes a linear relationship, whereas we have an exponential one, so our result is only approximate. However, for capital-budgeting applications it will normally be precise enough. We should generally give interpolated answers to only one decimal or the nearest percent or tenth of a percent in order not to convey the impression of greater precision than we in fact have. The actual rate, correct to the nearest tenth of a percent, *is* 50.3 percent in this case. In general, the smaller the range over which we bracket the rate, the more precise our interpolated result will be.

By this point it should be clear that calculation of IRR is a tedious task when cash flows are not uniform. In fact, to ease the computational burden, computer programs have been developed to calculate IRR and today some hand-held calculators are programmed to solve for IRR.[3] Programs to calculate IRR are not difficult to write; the Newton-Raphson or interval bisection methods, in conjunction with Horner's method of polynomial evaluation, both yield good results efficiently.

---

[3]Texas Instruments, Hewlett-Packard, and others make such calculators.

A CAUTION AND A RULE FOR IRR

Assume we have a project costing $4000 that will last only two years and provides cash flows of $1000 and $5000 in years one and two. To find the IRR for this project we may use the quadratic formula $(-b \pm \sqrt{b^2 - 4ac})/2a$, since (dropping the $ signs):

$$4000 = \frac{1000}{1 + r} + \frac{5000}{(1 + r)^2} \tag{7.7}$$

is equivalent to:

$$-4 + \frac{1}{1 + r} + \frac{5}{(1 + r)^2} = 0 \tag{7.8}$$

Multiplying by $(1 + r)^2$, we get:

$$-4(1 + r)^2 + (1 + r) + 5 = 0 \tag{7.9}$$

Letting $x = 1 + r$, we obtain the quadratic equation:

$$-4x^2 + x + 5 = 0 \tag{7.10}$$

which has roots given by:

$$\frac{-1 \pm \sqrt{1 + 80}}{-8}$$

of $x = -1.0$ and $+1.25$. Converting to r, we have IRR of -200 percent *and* $+25$ percent! Which do we take as *the* IRR for this project? The rule to follow in such cases is:

In the case of one positive or zero root and one negative root, choose the negative root only if the project cost is strictly greater than the undiscounted sum of the cash flows in periods 1 through N.

In this case $4000 < 1000 + 5000$, so we choose $+25$ percent for IRR. *A negative IRR makes no economic sense in cases in which the total cash return is greater than or equal to the project cost.* Conversely, in cases in which the cost exceeds the undiscounted cash flows, a positive IRR makes no economic sense. *A negative IRR < −100 percent makes no economic sense* because it is not possible to lose more than all of what is lost on a bad investment when all cash flows attributable to the project are included.

PAYBACK AND IRR RELATIONSHIP

In Chapter 5 the naive rate of return (NROR) was defined as the reciprocal of payback. Is there any relationship between NROR and IRR? Yes. Provided that certain conditions are met, the NROR may approximate the IRR.

Assuming uniform cash flows, $R = R_1 = R_2 = \ldots = R_N$. Then payback $= C/R$, NROR $= 1/\text{payback} = R/C$, and IRR is the r such that:

$$C = \sum_{t=1}^{N} \frac{R}{(1 + r)^t} = R \sum_{t=1}^{N} (1 + r)^{-t} \qquad (7.11)$$

$$\frac{C}{R} = \sum_{t=1}^{N} (1 + r)^{-t} \qquad (7.12)$$

so that:

$$\frac{R}{C} = \frac{1}{\sum\limits_{t=1}^{N} (1 + r)^{-t}} = \frac{r(1 + r)^N}{(1 + r)^N - 1} = \frac{r}{1 - (1 + r)^{-N}} \qquad (7.13)$$

which is defined as the *capital recovery factor* for N periods at rate r per period. Now, letting N increase without limit, we obtain:

$$\frac{R}{C} = \lim_{N \to \infty} \frac{r}{1 - (1 + r)^{-N}} = r \qquad (7.14)$$

which is the same result as the NROR provides.

Therefore, under certain conditions, the NROR may provide a useful approximation to IRR. What are the conditions? The first condition is that the project life should be at least twice the payback period. The second is that the cash flows be at least approximately uniform:

1. $N \geq 2C/R$ *and*
2. uniform R.

Today, some hand-held calculators make the task of finding the IRR of a uniform cash flow series almost trivial. For projects with nonuniform cash flows, however, it may be useful to employ a computer if one is readily accessible, especially if many cash flow periods are involved, or if it is desired to deal with the problem of mixed cash flows according to methods described in Chapter 10 and those following.

MATHEMATICAL LOGIC FOR FINDING IRR

For projects that we know will have only one real, positive root, by Descartes' rule of signs,[4] several methods can be easily programmed for computer solution. The most straightforward are interval bisection and Newton-Raphson. A capital investment with one real positive IRR yields a net present value polynomial function that looks like Figure 7-1, that is, concave from above.

Note that the IRR is the discount rate for which the discounted value of the project, including the cost $C(R_0)$, is zero. In other words, the IRR is the discount rate for which the project NPV is zero. Thus, to find the IRR we must find the rate for which the polynomial intersects the horizontal axis.

Interval Bisection

With the interval bisection method, we select a high value and a low value that we think will bracket the IRR. If we are wrong, we will try higher values the next time. Assume we first select 0

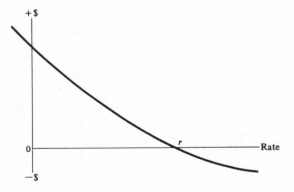

Figure 7-1.   IRR Polynomial.

[4]Descartes' rule states that the number of unique real roots to a polynomial with real coefficients cannot exceed the number of changes in the sign of the coefficients and that complex roots must be in conjugate pairs. That is, if $x + ci$ is a root, $x - ci$ is also a root.

as our low value and h as our high value. This is shown in Figure 7-2. We evaluate the NPV polynomial at rate 0 and at rate h. Since the NPV is positive for rate 0 and negative for rate h, we know the function has a root (crosses the horizontal axis) between these rates.

Next we improve our results by bisecting the interval between 0 and h and testing to determine in which subinterval the function crosses. We also test for the possibility that the midpoint of our earlier range, m, may actually be the IRR, even though unlikely. If we determine that the IRR lies in the interval between m and h, we bisect this range again, and repeat the process. We determine at the outset to stop when the difference between the low and high interval values is less than or equal to an arbitrarily small value. This error tolerance cannot be too small, however, because all digital computers have intrinsic round-off errors in computation and different capability for precision calculation.[5] In general, however, a tolerance of .0001 or .01 percent should cause no problems. If it does, a change to double-precision calculation may remedy the difficulty. If it does not, a computer specialist may have to be called in or a different computer used. The manual method of IRR solution is similar to this, except that the final IRR estimate is made by interpolation rather than continued iteration, once it is known that the IRR value has been bracketed.

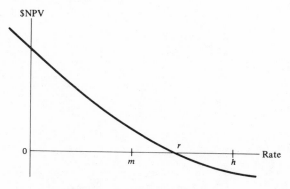

Figure 7-2. Interval Bisection.

[5]This is potentially a very serious problem, especially as the number of cash flows becomes large. Logically correct programs may yield totally incorrect results for which the program user is unprepared after testing the program with small problems having few cash flows and getting correct results.

Newton-Raphson Method

This method is somewhat more sophisticated than the interval bisection approach, and in some cases marginally more efficient.[6] Any increase in efficiency it yields will likely result in very small savings in computer time, however.

The approach with this method is to modify the original "guess" at the IRR by using the intersection of the tangent line to the NPV curve with the rate axis as the improved "guess." The process is repeated until the NPV is sufficiently close to zero. This might be expressed as an error less than or equal to some small percentage of the project cost, for example, or alternatively an NPV less than some small money amount.

The Newton-Raphson method requires that the numerical value of the derivative with respect to rate of the NPV be obtained at the current rate estimate. If we refer to r_n as the current IRR estimate and r_{n+1} as the revised estimate, $f(\ )$ as the NPV function, and $f'(\ )$ its derivative, then:

$$r_{n+1} = r_n - \frac{f(r_n)}{f'(r_n)}$$

The value of r_{n+1} is our revised estimate of the IRR. Graphically, the Newton-Raphson approach may be visualized as shown in Figure 7-3.

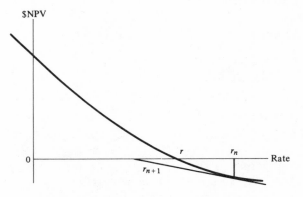

Figure 7-3. Newton-Raphson Method.

[6]Marginal is used here in the sense that one or two seconds of computer time is not usually significant unless a program is run very frequently in a commercial environment.

For the NPV function at rate i, the polynomial is:

$$\text{NPV} = f(i) = R_0(1 + i)^{-0} + R_1(1 + i)^{-1} + \cdots + R_n(1 + i)^{-n}$$

and the derivative:

$$f'(i) = -R_1(1 + i)^{-2} - 2R_2(1 + i)^{-3} - \cdots - nR_n(1 + i)^{-(n-1)}$$

Computer evaluation of $f'(i)$ involves modification of $f(i)$ by dropping the first term containing R_0, negating all the subsequent cash flow terms, multiplying each by the corresponding exponent, and then decrementing each of the exponent powers by one.

Strong Points of IRR

1. It is conceptually superior to payback and accounting methods.
2. It does not ignore any periods in the project life nor any cash flows.
3. It takes into account the time-value of funds.
4. It is consistent with the basic valuation model expressed in Chapter 2.
5. It yields a percentage that management can examine and make judgment about when k is not known with confidence.
6. It favors early cash flows over later ones.

Weak Points of IRR

1. It requires an estimate of the organization's cost of capital, or at least a range of values in which this is likely to be found.
2. It is much more difficult to apply without a computer than payback or accounting methods, and when cash flows are nonuniform, much more difficult to apply than the net present value method.
3. It does not distinguish between projects of different size and/or different economic lives. However, adjustment for

this may be made along lines similar to such adjustments for net present value.

4. It often yields multiple, and thus ambiguous, results when there is more than one sign change in the cash flows.

5. Some have criticized the method on the basis that it implicitly assumes that cash flows may be reinvested at a return equal to the IRR.

A DIGRESSION ON NOMINAL AND EFFECTIVE RATES

Investment-Financing Relationship

The mathematics of the internal rate of return are identical to those required for finding the effective interest rate on a loan or the yield to maturity or call on a bond. To the lender, a loan or a bond purchase is an investment. Symmetry of the loan or bond relationship requires that the effective cost rate to the borrower (bond issuer) be the same as the rate of return to the lender (bond purchaser) on a pretax basis. Mathematically, the only difference in a loan or bond from the perspectives of borrower and lender is that the signs of the cash flows will be reversed.

Consider a bond that has a face value of $1000, a nominal interest yield or coupon rate of 7 percent, and a 20-year maturity. It sells when first issued for $935. Interest will be calculated semiannually and we assume the bond will not be called prior to its maturity date. To the purchaser of the bond who buys at issue, it is an investment with cash flows in periods zero through 40 (semiannual payments over 20 years) and the IRR equation is, dropping the $ signs:

$$-935 + 35(1 + r_s)^{-1} + 35(1 + r_s)^{-2} + \cdots \\ + 35(1 + r_s)^{-40} + 1000(1 + r_s)^{-40} = 0 \qquad (7.15)$$

To the issuer of the bond, the equation to calculate the effective cost is:

$$+935 - 35(1 + r_s)^{-1} - 35(1 + r_s)^{-2} - \cdots \\ - 35(1 + r_s)^{-40} - 1000(1 + r_s)^{-40} = 0 \qquad (7.16)$$

The solution to the real, positive root of Eq. (7.15) is the same as that to Eq. (7.16).

Nominal Rate and Effective Rate

Note that the rate in Eqs. (7.15) and (7.16) is denoted by r_s. This is to flag it as a semiannual rate. The corresponding nominal annual yield or cost rate is two times r_s. The effective annual rate is that rate that would be equivalent if interest payments were made annually at the end of each year instead of at the end of each semiannual period.

For the bond in question the (pretax) rates are:

Semiannual Effective Yield $\quad r_s = 3.81964\%$
Nominal Annual Yield $\quad\quad r_n = 2r_s = 7.63928\%$
Effective Annual Yield $\quad\quad r = (1 + r_s)^2 - 1 = 7.78518\%$

It is usual United States financial practice to report yields in terms of nominal annual rates rather than effective annual rates. If the investor has the opportunity to reinvest interest payments as they are received at the effective per-period rate, however, the period-to-period compounding implicit in this should be recognized. The effective annual yield recognizes such compounding; the nominal annual rate does not.

Clarification of Nominal and Effective Rates

Let us examine here a problem that may help to clarify the relationship between and meaning of the various rates. In the case of a bond, the *coupon rate* is the rate applied to the face or par value of the bond to determine the dollar interest to be paid. The coupon rate is a nominal annual rate. The rate advertised by thrift institutions, which is compounded so many times per year, is also a nomical annual rate.For example, $5\frac{3}{4}$ percent compounded quarterly is a nominal annual rate. If we divide it by the number of compounding periods, we obtain the effective rate per quarter, which is 1.4375 percent per quarter. Money left on deposit will thus earn 1.4375 percent every three months. If $1000 is deposited at the beginning of a year under these terms, it will grow to $1058.75 at year end. This is thus an effective increase of 5.875 percent, not 5¾ percent.

In general, nominal annual (coupon) rate, per period effective rate, and effective annual rate are related as follows:

I. Nominal annual rate (r_N) ÷ number of compounding periods in a year (M) = effective per period rate (r_p).
II. The quantity one plus the effective per period rate raised to the power corresponding to the number of compounding periods in a year = one plus the effective annual rate.

$$\frac{r_N}{M} = r_p$$
$$(1 + r_p)^M - 1 = r$$

Or, comprehensively in one equation:

$$r = \left(1 + \frac{r_N}{M}\right)^M - 1$$

Unless it is perfectly clear from the context in which the term is used, r_N should never be called the "annual rate," but should be called the "nominal annual rate" or "annual rate compounded M times per year." To do otherwise is imprecise, confusing, and misleading.[7]

IRR With Quarterly Cash Flows

Consider an investment project costing $5000 that will last an estimated five years and provides net, after-tax cash flows at the end of each *quarter* of $300 in all, but in the final quarter which, with salvage, amounts to $1000.

The quarterly, per-period IRR is r_p = 2.701 percent. The nominal annual IRR, r_N is 10.804 percent *compounded quarterly*. The effective annual IRR rate, r = 11.249 percent. If we were to ignore

[7]See, for example, Anthony F. Herbst, "Truth in Lending, Regulation Z: Comments on Closed-End Contract Interest Rate Disclosure Requirements," *Journal of Bank Research,* Vol. 3, No. 2 (December 1972).

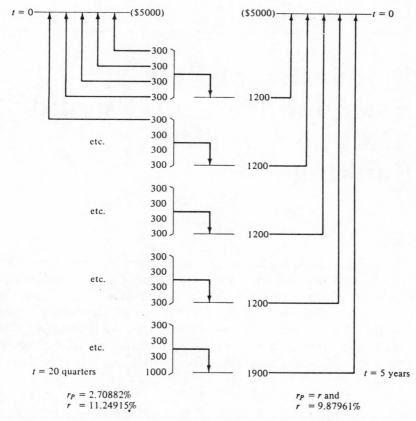

Figure 7-4. Quarterly Versus Annual Cash Flows for IRR Calculation.

the fact that the cash flows occur quarterly and instead treat the flows for each year as if they fell on the last day of the year, we would get an IRR of $r = 9.880$ percent. Note that this is significantly less than if the cash flows were treated as falling at the end of every three months, because the cash flows, on average, are pushed into the future some one-and-one-half quarters or some four-and-one-half months (see Figure 7-4).

8

Reinvestment Rate Assumptions for NPV and IRR and Conflicting Rankings

This chapter discusses some unsettled conceptual problems that have figured prominently in the literature of capital budgeting. Discussion contained here may be somewhat controversial to other writers in the field of capital investments. The author hopes that this chapter will move readers who are already familiar with the standard lore of capital budgeting to think critically of some things that may have been taken for granted, and judge for themselves.

REINVESTMENT RATE ASSUMPTIONS FOR NPV AND IRR

Comparison of Eqs. (7.3) with (6.1) and (6.2) shows that the internal rate of return (IRR) is nothing more nor less than a special case of net present value (NPV). The IRR is defined as the rate for which NPV is zero. With this in mind, let us examine a general equation combining (7.3) and (6.1):

$$X = \frac{R_0}{(1 + d)^0} + \frac{R_1}{(1 + d)^1} + \cdots + \frac{R_N}{(1 + d)^N} \qquad (8.1)$$

or

$$X = \sum_{t=0}^{N} \frac{R_t}{(1 + d)^t} = \sum_{t=0}^{N} R_t(1 + d)^{-t} \qquad (8.2)$$

If the discount rate d is such that $X = 0$, we say that d is the IRR. If $X \neq 0$, we say that X is the NPV for cost of capital $k = d$. Therefore, by employing Eqs. (8.1) and (8.2) we can deal simultaneously with both IRR and NPV.

So far, all mathematical formulations for IRR and NPV have been in terms of present value. We can convert to *future value* by multiplying both sides of the equation by $(1 + d)^N$, where d is either the IRR or cost of capital k, as the case may be. If we do this with Eqs. (8.1) and (8.2), we obtain:

$$X(1 + d)^N = R_0(1 + d)^N + R_1(1 + d)^{N-1} + \cdots + R_N \qquad (8.3)$$

$$X(1 + d)^N = \sum_{t=0}^{N} \frac{R_t}{(1 + d)^{t-N}} = \sum_{t=0}^{N} R_t(1 + d)^{N-t} \qquad (8.4)$$

Note that if d is the IRR, then $X = 0$ and $X(1 + d)^N$ is zero. Therefore, IRR could be as easily obtained from a future value formulation as from the conventional present value formulation. Also, if X were not zero, that is, if X were an NPV for $k = d$, the effect of multiplying by $(1 + d)^N$ simply moves the reference point from $t = 0$ to $t = N$.

In other words, looking at Eq. (8.3), we obtain the same results except for a constant of $(1 + d)^N$ times the NPV by assuming the cash flows are *reinvested* at earning rate d, rather than being discounted at that rate. The R_0, which for most projects will be the cost or initial outlay, is "invested" for N periods at rate d compounded each period. For the initial outlay this may be interpreted as the *opportunity* cost of committing funds to this project instead of to another purpose in which rate d could be earned. Or in the case where $d = k$, the opportunity cost may arise from the decision to undertake the project requiring funds to be raised, whereas without the project no new funds would need to be raised. The mathematical symmetry between these formulations has been a cause for concern among finance theorists. Let us consider the source of their concern.

The implication of future value formulation is that the project return, whether measured by IRR or by NPV, will depend on the rate at which cash flows can be reinvested. For a firm in a growth situation in which profitable investment opportunities abound, the IRR assumption that cash flows may be reinvested at a rate of earning equal to the IRR may thus not be unreasonable. For other firms, and government institutions, analysts think it more realistic to assume that the cash flows can be reinvested at a rate equal to the cost of capital k. Here we have the usual formulation of the reinvestment rate assumption.

Let us now consider the IRR and reinvestment rate in another light. Consider a loan of $100,000 that is made by a bank to an individual business proprietor for a period of five years. The loan is to be repaid in equal installments of $33,438.[1] From the bank's viewpoint this is an investment, with cash flows:

$t = 0$	$t = 1$	$t = 2$	$t = 3$	$t = 4$	$t = 5$
−$100,000	$33,438	$33,438	$33,438	$33,438	$33,438

and yield (that is, IRR) of 20 percent.

From the borrower's point of view, the cash flows are identical except that the signs are reversed. The cash flows of the borrower are the cash flows of the lender multiplied by minus one. Therefore, the borrower has cash flows:

$t = 0$	$t = 1$	$t = 2$	$t = 3$	$t = 4$	$t = 5$
+$100,000	−$33,438	−$33,438	−$33,438	−$33,438	−$33,438

and his effective *cost* is 20 percent on the loan. The *borrower* must earn at least 20 percent per period on the loan just to be able to repay it. The pretax return to the lender on the investment (loan) cannot be less than the cost to the borrower. Even if the bank does not reinvest the cash flows as the loan is repaid, its implicit return will still be 20 percent. The return is measured as a time-adjusted percentage of the principal amount outstanding, and is independent of what disposition is made of the cash flows as they are received. This is not to say that the uses to which the cash flows are put will have no effect on the organization, for they will. However, although the yield on the funds originally invested may be increased by such uses, it cannot be reduced by lack of such investment opportunities. This is a strong position to take, and requires explanation.

The payments made by the borrower, once given over to the lender, can earn nothing for the borrower. The borrower must, in the absence of other sources of funds, be able to earn 20 percent per period on the remaining loan principal. If the borrower is unable to earn anything on the remaining loan principal, he or she

[1]To the nearest whole dollar.

must still make the required periodical payments. The payments, even if made from other sources of funds, will be the same as those required if the loan were to generate funds at 20 percent per period. If funds must be diverted from other projects to repay the loan, the *opportunity* cost to the borrower may be *more* than 20 percent, if the funds could have earned more than this percentage in other uses. The cost internal to the loan itself, however, is 20 percent.

Table 8-1 provides a breakdown of the loan payments into the principal and interest components implicit in the IRR method of rate calculation. Note that the *interest is computed* at 20 percent per year on the *beginning-of-period principal balance.* The excess of payment over this amount is used to reduce the principal.

The following loan (to the borrower) will have identical cost of 20 percent, but the principal is not amortized but paid in full at the end of the loan:

$t = 0$	$t = 1$	$t = 2$	$t = 3$	$t = 4$	$t = 5$
+$100,000	−$20,000	−$20,000	−$20,000	−$20,000	−$120,000

The borrower may place the loan principal in a (hypothetical) bank account that pays him or her exactly 20 percent annually on the deposit. At the end of each year the borrower withdraws the interest and pays it to the lender. At the end of the loan the borrower withdraws the principal plus interest and repays the loan. Since he or she pays the interest to the lender as soon as it is earned, the person does not earn interest on interest. The

Table 8-1. Component Breakdown of Cash Flows (Amounts Rounded to Nearest $)

t	Beginning Principal	Interest on Principal	Principal Repayment
1	100,000	20,000	13,438[a]
2	86,562	17,312	16,126
3	70,437	14,087	19,351
4	51,086	10,217	23,221
5	27,865	5,573	27,865

[a]Assumes that end-of-year payment of $33,438 is composed of interest of 20% on the beginning balance *plus* a repayment of principal (that is, $20,000. + $13,438)

bank pays the borrower exactly 20 percent annually on the deposit, which he or she immediately turns over to the lender. The loan costs exactly equal the 20 percent annual interest the bank pays the borrower for the deposit, so there is no net gain to him or her. (We have ignored transactions costs to simplify discussion.)

For the lender the loan also yields exactly 20 percent. However, there is an important difference: The lender may reinvest the interest payments if desired and thus *increase* the gain. Such increase, significantly, does not depend on the loan itself, but on reinvestment opportunities available for the loan interest when it is received. The 20 percent return is thus a *minimum* return on the loan, and this minimum is independent of reinvestment opportunities. The reinvestment rate could be zero and still the lender would earn 20 percent on the loan.

The only difference between these two loans is the handling of principal repayment: In the first, the principal is amortized over the life of the loan. In the second loan, the entire principal repayment is made at the loan maturity date. The first loan does provide better reinvestment opportunities to the lender since larger payments are received in all but the last year, and the lender may be able to reinvest them and so raise the return on the loan. Once again, however, 20 percent is the minimum return to be expected, even if the reinvestment opportunity rate were to be zero. *The lender earns exactly 20 percent on the principal amount still in the hands of the borrower.* If the lender can earn 20 percent or more on the recovered principal, so much the better for the lender. If he or she cannot, the lender nevertheless continues to earn 20 percent on the still unrecovered principal.

Let us assume a zero reinvestment rate. With the first loan, let us consider that the $100,000 principal is returned in equal annual installments of $20,000 over the five-year loan maturity. This means that $13,438 over and above the principal repayment is earned on the *remaining* principal. The percentage return on the remaining principal in each year is then as shown in Table 8-2. The geometric mean return is 29.4 percent, the arithmetic mean return 30 percent, and the median return 22.4 percent. This treatment differs from the IRR formulation in assuming a fixed allocation of periodical payments to principal amortization[2] rather than

---

[2]Straight-line amortization of the principal.

a gradually increasing amortization payment. Therefore, the principal is more quickly reduced, consequently yielding a higher return on that which remains.

These results do not require any reinvestment rate other than zero. They show that the percentage return on an investment does not depend on the available reinvestment rate. The actual gain to the investor (or lender) may, of course, be higher than this minimum amount if the available reinvestment rate is greater than zero, but that is a condition *external* to the investment. The IRR is concerned with the internal characteristics only, and therefore provides a measure of the minimum return on the investment.

In summary, the conceptual difficulty with the reinvestment rate assumption arises from focusing on the superficial aspects of the mathematics of the IRR while neglecting the economic interpretation of the initial investment and the subsequent cash flows. Mathematics is a tool in financial mathematics, and economics the master. The reinvestment rate problem arises from confusion of this hierarchy—from trying to make the economics conform to the mathematics. The IRR might be called more properly *return on invested capital* to make clear its economic assumptions. However, this term has another specific meaning that is covered later, and is thus reserved for that.

Treatment of the reinvestment rate with the NPV, along lines similar to that of the IRR, is left as an exercise.

Table 8-2. Per Period Return on Remaining Principal (Constant Amortization of $20,000 Per Period)

t	Principal Remaining	% Return
1	$100,000	13.438
2	80,000	16.798
3	60,000	22.397
4	40,000	33.595
5	20,000	67.190

CONFLICTING RANKINGS AND FISHER'S INTERSECTION[3]

The rules for project acceptance once again are:

	IRR	NPV
Accept if	$r > k$	NPV > 0
Reject if	$r \leq k$	NPV ≤ 0

Now it would seem that if we are comparing two acceptable, yet mutually exclusive, projects, that we should get the same preference ranking by NPV as we do by IRR. However, this will not always be the case. Conflicting rankings may arise because one or both projects have nonuniform cash flows.

To begin, let us consider two projects each costing $7000 at $t = 0$, and each having an economic life of five years, in order that we do not need to correct for unequal project size or life. The projects have the following cash flows (dropping the $ signs):

Cost, R_0	Project H 7,000	Project I 7,000
CASH FLOW		
$t = 1$	6,000	250
$t = 2$	3,000	500
$t = 3$	1,500	750
$t = 4$	750	4,000
$t = 5$	375	10,000

The internal rates of return are IRR$_H$ = 35.120 percent, IRR$_I$ = 19.745 percent. As shown in Figure 8-1, the IRR values are fixed. However, the NPV values change, since they depend on the value of d that is used. For $d = 0$ (that is, zero discount) they are for projects H and I $4625 and $8500, respectively.

Notice that the two NPV curves intersect at a discount rate of approximately 11 percent (11.408 percent), which we denote as r_f. For smaller discount rates, project I has an NPV greater than that of project H. However, IRR$_H$ > IRR$_I$ always. Therefore, for discount rates less than r_f, there will always be a conflict

---

[3]A. A. Alchian, "The Rate of Interest, Fisher's Rate of Return over Cost, and Keynes' Internal Rate of Return," *The American Economic Review* (December 1955), pp. 938–943.

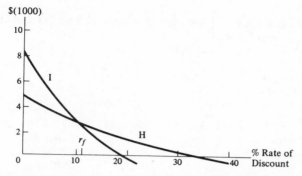

Figure 8-1. Fisher's Rate, r_f, and Conflicting IRR-NPV Project Rankings.

between the NPV ranking and the IRR ranking, but, for discount rates greater than r_f, both IRR and NPV will yield the same ranking.

Let us examine these projects further by treating them each as loans and inspecting their repayment schedules. We assume that each net cash flow is composed of two components: an interest payment and a principal repayment. First, we will use as discount rate the Fisher's rate of 11.408 percent.

The project NPVs at $t = 0$ can be found by discounting the amounts in column 4. For project H we have $996.26(1.11408)^{-2}$ + $1500(1.11408)^{-3}$ + $750(1.11408)^{-4}$ + $375(1.11408)^{-5}$, equaling $2592.80. For project I we have $4449.93(1.11408)^{-5}$ or $2592.80. As we should have expected, at Fisher's rate the NPVs of projects H and I are equal, for that is how Fisher's rate is defined.

Notice an important difference between the two projects with respect to column 1, the beginning-of-period principal remaining. The net cash flows for project H were sufficiently high at the end of periods one and two to pay off the entire principal after paying the required interest. In fact, at the end of period two the net cash flow was $996.26 *in excess* of what was required to pay off the interest and remaining principal. This is the meaning of NPV, and why some authors choose to call it *excess present value*. The NPV is the amount, at discount, by which the net cash flows of an investment project exceed what is required for payment of interest on remaining principal and principal repayment. Note that although project H paid off the entire principal by the end of period two, project I did not pay off its principal until the end of period five.

Table 8-3. Component Treatment of Projects H and I at Fisher's Rate of 11.408% (Amounts in $)

PROJECT H

t	(1) Beginning Principal	(2) Interest on Principal	(3) Principal Repayment	(4) Excess over (2) + (3)	(5) Total Net Cash Flow
1	7000.00	798.56	5201.44	0	6000.00
2	1798.56	205.18	1798.56	996.26	3000.00
3	0	0	0	1500.00	1500.00
4	0	0	0	750.00	750.00
5	0	0	0	375.00	375.00

PROJECT I

t	(1) Beginning Principal	(2) Interest on Principal	(3) Principal Repayment	(4) Excess over (2) + (3)	(5) Total Net Cash Flow
1	7000.00	798.56	−548.56	0	250.00
2	7548.56	861.14	−361.14	0	500.00
3	7909.70	902.34	−152.34	0	750.00
4	8062.04	919.72	3080.28	0	4,000.00
5	4981.75	568.32	4981.75	4449.93	10,000.00

We know that projects H and I are not loans, but are capital investment projects. The principal repayments represent recovery of the initial investment, whereas the interest payments represent the opportunity cost of funds committed to the projects and as yet unrecovered. Which project is preferable? Both have the same NPV of $2592.80 at Fisher's rate. Does this mean that we should feel indifferent about the two projects?

Although projects H and I have identical NPVs at Fisher's rate of 11.408 percent, project H is clearly preferable. The reason is that project H provides for faster recovery of the funds invested in it than does project I. In fact, project I is incapable of paying the interest on beginning-of-period principal in any of periods one through three. Therefore, instead of giving us back our original investment with interest from the start, project I requires that we wait until the end of period four before any reduction in principal plus accumulated interest can be made. On the principle that a bird in the hand is worth two in the bush, or rather that a dollar today is better than a dollar plus interest tomorrow (if there is any doubt about getting the dollar tomorrow), we prefer project H to project I. The fact that the NPVs of the two projects are identical should not cause us to be indifferent between projects such as H and I, for the NPV is only one criterion by which project merit may be gauged. If the NPVs are equal, we will, of course, prefer the project that offers the more rapid capital recovery. Invested funds recovered early are subject to less uncertainty of receipt than funds to be recovered later, and funds recovered early can be reinvested for a longer period to enhance the earnings of the firm.

We have seen that, at Fisher's rate, project H is preferable to project I even though the NPVs are identical. This preference is consistent with what we would have obtained by choosing between the projects on the basis of their IRRs. Now let us examine these same projects for a rate of discount substantially less than r_f, Fisher's rate. For illustration we will use a discount rate of 5 percent. Table 8-4 contains the results of our calculations.

We may again determine the NPVs by bringing the column 4 amounts to $t = 0$ at a discount rate of 5 percent per period. For project H we obtain an NPV of $3641.98 and for project I an NPV of $5465.56. Since NPV of I > NPV of H, which we would expect for a discount rate less than Fisher's rate, the NPV criterion favors project I. The profitability indexes (PIs) would not suggest a different relationship, because both projects require the same initial investment outlay.

Table 8-4. Component Treatment of Projects H and I at 5%, a Rate Less Than Fisher's Rate (Amount in $)

PROJECT H

t	(1) Beginning Principal	(2) Interest on Principal	(3) Principal Repayment	(4) Excess over (2) + (3)	(5) Total Net Cash Flow
1	7000.00	350.00	5650.00	0	6000.00
2	1350.00	67.50	1350.00	1582.50	3000.00
3	0	0	0	1500.00	1500.00
4	0	0	0	750.00	750.00
5	0	0	0	375.00	375.00

PROJECT I

1	7000.00	350.00	−100.00	0	250.00
2	7100.00	355.00	145.00	0	500.00
3	6955.00	347.75	402.25	0	750.00
4	6552.75	327.64	3672.36	0	4,000.00
5	2880.39	144.02	2880.39	6975.59	10,000.00

At a cost of capital of 5 percent we find that the NPV (or PI) criterion favors project I. The IRR criterion, however, favors project H. Which criterion should we use? For a cost of capital (discount rate) greater than or equal to Fisher's rate we would have no problem, for both the IRR and the NPV would favor project H. But we have under consideration a rate of 5 percent and a conflict in ranking that must be resolved.

To help us decide which project is preferable, let us again examine columns 1 and 4 of Table 8-4. Notice that project H (column 1) allows us to recover our entire investment plus interest (opportunity cost on the funds committed) and yields an excess of $1582.50 at the end of the second year (column 4). Project I, in contrast, cannot even compensate for our opportunity cost in year one. It does not yield recovery of our investment until the end of the fifth year. In fact, *the entire NPV of project I depends on the large cash flow in period five.* If unanticipated events in year three, four, or five caused all cash flows to be zero, project H would still have a positive NPV of $1582.50(1.05)^{-2} = $1435.37, but project I would have a negative NPV of $-$6308.39. Not only does project H have a higher IRR (35.120 percent) than project I (IRR = 19.751 percent), but also it does not depend on the accuracy of our cash flow estimates beyond year two to be acceptable.

Hopefully the foregoing analysis illustrates the danger of relying on any single measure of investment merit. This applies to the NPV and the PI as it does to other measures. Some have emphasized the NPV-PI criterion to an extent tantamount to recommending it as a universal prescription for capital-budgeting analysis. We have just seen that the NPV alone does not provide sufficient information to choose between two projects that have the same required investment and useful lives. A formal treatment of risk in capital budgeting is deferred until the latter chapters. However, we must realize that risk is our constant companion whether we deal with it formally or ignore it.

On the premise that point estimates are subject to error, and that the expected error becomes greater the further from the present the event we estimate, *ceteris paribus* we prefer an investment that promises early recovery of funds committed, and early receipt of funds above this amount. In the applied world of capital investments, no single measure has adequately captured the multiple-faceted character of capital-budgeting projects. For this reason industrial firms often examine several measures of a capital investment in their decision-making processes.

RELATIONSHIP OF IRR AND NPV

Mao[4] has explicitly shown the relationship of IRR to NPV in an interesting way. Let us again examine Eqs. (7.3) and (6.2).

$$0 = \sum_{t=0}^{N} R_t(1 + r)^{-t} \tag{7.3}$$

$$\text{NPV} = \sum_{t=0}^{N} R_t(1 + k)^{-t} \tag{6.2}$$

If we subtract (7.3) from (6.2), we obtain

$$\text{NPV} = \sum_{t=0}^{N} R_t[(1 + k)^{t} - (1 + r)^{t}] \tag{8.5}$$

Now, taking any term beyond $t = 0$, we assume that k and r are both positive and R_t nonnegative. For NPV to be positive it is necessary only for the relation $r > k$ to be true. Conversely, for NPV to be negative, it is necessary that the relation $r < k$ be true. This shows the equivalence of the NPV and IRR criteria for projects that have $R_t \geq 0$ for $t > 0$, *in terms of the accept/reject decision.*

ADJUSTED, OR MODIFIED, IRR

The controversy over whether or not the IRR should be used when there is doubt that the project's cash flows can be reinvested at the IRR led to the development of the adjusted IRR. The idea behind the adjusted IRR is to assume that all cash flows after the initial outlay or outlays are invested to earn at the firm's cost of capital or some other conservative reinvestment rate. Thus all cash flows except for the initial outlay are taken out to a future value at the terminal year of the project's life, and zeroes are used to replace them in the adjusted series. After this adjustment it is easy to calculate the implicit rate of return that would take the

[4]J.C.T. Mao, *Quantitative Analysis of Financial Decisions* (New York: Macmillan, 1969), p. 196.

initial investment to the terminal amount that contains the compounded sum of all cash flows from $t=1$ through $t=N$.

The adjusted, or modified, IRR is analogous to the rate of
return on a zero coupon bond. Since there are no cash flows to
be reinvested, the rate at which the firm can reinvest cash is no
longer material to the rate of return. The procedure for calculating
an adjusted IRR is clearly a type of sinking fund method. Sinking
fund methods in general are covered in another chapter.

The modified IRR has been more widely accepted by engineering economists than by finance writers. However, that situation
is changing.

The following application of the adjusted IRR to projects H
and I will serve to clarify the procedure involved:

Using Cost of Capital/Reinvestment Rate of 12.00%:

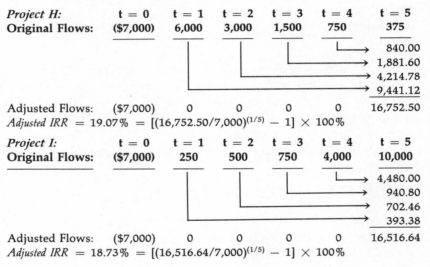

Project H:	t = 0	t = 1	t = 2	t = 3	t = 4	t = 5
Original Flows:	($7,000)	6,000	3,000	1,500	750	375
						840.00
						1,881.60
						4,214.78
						9,441.12
Adjusted Flows:	($7,000)	0	0	0	0	16,752.50

Adjusted IRR = 19.07% = $[(16,752.50/7,000)^{(1/5)} - 1] \times 100\%$

Project I:	t = 0	t = 1	t = 2	t = 3	t = 4	t = 5
Original Flows:	($7,000)	250	500	750	4,000	10,000
						4,480.00
						940.80
						702.46
						393.38
Adjusted Flows:	($7,000)	0	0	0	0	16,516.64

Adjusted IRR = 18.73% = $[(16,516.64/7,000)^{(1/5)} - 1] \times 100\%$

SUMMARY AND CONCLUSION

In this chapter we have examined (1) the reinvestment assumptions implicit in the discounted cash flow methods, IRR and NPV,
(2) the reasons for conflicting rankings between IRR and NPV,
and (3) Mao's treatment of the IRR-NPV relationship.

The reinvestment rate assumptions were seen to arise from the
mathematical relationship between present value and future

value formulations of the discounted cash flow methods. It was shown that the return on investment, that is, the remaining un- recovered initial investment, is not dependent on reinvestment opportunities. To do this the net cash flows were separated into two components: a payment of "interest" (return) on remaining "principal" (investment), and a repayment of "principal" (recov- ery of investment).

A treatment similar to that used to deal with the reinvestment assumptions was employed to analyze, in conjunction with Fisher's rate (r_f), the reason for contradictory rankings between IRR and NPV. It was seen that for rates less than r_f that the NPV alone is inadequate to judge which of two projects is better, since the NPV does not distinguish between the timing of cash receipts to recover the investment and those that provide a net return.

Mao's mathematical connection of IRR and NPV in a single equation serves to illustrate the conditions under which the NPV is positive or negative, and to focus more clearly on the IRR-NPV relationship.

9

The MAPI (Terborgh) Method

George Terborgh, Research Director of the Machinery and Allied Products Institute (MAPI), authored *Dynamic Equipment Policy,* published in 1949. This work still provides perhaps the most useful and theoretically sound practical means for analyzing component projects, despite its early publication date. In 1958 a simplified and streamlined version of the methodology proposed in 1949 was published in *Business Investment Policy,* many points of which are contained in *An Introduction to Business Investment Analysis,* based on an address delivered in 1958 by George Terborgh. Newer publications are available from the Institute.

In order to appreciate how the MAPI method relates to the other methods that employ discounted cash flow, it will be useful if first the concept of *duality* is understood. Those familiar with mathematical programming may skip the following section without loss of continuity.

THE CONCEPT OF DUALITY

One of the important contributions of mathematical programming is that of duality. Simply stated, duality means that for every maximization problem there corresponds a minimization problem yielding identical solution values. If the problem at hand, called the *primal* problem, is one of maximization, the *dual* problem will always be a minimization problem. The converse is also true: If the primal is a minimization formulation, the dual will be a maximization formulation. Furthermore, the dual of the dual will be the primal.

Let us examine the general linear programming problem:

110

$$
\begin{aligned}
\text{Maximize} \quad & p_1 q_1 + p_2 q_2 + \cdots + p_n q_n & (9.1) \\
\text{Subject to} \quad & a_{11} q_1 + a_{12} q_2 + \cdots + a_{1n} q_n \leq b_1 \\
& a_{21} q_1 + a_{22} q_2 + \cdots + a_{2n} q_n \leq b_2 \\
& \ \ \vdots \qquad\qquad\qquad\qquad\quad \vdots \qquad \vdots \\
& a_{m1} q_1 + a_{m2} q_2 + \cdots + a_{mn} q_n \leq b_m \\
& \text{and for all } i \ q_i \geq 0
\end{aligned}
$$

which in the shorthand notation of matrix algebra becomes:

$$
\begin{aligned}
\text{Maximize} \quad & p \cdot q & (9.2) \\
\text{Subject to} \quad & A \cdot q \leq b \\
& q_i \geq 0 \text{ for all } i
\end{aligned}
$$

This particular linear programming problem may be considered that of maximizing total firm profit (price times quantity for each product) subject to constraints on the output of each product associated with limitations on machine time, labor, and so on, and the relative requirements of each product for these limited resources.

If the above maximization problem has a feasible solution, the dual formulation will also have a feasible solution, and the dual will yield the same amounts of each product to be produced. The corresponding dual problem is:

$$
\begin{aligned}
\text{Minimize} \quad & b_1 u_1 + b_2 u_2 + \cdots + b_m u_m & (9.3) \\
\text{Subject to} \quad & a_{11} u_1 + a_{21} u_2 + \cdots + a_{m1} u_m \geq P_1 \\
& a_{12} u_1 + a_{22} u_2 + \cdots + a_{m2} u_m \geq P_2 \\
& \ \ \vdots \qquad\qquad\qquad\qquad\quad \vdots \qquad \vdots \\
& a_{1n} u_1 + a_{m2} u_2 + \cdots + a_{mn} u_m \geq P_n \\
& \text{and for all } i \ u_i \geq 0
\end{aligned}
$$

which in matrix algebra notation corresponding to the primal becomes:

$$
\begin{aligned}
\text{Minimize} \quad & b'u & (9.4) \\
\text{Subject to} \quad & A'u \geq p' \\
& u_i \geq 0 \text{ for all } i
\end{aligned}
$$

where b' is the transpose of the vector of constraint constants in the primal problem, and so on. The u variables are called *shadow prices* and represent the opportunity costs of unutilized resources. Thus, if we minimize the opportunity costs of nonoptimal employment of our machine, labor, and other resources, we achieve a lowest cost solution.

The important point of all this is that the primal and the dual formulations *both* lead to the *same* allocation of available resources. Therefore, it is not important which of the two formulations we solve. For reasons of ease of formulation, calculation, or computer efficiency, we may choose to work with *either* the primal or the dual formulation.

Now, getting back to the MAPI method of capital-budgeting project evaluation, we may say that the method is analogous to a dual approach to the goal of maximization of the value of the firm expressed in Eq. (2.1). It will be useful to again state Eq. (2.1) here as:

$$\text{Maximize } V = \sum_{t=0}^{\infty} \frac{R_t}{(1 + k)^t} \qquad (9.5)$$

If we recognize that the net cash flows R_t are composed of gross cash profits P_t as well as cash costs C_t, then

$$R_t = P_t - C_t \qquad (9.6)$$

And for component projects we may assume that the P_t are fixed: We cannot directly associate cash inflows with the project. Even for major projects we may have to take the cash inflows as given, since to some extent they are beyond our control, at least as far as finance and production are concerned. Marketing staff may influence gross revenues through advertising, salesmanship, and marketing logistics, but still they will be subject to the state of the general economy, the activities of our competition, and "acts of God."

If we take the P_t as given, or fixed, and is thus independent of the capital equipment used in production, then we may reformulate our objective as:

$$\text{Minimize cost} = \sum_{t=0}^{\infty} \frac{C_t}{(1 + k)^t} \qquad (9.7)$$

which may be operationalized by accepting the lowest cost projects for performing any given task, subject to their capability of performing the task to our requirements.

This is the basic idea behind the MAPI method, which we will now examine.

THE MAPI FRAMEWORK

The methodology of the MAPI method involves calculating the time-adjusted annual average cost of the project or projects under consideration. However, several concepts vital to intelligent application of the method must first be understood.

Challenger and Defender

In Terborgh's colorful terminology, the capital equipment currently in use is referred to as the *defender*, and the alternative that may be considered for replacement as the *challenger*. The MAPI method as originally developed emphasized capital equipment replacement, but is applicable to nonreplacement decisions as well since, in such cases, the status quo may be considered the defender. Various potential challengers may be compared against one another in a winnowing process, with the project promising the lowest time-adjusted annual average cost selected as *the* challenger.

If the challenger is superior to the defender as well as to presently available rivals, it may still be inferior to future alternatives. The current challenger is the best replacement for the defender only when there is no future challenger worth delaying for. This requires that a series of capital equipment not currently in existence be appraised, and this presents some difficulties:

> Now obviously it is impossible as a rule for mere mortals to foresee the form and character of machines not yet in existence. In some cases, no doubt, closely impending developments may be more or less dimly discerned and so may be weighted, after a fashion, in the replacement analysis, but in no case can the future be penetrated more than a fraction of the distance that is theoretically necessary for an exact, or even a close solution of the problem. What then is the answer? *Since the machines of the future cannot be foreseen, their character must be assumed.* [1]

---

[1]George Terborgh, *Dynamic Equipment Policy* (Washington: Machinery and Allied Products Institute, 1949), pp. 57, 58.

The exact nature of the necessary assumptions is dependent on some additional terminology, which will be introduced at this point.

Capital Cost

The mechanics of the MAPI method require that we obtain the time-adjusted annual average cost of the project under consideration. The two components that determine what the average cost will be: (1) capital cost and (2) operating inferiority. Capital cost must not be confused with the firm's cost of capital, because they are different things despite the similarity in labels.

Capital cost in the MAPI framework is the uniform annual dollar amount, including the opportunity cost of funds tied up in the project, that must be recovered if the project is retained for one year, or for two years, or for three years, and so on. To clarify this concept, assume we are examining a project that costs $10,000, and our firm has a 15 percent annual cost of capital. Our opportunity cost for funds committed to the project is at least 15 percent annually since, if funds were not committed to it, our cost of funds would be lower by this amount. That is, our firm would require $10,000 less, for which it is incurring an annual 15 percent cost.

Now, if we accept this project, and then at the end of one year abandon it, what is the capital cost? It is $10,000 *plus* the opportunity cost at 15 percent, or $11,500. What if the project is abandoned at the end of the second year? In this case the total capital cost is $10,000(1.15)^2 or $13,225. However, since the project will be kept for two years, the *annual* capital cost will be much less, not even one-half of the $13,225. The reason for this is that funds recovered in the first year do not incur opportunity cost during the second year. At a 15 percent annual cost of capital, the time-adjusted annual average capital cost in each of the two years will be $6151. If the project were retained for three years, the time-adjusted annual average cost will be $4380. These amounts are obtained by multiplying the initial investment by the *capital recovery factor* corresponding to the annual percentage cost of capital and the number of years the project is retained. The capital recovery factor is the reciprocal of the annuity (uniform series) present worth factor.

The longer a project is retained and kept in service, the lower the amount of investment that must be recovered in each individual year of the project's life. A project that is retained only one or two years must therefore yield a larger cash flow each year to allow recovery of the initial investment, plus opportunity cost of the committed funds, than the same project if kept for many years.

In the present value and internal rate of return methods for capital budgeting, the initial investment is considered only at time period zero. In the MAPI method, the initial investment is spread over the years of the projects's life. With the NPV method, since the discount rate is assumed to be known, that is, it is the firm's cost of capital, it is possible that the initial investment could be treated in the same way as in MAPI; nevertheless, in practice it is not treated thus.

Operating Inferiority

Operating inferiority is defined as the deficiency of the defender, the incumbent, existing project or the status quo, relative to the best available alternative for performing the same functions. Operating inferiority is considered to be composed of two components: physical deterioration and technological obsolescence. In the MAPI method we measure operating inferiority using the best capital equipment as a benchmark:

> In the firmament of mechanical alternatives there is but one fixed star: the best machine for the job. This is base point and the standard for evaluating all others. What an operator can afford to pay for any rival or competitor of this machine must therefore be derived by a top-down measurement. *But the process is not reversible.* He cannot properly compute what he can afford to pay for the best by measurement upward from its inferiors.[2]

Physical Deterioration

Physical deterioration of capital can be determined by comparing the equipment in service with the *same* equipment when new and undegraded by past operation. Physical deterioration, then, will be the excess of the operating cost of the old machine over its new replica's operating cost. We normally would expect rapid physi-

[2]Ibid., p. 35.

cal deterioration in the first few years of a project's life, then to accumulate more slowly, perhaps reaching a steady-state equilibrium, with repair costs at a relatively constant level per period, keeping the quality of service approximately constant. The comparison of the equipment in service with its new replica should be in terms of operating costs, including maintenance and repair, additional direct labor required, extra indirect labor required (such as for quality control inspection), and the cost of higher scrap output.

Technological Obsolescence

Although physical deterioration may be considered an internal, age-related aspect of capital degradation, technological obsolescence is external to it and not necessarily related to age. Obsolescence consists of the sum of the excess operating cost of the same capital that is new over that of the *best* alternative now available plus the deficiency in the value of service relative to the best alternative. Physical deterioration is degradation of the firm's existing capital relative to new, *identical* capital. Technological obsolescence is the inferiority of the existing capital relative to the latest generation of capital for doing the job.

Two Basic Assumptions

Unfortunately, although the concept of operating inferiority is not difficult to grasp, implementation poses some problems. Although we may be able to estimate the cost of operating inferiority for this year, and perhaps the next as well, the task becomes increasingly difficult and tenuous as we attempt to carry the process into the future. Physical deterioration may not occur uniformly: It may be substantial in the early years, tapering off later, or it may be just the opposite. Technological developments tend to occur randomly over time. Although some may be anticipated in advance in rapidly developing fields, such as computer technology, prediction of when they will be brought to market is still a somewhat uncertain enterprise.

In addition to the problems inherent in estimating operating inferiority, there is yet another obstacle. This is related to the characteristics of future challengers.

It is true that the challenger has eliminated all *presently available* rivals. But it has not eliminated *future* rivals. The latter, though at present mere potentialities, are important figures in the contest. For the current challenger can make good its claim to succeed the defender only *when there is no future challenger worth waiting for.* It must engage, as it were, in a two-front war, attacking on one side the aged machine it hopes to dislodge and on the other an array of rivals still unborn who also hope to dislodge the same aged machine, but later.[3]

The MAPI analysis emphasizes the importance of future capital equipment:

For since the choice between living machines can be made only by reference to the machines of tomorrow, the latter remain, whether we like it or not, an indispensable element in the calculation. It may be said . . . that the appraisal of the ghosts involved is the heart of the . . . analysis. No replacement theory, no formula, no rule of thumb that fails to take cognizance of these ghosts and to assess their role in the play can lay claim to rational justification.[4]

In order to deal with these problems Terborgh proposed two "standard" assumptions on the basis that "The best the analyst can do is to start with a set of standard assumptions and shade the results of their application as his judgment dictates."[5] In other words, if we have information we will use it; if not, we will employ reasonable standard assumptions.

Adverse Minimum

The key to the MAPI method is the "adverse minimum" for the capital project. This is defined as the lowest combined time-adjusted average of capital cost and operating inferiority that can be obtained by keeping the project in service the number of years necessary to reach this minimum, and no longer.

First Standard Assumption

Future challengers will have the same adverse minimum as the present one.[6]

---

[3]Ibid., p. 55.
[4]Ibid., p. 57.
[5]Ibid., p. 60.
[6]Ibid., p. 64.

Second Standard Assumption

The present challenger will accumulate operating inferiority at a constant rate over its service life.[7]

The first standard assumption is justified on the basis that there is no alternative that is more reasonable. In the absence of information to the contrary, what compulsion is there for us to assume that future challengers will have either higher or lower adverse minima? If we have information that leads us to believe that future challengers will have different adverse minima, then we may modify the standard assumption. Furthermore, this standard assumption facilitates developing a simpler replacement formula than would be otherwise possible.

The second standard assumption again is justified on the basis of methodological necessity, since the analyst typically does not have data on a sufficient sample size of similar equipment to make a more reasonable assumption. In the absence of information to the contrary, the best we can do is predict the future by extrapolation from the present and past experiences on the basis that there are elements of continuity and recurrence that will be repeated into the future. If we were to reject entirely this continuity and recurrence over time, we would be utterly incapable of dealing with the future in all but those situations in which change is at least dimly visible on the horizon.

APPLICATION OF THE MAPI METHOD

To apply the MAPI method to a potential challenger, we require an estimate of the firm's cost of capital, the cost of the project, and an estimate of the project's first-year accumulation of operating inferiority. From this information we derive the adverse minima of potential challengers, thereby selecting the project with the lowest adverse minimum as *the* challenger. The adverse minimum of the defender, if there is existing capital equipment that may be replaced by the challenger, is determined similarly. In many cases the defender will be found to have already passed the point in time at which its adverse minimum occurs. In such cases Terborgh has recommended that the next-year total of capi-

[7]Ibid., p. 65.

tal cost and operating inferiority be used as the defender's adverse minimum.

Let us assume the firm's cost of capital is 15 percent per annum, and that we have an existing machine (defender) that will have a combined capital cost and operating inferiority of $70,000. There is only one potential challenger. It costs $100,000 and is estimated to accumulate operating inferiority during the first year of service amounting to $7000. Application of the second standard assumption means we assume operating inferiority will be accumulated at $7000 each year the challenger would be in service. We ignore salvage value for now to simplify the exposition. Table 9-1 illustrates the technique of finding the challenger's adverse minimum.

Since the adverse minimum of the challenger of $41,105 per year if held six years is substantially lower than the next-year operating inferiority of the defender, we would replace the defender this year. In fact, even if the challenger were to be replaced itself at the end of the second year of its service by a still better but yet unbuilt new challenger, the decision would still be correct. If kept in service two years, the challenger costs $64,768, whereas the defender will cost $70,000 next year and, if it continues to accumulate operating inferiority, still more the following year. The figures in column 8 of Table 9-1 are average annual costs, adjusted for the time-value of money. The lowest of these, as stated earlier, is the adverse minimum.

The time-adjusted annual average costs are composed of a capital cost component that declines over time, and an operating inferiority component that increases over time. For the project analyzed in Table 9-1, capital cost declines rapidly in the early years of the project's life, whereas operating inferiority rises rapidly. Therefore, this challenger will obtain its adverse minimum in only six years. Some projects may not reach their adverse minimum for many years. For instance, management may have a policy of abandoning equipment at the end of, say, 15 years regardless of its condition. In such an environment the adverse minimum may not be reached. However, if the time-adjusted annual average cost declines constantly, we may then take the last year of service's value as our adverse minimum. Of course, as we go into the future further and further, the reliability of the two standard assumptions employed in the beginning begins to wane. Thus, other things being equal, we would prefer a chal-

Table 9-1. Derivation of the Adverse Minimum of a Challenger Costing $100,000 with Inferiority Gradient of $7000 a Year. Assumes No Capital Additions and No Salvage Value. Cost of Capital Is 15%.

Year of Service	(1) Operating Infr[a] for Year Indicated	(2) Present Worth Factor for Year Indicated	(3) Present Worth of Operating Infr[a] (1) × (2)	(4) Present Worth of Operating Infr Accm[b] (3) Accm	(5) Capital Recovery Factor for Year Indicated	(6) Operating Infr[a] (4) × (5)	(7) Capital Cost (5) × $100,000	(8) Both Combined (6) + (7)
1	$ 0	.86957	$ 0	$ 0	1.15000	$ 0	$115,000	$115,000
2	7,000	.75614	5,293	5,293	.61512	3,256	61,512	64,768
3	14,000	.65752	9,205	14,498	.43798	6,350	43,798	50,148
4	21,000	.57175	12,007	26,505	.35027	9,284	35,027	44,311
5	28,000	.49718	13,921	40,426	.29832	12,060	29,832	41,892
6	35,000	.43233	15,132	55,558	.26424	14,681	26,424	41,105[c]
7	42,000	.37594	15,789	71,346	.24036	17,149	24,036	41,185
8	49,000	.32690	16,018	87,364	.22285	19,469	22,285	41,754
9	56,000	.28426	15,919	103,283	.20957	21,645	20,957	42,602
10	63,000	.24718	15,572	118,855	.19925	23,682	19,925	43,607
11	70,000	.21494	15,046	133,901	.19107	25,584	19,107	44,691
12	77,000	.18691	14,392	148,293	.18448	27,357	18,448	45,805

[a]Infr = inferiority
[b]Accm = accumulated
[c]Adverse minimum

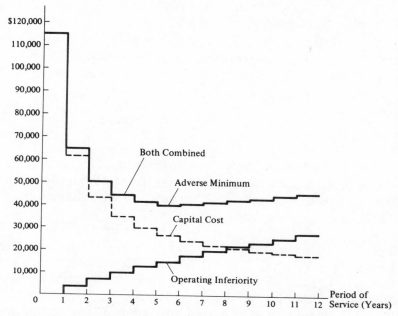

Figure 9-1. Graphic Representation of Columns 7, 8, and 9 of Table 9-1. Time-Adjusted Annual Averages for Period Ending with Year Indicated.

lenger that reached its adverse minimum within just a few years to one that took 15 or 20 years to reach it.

Figure 9-1 illustrates graphically how the adverse minimum is determined as the minimum point on the total cost function, which is the vertical sum of the individual costs of the component functions for capital cost and for operating inferiority. Readers who are familiar with the derivation of the basic economic order quantity model will note some similarity of the graphs.

The Problem of Capacity Disparities

The existence of alternatives that provide for different production capacities requires some modification to the MAPI method. Assume that the defender, having a next-year operating inferiority of $50,000, is capable of producing 10,000 units of output annually. Assume further that potential challengers A and B have respective adverse minima of $500,000 and $1 million and annual production capabilities of 150,000 and 400,000 units.

At first glance it would appear that the defender should not be

Table 9-2.   Comparison of Alternatives

Machine	Adverse Minimum	Annual Production Capability	Cost per Unit
Defender	$ 50,000	10,000	$5.00
Alternative A	500,000	150,000	3.33
Alternative B	1,000,000	400,000	2.50

replaced, for it has the lowest adverse minimum (next-year operating inferiority). However, if we express the adverse minima in
terms of the units of annual production, we find that alternative
B promises the lowest cost *per unit* (see Table 9-2).

Now we see that the ordering of the per unit costs is the
opposite of the ordering of the adverse minima for the three
alternatives. Which should be selected? The answer depends on
the firm's annual production requirements. For instance, if the
firm requires that 35,000 units be produced each year, then the
cost per unit will be $14.28 with alternative A and $28.57 with
alternative B. The defender alone cannot produce more than
10,000 units annually. However, if exact duplicates of the defender may be acquired (with the same adverse minimum as the
defender), then we would need to add three machines. This
would raise capacity to 40,000 units in total—5000 more than
required. The cost per unit will be $5.71, which is much less than
the per unit costs of machines A and B.

Therefore, adverse minima in themselves are meaningless unless the alternative machines have the same annual productive
capacity. If they do not, it is necessary to make adjustments. Cost
should be expressed in terms of cost *per unit,* since to do otherwise
may lead to improper selection of the challenger and on to a
wrong replacement decision. And the cost per unit must be based
on the firm's requirements, not on the rated machine capacities
that may be lesser or greater than the production required by
the firm.

CONCLUSION

The MAPI method of capital equipment analysis provides an
alternative means of investment evaluation that is based on
minimization of costs. It is thus, in a sense, a dual formulation of

methods based on maximization of some measure of investment return such as the discounted cash flow (DCF) measures.

Because the MAPI method is based on cost minimization, it is suitable for analysis of projects where the DCF measures are much more difficult, if not impossible, to apply. Such projects are those this author has defined as component projects—they do not have cash revenues directly attributable to them alone. For these projects the cash inflows may be assumed invariant with respect to the production equipment employed, whereas cash costs will vary directly with respect to the choice of equipment. The MAPI method, unlike the DCF methods, requires no estimates of cash inflows. Instead it requires cost estimates that often may be provided more easily, and provided by those personnel whose experience in production promises they may be the best obtainable estimates. Conversely, revenue estimates for component projects are likely to be based on tenuous premises if not pure guesses.

Proper application of the MAPI method requires that the adverse minima of alternative projects be adjusted to reflect production capacity differences or the firm's production requirements. Otherwise the per unit cost of one alternative may be greater than that of another even though it may have a lower adverse minimum.

10

The Problem of Mixed Cash Flows: I

When the internal rate of return (IRR) was discussed in Chapter 7, a restriction was placed on the cash flows that assured there would be only one real IRR in the range -100 percent to ∞—that there be only one change in the arithmetic sign in the flows. In this chapter the restriction is removed, the consequences examined, and a method analyzed that is claimed to provide a unique measure of return on investment.

INTERNAL RATE OF RETURN DEFICIENCIES

Under certain circumstances the IRR may not be unique, and thus we would seem to have to decide which, if any, of the IRR is a correct measure of return on investment. As we shall see, when there are two or more IRRs, none of them is a correct measure of return on investment.

The difficulties with IRR arise because of mixed cash flows. We define mixed cash flows as existing whenever a project has more than one change in arithmetic sign. There must, of course, be one change in sign for us to find any IRR. However, when there is more than one change in sign, the IRR, even if unique, may not measure the return on investment.

EXAMPLE 10-1

Let us consider the following capital-budgeting project, for which we have mixed cash flows of:

$t = 0$	$t = 1$	$t = 2$
$-\$100$	$+\$320$	$-\$240$

This project has two IRRs: 20 percent and 100 percent. The net present value (NPV) is positive for any cost of capital greater than

$NPV

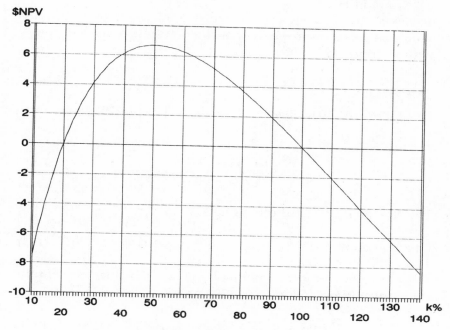

Figure 10-1.   Net Present Value.

20 percent but less than 100 percent. Figure 10-1 illustrates the NPV function for this project. The NPV reaches a maximum of $6.25 for a cost of capital of 60 percent. The profitability index (PI) of .0625 (or 1.0625 by the common, alternative definition of PI) is not likely to cause much enthusiasm, but let us retain this example for further analysis.

DESCARTES' RULE

Descartes' rule of signs states that the number of unique, positive, real roots to a polynomial equation with real coefficients (such as the equation for IRR) must be less than or equal to the number of sign changes between the coefficients. If less than the number of sign changes, the number of positive,[1] real roots must be less

___

[1]We are interested in positive, real roots since in solving any given polynomial, we will find the values of $x = 1 + r$, where r is the IRR value in decimal form. Therefore, after solving for the roots of the IRR polynomial, we must make the transformation $r_j = x_j - 1$ for each root, $j = 1, \ldots, n$. Since we work with all net cash flows attributable to the particular project, we therefore cannot lose more than 100 percent or our investment. Thus limiting the r_j to ≥ -1.00 restricts the x_j to ≥ 0.

by any even number, since complex roots come in conjugate pairs, and an nth degree polynomial will have n roots, not necessarily distinct.

EXAMPLE 10-2

The following cash flows yield a third-degree IRR polynomial equation:

$t = 0$	$t = 1$	$t = 2$	$t = 3$
$-\$1000$	$+\$3800$	$-\$4730$	$+\$1936$

The IRR equation is (dropping \$):

$$-1000 + 3800(1 + r)^{-1} - 4730(1 + r)^{-2} + 1936(1 + r)^{-3} = 0 \quad (10.1)$$

or, alternatively, by multiplying by $(1 + r)^3$ to put into future value form, then dividing by 1000 and letting $x = 1 + r$:

$$1x^3 - 3.8x^2 + 4.73x - 1.936 = 0 \quad (10.2)$$

This equation has three real roots, one with a multiplicity of two (double root). The roots are 10 percent, 10 percent, and 60 percent, which we can verify by generating the equation by multiplication and by comparing with Eq. (10.2). If $r = 10$ percent $= .10$, then $x = 1.1$ and $x - 1.1$ is a zero (root) to the equation. Similarly, $x - 1.6$ is a zero to the equation. Multiplying, we obtain:

$$
\begin{array}{r}
x - 1.1 \\
\underline{x - 1.1} \\
x^2 - 2.2x + 1.21 \\
\underline{x - 1.6} \\
x^3 - 2.2x^2 + 1.21x \\
\underline{-1.6x^2 + 3.52x - 1.936} \\
x^3 - 3.8x^2 + 4.73x - 1.936
\end{array}
\quad (10.3)
$$

which is identical to Eq. (10.2).

We shall leave the matter of multiple roots now, because, as we shall see, when a project has mixed cash flows, even a unique, real IRR is no assurance that the IRR is a correct measure of investment return.

THE TEICHROEW, ROBICHEK, AND MONTALBANO (TRM) ANALYSIS

Teichroew, and later Teichroew, Robichek, and Montalbano[2] (TRM) explained that the existence of multiple IRR provided a meaningful interpretation, and proposed an algorithm for determining a unique measure of return on invested capital (RIC). James C. T. Mao was the first to offer a lucid summary of the main points of the TRM work,[3] and his work is still a valuable reference on the topic.

The analysis of TRM realized that projects with mixed cash flows may be neither clearly investments nor clearly financing projects. If, for example, the firm makes a loan, the cash flow sequence will be $- + + \cdots + +$ if the loan is amortized with periodic payments. This is identical to a capital investment with the same net cash flows. From the viewpoint of the borrower (or the capital asset, if we can attribute a viewpoint), the cash flow sequence will be the negative of our firm's: $+ - - \cdots - -$. Depending on whether we view the cash flow sequence through the firm's eyes or those of the borrower, we have what is unambiguously either an investment or a financing project. Since there is only one change in sign between the cash flows, we know the IRR will be unique.

Now, what if we have instead a cash flow sequence of $- + + - +$, or $+ - - + - +$? Can we say a priori that we have an investment or a financing project based only on examining the signs of the cash flows? The answer is no, we cannot. The TRM analysis recognizes that some projects with mixed cash flows have attributes of *both* investment and financing projects. The returns on such projects are not, as the IRR method assumes, independent of the firm's cost of capital. To understand the TRM analysis, we need to define some terms.

[2]D. Teichroew, *An Introduction to Management Science* (New York: Wiley, 1964).
———, A. Robichek, and M. Montalbano, "Mathematical Analysis of Rates of Return Under Certainty," *Management Science*, Vol. II (January 1965).
———, "An Analysis of Criteria for Investment and Financing Decisions Under Certainty," *Management Science*, Vol. 12 (November 1965).
[3]J. C. T. Mao, "Financing Urban Change in the Great Society: Quantitative Analysis of Urban Renewal Investment Decisions," *The Journal of Finance*, Vol. XXII, No. 2 (May 1967).
———, *Quantitative Analysis of Financial Decisions* (New York: MacMillan, 1969).

Definitions

Let

$$a_0, a_1, \ldots, a_n$$

denote the project cash flows.

Let

$$s_t(r) = \sum_{i=0}^{t} a_i(1 + r)^{t-i}, 0 \leq t < n,$$

and

$$s_t(r) = (1 + r)s_{t-1} + a_t$$

denote the *project balance* equations, and

$$s_n(r) = \sum_{i=0}^{n} a_i(1 + r)^{n-i}$$

denote the *future value* of the project.

The minimum rate is $r_{\min}$ for which all the project balance equations are less than or equal to zero: $s_t(r_{\min}) \leq 0$ for $0 < t < n$.

The project balance at the end of period t, at rate r, is interpreted as the future value of (1) the amount the firm has invested in the project or (2) the firm has received from the project from period zero to the end of period t. By using TRM's classifications, *at rate r*, the following occur:

1. If $s_t(r) \leq 0$ for $0 \leq t < n$, we have a *pure investment project*.
2. If $s_t(r) \geq 0$ for $0 \leq t < n$, we have a *pure financing project*.
3. If $s_t(r) \leq 0$ for *some t*, $s_t(r) > 0$ for *some t*, and $0 \leq t < n$, we have a *mixed project*.

A *simple project* is one in which the sign of a_0 is different from the sign of a_i for all $i > 0$. In a mixed project, the firm has money invested in the project during some periods, and "owes" the project money during some other periods.

It can be shown that all simple investments are pure investments. However, the converse is not true: Not all pure investments are simple investments.

Let us follow TRM's notation in using PFR to denote the *project financing rate*, the rate applied for periods in which the project can be viewed as providing funds to the firm; that is, as a net financing source, with positive project balance. We use k, the firm's cost of capital for PFR, and PIR to denote the *project investment rate, $r°$* (TRM use r for this), the rate that the project yields when the project balance is negative. We also refer to the PIR as the RIC, the *return on invested capital*.

To determine the PIR, or RIC, we proceed as follows, first negating all cash flows if $a_0 > 0$:

$$s_0(r, k) = a_0$$
$$s_1(r, k) = (1 + r)s_0 + a_1 \text{ if } s_0 < 0$$
$$= (1 + k)s_0 + a_1 \text{ if } s_0 \geq 0$$
$$s_2(r, k) = (1 + r)s_1 + a_2 \text{ if } s_1 < 0$$
$$\vdots = (1 + k)s_1 + a_2 \text{ if } s_0 \geq 0$$
$$s_n(r, k) = (1 + r)s_{n-1} + a_n \text{ if } s_{n-1} < 0$$
$$= (1 + k)s_{n-1} + a_n \text{ if } s_{n-1} \geq 0$$

In order to find whether, for any $j (0 < j \leq n)$, $s_j(r, k) < 0$ or ≥ 0, we substitute r_{min} for r in evaluating it. Since we will use an estimate of the firm's cost of capital for k, the only unknown in $s_n(r, k)$ is r. We solve this equation for r, and since the solution is a particular value, the RIC, we refer to it as $r°$.

Note that because r_{min} is defined as the smallest real root for which all the project balance equations, $s_t(r_{min})$, *are* ≤ 0, *with* $0 \leq t < n$, *it is a_n which determines whether the project is pure or mixed*. If $s_n(r_{min}) \geq 0$, a greater discount rate r, one for which $s_n(r_{min}) = 0$, will retain the condition that $s_t(r) \leq 0$ for $0 \leq t < n$. In this case, the r for which $s_n(r) = 0$ will be the $r°$ of the project. It will also be the IRR of the project. *From this it follows that the IRR is found by assuming that the project financing rate equals the project investment rate,* so that k does not enter the equation for IRR. In general, this will not be a correct assumption. However, it does not affect our results when $s_n(r, k) = s_n(r)$, a condition we have for all pure investments. *In other words, for pure investments only, $r° = IRR$, and k does not affect $r°$: the IRR is "internal" to the project.*

THE TRM ALGORITHM

The foregoing leads to an algorithm for determining the RIC on an investment, either simple or with mixed cash flows. The steps of the algorithm are:

I. If $a_0 > 0$, negate all cash flows before beginning. Find r_{min}, the minimum real rate for which all the project balance equations, $s_t(r_{min})$ are ≤ 0, for $0 \leq t < n$.

II. Evaluate $s_n(r_{min})$.
   (1) If $s_n(r_{min}) \geq 0$, then $s_t(r, k) = s_t(r)$ and $r°$ equals the unique IRR as traditionally found.
   (2) If $s_n(r_{min}) < 0$, then we proceed to step III.

III. Let k be the firm's cost of capital.

$$
\begin{aligned}
s_0 &= a_0 \\
s_1 &= (1 + r)s_0 + a_1 \text{ if } s_0 < 0 \\
    &= (1 + k)s_0 + a_1 \text{ if } s_0 \geq 0 \\
s_2 &= (1 + r)s_1 + a_2 \text{ if } s_1 < 0 \\
    &= (1 + k)s_1 + a_2 \text{ if } s_1 \geq 0 \\
&\quad\vdots \\
s_n &= (1 + r)s_{n-1} + a_n \text{ if } s_{n-1} < 0 \\
    & (1 + k)s_{n-1} + a_n \text{ if } s_{n-1} \geq 0
\end{aligned}
$$

In every $s_t(r, k)$, use r_{min} for r to determine whether the project balance is less than zero or greater than or equal to zero.

IV. Solve $s_n(r, k)$ for unique r; call this $r°$, the return on invested capital.

Note that the return on invested capital $r°$ may be the IRR, but in general will not be.

EXAMPLE 10-3

Let us now take up the project discussed earlier, which had cash flows:

$t = 0$	$t = 1$	$t = 2$
$-\$100$	$+\$320$	$-\$240$

and apply the TRM algorithm.

I. Find r_{min}:

$$-100(1 + r) + 320 = 0$$
$$r = 3.2 - 1 = 2.2 \text{ or } 220\%$$
$r_{min} = r$ (In this example there is only one project balance equation.)

II. Evaluate

$$s_n(r_{min}) = -100(1 + r)^2 + 320(1 + r) - 240$$
$$= -240$$
$$-240 < 0$$

So we have a mixed investment.

III. Let k be the firm's cost of capital:

$$s_0 = a_0 = -100 < 0$$
$$s_1 = s_0(1 + r) + a_1 \text{ since } s_0 < 0$$
$$= 0 \text{ when evaluated for } r = r_{min}$$
$$s_2 = s_1(1 + k) + a_2 \text{ since } s_1 \geq 0$$
$$= -100(1 + r)(1 + k) + 320(1 + k) - 240$$

IV. Solve for $r° = r$:

$$1 + r = \frac{320(1 + k) - 240}{100(1 + k)} \tag{10.4}$$

$$r° = r = 2.2 - \frac{2.4}{1 + k} \tag{10.5}$$

Under the IRR assumption of $r = k$, we find that

$$r = 2.2 - \frac{2.4}{1 + r}$$
$$r^2 - 1.2r + .2 = 0$$

and, using the quadratic formula,

$$r = \frac{1.2 \pm \sqrt{1.44 - .8}}{2} = \frac{1.2 \pm .8}{2}$$
$$= 1.0, .20$$
$$= 100\%, 20\%$$

What if $r \neq k$? Figure 10-2 shows the function for $r°$ in terms of k. The figure shows clearly that for only two values of k will $r° = k$ for this project. Under the rule that we accept a project if

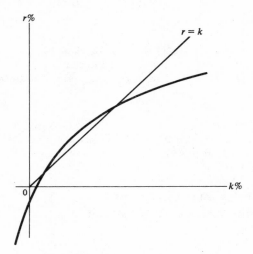

Figure 10-2. r^* Function of k.

$r° > k$ and reject if $r° ≤ k$, this project is acceptable for the same values of k that we found with the NPV criterion.

EXAMPLE 10-4

For a second application of the TRM algorithm let us take the project considered earlier that had cash flows:

$t = 0$	$t - 1$	$t = 2$	$t = 3$
$-\$1000$	$+\$3800$	$-\$4730$	$+\$1936$

I. Find r_{min}:
   (1)

$$-1000(1 + r) + 3800 = 0$$
$$r_1 = 3.8 - 1 = 2.8 \text{ or } 280\%$$

(2)

$$-1000(1 + r)^2 + 3800(1 + r) - 4730 = 0$$

$$r_2 = \frac{-3.8 \pm \sqrt{(3.8)^2 - (4)(4.73)}}{-2}$$

$$= \text{complex roots}$$

Therefore, $r_{min} = 2.8 = r_1$.

II. Evaluate $s_n(r_{min})$:

$$s_n(r_{min}) = -1000(3.8)^3 + 3800(3.8)^2 - \\ 4730(3.8) + 1936 \\ = -16{,}038 < 0$$

Hence this is a *mixed project.*

III. Let k be the firm's cost of capital:

$$\begin{aligned}
s_0 &= a_0 = -1000 < 0 \\
s_1 &= s_0(1 + r) + a_1 = 0 \\
&= -1000(1 + r) + 3800 = 0 \text{ at } r = r_{min} \\
s_2 &= s_1(1 + k) + a_2 \\
&= -1000(1 + r)(1 + k) + 3800(1 + k) - 4730 \\
&< 0 \text{ at } r = r_{min} \\
s_3 &= -1000(1 + r)^2(1 + k) + 3800(1 + r)(1 + k) - \\
&\quad 4730(1 + r) + 1936
\end{aligned}$$

IV. Solve for $r° = r$:

This yields a fairly complicated expression for r in terms of k, although for a specific value of k, the solution can be easily accomplished with the quadratic formula. The expression for k in terms of r is:

$$k = \frac{1.936 - 4.73(1 + r)}{(1 + r)^2 - 3.8(1 + r)} - 1 \tag{10.6}$$

from which we may generate values of k corresponding to various $r° = r$ and plot the function (see Figure 10-3).

Note that $r°$ is a double-valued function of k. Since we cannot lose more than we have invested in the project,[4] values of $r < -100$ percent are not economically meaningful and may thus be ignored. We cannot lose more than 100 percent of what we invest in the project, because the cash flows reflect the total effect of the project on the firm; *all* costs and revenues attributable to the project are incorporated in the cash flows. At 10 percent, a double root to the IRR equation, it is interesting that the function touches, but does not cross, the $r° = k$-axis. This project is acceptable for $0 \leq k < 10$ percent and 10 percent $< k < 60$ percent, the same as by the NPV criterion. The NPV function is shown in Figure 10-4.

---

[4]We are still assuming project independence in this chapter.

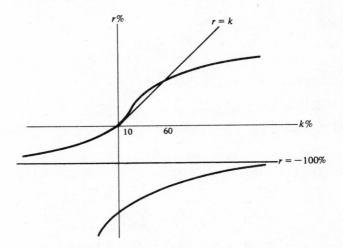

Figure 10-3. r^* as Function of k.

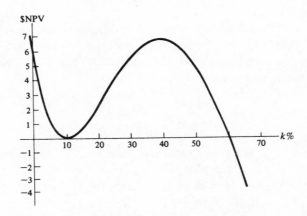

Figure 10-4.   NPV Function.

EXAMPLE 10-5

Let us now solve for the RIC of a project having cash flows in six periods:

$t = 0$	$t = 1$	$t = 2$	$t = 3$	$t = 4$	$t = 5$
$-\$100$	$+\$600$	$-\$1509$	$+\$2027$	$-\$1436$	$+\$418$

This project has real IRR values of 0 percent, 10 percent, and 90 percent. The IRR equation also has complex roots of $0 + i$ and $0 - i$.

I. Find r_{min}:

(1)

$$-100(1 + r) + 600 = 0$$
$$r_1 = r = 5 \text{ or } 500\%$$

(2)

$$-100(1 + r)^2 + 600(1 + r) - 1509 = 0$$

$$r = \frac{-600 \pm \sqrt{(600)^2 - (4)(-100)(-1509)}}{-200}$$

Since r is a complex root, skip r_2.

(3) We can approach this in two ways. First, we could solve the equation:

$$-100(1 + r)^3 + 600(1 + r)^2 - 1509(1 + r) + 2027$$

after setting it equal to zero. This is a laborious process, conducive to errors in calculations, unless we use a computer program. Even in this case there may be time lost in accessing a computer and waiting for results. Once we did find r we would set $r_3 = r$. The second approach may save us this trouble.

Let us substitute the r_{min} thus far obtained—$r_1 = 500$ percent. If this equation value is less than zero for r_1, we do not need to solve for the value of r_3. Using this approach, we find the equation value is -7027, so we need not solve for r_3.

(4) As in (3), we could solve for r in the equation:

$$-100(1 + r)^4 + 600(1 + r)^3 - 1509(1 + r)^2 + 2027(1 + r) - 1436$$

after setting it equal to zero. But again, let us first try the second approach. We obtain a value of $-43,595$; so again we need not solve for r_4.

We have found that $r_{min} = r_1 = 500$ percent, since for this rate, and no lesser rate, all project balance equations are less than or equal to zero.

II. Evaluate $s_n(r_{min})$:

$$s_n(r_{min}) = -100(6)^5 + 600(6)^4 - 1509(6)^3 + 2027(6)^2 - 1436(6) + 418$$
$$= -261,152 < 0$$

So this is a mixed project.

III. Let k be the firm's cost of capital:

$$s_0 = a_0 = -100$$
$$s_1 = -100(1 + r) + 600 = 0 \text{ at } r = r_{min}$$
$$s_2 = -100(1 + r)(1 + k) + 600(1 + k) - 1509 < 0$$
$$s_3 = -100(1 + r)^2(1 + k) + 600(1 + r)(1 + k) - 1509(1 + r) + 2027 < 0$$
$$s_4 = -100(1 + r)^3(1 + k) + 600(1 + r)^2(1 + k) - 1509(1 + r)^2 + 2027(1 + r) - 1436 < 0$$
$$s_5 = -100(1 + r)^4(1 + k) + 600(1 + r)^3(1 + k) - 1509(1 + r)^3 + 2027(1 + r)^2 - 1436(1 + r) + 418$$

IV. Solve for $r° = r$.

Because this involves solution of a fourth degree equation, we will present the solutions for $k = 15$ percent and $k = 25$ percent. At $k = 15$ percent, $r° = r = 15.08$ percent, and the project is marginally acceptable. At $k = 25$ percent, $r° = r = 25.28$ percent, and again the project is marginally acceptable.

THE UNIQUE, REAL INTERNAL RATE OF RETURN: CAVEAT EMPTOR![5]

The internal rate of return (IRR), even when unique and real, may nevertheless be an incorrect measure of the return on investment. All projects characterized by negative flows occurring only at the beginning and the end will be mixed investments for which the IRR, whether unique and real or not, is not a correct measure of investment return.

Several years ago, W. H. Jean[6] proved that for capital-budgeting projects in which only the first and last cash flows were negative that there would be a unique, real, positive internal rate of return or no positive IRR. J. Hirschleifer[7] subsequently showed that if the sum of cash flows beyond the first was less than or equal to the first cash flow, then multiple IRRs can exist for the

[5]Reprinted with permission of *Journal of Financial and Quantitative Analysis,* Copyright © 1978. With Corrections.
[6]W.H. Jean, "On Multiple Rates of Return," *The Journal of Finance,* Vol. XXIII, No. 1 (March 1968).
[7]J. Hirschleifer, "On Multiple Rates of Return: Comment," *The Journal of Finance,* Vol. XXXIV, No. 1 (March 1969).

project. This prompted Professor Jean[8] to extend his treatment, and further specify the conditions for unique IRR for such cases as Hirschleifer cited.

Although Jean's results are mathematically interesting, they do not take into account the way in which such projects violate the assumption of independence between the IRR and the firm's cost of capital, which destroys the economic meaningfullness of the resulting IRR. The conditions under which the IRR of a project may not be independent of the firm's cost of capital have been widely ignored in the literature, one noteworthy exception being Mao's text. Jean's article and examples are cited here for purposes of illustration, since his article is mathematically rigorous.

However, mathematical uniqueness of a real root to the traditional IRR equation is, although a *necessary* condition, nevertheless not a *sufficient* condition to insure that one has obtained a rate independent of the firm's cost of capital, and thus a measure of investment return "internal" to the cash flow of the project. In fact, we shall prove that in the case of a project with negative flows only at beginning and end, for which Professor Jean proved a unique, positive IRR can always be found, that the IRR will *never* (excluding rare events in which the firm's cost of capital is the same as the rate r_{min}, which is discussed later) be independent of the firm's cost of capital.

The TRM Algorithm Applied to Jean and Hirschleifer Cases

A theorem will be proved later that has two corollaries relating to the discussion of Professors Jean and Hirschleifer. First, however, the examples provided by Jean and Hirschleifer will be analyzed within the framework provided by TRM. A cost of capital $k = 10$ percent will be assumed for all cases.

Case 1.   Cash flows are -1, 5, -6

$$IRR = -100\%, 200\%$$
$$r_{min} = 400\%$$
$$s_n(r_{min}) = -6 < 0$$

Hence this is a mixed investment.

[8]W. H. Jean, "Reply," *The Journal of Finance,* Vol. XXIV, No. 1 (March 1969).

$$s_0 = a_0 = -1 < 0$$
$$s_1 = s_0(1 + r^\circ) + a_1$$
$$= -1(1 + r^\circ) + 5 = 0 \text{ (using } r_{min} \text{ for } r^\circ\text{)}$$
$$s_2 = s_1(1 + k) + a_2$$
$$= -1(1 + r^\circ)(1 + k) + 5(1 + k) - 6$$

Therefore $r^\circ = -145.45\%$, the rate for which $s_2 = 0$

Case 2.   First m inflows are negative. Cash flows are $-5, -1, 2, 2$.

$$IRR = -15.9\%$$
$$r_{min} = -45.9\%$$
$$S_n(r_{min}) = +2 > 0$$

Hence this is a pure investment and the IRR is a unique, real measure of project return, independent of k.

Case 3.   In middle life, m inflows are negative. Cash flows are $-1, 2, -4, 2$.

$$IRR = -36.0\%$$
$$r_{min} = 100\%$$
$$S_n(r_{min}) = -6 < 0$$

Hence this is a mixed project.

$$s_0 = a_0 = -1 < 0$$
$$s_1 = s_0(1 + r^\circ) + a_1$$
$$= -1(1 + r^\circ) + 2 = 0 \text{ (using } r_{min} \text{ for } r^\circ\text{)}$$
$$s_2 = -1(1 + r^\circ)(1 + k) + 2(1 + k) - 4 < 0$$
$$s_3 = s_2(1 + r^\circ) + a_3$$
$$= -1(1 + r^\circ)^2(1 + k) + 2(1 + r^\circ)(1 + k) - 4(1 + r^\circ) + 2$$
$$r^\circ = -24.09\%, \text{ the rate for which } s_3 = 0$$

Of the three cases considered, only Case 2 has a return "internal" to the project. Case 1 has two IRRs and thus the IRR is not only an incorrect measure of investment return, but also ambiguous. Case 3 has a unique, real IRR. However, it is not a proper measure of return on investment. *This is a crucial criticism of the IRR—even though it may be unique and real in the mathematical sense, this in itself is not a sufficient condition for it to be a correct measure of return on investment.*

An example presented by Professor Mao vividly emphasizes this point in Case 4.

Case 4.　Cash flows are -10, $+40$, -40.

$$IRR = 100\%$$
$$r_{min} = 300\%$$
$$s_n(r_{min}) = -40 < 0$$

Hence this is a mixed project.

$$s_0 = a_0 = -10 < 0$$
$$s_1 = s_0(1 + r°) + a_1$$
$$= -10(1 + r°) + 40 = 0 \text{ (using } r_{min} = r°)$$
$$s_2 = s_1(1 + k) + a_2$$
$$= -10(1 + r°)(1 + k) + 40(1 + k) - 40$$
$$r° = -63.64\%, \text{ the rate for which } s_2 = 0$$

This is a mixed investment with return on invested capital of *minus* 63.64 percent, even though the project has a unique, real, positive IRR of 100 percent. Thus, use of the IRR would lead to acceptance of the project for any cost of capital $k < 100$ percent—a very undesirable consequence for a firm with normal financial management goals.

A NEW THEOREM

To generalize our findings, we now present a theorem that has significant implications on the class of investment projects with negative cash flows only at the beginning and the end.

Theorem

Given that $a_0 < 0$, $a_n < 0$, $a_t \geq 0$ for $t = 1, \ldots, n - 1$ with *some* $a_t > 0$ for a project, *the project will always be a mixed investment* (a mixed financing project[9] if $a_0 > 0$, $a_n > 0$, and $a_t \leq 0$ for $t = 1, \ldots, n - 1$ with some $a_t < 0$).

Proof.　Since $a_0 < 0$, and $a_t \geq 0$ for $t = 1$ to $n - 1$, if we look only at the cash flows a_0 through a_{n-1}, they form in themselves a *simple investment* that TRM have proved has a unique, real rate r for which all the $s_t \leq 0$ for $t = 1, 2, \ldots, n - 1$. In particular, $s_{n-1} = 0$. Therefore, this r is the r_{min} of the project, for any larger r would cause all s_t to be less than zero for $t \leq n - 1$.

[9]In this case we negate all cash flows before applying the TRM algorithm.

In evaluating s_n at rate $r = r_{min}$, we simply add a_n, which is less than zero to $(1 + r_{min})s_{n-1}$, which is equal to zero. Then, since $s_n < 0$, we have a mixed investment as defined by TRM, and the project rate $r°$ is *not* independent of the firm's cost of capital.

Corollary I

If

$$a_t < 0 \text{ for } m < n - 1$$

and

$$a_n < 0$$

with

$$a_t \geq 0 \text{ for } m \leq t \leq n \text{ and some } a_t > 0$$

then the project will be a mixed investment.

11

The Problem of Mixed Cash Flows: II

In the previous chapter the problem of mixed cash flows was introduced, and a particular method of analysis, that of Tei-chroew, Robichek, and Montalbano (TRM), was discussed. Although the theoretical merits of the rigorously developed TRM approach may be superior, other methods are more widely used in practice to deal with projects having mixed cash flows. The question of which, if any, of the existing methods is universally "best" may be unresolvable. The appropriateness of any of the methods to a given situation depends on the extent to which the method's underlying assumptions match the particular situation and the goals of the enterprise's management. Different circumstances may require different analytical assumptions, and these in turn may imply different methods of analysis.

The methods examined in this chapter are the *Wiar method* and the *sinking fund family of methods.* Because it is substantially different in nature from the others, the Wiar method is discussed first.

THE WIAR METHOD

Robert Wiar[1] developed this method for analysis of the investment returns on leases,[2] for which he asserted it is inappropriate to analyze directly the net cash flows to equity. His approach was to employ that aspect of the Keynesian theory that states that the supply cost of funds cannot exceed the imputed income stream yield. In other words, analysis must be handled by simultaneous

[1]Robert Wiar, "Economic Implications of Multiple Rates of Return in the Leveraged Lease Context," *The Journal of Finance,* Vol. XXVIII, pp. 1275–1286.

[2]Leveraged leases are covered in detail in a later chapter. The characteristic of leveraged leases of concern to us now is that they generally have mixed net, after-tax cash flows to equity.

treatment of three components: (1) positive cash inflows; (2) mortgage bond amortization flows; and (3) the required equity investment. This analysis can be stated in two equivalent ways:

$$E_0(1 + r_e)^t = \sum_{i=1}^{t} R_i(1 + r^\circ)^{t-1} - \sum_{i=1}^{t} M_i(1 + r_b)^{t-1} \qquad (11.1)$$

or

$$R_0(1 + r^\circ)^t = M_0(1 + r_b)^t + E_0(1 + r_e)^t \qquad (11.2)$$

where

M_0 is the amount financed by bonds
M_i is the fixed amortization payment
r_b is the effective yield to the bond holders
E_0 is the equity investment
r_e is the return on equity, ignoring bond service
R_0 is the initial outflow—investment—equity plus bond financing
r° is the overall return on aggregate investment
R_i is the future income stream

In the case of capital-budgeting projects it will normally be appropriate to consider the supply cost of funds as the firm's overall marginal cost of capital k.[3] Let us examine Eq. (11.2), letting $M_0 = 0$, $k = r_e$, and $R_0 = E_0$. Then

$$R_0(1 + r^\circ)^t = R_0(1 + k)^t \qquad (11.3)$$

and it is clear that $r^\circ = k$. This means that the imputed income stream yield, r°, equals the supply cost of funds k. This is what we would expect, in equilibrium, at the cut-off point, for a firm not constrained by capital rationing, and it is consistent with the IRR criterion or Keynesian marginal efficiency of capital (MEC).[4]

[3]This is because of risk considerations. No individual capital-budgeting project, unless independent of the firm's existing assets, can be properly considered in isolation and without regard to its effect on the firm's risk characteristics that affect the firm's cost of capital.

[4]The Keynesian term "MEC" is normally used in macroeconomic discussions concerning the aggregate investment return curve for an entire national economy, whereas IRR is normally used by noneconomists to refer to the return on individual projects.

EXAMPLE 11-1. AN APPLICATION OF THE WIAR METHOD

Consider a project costing $10 million that is expected to yield net, after-tax cash flows of $1.5 million at the end of each year of its useful lifetime of ten years. There is expected to be a salvage value of zero.

The firm's existing capital structure is 25 percent debt, 75 percent equity, and is considered optimal. The project, if accepted, will be financed by a private placement of $2.5 million in bonds yielding 10 percent and maturing in ten years, and the balance by equity.

Assuming the bonds are sold at par value, the payment (assumed to be made at year end) will be $250,000. The entire $2.5 million must be retired in the tenth year, the year of maturity for the bond.

The overall cash flow stream is composed of two component streams, as shown in Table 11-1. It is the return on *equity* we are interested in. The equity cash flow stream has mixed cash flows. Applying the Wiar method, we obtain from (11.2) the equation to be solved for r_e:

$$.75(1 + r_e)^{10} = 1.0(1.0814)^{10} - .25(1.1000)^{10}$$

and

Table 11-1.   Cash Flows for Wiar Method Example

Year	Project Cash Flow	For Bond Service	Net Cash Flow to Equity
0	−$10,000,000	$2,500,000	−$7,500,000
1	1,500,000	−250,000	1,250,000
2	1,500,000	−250,000	1,250,000
3	1,500,000	−250,000	1,250,000
4	1,500,000	−250,000	1,250,000
5	1,500,000	−250,000	1,250,000
6	1,500,000	−250,000	1,250,000
7	1,500,000	−250,000	1,250,000
8	1,500,000	−250,000	1,250,000
9	1,500,000	−250,000	1,250,000
10	1,500,000	−2,750,000	−1,250,000
IRR of cash Flow stream =	8.14%	10.00%	7.03%

$$r_e = 7.45\%$$

which is greater than the IRR of 7.03 percent on the equity stream. The ordinary IRR on the mixed equity stream is unique in this particular problem, but it need not be so. The previous chapter showed that, when mixed cash flows are considered, even a unique IRR does not measure return on investment.

The r_e obtained is then compared with the required return on equity. If it is greater than the required rate, the project will be acceptable.

The Wiar method will be discussed again in Chapter 13, which deals with leveraged leases. For now we recognize that for capital budgeting projects as a class, the method reduces to the IRR method already treated in detail, and that it is inadequate for analyzing projects having mixed cash flows.

SINKING FUND METHODS

Sinking fund methods, as a class, are characterized by some adjustment being made to the original cash flows series, aimed at making the adjusted cash flow series amenable to treatment by internal rate of return analysis. To apply any of them, we first follow some procedure for systematically modifying the cash flow series to remove all negative flows except those at the beginning,[5] which represent the initial cash outlay or outlays. All negative cash flows beyond the initial outlay sequence are forced to zero. Next, because the adjusted cash flows have only one sign change, the internal rate of return procedure is applied. Under this definition, the Teichroew, or Teichroew, Robichek, and Montalbano method discussed in the previous chapter can also be considered a sinking fund method.

To avoid, or perhaps clear up some semantic difficulties, let us state here that (at least) three sinking fund methods have been used in practice. One is the *initial investment method* (IIM), another is the *sinking fund method* (SFM), the third is the *multiple investment sinking fund method* (MISFM). A possible semantic problem exists because *the* SFM, although a *particular* method, carries the name of the *entire class* of methods. In other words, the sinking fund method is really only one of several methods, all of which can be

---

[5]The multiple investment sinking fund method is an exception to this because not all negative cash flows are removed beyond the initial negative flow or flows.

characterized as sinking fund methods. As a class they include all of these methods as well as the TRM method. To avoid confusion, we shall refer to "the" sinking fund method as the *traditional sinking fund method* (TSFM).

The *sinking fund earnings rate* refers to the assumed rate at which funds that are set aside in a (hypothetical) sinking fund will accrue interest earnings. The *sinking fund rate, sinking fund rate of return,* or *sinking fund return on investment* refers to the internal rate of return on the adjusted cash flow sequence. Similarly, the *initial investment rate,* and so on, refers to the analogous internal rate of return on the adjusted cash flow series with the initial investment method.

To avoid complicating matters, we rule out the possibility of early project abandonment in this chapter. That is, we assume all projects will be held until the end of their economic lives. Furthermore, a uniform period-to-period sinking fund earnings rate is assumed in order to simplify and streamline exposition.

The Initial Investment Method

The initial investment method (IIM) is a type of sinking fund method. In the standard, conservative IIM it is assumed that an additional amount is invested, at the beginning of the project, specifically for the purpose of accumulating funds exactly sufficient to cover all negative cash flows occurring after the first positive flow.[6] Such *initial investment* is assumed to earn at some rate of return compounded from period to period. The rate of return is calculated on the revised initial investment and the subsequent positive cash flows. Negative flows are zeroed inasmuch as they are assumed to be exactly offset by the additional initial investment. Another way of applying the IIM is to assume that the *earliest* positive cash flows are set aside into a sinking fund earning just sufficiently to match exactly later negative cash flows.

To gain an understanding of the IIM, it will help to analyze an example. However, in order that the two similar methods may be compared together, this will be postponed until after the following discussion of the traditional sinking fund method.

---

[6]A series of *m* negative cash flows followed by a series of positive flows would cause no problem in determining return, for we could use the IRR directly in such cases.

The Traditional Sinking Fund Method

The traditional sinking fund method (TSFM), like the initial investment method, assumes that positive cash flows can be invested at some nonnegative rate of return so that later negative cash flows may be exactly covered. Unlike the IIM, however, the TSFM assumes that the most proximate positive cash flows preceding the negative flow will be put into a sinking fund to the extent required to offset the negative flow or flows. The TSFM, therefore, can be considered a much less conservative method than the IIM, to the extent it delays investment for some time and thus does not provide the benefit of having at least some accumulated earnings should the actual available earnings rate decline later in the project life.

Initial Investment and Traditional Sinking Fund Methods

The initial investment and traditional sinking fund methods are based on similar assumptions. Both the IIM and the TSFM are based on a technique that modifies the cash flows of a project

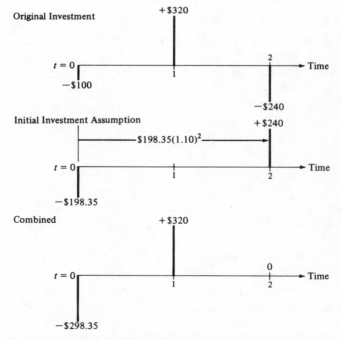

Figure 11-1. Initial Investment Method Applied to Example 11-2 Cash Flows.

having mixed cash flows (and thus often a mixed project in the TRM sense) to produce a simple, pure project that has zeros where the original had negative flows, in all but the initial outlays.[7] In fact, the TRM algorithm of the preceding chapter is closely related, with the earning rate on "sinking fund" equal to k, the firm's cost of capital. However, with the TRM method the timing and the amount of investment in a "sinking fund" are perhaps obscured by the nature and the complexity of the algorithm, with the cash flows "compressed"[8] prior to the solution for return on invested capital. With the IIM and TSFM, cash flows that had been negative are zeroed prior to solution for rate of return. Thus, the order of the polynomial that will be solved for a unique, real root will be less for the TRM than for the IIM or TSFM. This will be clarified by using two of the same examples that were used in the previous chapter with the TRM algorithm, but this time with the IIM and TSFM.

EXAMPLE 11-2

This example is the same as Example 10-1 used in Chapter 10. The cash flow is:

$t = 0$	$t = 1$	$t = 2$
$-\$100$	$+\$320$	$-\$240$

As stated in Chapter 10, this project has two IRRs: 20 percent and 100 percent. The NPV reaches a maximum of $6.67 at 50 percent cost of capital. The return on invested capital for this project, for $k = 10$ percent, is 1.82 percent. Figure 11-1 indicates the procedure used in applying the initial investment method to the cash flows. The IIM rate of return on investment is 7.26 percent for this example. Figure 11-2 suggests the procedure followed in applying the traditional sinking fund method. It is assumed that the applicable sinking fund's earning rate is 10 percent.

The essence of application of the TSFM to this project is to set aside sufficient cash, at some earnings rate, to accumulate to an amount exactly sufficient, one period later, to match the negative cash flow.

[7]The nonpositive cash flows preceding the first positive cash flow.

[8]Compressed in the sense that the polynomial that must be solved for the return on invested capital, $r°$, is of lesser degree than the IRR polynomial would be for the same project.

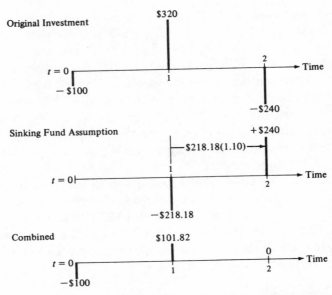

Figure 11-2.   Traditional Sinking Fund Method Applied to Example 11-2 cash flows.

Thus, for any positive cost of capital above 1.82 percent, the project would be unacceptable for investment under either method. Like the IRR method or that of TRM, we compare the project yield to the enterprise's cost of capital and reject the project if the yield rate is less than the cost of capital. For this project, if the earnings rate on the funds set aside[9] is 10 percent, and the cost of capital is $k = 10$ percent, then $r_{TSFM} = 1.82$ percent—the same as that obtained with the TRM method in Chapter 10. In general, they will not be the same. However, it is indicative of the relationship between the methods.

Let us next examine another example, this one the same as Example 10-2.

EXAMPLE 11-3

Figure 11-3 displays the net cash flows for this project and indicates the application of the initial investment method.

[9]In practice, it will be rare to find an investor actually depositing or setting aside cash to meet outflows later in the life of a project. Rather, the firm will usually employ the positive cash flows in its operations. To be conservative, we could assume that a zero earnings rate is applicable. However, it would be normally appropriate to assume that funds earn at the firm's cost of capital.

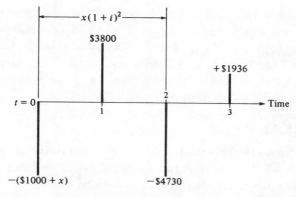

Figure 11-3. Initial Investment Method: Application to Example 11-3.

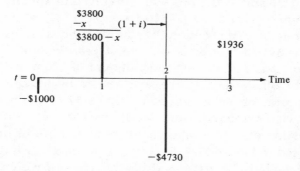

Figure 11-4. Traditional Sinking Fund Method: Application to Example 11-3.

Note that positive cash flows are compounded forward in time. They are not discounted back to an earlier point in time with the various sinking fund methods.[10] Otherwise, the $1936 positive cash flow at the end of year three could have been discounted back one year to offset partially the negative flow of $4730 at the end of year two.

The cash flow sequence that must be solved for r_{IIM} is: $-(\$1000 + x)$ at $t = 0$; $3800 at $t = 1$; 0 at $t = 2$; and $1936 at $t = 3$. The value of x depends on the assumed earnings rate on the sinking fund. It is equal to $\$4730/(1 + k)^2$, where i is the applicable rate. For $i = 10$ percent, we obtain $x = \$3909.10$ and $r_{IIM} = 10$ percent.

[10]An exception to this general rule is to be found in what is referred to as the modified sinking fund method (MSFM). We shall not discuss this method here, since it is a straightforward variation of the TSFM in which later positive cash flows may be discounted to pay off earlier negative flows.

Figure 11-4 illustrates application of the traditional sinking fund method to the same project. The adjusted cash flows from which we find the r_{TSFM} are: $-\$1000$ at $t = 0$; $\$3800 - x$ at $t = 1$; 0 at $t = 2$; and $\$1936$ at $t = 3$. The value of x is $\$4730/(1 + i)$, where i is the sinking fund earnings rate. For $i = 10$ percent, we obtain $r_{TSFM} = 10$ percent.

EXAMPLE 11-4

The cash flows for this project are illustrated in the time diagram of Figure 11-5. This project has two positive cash flows at the end of the years preceding the final cash flow of minus $22 at the end of year three.

Figure 11-6 shows the procedure involved in applying the traditional sinking fund method to Example 11-4. At an assumed earnings rate of 10 percent on the sinking fund, a set-aside of $20 (out of the $90 cash flow) at the end of year two will increase to $22 a year later. The sinking fund amount of $20 plus $2 interest will exactly offset the negative cash flow at the end of year three. After set-aside of $20 at end of year two, $70 remains for other uses. The yield on the adjusted cash flows is 25.7 percent $= r_{TSFM}$.

Application of the initial investment method to Example 11-4 is illustrated in Figure 11-7. Again, the assumed earnings rate on funds set aside is 10 percent. With this method we must invest an extra $16.53 at $t = 0$ to offset the negative $22 cash flow

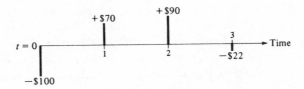

Figure 11-5. Original Cash Flow Series for Example 11-4.

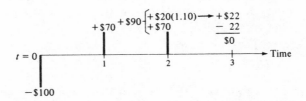

Figure 11-6. Traditional Sinking Fund Method, Adjusted Cash Flows for Example 11-4 with $i = 10$ Percent

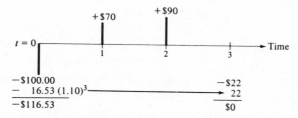

Figure 11-7. Initial Investment Method: Adjusted Cash Flows for Example 11-4 with $i = 10$ Percent.

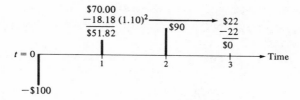

Figure 11-8. Initial Investment Method: Adjusted Cash Flows for Example 11-3 with $i = 10$ Percent.

at $t = 3$. The r_{IIM} on the adjusted cash flow series is 22.91 percent.

The initial investment method, a special case of the sinking fund method, may be considered more conservative than the traditional sinking fund method. This difference relates to the manner of selecting the timing and amounts to be set aside.

One might argue that it is extreme conservatism to assume that sufficient extra funds must be put into a sinking fund at $t = 0$ to cover the later negative cash flows. The initial investment method so far discussed is the limiting case on the conservative end of the spectrum (especially so if the assumed earnings rate were to be zero). As an alternative initial investment approach, we could assume that sufficient funds are set aside from the *earliest positive* cash flows to offset later negative flows. Figure 11-8 illustrates this variation of the IIM. The r_{IIM} in this case is 24.25 percent.

EXAMPLE 11-5

Now let us consider a somewhat more complex project than those in the previous examples of this chapter. Consider, for instance, a replacement chain of one capital investment following another. Let us assume we have a mine, which will cost $100 initially to develop and which will provide net, after-tax cash flows of $150 at the end of each year of its three-year economic life. Furthermore, assume that undertaking this mining project commits our organization to a project for secondary mineral recovery costing $350 to initiate and providing net, after-tax cash flows of $100 at the end of each year of its three-year useful life. Finally, at the end of the secondary recovery, our organization will have to pay out $350 to close down operations and rehabilitate the land on which the mine is situated to comply with environmental legislation. Since we have some positive cash flows from the projects at the end of years three and six, the overall net outlays in those years are not $350, but are $200 and $250, respectively. Figure 11-9 contains a time diagram illustrating the cash flows for this example.

This project has two positive internal rates of return: 10.23

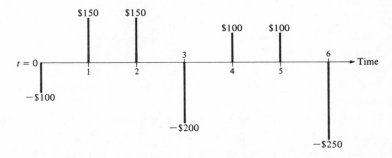

Figure 11-9.   Original Cash Flow Series for Example 11-5.

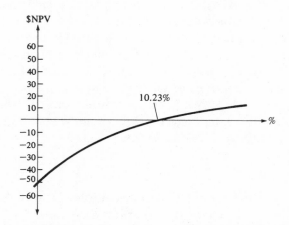

Figure 11-10.   Net Present Value as a Function of Cost of Capital for Example 11-5.

percent and 85.47 percent. From Chapter 10 we know that neither is a correct indication of the return on investment. The net present value function for the project is plotted in Figure 11-10. Note that under the net present value criterion the project would be considered acceptable for values of cost of capital k, such that 10.23 percent $< k <$ 85.47 percent.

Since this project is more complex than those considered previously in this chapter, application of the traditional sinking fund and initial investment methods is illustrated in the tables. Table 11-2 shows, for a 10 percent traditional sinking fund earnings rate, the adjustment to the cash flows that will be made employing the traditional sinking fund method. The traditional sinking fund method yield rate can be seen by inspecting the adjusted cash flows to be 9.27 percent. Figure 11-11 contains a time diagram showing the adjusted cash flows.

Table 11-3 shows, for a 10 percent sinking fund earnings rate, the procedure employed for adjusting the cash flows with the less conservative variation of the initial investment method. Figure 11-12 contains the time diagram corresponding to the adjusted cash flows. The initial investment method yield rate cannot be obtained by inspection (in contrast to the sinking fund yield rate). By calculation we find it to be 9.84 percent.

Table 11-2. Traditional Sinking Fund Method Adjustment to Original Cash Flows for Example 11-5.

Time Period Original Cash Flows	t = 0 -100	t = 1 150	t = 2 150	t = 3 -200	t = 4 100	t = 5 100	t = 6 -250
Step 1						-100 $\times(1.1) \longrightarrow 110$	
Step 2					-100 $\times(1.1)^2 \longrightarrow 121$		
Step 3			-12.98 $\times(1.1)^4 \longrightarrow 19$				
Step 4			-137.02 $\times(1.1) \to 150.72$				
Step 5		-40.73 $\times(1.1)^2 \longrightarrow 49.28$					
Sinking Fund Method Cash Flows	-100	109.27	0	0	0	0	0

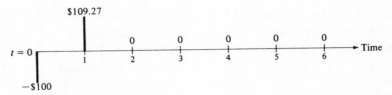

Figure 11-11. Modified Initial Investment Method: Adjusted Cash Flows for Example 11-5 with $i = 10$ Percent.

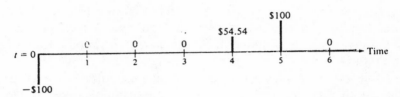

Figure 11-12. Modified Initial Investment Method: Adjusted Cash Flows for Example 11-5 with $i = 10$ Percent.

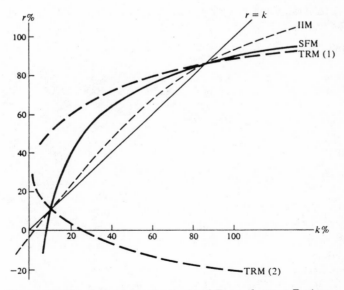

Figure 11-13. Sensitivity Analysis of Example 11-5 Project.

Figure 11-13 and Table 11-4 contain sensitivity analyses of the (less conservative) initial investment, traditional sinking fund, and TRM rates of return associated with various cost of capital percentages (traditional sinking fund earnings rates). Note that for $k = 0$ there is no real solution to the TRM return on investment equation.

Table 11-3. Modified Initial Investment Method Adjustment to Original Cash Flows for Example 11-5.

Time Period Original Cash Flows	t = 0 $-100	t = 1 $150	t = 2 $150	t = 3 $-200	t = 4 $100	t = 5 $100	t = 6 $-250
Step 1		-150 $\times(1.1)^2$⟶	⟶181.50				
Step 2			16.82 $\times(1.1)$⟶	⟶18.50			
Step 3			-133.18 $\times(1.1)^4$	⟶		⟶194.99	
Step 4					-45.46 $\times(1.1)^2$⟶	⟶55.01	
Initial Investment Method Adjusted Cash Flows	-100	0	0	0	54.54	100	0

Table 11-4. Sensitivity Analysis of Example 11-5 Project

k%	TRM(1)%	TRM(2)%	IIM%	TSFM%
0			3.19	50.00
10	51.01	10.11	0.61	0.87
20	60.74	2.80	23.10	39.08
30	67.07	-2.40	35.81	54.85
40	71.94	-6.40	47.50	64.25
50	75.87	-9.66	58.01	70.89
60	79.14	-12.40	67.25	76.08
70	81.90	-14.77	75.26	80.28
80	84.29	-16.86	82.14	83.79
90	86.38	-18.72	88.02	86.76
100	88.21	-20.39	93.02	89.31
110	89.85	-21.91	97.29	91.53
120	91.31	-23.30	100.94	93.49
130	92.63	-24.58	104.06	95.22

THE MULTIPLE INVESTMENT SINKING FUND METHOD

The final sinking fund variant we shall discuss in this chapter is the multiple investment sinking fund method (MISFM). The idea underlying the MISFM is to adjust the cash flow sequence to obtain two distinct, nonoverlapping investment sequences having identical internal rates of return. For example, the project having a five-year useful life can be decomposed as follows into adjusted cash flows plus sinking fund. We assume the sinking fund earns at 15 percent per period.

The adjusted cash flows can be considered to be two nonoverlapping investments, each having a unique, positive internal rate of return of 50.0 percent. For this particular project the r_{IIM} is 28.93 percent, r_{TSFM} is 40.95 percent, and the RIC is 52.24 percent.

	t = 0	t = 1	t = 2	t = 3	t = 4	t = 5
Original Cash Flows	−$1000	765	2500	−3500	1000	3000
Adjusted Cash Flows	−$1000	500	1500	−2000	1000	3000
Sinking Fund		265	1000	−1500		

The MISFM is much more difficult to apply than the IIM or TSFM, because it requires that the original cash flows be adjusted so that one, two, or several nonoverlapping subsequences remain, all of these having the same unique, real IRR, which is the r_{MISFM}. The method has been used by several major organizations in their leveraged lease analysis. Limited experience with results of the MISFM suggests that the rate is generally close to the TRM RIC rate. This suggests that the RIC could be used as a first approximation to the r_{MISFM}.

Strong Points of the Methods

1. Both the traditional sinking fund and initial investment methods are based on theoretically defensible assumptions.
2. The methods take into account the time-value of money and do not exclude any cash flows.
3. The methods are much easier to apply than the Teichroew, Robichek, and Montalbano algorithm, except for the MISFM.

4. Both methods assure a unique, real measure of return on investment.
5. Application of the methods is not difficult and can be easily learned.

Weak Points of the Methods

1. Both the traditional sinking fund and initial investment methods may require, in addition to an estimate of the organization's cost of capital, an estimate of the sinking fund rate at which cash may be invested. For reinvestment of funds within the firm this rate could be the same as the cost of capital.
2. Both methods are more difficult to apply without a computer than the net present value method.
3. The methods do not distinguish between projects of different size and/or different economic lives. However, adjustment may be made for this.
4. In general, the methods may not adequately reflect the interrelated nature of investment and financing imbedded within mixed projects.

APPENDIX: THE PROBLEM OF MIXED CASH FLOWS—III: A TWO-STAGE METHOD OF ANALYSIS

INTRODUCTION

The two preceding chapters present the Teichroew, Robichek, and Montalbano method and other methods classifiable as sinking fund approaches to obtaining a unique, real rate of return measure on those investments having mixed cash flows. It was shown in Chapter 10 that even a mathematically unique, real internal rate of return is no assurance, under the TRM assumptions, of a measure of return on investment independent of the enterprise's cost of capital. This chapter presents an alternative, developed by the author, to the various sinking fund methods.

The algorithm, or method of analysis, presented here is designed to separate explicitly the analysis of investments with mixed cash flows into two separate but related decision phases, or stages. The method yields two measures by which investments with mixed cash flows, such as leveraged leases, may be evaluated:

1. The *time* required to recover the initial investment *plus* the opportunity cost associated with the funds committed to the project.
2. The implicit "borrowing" *rate* contained within the cash flows occurring beyond the capital recovery time.

Together the two measures provide a decision rule: If the capital recovery period is acceptable *and* the implicit borrowing rate less than the rate at which the firm can acquire funds (the firm's cost of capital), or reinvest the second stage cash flows, the project is acceptable.

RELATIONSHIP TO OTHER METHODS

The net present value (NPV) method assumes that the enterprise cost of capital is the appropriate rate at which to discount the cash flows, whether they be positive or negative. The NPV itself is a measure of monetary return over and above the investment outlay. Although it is implicit in the NPV, the method and the measure provide no information pertaining to the timing of recovery of the funds invested in the project. The NPV method relates directly to the basic valuation model of modern financial management and is generally preferred by academic writers to other capital-budgeting methods. It will be shown in this chapter that the two-stage method is, unlike the internal rate of return (IRR), perfectly compatible with the NPV. The two-stage method yields identical accept/reject decisions to those obtained with the NPV, when the acceptable time span to recover the invested funds is unconstrained.

The two-stage method, although yielding results identical to NPV, provides decision measures in the separate stages that are in terms of time and percentage rate. Thus, the first stage, by providing a time measure, relates to the ubiquitous payback method. As shall be seen, however, it does not suffer from the well-known shortcomings of the payback method. The second stage relates to the IRR, except that the rate found will be a cost rate rather than a return rate.

THE TWO-STAGE METHOD

That business people employ the payback method very heavily, much to the dismay of academics who have dwelt upon and publicized its shortcomings, has been documented by many authors. The major shortcomings of the payback method are that it ignores the time-value of money and ignores cash flows beyond the end of the payback period. Or, equivalently, a zero opportunity cost rate is assigned during the payback period, with an infinite rate thereafter.

In stage one of the method proposed here, a payback period for the initial investment is determined. However, this payback period takes the time-value of money into account by requiring not only that the initial investment be recovered but, in addition, the opportunity cost of the unrecovered funds remaining invested in the project. This is related to Durand's unrecovered investment: At this payback, and not before, unrecovered investment is zero. Unrecovered investment is discussed in Chapter 14. Because the time-value of funds is taken into account, this payback measure is economically justifiable.[1]

In stage two, the cash flows remaining beyond the payback are analyzed, in the "negative investment" or "loan" phase of the project. Thus the second major objection to the traditional payback method is of no consequence. In the second stage, an imputed rate is determined that can be compared to the enterprise's cost of capital or the investment opportunity rate available to the firm over the periods remaining in the project life from payback to the end of the project life.[2] If the "loan" rate is less than the firm's cost of capital, or rate the firm expects to be able to earn on the cash flows from the project, it is acceptable on the rate basis. Since the firm's cost of capital would be less than or equal to the reinvestment rate offered by future acceptable projects,[3] we shall assume that comparison will be with the cost of capital.

---

[1] For the remainder of this chapter "payback" will refer to this time-value-of-money-adjusted payback—"traditional payback" to the method as it is usually applied.

[2] Or, if abandonment is to be considered, rates can be found corresponding to abandonment at any time prior to the end of the project's economic life.

[3] If the "loan" rate is less than the cost of capital, the project is providing funds at a cost less than the combined total of other sources. Such funds can be invested as they are received to earn the opportunity rate available to the firm. In the idealized construct of a world without capital rationing, the enterprise would be expected to invest funds up to the point at which the marginal rate of return equaled the marginal cost of capital.

Otherwise, it could be possible to accept a project with an implicit cost greater than the enterprise cost of capital because the reinvestment rate of return is greater.

The two-stage method can perhaps be best explained by detailed treatment of examples.

EXAMPLE 11A-1

We shall analyze the cash flows to equity on a leveraged lease discussed by Childs and Gridley.[4] Chapter 13 examines leveraged leases in detail, and this same leasing project is examined further. For now it will suffice to take the net cash flows to equity as given and note that our purpose here is to illustrate the two-stage method of project analysis and not to discuss leveraged leases. Table 11A-1 contains the original net cash flows and the adjusted cash flow series. We assume a cost of capital $k = 10$ percent.

The project (lease) requires an initial equity outlay of $20. With $k = 10$ percent the enterprise must recover $20 plus 10 percent of $20, $20(1 + k)$, at the end of the following year. The enter-

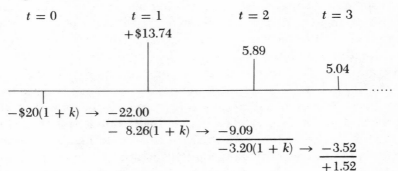

Original Cash Flows

Adjusted Cash Flows

The payback is thus $2 + 3.52/5.04$ years, or 2.7 years.

Figure 11A-1. Stage I Analysis.

[4]C. Rogers Childs, Jr., and William G. Gridley, Jr., "Leveraged Leasing and the Reinvestment Rate Fallacy," *The Bankers Magazine,* Vol. 156 (Winter 1973), pp. 53–61.

prise will be no better off nor worse off if it can recover the capital committed to the project along with the cost of those funds; its capital will still be preserved. Because the cash flow at $t = 1$ is only $13.74, with $8.26 of the $22 remaining to be recovered a year later, which with opportunity cost amounts to $9.09. The cash flow of $5.89 at $t = 2$ cannot quite suffice, and therefore $3.52 must be recovered at $t = 3$. Figure 11A-1 illustrates the procedure.

By allowing a noninteger value for payback, we violate the assumption that cash flows occur only at the end of each period. To be consistent with this assumption we would take three years as the payback period required to recover the initial investment plus opportunity cost of funds. However, if we recognize that the assumption of end-of-period cash flows is only to facilitate calculations, and that cash flows do, in fact, occur more or less uniformly over time, we will be comfortable with the fractional result as calculated.

The residual $1.52 after investment recovery, or capital recovery, is the first nonzero cash flow in the adjusted series. If it were not for the final cash flow of $+$2.40 at $t = 16$ we would have, in the remaining cash flows, the series of a simple *financing* project with only one sign change in the cash flows. Before applying stage II of the method, we must first get rid of this last cash flow.

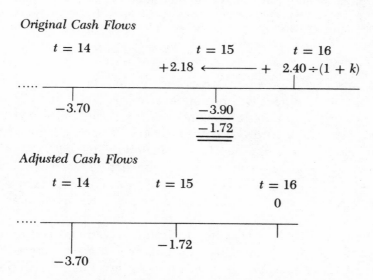

Figure 11A-2. Preparation for Stage II Analysis.

Table 11A-1.   Assumed Per-Annum Opportunity Cost of Funds (Cost of Capital) Is 10%.

t	Original Investment Plus Opportunity Cost	Original Net After-Tax Cash Flows	Adjusted Cash Flow Series°	
0	0	$−20.00	$−20.00	2.698
1	$−22.00	13.74	−8.26	Year
2	−9.09	5.89	−3.20	Payback
3	−3.52	5.04	1.52	
4		4.19	4.19	
5		3.32	3.32	
6		2.43	2.43	
7		1.54	1.54	
8		.63	.63	
9		−.51	−.51	
10		−2.68	−2.68	
11		−2.90	−2.90	
12		−3.16	−3.16	
13		−3.41	−3.41	
14		−3.70	−3.70	
15		−3.90	−1.72	
16		+2.40	0	

°The payback is in 2.7 years. The $1.52 remaining after payback in year three is assumed to occur at the end of the period, just as the original flow of $5.04 is.

   Before solving for the implicit loan rate, the last flow of +$2.40 is discounted back at the opportunity cost rate, using a sinking fund approach until absorbed by the negative flows. This may be interpreted as assigning, at discount, the last positive flow to the project—in other words, using it to prepay a portion of the loan.

One approach, a conservative one, would be to ignore the +$2.40, to assume it will not be received. A better approach, in the author's opinion, is to assume that funds can be borrowed at rate k, and the loan proceeds used to offset one or more of the immediately preceding negative cash flows. The +$2.40 would be used at $t = 16$ to repay the loan. Equivalently, we may assume the +$2.40 is assigned (at discount of k) to a creditor. This latter approach is the one that will be used. Figure 11A-2 illustrates the method.

   The enterprise has recovered its initial investment and the associated cost of the unrecovered funds remaining committed by the end of the first 2.7 years. The remaining adjusted cash flows occurring subsequent to that time are gratuitous to capital recovery of the initial investment. They are characteristic of a loan, and therefore we are interested in the rate implied by these cash flows. This "loan" rate is determined to be 3.9 percent, much less than our assumed 10 percent cost of capital. If we can obtain funds at a rate lower than our cost of capital, we should do so,[5] and the project is acceptable on this basis.

As will become apparent in the formal development of the two-stage method, *if a project is not rejected on the basis of an unacceptable payback, the accept/reject decision obtained from stage II will be identical to that obtained with the NPV method.* This is an important result. Although the stage II results are perfectly compatible with the NPV, the stage I payback may mark a project as unacceptable because capital recovery takes longer than is considered acceptable.

Before getting into the formal, mathematical treatment of the two-stage method, it will be useful to analyze one more example. This is the same as Example 10-2 from Chapter 10.

EXAMPLE 11A-2

This project has cash flows:

$t = 0$	$t = 1$	$t = 2$	$t = 3$
$-\$1000$	$+\$3800$	$-\$4730$	$+\$1936$

Again assuming $k = 10\%$, the $1000 initial investment plus cost of the funds committed (a total of $1100) is fully absorbed by the large positive cash flow at $t = 1$. The stage I payback for this project is $1100/3800 = .289$ or $.3$. The adjusted cash flows are:

$t = 0$	$t = 1$	$t = 2$	$t = 3$
0	$+\$2700$	$-\$4730$	$+\$1936$

Before finding the stage II rate, we assume the $1936 is assigned to a creditor, at a discount of k percent, and the proceeds received at $t = 2$. Thus, the adjusted cash flow at $t = 2$ is $-\$4730 + (\$1936/1.10) = -\$2970$. To find the stage II rate, r_B, we solve for the IRR of the cash flow series:

---

[5]Even if we recognize that risk considerations may alter this conclusion, the effect of the project itself on k could have been incorporated into the rate itself prior to this analysis.

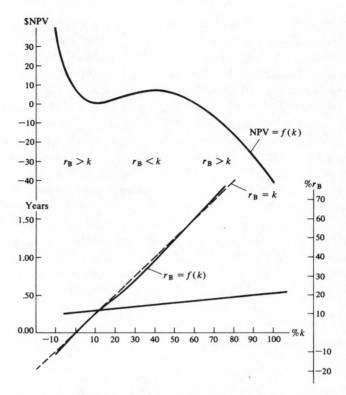

Figure 11A-3.   NPV and Two-Stage Measures for Example 11A-2.

$t = 0$	$t = 1$	$t = 2$	$t = 3$
0	+$2700	−$2970	0

And

$$\$2700(1 + r_B) = \$2970$$

so that

$$r_B = 10 \text{ percent}$$

Since $r_B = k$ the project is not acceptable. This project, not coincidentally, as will be shown, has a zero NPV for $k = 10$ percent. Figure 11A-3 contains a plot of the two-stage method results and NPV for various values of k.

FORMAL DEFINITION AND RELATIONSHIP TO NPV

It was stated earlier in this chapter that the two-stage method yields results identical to those obtained with the NPV provided that time for full capital recovery is unimportant. To make the two-stage NPV relationship explicit and at the same time provide a formal definition of the two-stage method, we first write the formula for NPV as:

$$\text{NPV} = \sum_{t=0}^{n} \frac{R_t(1 + r_r)^{n-t}}{(1 + k)^n} \qquad (11A.1)$$

where R_t are the net, after-tax cash flows, r_r the reinvestment rate.

$$\text{NPV} = \sum_{t=0}^{n} \frac{R_t}{(1 + k)^t} = \sum_{t=0}^{n} R_t(1 + k)^{-t} \qquad (11A.2)$$

also by reduction of (11A.1).

Similarly, the two-stage method may be written as the following:

Payback Stage

$$\sum_{t=0}^{P} \frac{R_t(1 + r_r)^{P-t}}{(1 + k)^P} = 0 \to P \qquad (11A.3)$$

$$\sum_{t=0}^{P} \frac{R_t}{(1 + k)^t} = \sum_{t=0}^{P} R_t(1 + k)^{-t} = 0 \to P \qquad (11A.4)$$

Multiplying Eq. (11A.4) by $(1 + k)^n$ yields the equivalent form actually employed in the problem treated earlier:

$$\sum_{t=0}^{P} R_t(1 + k)^{n-t} = 0 \to P \qquad (11A.5)$$

"Borrowing" Rate

$$\sum_{t=P+1}^{n} \frac{R_t(1 + r_B)^{n-t}}{(1 + r_B)^{n-P}} = \sum_{t=P+1}^{n} R_t(1 + r_B)^{-t} = 0 \to r_B \qquad (11A.6)$$

where r_B is the implicit cost of funds inherent in the flows remaining after payback.[6] Formula (11A.6) assumes the opportunity cost rate equals the implicit cost of funds. If necessary, the last cash flow at the end of the project can be forced to zero as illustrated earlier.

Formula (11A.6) can be modified to incorporate the firm's cost of capital and to obtain a present value formulation:

$$\sum_{t=P+1}^{n} \frac{R_t(1 + r_B)^{n-t}}{(1 + k)^{n-P}} = \text{present value} \qquad (11A.7)$$

Now, adding (11A.3) and (11A.7), we obtain:

$$\sum_{t=0}^{n} \frac{R_t(1 + r_r)^{P-t}}{(1 + k)^{P}} + \sum_{t=P+1}^{n} \frac{R_t(1 + r_B)^{n-t}}{(1 + k)^{n-P}} \qquad (11A.8)$$

which, for reinvestment rate r_r = "borrowing" rate r_B = r, reduces to:

$$\sum_{t=0}^{n} \frac{R_t(1 + r)^{n-t}}{(1 + k)^{n}} \qquad (11A.9)$$

which is identical to the NPV formulation of (11A.1).

In this chapter we have so far considered projects with mixed cash flows. What if we now apply the two-stage method to a simple investment? Consider the cash flows in the following example.

EXAMPLE 11A-3

$t = 0$	$t = 1$	$t = 2$	$t = 3$	$t = 4$
−$1000	1000	1000	1000	1000

If we again let k = 10 percent, the stage I payback is 1.11 periods and the revised cash flow series is:

$t = 0$	$t = 1$	$t = 2$	$t = 3$	$t = 4$
0	0	+$890	1000	1000

[6]The rates r_r, r_B, and k are assumed to be greater than or equal to zero in order that they have a meaningful economic interpretation.

There is no real rate that satisfies the second stage rate equation. However, because the remaining cash flows are all positive, they constitute in themselves a "loan" that does not have to be repaid, or a gift to the firm, and the project is acceptable on this basis. The two-stage method may be used for simple investments as well as those with mixed cash flows. It is generally applicable, which was to be expected from what is basically a special formulation of the NPV.

CONCLUSION

The NPV method of analysis has been largely ignored by those decision makers who have shown continuing preference for the traditional payback method and to a lesser extent the (internal) rate of return. The two-stage method discussed in this chapter presents the NPV in terms decision makers are accustomed to: payback and percentage rate. The payback, however, takes into account the time-value of funds at the enterprise's cost of capital; the percentage rate, for nonsimple investments, is a cost rate implicit in the cash flows after payback. If payback is not constrained, the two-stage method will always yield the same accept/reject decision as the NPV method.

Because decision makers have shown long-standing tenacity for the traditional payback method, the two-stage algorithm may find better acceptance by practitioners than the NPV method has received. And the two-stage method makes explicit, in the payback measure, the time required to recover the capital committed to a project. This is something the NPV method does not do, as it is usually stated.

A BRIEF DIGRESSION ON UNCERTAINTY

Up to this point we have considered the environment in which capital investment decisions are to be made one of certainty. If we relax this assumption, as we do in the next section, we are compelled to admit that, to the extent that cash flow estimates become increasingly tenuous and subject to error the further they occur from the present, a project that returns the initial investment early is to be preferred to one that does not, *ceteris paribus*. This is particularly so during times of economic, political, and social instability, the combined effects of which may cause cumulative exogenous effects to the enterprise that are impossible to predict far in advance.

Some years ago the distinction was often made between risk and uncertainty. Today it seems the distinction is often ignored, perhaps because the theory of finance in general and investments in particular have been developed to their present state by assuming risk rather than the more intractable uncertainty. The distinction is this: With risk we take as known the probability distributions of the variables; with uncertainty we assume ignorance of the distributions of the variables.

The two-stage algorithm for investment analysis provides, in its payback measure, a means of addressing uncertainty. *Two investments with identical NPV may have substantially different capital recovery paybacks and, in a world characterized by uncertainty, the investment with the shorter payback is to be preferred.* Because the two-stage method provides a capital recovery measure, it allows management to determine whether or not the capital recovery is swift enough. Because capital preservation may be a goal that overrides possible investment returns, the payback should be of interest.

12

Leasing

A lease is a contract under which the user (lessee) receives use of an asset from its owner (lessor) in return for promising to make a series of periodic payments over the life of the lease. A lease separates use from ownership. The two basic types of leases are operating and financial. *Operating leases* have relatively short terms, provide less than full payout,[1] and may be canceled by the lessee. A hotel room, or home telephone, water or electrical service may thus be considered forms of operating lease. In contrast, a *financial lease* is for a long term, provides for full payout, and is not cancelable without penalty by the lessee. We shall not be concerned with operating leases, but instead focus on financial leases.

Financial leases may be separated into two main categories: ordinary and leveraged. This chapter is concerned with ordinary financial leases. Chapter 13 considers leveraged leases and their unique attributes and problems. Both kinds of financial leases have assumed increasing importance in recent years and we may expect growth in leasing to continue over the next decade, barring major changes in tax laws that apply to them.

ALLEGED ADVANTAGES TO LEASING

Many advantages over conventional financing have been attributed to leasing. Although some have genuine value, others may have advantages only to certain firms in particular circumstances, and still others may have dubious value altogether. Among the claimed advantages are the following:

1. *Off-Balance-Sheet Financing* This is of dubious value, since the existence of financial leases must be footnoted and

---

[1]Full payout for a lease requires that the total of payments be sufficient for the lessor to recover, in addition to the capital investment, the cost of funds and profit.

analysts will treat a lease as if its capitalized value were a listed liability.

2. *Provides 100 Percent Financing* This may be advantageous when other financing is not available or available only under unacceptable terms.

3. *Longer Maturity Than Debt* For a long-lived asset this may be a significant advantage. Financial leases generally run for the life of the asset. Loan terms, on the other hand, are generally set by the policy of the lender and maturity may be much shorter than the asset life.

4. *Entire Lease Payment Tax Deductible* This can be advantageous if land is involved since it is not depreciable if owned.

5. *Level of Required Authorization* Leases may sometimes be authorized by plant managers, whereas purchase of the same asset may require approval higher in the organization.

6. *Avoids Underwriting and Flotation Expense* Leasing also avoids the public disclosure associated with sale of securities.

7. *Front-End Costs Reduced* Delivery and installation costs are spread over the life of the lease.

8. *Lease Payments Fixed Over Time* Both the lessee and the lessor know the costs over the life of the lease.

9. *Less Restrictive, Quicker, More Flexible.*

10. *May Conserve Available Credit* Possibly, but consider comment under number 1.

11. *Lease May "Sell" Depreciation* The lessee, if unable to use depreciation and investment tax credit directly because of losses, in essence "sells" them to the lessor for more favorable leasing terms and thus gains from what would otherwise be lost.

12. *Leased Assets Provide Own Collateral* The lessee does not have to pledge other assets that might have to be pledged to secure debt financing for the same leased equipment. Because the lessor owns the leased asset, he can recover it in the event the terms of the lease are broken.

ANALYSIS OF LEASES

The analysis of ordinary financial leases in the literature has focused almost exclusively on lease evaluation from the viewpoint of the lessee, the user of the equipment. Very little has been written on lease analysis from the lessor's view until recently. Evaluation by the lessor is in itself a capital-budgeting problem that, depending on the terms of the lease and the quality of the lessee, may approach a certainty environment in many respects. In this chapter the analysis of leases will be considered from both the lessee and the lessor viewpoints. First, the traditional analysis from the lessee's position will be considered. Then an integrated treatment of the lessee's and the lessor's positions will be discussed.

It should be made clear at the outset that lease analysis itself does not address the question of whether a particular asset should be acquired or not. Rather, *lease analysis starts with the premise that the asset should be acquired by the lessee.* [2] The question that lease analysis tries to answer is whether the asset in question should be purchased or leased. This is often expressed as "lease or buy" or "lease or borrow." The traditional analysis, through the lessee's eyes, involves finding the least cost alternative to acquiring an asset: the minimum of the lease cost and the alternative financing cost. The alternative financing is generally assumed to be 100 percent debt financing, since leasing commits the lessee to making periodic payments just as a fully amortized bond would do. And contrary to alleged advantages 1 and 10 above, it has become widely recognized that leases do displace debt.

Traditional Analysis

Many approaches to the valuation of leases have been proposed. The one proposed by Bower[3] is representative of a broad class of net present value (NPV) models, and thus will be discussed first. The Bower model (in this author's notation) is:

$$\text{NAL} = C - \sum_{t=1}^{H} \frac{L_t}{(1 + r_1)^t} + \sum_{t=1}^{H} \frac{TL_t}{(1 + r_2)^t} - \tag{12.1}$$
$$\sum_{t=1}^{H} \frac{TD_t}{(1 + r_3)^t} - \sum_{t=1}^{H} \frac{TI_t}{(1 + r_4)^t} +$$
$$\sum_{t=1}^{H} \frac{O_t(1 - T)}{(1 + r_5)^t} - \frac{S_H}{(1 + r_6)^H}$$

---

[2] This question having been answered by the capital-budgeting methods generally applied to determine project acceptance.

[3] R. Bower, "Issues in Lease Financing." *Financial Management.* (Winter 1973), pp. 25–34.

where

NAL = Net Advantage to Leasing
C = Asset Cost if Purchased
H = Life of the Lease
L_t = Periodic Lease Payment
T = Marginal Tax Rate on Ordinary Income
D_t = Depreciation Charged in Period t
I_t = Interest Portion of Loan Payment
O_t = Operating Maintenance Cost in Period t
S_H = Realized, After-Tax Salvage Value
r_i = Applicable Discount Rate

This model allows for discount rates that are different for each of the terms. However, Bower concludes that the appropriate discount rate is the firm's cost of capital. With this in mind, we drop the term containing I_t since the interest tax shelter is implicitly contained in the cost of capital. The model then becomes:

$$NAL = C - \sum_{t=1}^{H} \frac{L_t}{(1+k)^t} + \sum_{t=1}^{H} \frac{TL_t}{(1+k)^t} - \sum_{t=1}^{H} \frac{TD_t}{(1+k)^t} + \sum_{t=1}^{H} \frac{O_t(1-T)}{(1+k)^t} - \frac{S_H}{(1+k)^H} \tag{12.2}$$

or, by combining terms:

$$NAL = C - \sum_{t=1}^{H} \frac{L_t(1-T) + TD_t - O_t(1-T)}{(1+k)} - \frac{S_H}{(1+k)^H} \tag{12.3}$$

At this point let us consider a numerical example.

EXAMPLE 12-1

A firm with 12 percent overall marginal cost of capital has decided to acquire an asset that, if purchased, would cost $100. This same asset may be leased for five years at an annual lease payment of $30. Operating maintenance is expected to be $1 a year, and straight-line depreciation to a zero salvage value would be used if the asset were to be purchased. The prospective lessee is in the 48 percent marginal tax category.

Applying Eq. (12.3) we obtain:

$$NAL = 100 - \sum_{t=1}^{5} \frac{30(1 - .48) + (.48)20 - (1 - .48)}{(1.12)^t}$$

$$= 100 - \sum_{t=1}^{5} \frac{15.60 + 9.60 - .52}{(1.12)^t}$$

$$= 100 - \sum_{t=1}^{5} \frac{24.68}{(1.12)^t}$$

$$= \$11.03$$

Since $\$11.03 > 0$, the leasing alternative is preferable to purchase of the asset. But what if the net, realized after-tax salvage was estimated to be $20? In this case the NAL would be only $6.61 and the lease would be less attractive.

Alternative Analysis[4]

The discussion so far has been limited to the case of the *lessee.* Also, the impact of the lease on the lessee's debt capacity has not yet been considered. Myers, Dill, and Bautista (MDB) developed a model that allowed for the impact of the lease on the lessee's debt capacity.[5] The MDB model assumes that the lessee borrows 100 percent of the tax shields created by interest payments, lease payments, and depreciation. This debt constraint is used to eliminate the debt displacement term normally used in the lease valuation equation, assuming that a dollar of debt is displaced by a dollar of lease. Myers, Dill, and Bautista generalize their model by removing the constraint that a dollar of lease displaces a dollar of debt. However, they constrain the proportion of debt displaced by a dollar of the lease, λ, to be equal to the proportion of the tax shields the lessee borrows against, γ.

Here the effects of allowing λ to vary from 1.0 are examined. At the same time it is assumed that the lessee borrows 100 percent

[4]This section is based on the extension to the MDB work by Perg and Herbst. Wayne F. Perg, and Anthony F. Herbst, "Lease vs. Conventonal Financing: Integrating the Lessor's Gains and Losses," *Proceedings of the 1980 Meeting, Eastern Finance Association.*

[5]Stewart C. Myers, David A. Dill, and Alberto J. Bautista, "Valuation of Financial Lease Contracts," *Journal of Finance,* Vol. XXXI (June 1976), pp. 799–820.

of the tax shields ($\gamma = 1.0$) in order to maintain an optimal capital structure. The generalized model, using MDB's model as the starting point, is:[6]

$$V_0 = 1 - \sum_{t=1}^{H} \frac{P_t(1 - T) + Tb_t}{(1 + r - \gamma rT)^t}$$
$$+ \sum_{t=0}^{H-1} \sum_{\tau=t+1}^{H} \frac{rTP_r(\gamma - \lambda)}{(1 + r - \gamma rT)^{t+1}(1 + r)^{\tau-t}} \tag{12.4}$$

where

V_0 = Value of the Lease to the lessee

P_t = Lease Payment in Period t (normalized by dividing by the purchase price of the asset leased).

b_t = The Normalized Depreciation Foregone in Period t If the Asset Is Leased Instead of Purchased

r = Lessee's Borrowing Rate

T = Lessee's Marginal Tax Rate on Income

H = Life of the Lease

λ = Proportion of Debt Displaced by a Dollar of the Lease

γ = Proportion of the Tax Shields the Lessee Borrows Against

Equation (12.4) follows MDB's notation except for the inclusion of γ. Salvage value and foregone investment tax credit are assumed to be zero to simplify the model, and operating maintenance expenses absorbed by the lessor are also assumed to be zero.

The valuation model in (12.4), once again *is for the lessee.* To determine the value of the lease to the lessor may be somewhat more controversial if for no other reason than little work in this area has been published. The claim of MDB is that the lessor's valuation is the lessee's valuation model multiplied by -1.0 to reflect the reverse direction of the cash flow. And for the lessor they claim that λ is the proportion of debt *supported by* the lease, because the lease is an investment to the lessor (Remember that for the lessee, λ represents the proportion of debt *displaced by* the

[6]The derivation is contained in the appendix to this chapter.

lease.) The lessor's λ will very likely be different from the lessee's; so may the tax rate, *T*.

If λ were to be the proportion of the lessor's debt *supported by* the lease [in (12.4) multiplied by −1.0 and with λ = γ], however, then *r* would be the lessor's borrowing rate, *not* the lessee's borrowing rate. This presents a problem. If the lessor acts as financial intermediary, then the lessor's borrowing rate will generally be less than the lessee's borrowing rate, because the debt obligations of the lessor are less risky. This lower risk is due to the lessor's equity cushion, the likely more liquid nature of the lessor's obligations, and the diversification through holding many different leases. Financial intermediaries also tend to keep the maturity of their obligations shorter than their assets in order to take advantage of a yield curve, that is, an average, upward sloping. Myers, Dill, and Bautista made a valuable contribution to the literature on leasing. The problem, however, of two different discount rates (the lessee's and the lessor's) make the MDB approach to determining the lessor's valuation of the lease unsuitable. We will now look at an alternative model for the lessor.

We base our approach to determining the value of a lease to the lessor on the fact that, *to the lessor, the lease is an investment.* The NPV of the lease is equal to the present value of its after-tax cash flows, valued at the after-tax discount rate appropriate for the level of risk associated with investment in the lease, less the purchase price of the asset to be leased. It is assumed that the lessor is also a lender, a share value maximizer, and financial markets are competitive. From this we can say that the lessor will invest in bonds, including those of the lessee, until their after-tax return is equal to the lessor's after-tax cost of capital appropriate to the risk associated with holding the bonds.

If the lease is equivalent in risk[7] to the lessee's bonds, then the cost of capital associated with investing in the lease is equal to the cost of capital associated with investing in those bonds: the after-tax borrowing rate of the lessee. If the risk is *not* equal, then

[7]Strictly speaking, this section deals with a certainty environment. However, in discussing analysis of leases it is necessary to bring risk into consideration. The awkward alternative would be either to deal with leases under certainty here and bring in risk in a later chapter or to postpone treatment of leasing until later, and out of this author's desired sequence of topics. Risk treatment *in a formal sense* is deferred, however, until later chapters.

the lessor's cost of capital for the lease equals X times the after-tax borrowing rate of the lessee, where $X > 1.0$ if the lease is riskier than the lessee's bonds, and $X < 1$ if the lease is less risky than the bond. Recognizing this we obtain the model for the value of the lease to the lessor:

$$V_0 = \sum_{t=1}^{H} \frac{P_t(1 - T) + Tb_t}{[1 + Xr(1 - T)]^t} - 1 \qquad (12.5)$$

Here P_t, b_t, and r are the same as in (12.4). But T now represents the *lessor's* marginal tax rate, not the lessee's, and X is a risk adjustment factor. The factor X can be reasonably expected to be related to the debt displacement factor λ in (12.4). For example, if leases have financial characteristics similar to subordinated debt, then the lessor's cost of capital for the lease will exceed his cost of capital for the bonds ($X > 1$), and a dollar of lease will displace *less than* a dollar of bonds ($\lambda < 1$). On the other hand, if leases possess financial characteristics that make them senior to the firm's bonds, we would expect $X < 1$ and $\lambda > 1$. These possible relationships are discussed in the following analysis.

Analysis

The factors that enter into the possible superiority of leasing over conventional financing are (1) the marginal tax rates (T) of the lessor and the lessee and (2) the relationship between λ and X. In order to explore the effects of the interactions of these variables on the value of a lease, we compute the breakeven lease payment of the lessee for various combinations of the lessee's tax rate and λ. The breakeven lease payment is then used to compute the value of the lease to the lessor for various combinations of the lessor's tax rate and X. The patterns of the results are of major interest. They are not affected by varying H, r, or the use of accelerated depreciation since these factors are common to both the lessee's and the lessor's valuation models. Therefore, only the results for $H = 15$, $r = 10\%$, and straight-line depreciation are presented in Table 12-1. In calculating the values for Table 12-1 the value of γ is kept equal to 1.0 because it is thought the results will be more meaningful if the lessee always maintains an optimal capital structure.

The topmost section of Table 12-1 confirms the conventional

results that hold when leases are financially equivalent to loans. Thus, if a dollar of lease displaces a dollar of debt (that is, $\lambda = 1$) and leases have the same risk as loans ($X = 1$), then leasing is advantageous if, and only if, the lessee's marginal tax rate is less than that of the lessor. The advantage occurs because the lease is tantamount to the sale of depreciation tax shields by the lessee to the lessor. If the lessor has a higher tax rate, then the value of the tax shields is greater to the lessor than the cost to the lessee for giving up the tax shields. The lower the lessee's tax rate, and the higher the lessor's, the more mutually advantageous leasing becomes.

Results change dramatically once the assumption of financial equivalency is dropped. The second and third panels of Table 12-1 illustrate what happens if a dollar of lease displaces only 80 cents of debt ($\lambda = .8$). With this value of lambda the lessee's breakeven lease payment actually *increases* as the tax rate increases, rather than decreasing as we might have expected from the standard result at the top of the table. To understand this we refer to an important point made by MDB. The lessee's lease valuation rests upon the well-known Modigliani and Miller assumptions, which imply (among other things) that the only advantage to borrowing is the interest tax shield. If $\lambda = 1.0$, then leasing decreases the present value of the available tax shields because depreciation tax shield is surrendered. Therefore, as the lessee's tax rate rises, his breakeven lease payment falls. But if λ is sufficiently less than one ($\lambda = .8$ is sufficiently less), then leasing actually *increases* the present value of the tax shields available since the increase in debt capacity—and therefore interest tax shields—more than outweighs the loss of depreciation tax shield. Because of this the lessee's breakeven lease payment rises as the tax rate rises.

It follows that if λ is sufficiently less than one, the value of leasing is a positive function of the tax rates of *both* the lessor *and* the lessee. How high the tax rates must be for lessor and lessee to make leasing advantageous depends on how much riskier these debt-capacity-increasing leases are than the lending/borrowing alternative. If they are no more risky than lending (that is, $X = 1$), leasing is then advantageous for *all positive tax rates,* regardless of whether the lessee's or lessor's tax rate is higher.

The two panels at the bottom of Table 12-1 show the case in which $1 of lease displaces $1.20 of debt. In this case the lessee's

Table 12-1. $H = 15, r = .10$, Straight-Line Depreciation $\gamma = 1$

Lessee's Marginal Tax Rate		Lessee's Breakeven Lease Payment	Value of Lease to Lessor		
	$\lambda = 1$		$X = 1$		
			$T = 0$	$T = .25$	$T = .50$
$T = 0$		.1314738	0	.0175207	.0283163
$T = .25$		.1288274	−.0201286	0	.0145813
$T = .50$		.1260179	−.0414979	−.0185998	0
	$\lambda = .8$		$X = 1.2$		
			$T = 0$	$T = .25$	$T = .50$
$T = 0$		.1314738	−.1045497	−.0708275	−.0378043
$T = .25$		.1337616	−.0889678	−.0569969	−.0266946
$T = .50$		.1410994	−.0389911	−.0126358	.0089385
	$\lambda = .8$		$X = 1$		
			$T = 0$	$T = .25$	$T = .50$
$T = 0$		.1314738	0	.0175207	.0283163
$T = .25$		.1337616	.0174014	.0326661	.0401897
$T = .50$		.1410994	.0732132	.0812453	.0782708
	$\lambda = 1.2$		$X = .8$		
			$T = 0$	$T = .25$	$T = .50$
$T = 0$		.1314738	.1253474	.1195513	.1015017
$T = .25$		.1242443	.0634667	.0668896	.0613131
$T = .50$		.1138490	−.0255119	−.0088307	.0035225
	$\lambda = 1.2$		$X = 1$		
			$T = 0$	$T = .25$	$T = .50$
$T = 0$		.1314738	0	.0175207	.0283163
$T = .25$		.1242443	−.0549879	−.0303416	−.0092031
$T = .50$		.1138490	−.1340555	−.0991614	−.0631539

breakeven lease payment falls even faster as his or her tax rate rises than it does when $\lambda = 1$. The reason this happens is that the lessee gives up the present value of reduced interest tax shields as the lessee's debt capacity falls, in addition to the present value of the depreciation tax shield.[8] Here the lessee's marginal tax rate must be as low as possible if leasing is to be advantageous. However, it does not follow that it is necessarily best for the *lessor's* tax rate to be as high as possible to make the lease most

[8]Note that for $T = 0$ the lessee's breakeven lease payment is not affected by λ since the value of the tax shields is zero.

advantageous. When the debt-capacity-reducing effect of the lease (perhaps as a result of its senior claim on the leased asset or assets) is reflected in lower risk and a lower cost of capital for the lessor (for example, $X = .8$), the greatest gain to leasing occurs if both the lessee and the lessor were to have zero tax rates.

Implications

From the foregoing it is clear that the conventional condition for leasing to be advantageous—that the lessee's tax rate be less than the lessor's—applies only if leasing and borrowing are financially equivalent (that is, both $\lambda = 1.0$ and $X = 1.0$). In the literature it has become traditional to argue that financial equivalency should hold. However, for such equivalency to prevail would require that product differentiation of financial instruments not influence their sales. Whether or not product differentiation can affect sales may not be settled to everyone's satisfaction. But until empirical evidence refuting parallel effects to those among consumer goods are published and confirmed, it would seem reasonable to expect differentiation to apply. If there really were no marketable differences between debentures, mortgage bonds, leases, and so on, one would be hard-pressed to explain why different financial instruments and arrangements persist.

If λ and X may differ from 1.0, we may ask how they may do so. First, let us consider a lessee in sound financial condition; all debt is on an unsecured basis. A lease, however, is a highly secured form of debt.[9] This extra security—actual ownership of the physical asset—makes the lease senior to the firm's debt and impairs the security of the other debt.[10] It follows that if the riskiness of this debt is not going to increase (and it cannot if γ, the cost of capital, is to stay constant), total borrowings—including the obligation on the lease—must fall, and this means $\lambda > 1$. The senior claim of the lease makes it somewhat less risky than the lessee's debt. To the extent that proceeds from the sale or re-lease of the asset, if it were to be seized from the delinquent lessee, would be insufficient to cover the unpaid rentals and expenses caused by the default, the lessor becomes a general creditor. Altogether, this implies that $X < 1$.

[9]The lessor holds title to the asset and thus may recover it more easily than if title were held by the lessee.

[10]If the asset were purchased, the title would be held by the firm that otherwise would be the lessee and it would serve to secure all that firm's debt along with all its other assets.

Now, in contrast, let us consider a highly leveraged firm whose debt is virtually all secured. In such a case existing creditors would not perceive themselves as being harmed by leasing, relative to financing the asset with debt, because the new debt would have been secured in any case. But prospective creditors might find themselves more willing to make new leases than new secured loans because of their superior position with respect to recovering the asset they hold title to if the lessee were to encounter financial difficulty. This enhanced recovery ability may cause such prospective creditors to be more willing to make leases rather than loans ($\lambda < 1.0$) even though risk were to be increased ($X > 1.0$).

Practical Perspective

It is probably reasonable to assume that much, if not most, leasing is done in situations where $\lambda \neq 1.0$ and $X \neq 1.0$. For high-quality, low-risk lessees it is likely that $\lambda > 1.0$ and $X < 1.0$. From the bottom two panels of Table 12-1 we see that a low tax rate for the lessee is of the greatest importance in this situation. It is also in the lessee's vital interest to negotiate terms for the lease that reflect the low risk associated with the lease. Because most standardized leases are set up to protect the lessor from the higher risk lessees, this would tend to limit low-risk prospective lessees to large, negotiated, and (usually) leveraged leases. Leveraged leases are discussed in the following chapter.

In high-risk leases, $\lambda < 1.0$ and $X > 1.0$. As shown by the middle two panels of Table 12-1, it may make leasing advantageous if the lessee were to have a high tax rate, provided that λ is sufficiently less than one. In this case expansion of his or her debt capacity is of prime concern to the lessee; the foregoing analysis may understate the value of leasing because the value of additional debt capacity to the lessee may well exceed the present value of the tax shields since the future of the firm as a viable, going concern may well lie in the balance.

SUMMARY AND CONCLUSION

A financial lease is a financing arrangement in which the lessee purchases the use of an asset owned by the lessor. Asset use is separate from asset ownership. Lease analysis does not determine whether or not an asset should be acquired; it starts with the premise that the asset should be acquired and attempts to determine if leasing provides an attractive alternative for financing the asset. The associated question is normally phrased as "lease or buy" or "lease or borrow."

Traditional analysis of leases has focused almost exclusively on the problem of the lessee. However, to the lessor the lease is even more of a capital-budgeting decision; it is an investment. The lessor's decision is not simply the mirror image of the lessee's decision, because of different tax rates and different risk implications of the same lease to each of them. Traditional analysis has assumed that leases were substitutes for debt, but it did not address the impact of leasing on the lessee's debt capacity, or the measure of substitutability.

Myers, Dill, and Bautista extended the traditional analysis of leases to take into account the effect of leasing on the debt capacity of the lessee. Perg and Herbst extended the analysis to the lessor and integrated the analysis of lessee and lessor.

APPENDIX

The derivation of the generalized lease valuation equation for the lessee uses MDB's notation except for introducing γ to represent the proportion of the tax shields that the lessee borrows against. The starting point of the derivation is the debt constraint of the lessee. Y_t is the total debt of the firm in period t, L is the initial dollar value of the leased asset, D_t is the debt displaced in t per dollar of asset leased $(D_t \equiv \partial Y_t/\partial L)$, S_t is the lessee's total tax shield due to book depreciation on all assets owned in t, and $\hat{Z}$ is optimal borrowing excluding any contribution to debt capacity made by depreciation and interest tax shields.

$$
Y_t = \lambda \sum_{\tau=t+1}^{H} \frac{P_r L}{(1 + r)^{\tau-t}} = \hat{Z}
$$
$$
+ \gamma \left\{ \sum_{\tau=t+1}^{\infty} \frac{S_\tau + rTY_\tau}{(1 + r)^{\tau-t}} + \sum_{\tau=t+1}^{H} \frac{TP_\tau L}{(1 + r)^{\tau-t}} \right\} \text{(A.1)}
$$

Differentiating Y_{H-1} with respect to L and solving for D_{H-1}:

$$
D_{H-1} = \frac{-P_H(\lambda - \gamma T) - \gamma Tb_H}{1 + r - \gamma rT} \tag{A.2}
$$

Substituting D_{H-1} into the expression for V_{H-1} and simplifying,

$$V_{H-1} = \frac{-P_H(1 - T) - Tb_H}{1 + r - \gamma rT} + \frac{rTP_H(\gamma - \lambda)}{(1 + r)(1 + r - \gamma rT)} \quad \text{(A.3)}$$

Going back to the debt constraint, (A.1), for Y_{H-2}, differentiating with respect to L, and solving for D_{H-2}:

$$D_{H-2} = \frac{-P_{H-1}(\lambda - \gamma T) - \gamma Tb_{H-1}}{1 + r - \gamma rT} + \frac{D_{H-1}}{1 + r - \gamma rT} \quad \text{(A.4)}$$

Substituting (A.2) into (A.4) and then substituting (A.4) into the expression for V_{H-2} and simplifying:

$$V_{H-2} = \frac{-P_{H-1}(1 - T) - Tb_{H-1} + V_{H-1}}{1 + r - \gamma rT}$$
$$+ \sum_{\tau=H-1}^{H} \frac{rTP_\tau(\gamma - \lambda)}{(1 + r - \gamma rT)(1 + r)^{\tau-H+2}} \quad \text{(A.5)}$$

Clearly, this reasoning repeats and in general (except for $t = 0$):

$$V_t = \frac{-P_{t+1}(1 - T) - Tb_{t+1} + V_{t+1}}{1 + r - \gamma rT}$$
$$+ \sum_{\tau=t+1}^{H} \frac{rTP_\tau(\gamma - \lambda)}{(1 + r - \gamma rT)(1 + r)^{\tau-t}} \quad \text{(A.6)}$$

For $t = 0$,

$$V_0 = 1 + \frac{-P_1(1 - T) - Tb_1 + V_1}{1 + r - \gamma rT} + \sum_{\tau=1}^{H} \frac{rTP_\tau(\gamma - \lambda)}{(1 + r - \gamma rT)(1 + r)^\tau} \quad \text{(A.7)}$$

By successive substitution, $V_1, V_2, \ldots, V_{H-1}$ are eliminated to obtain:

$$V_0 = 1 - \sum_{t=1}^{H} \frac{P_t(1 - T) + Tb_t}{(1 + r - \gamma rT)^t}$$
$$+ \sum_{t=0}^{H-1} \sum_{\tau=t+1}^{H} \frac{rTP_\tau(\gamma - \lambda)}{(1 + r - \gamma rT)^{t+1}(1 + r)^{\tau-t}} \quad \text{(A.8)}$$

13

Leveraged Leases

DEFINITION AND CHARACTERISTICS

Analytical techniques discussed in previous chapters are applicable to analysis of the lease versus purchase decision and to lease analysis in general. This chapter is concerned with the analysis of a particular category of financial lease termed *leveraged leases.*

Leveraged leases are tax-sheltered financial leases in the sense that some of the returns to the lessor are attributable to the tax legislation that was enacted to encourage capital investment. The investment tax credit, for example, has its raison d'être in encouraging capital investment. However, as Campanella points out, those companies that could benefit from new capital often could not benefit from the investment tax credit. Such firms might not have been producing taxable income, for instance, or carry-over from previous tax shelter may have made the credit useless. Those firms found it advantageouss to find a lessor who could use the tax benefits, and then arrange a lease in return for a lease cost lowered by those tax benefits. Leveraged leasing grew rapidly during the 1960s and is still significant. Changes in the tax laws have not, as some thought they might, negated the advantages of leveraged lease arrangements.

In terms of setting up a leveraged lease, it is typically done through a trust arrangement. The lessor contributes a small percentage (20 to 40%) of the capital equipment cost, and the trust then borrows the balance from institutional investors on a nonrecourse basis to the owner. The loans to the trust are secured by a first lien on the equipment along with an assignment of the lease and the lease payments. According to Campanella[1] "a leveraged lease is a direct lease wherein the lessor, through a trust, has borrowed a portion of the equipment cost to help finance the transaction. Under the 'true' lease concept, the lessor retains a

[1]Joseph A. Campanella, "Leveraged Leasing Financing and the Commercial Bank," Masters Thesis, The Stonier Graduate School of Banking, Rutgers University, June 1974.

material equity and ownership in the leased property and no option to purchase, other than a fair market value option at the expiration of the lease term, is given to the lessee." This is an important point because, with the similar railroad trust certificate leases, the lessee is treated as the owner for tax purposes, and no tax advantage exists.

The trust is usually administered by a commercial bank, called the *owner trustee.* This trustee takes title to the capital equipment and enters into the lease arrangement with the actual user, the lessee. The lease is a long-term, full-payment "true" lease. With a true lease the lessor retains a material equity ownership interest in the capital equipment and no option to purchase the equipment is provided to the lessee, at any price other than "fair market value." The tax treatment on which leveraged leases are predicated rests on their being true leases. After first servicing principal and interest on debt, the trustee remits any remaining funds, pro rata, to the equity investors. It is the profitability of the leasing arrangement to the equity investors that we are primarily concerned with in this chapter.

Although the returns to the creditors of the trust normally may be straightforwardly calculated as the yield on a fully amortized note, and the cost to the lessee may similarly be found, calculating the return to equity is much more troublesome. The reason for this difficulty is in the mixed cash flows to equity that is characteristic of leveraged leases. A number of methods for computing the attractiveness of returns to equity on leveraged leases have been proposed. Unfortunately, instead of resolving the issue, the various proposals themselves may have added to the confusion. When one applies the methods to the typical leveraged lease, the results may seemingly be contradictory. Leveraged leases provide us with an interesting application of analytical techniques that have been proposed for dealing with mixed cash flows. Furthermore, the assumption of certainty is not so unreasonable as it may be with most capital investment projects because the returns are governed by the contractural terms of the lease.

METHODS OF LEVERAGED LEASE ANALYSIS

The methods of analysis we shall consider are the net present value, the Wiar method, the sinking fund methods (including the

Teichroew, Robichek, and Montalbano (TRM) approach), and the two-stage method. Since these methods have been introduced in previous chapters, the reader is already familiar with the basic application of each. We shall therefore analyze several example problems to provide a structure for comparing the various methods.

APPLICATION OF THE METHODS

EXAMPLE 13-1

This example was proposed by Bierman[2] to illustrate the superiority of the net present value (NPV) method of analysis. The project has cash flows of $-\$400$, $\$1100$, and $-\$700$ at the end of years $t = 0$, 1, and 2. Figure 13-1 contains plotted results of NPV for different values of k, the cost of capital. The NPV function reaches a maximum at 27.0 percent. The project has IRR at 0 percent and 75 percent, and between these values the NPV is positive. This suggests that for 0 percent $< k <$ 75 percent the project is acceptable.

That this is a mixed project is apparent if we decompose the cash flows into two subsequences as follows:

	$t = 0$	$t = 1$	$t = 2$	
(a)	-400	$+400$		Return $= 0\%$
(b)		$+700$	-700	Cost $= 0\%$

or

	$t = 0$	$t = 1$	$t = 2$	
(c)	-400	700		Return $= 75\%$
(d)		400	-700	Cost $= 75\%$

Subprojects (a) and (c) are investments, whereas (b) and (d) are financing projects. In the particular subproject above, the investment returns are exactly offset by the corresponding financing costs. At rates between 0 percent and 75 percent the investment return dominates the financing cost. Consider the decomposition corresponding to 10 percent cost of capital, for example:

[2]Harold Bierman, Jr., "Leveraged Leasing: An Alternative Analysis," *The Bankers Magazine*, Vol. 157 (Summer 1974).

	t = 0	t = 1	t = 2
(e)	−400	463.64	
(f)		636.36	−700

The "loan" implicit in cash flow sequence (f) is at 10 percent. The NPV of sequence (e) is 21.49 and has an IRR of exactly 16 percent.

The TRM return on invested capital (RIC $= r°$) is plotted against k in Figure 13-2. The $r°$ values for $r° > k$ are for 0 percent $< k < 75$ percent—the same as obtained with the NPV approach. The initial investment method (IIM) yields r_{IIM} values of 0 percent and 75 percent for corresponding cost of capital percentages.

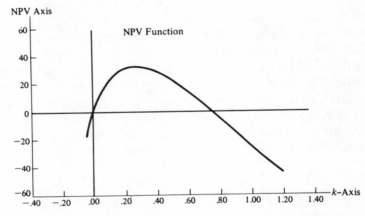

Figure 13-1.   Bierman Example. Plot of Investment Characteristics.

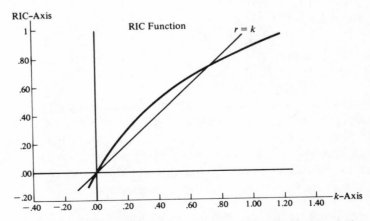

Figure 13-2.   Bierman Example. Plot of Investment Characteristics.

Furthermore, the traditional sinking fund method (TSFM) yields r_{TSFM} values of 0 percent and 75 percent. The two-stage method yields results consistent with these. Next let us consider a project that has two more cash flows.

EXAMPLE 13-2

This project has cash flows at end of years 0, 1, 2, 3, and 4 of −$1000, $2000, $2000, $2000, and −$5000, respectively. The NPV is positive between 0 and 400 percent as shown in the NPV versus k graph in Figure 13-3. The corresponding RIC or $r°$ plot is contained in Figure 13-4. Note that the $r°$ is a double-valued function of k. In this case the plot of interest is for positive values of $r°$. We reject the negative values on the basis that the adjusted cash flow series from which we find $r°$ for a given k value sums to greater than zero. In other words, the simple sum of the adjusted cash flows is positive, so we do not admit negative returns even though mathematically they are acceptable. Table 13-1 contains an outline of the TRM solution and some selected dual values of $r°$ for corresponding k. As we have noted before, returns of less than −100 percent have no economic significance because it is not possible to "lose more than we lose" with a project.

In contrast to the Bierman project in Example 13-1, for this case the NPV and the RIC are not totally in agreement. In fact, the RIC conflicts with the other, NPV-compatible methods also, as is to be expected. The NPV is greater than zero between the IRR boundary values of 0 percent and 400 percent. The $r°$ (RIC) is greater than k over much of the same range but not all of it. At a k value of 200 percent, for instance, the $r°$ is 176.65 percent whereas the NPV is still positive. One could dismiss this conflict as irrelevant in a world where k cannot be so great, since the $r°$ and NPV do agree over the range of k values that firms could, in fact, be expected to have. However, because they *are* different over part of the range of k, we should abandon any complacency generated by the Bierman example and other examples involving only two cash flows beyond the initial outlay. The Bierman example underscores the hazards lurking in the shadows for those who would try to generalize from the three-cash-flow case to the N-cash-flow case.

The conflict between the NPV and the RIC for large values of k is attributable in this case to the assumption implicit in the NPV that the investment and financing rates are both equal to the cost

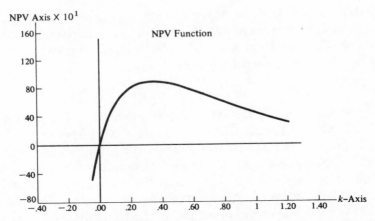

Figure 13-3. NPV-RIC Conflict. Plot of Investment Characteristics.

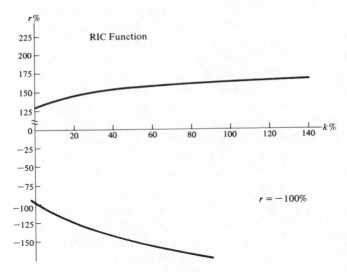

Figure 13-4. NPV-RIC Conflict.

of capital, whereas the RIC requires only that the financing rate be equal to k.

Let us next apply the Wiar method (WM), the initial investment method (IIM), traditional sinking fund method (TSFM), and the two-stage method (TSM) to this example and summarize the results obtained in Table 13-2.

The various methods are in agreement that for k values of 10, 20, and 30 percent the project is acceptable. The Wiar method could not properly be applied because it is predicated on overall

Table 13-1. TRM Analysis of Example 13.2

Original Cash Flows	Solution to Project Balance Equation[a]
−1000	
2000	100.00000%
2000	173.20508
2000	191.96396 $= r_{min}$
−5000	

Some Solution values are:

k	r°	r°
−5	−90.93%	124.50%
0	−100.00	130.25
5	−107.75	135.25
10	−114.55	139.25
20	−126.10	145.50
30	−135.73	150.25
40	−144.00	154.34
50	−151.29	157.55
100	−178.96	167.73
400	—	183.12

[a]This is mixed project, for which, to find $r°$ for a given k, we must solve the equation:
$$-(1 + k)(1 + r°)^3 + 2(1 + k)(1 + r°)^2 + 2(1 + k)(1 + r°) + [2(1 + k) - 5] = 0$$

debt service and equity-return cash flow streams. Since no debt was assumed for this example, the method could not yield results other than the IRR values of 0 and 400 percent. This would not be a proper test of the method.

ANALYSIS OF A TYPICAL LEVERAGED LEASE (CHILDS AND GRIDLEY)

EXAMPLE 13-3

This example was first proposed by Childs and Gridley[3] and since discussed extensively in the literature. Table 13-3 contains the salient data for the Childs and Gridley leveraged lease. A 7 per-

[3]C. Rogers Childs, Jr., and William G. Gridley, Jr., "Leveraged Leasing and the Reinvestment Rate Fallacy," *The Bankers Magazine,* Vol. 156 (Winter 1973).

Table 13-2.   Summary of Analytical Results for Example 13-2 Project

FOR $k = 10\%$

NPV Method	$558.64	Accept
TRM RIC	139.25%	Accept
Wiar Method Equity Return	Inapplicable	
IIM Return	17.06%	Accept
TSFM Return	71.45%	Accept
Two-Stage Measures	.55 years, 4.58%	Accept[a]

FOR $k = 20\%$

NPV Method	$801.70	Accept
TRM RIC	145.50%	Accept
Wiar Method Equity Return	Inapplicable	
IIM Return	34.57%	Accept
TSFM Return	109.09%	Accept
Two-Stage Measures	.60 years, 9.05%	Accept[a]

FOR $k = 30\%$

NPV Method	$881.59	Accept
TRM RIC	150.25%	Accept
Wiar Method Equity Return	Inapplicable	
IIM Return	52.01%	Accept
TSFM Return	125.70%	Accept
Two-Stage Measures	.65 years, 13.47%	Accept[a]

[a]Assumes management's requirement for capital recovery is not less than these fractions of a year.

cent investment tax credit applies to the equipment. Depreciation was calculated using sum-of-the-years' digits method and an 11-year lifetime. The equipment was depreciated to a salvage-for-tax amount of 5 percent of the original depreciable value. The depreciation for $t = 9$ (year ten) is shown as $4.09; the calculated amount was $4.55. This difference is due to the requirement that $5 remain for write-off at $t = 15$ (year 16). The column of data of most concern to the equity investor is the "Net-After-Tax Cash Flow" column. It is this column on which our analysis will focus, although the Wiar method incorporates additional information.

This series of cash flows is a mixed project in the TRM sense. The r_{min} can be calculated from the series by taking the cash flows for $t = 0$ through $t = 8$ and solving for the IRR. Verification that

Table 13-3. Childs and Gridley Leveraged Lease Example—a la Wiar's Analysis Borrow $80 at 8% for 15 Years, Invest $20 Equity, Tax Rate 48%

t	Year	Lease Payment	Deprec.	Mortgage Interest Payment	Effect on Earnings Before Taxes	Effect on Taxes	Effect on Earnings After Taxes	Mortgage Principal Payment	Net After-Tax Cash Flow (To equity)
0		0	0	0	0	0	0	0	−20.00
1	1	9.64	16.67	6.40	−13.43	−13.45[a]	.02	2.95	13.74[a]
2	2	9.64	15.15	6.16	−11.67	−5.60	−6.07	3.19	5.89
3	3	9.64	13.64	5.91	−9.91	−4.75	−5.16	3.44	5.04
4	4	9.64	12.12	5.63	−8.11	−3.90	−4.21	3.72	4.19
5	5	9.64	10.61	5.34	−6.31	−3.03	−3.28	4.01	3.32
6	6	9.64	9.09	5.02	−4.47	−2.14	−2.33	4.33	2.43
7	7	9.64	7.57	4.67	−2.60	−1.25	−1.35	4.68	1.54
8	8	9.64	6.06	4.29	−.71	−.34	−.37	5.06	.63
9	9	9.64	4.09	3.89	1.66	.80	.86	5.46	−.51
10	10	9.64	0	3.45	6.19	2.97	3.22	5.90	−2.68
11	11	9.64	0	2.98	6.66	3.19	3.47	6.37	−2.90
12	12	9.64	0	2.47	7.17	3.45	3.72	6.88	−3.16
13	13	9.64	0	1.92	7.72	3.70	4.02	7.43	−3.41
14	14	9.64	0	1.33	8.31	3.99	4.32	8.02	−3.70
15	15	9.64	0	.68	8.96	4.30	4.66	8.56	−3.90
Total		144.60	95.00	60.14	−10.54	−12.06	1.52	80.00	−3.48
16	Residual	0	5.00	0	−5.00	−2.40	−2.60	0	2.40
Total		144.60	100.00	60.14	−15.54	−14.46	−1.08	80.00	−1.08

[a] Includes 7% investment tax credit on the $100 investment.

Table 13-4. Analysis of Childs and Gridley Leveraged Lease Example—a la Wiar

t	Year	Lease Payment	Deprec.	Effect on Earnings Before Taxes	Effect On Taxes	Effect on Earnings After Taxes	Net After-Tax Cash Flow (Overall lease)
0		0	0	0	0	0	−100.00
1	1	9.64	16.67	−7.03	−10.37[a]	−3.34[a]	20.01[a]
2	2	9.64	15.15	−5.51	−2.64	−2.87	12.28
3	3	9.64	13.64	−4.00	−1.92	−2.08	11.56
4	4	9.64	12.12	−2.48	−1.19	−1.29	10.83
5	5	9.64	10.61	−.97	−.47	−.50	10.11
6	6	9.64	9.09	.55	.26	.29	9.38
7	7	9.64	7.57	2.07	.99	1.08	8.65
8	8	9.64	6.06	3.58	1.72	1.86	7.92
9	9	9.64	4.09	5.55	2.66	2.89	6.98
10	10	9.64	0	9.64	4.63	5.01	5.01
11	11	9.64	0	9.64	4.63	5.01	5.01
12	12	9.64	0	9.64	4.63	5.01	5.01
13	13	9.64	0	9.64	4.63	5.01	5.01
14	14	9.64	0	9.64	4.63	5.01	5.01
15	15	9.64	0	9.64	4.63	5.01	5.01
	Total	144.60	95.00	49.60	16.82	32.78	7.78
16	Residual	0	5.00	−5.00	−2.40	2.60	2.40
	Total	144.60	100.00	44.60	14.42	35.38	10.18

[a]Includes 7 percent investment tax credit on the $100 investment.

the result obtained, 28.5038 percent, is, in fact, the project r_{min} can be obtained by evaluating the project balance equations corresponding to the preceding cash flows at this rate; they will all be less than or equal to zero.

The Wiar analysis[4] can be carried out by evaluating the equation:

$$20(1 + r_W)^{16} = 100(1.045220)^{16} - 80(1.0416)^{16}$$

to find that $r_W = 5.80736$ percent after tax (or 11.16799 percent pretax). The rate of 4.52220 percent is the return on the *overall* cash flow to the leveraged lease, whereas the 4.16 percent rate is the *after-tax* interest on the debt financing. The overall cash flows to this lease are displayed in Table 13-4. Note that the Wiar rate does not depend on the lessor's cost of capital. The decision to accept the leasing project as an investment or not is made by comparing the r_W with the lessor's cut-off or hurdle rate.

The TRM-RIC function for the Childs and Gridley leveraged lease is plotted in Figure 13-5, along with the initial investment, traditional sinking fund, and two-stage measures. The functions are plotted on the same graph to illustrate the consistency of the methods: All but the Wiar equity return would mark the project acceptable for values of $k < 25$ percent, and unacceptable for $k > 25$ percent. The apparent symmetry of the "loan" phase measure of the two-stage method with the traditional sinking fund method is interesting. The lease is acceptable for $k < 25$ percent with the two-stage method, provided that the payback (recovery of investment plus opportunity cost) is acceptable, since the implicit loan embedded in the later cash flows is at a rate less than k in this range. The fact that the two-stage payback goes to infinite value after k reaches 28.5 percent is noteworthy, for that is the value of r_{min} in the TRM solution. An infinite value of the two-stage payback means that the initial investment and opportunity cost of the funds committed will never be fully recovered. Any such payback beyond the project's economic life may be similarly interpreted.

[4]Robert C. Wiar, "Economic Implications of Multiple Rates of Return in the Leveraged Lease Context," *Journal of Finance,* Vol. XXVIII (December 1973), pp. 1275–1286.

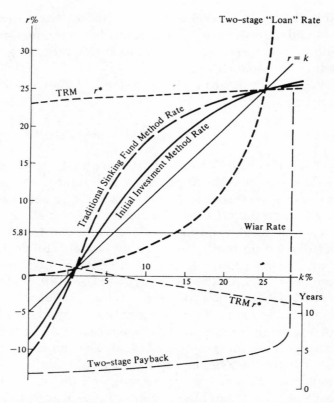

Figure 13-5. Several Measures on the Childs and Gridley Leveraged Lease Returns.

CONCLUSION

Leveraged leases provide perhaps the closest "real-world" approximation to the certainty environment we have considered to exist for capital-budgeting analysis to this point. Furthermore, growth in the use of leveraged leasing and the magnitude of funds involved make leveraged lease profitability analysis a significant area for investigation.

In this chapter we have examined leveraged leases as an interesting and practical application of analytical methods designed to deal with mixed cash flows. The results obtained suggest that accept/reject decisions may be correctly reached by several of the methods: NPV; two-stage method; initial investment method; traditional sinking fund method; and the TRM approach.

The Wiar method would reject projects acceptable under the

other criteria. In fact, the Wiar rate is truly internal to the project—the cost of capital does not enter into its calculation at all. It is solely a function of the internal rate of return to the overall lease cash flows and the interest rate on the debt component of the lease. Because of this the Wiar rate, r_W, is plotted on a straight-line parallel to the k-axis.

III

Special Topics and Methods

14

Alternative Investment Measures

The purpose of this chapter is to introduce several additional measures that may be applied to capital-budgeting projects. These include the geometric mean rate of return, the average rate of return, Boulding's time spread; and Macaulay's duration.

In this chapter, in order to simplify the exposition, capital outlays will be restricted to the initial outlay, and subsequent net cash flows will be assumed to be nonnegative. All cash flows are assumed to occur at the end of the corresponding time periods. In other words, only simple investments in the sense defined in Chapter 10 will be considered.

ADDITIONAL RATE OF RETURN MEASURES

Geometric Mean Rate of Return

In contrast to the more generally known arithmetic mean, the geometric mean is obtained by taking the nth root of the product of the n items, rather than dividing their sum by the number n. When considering the average of interest or growth rates over a period of time, the geometric mean is considered more appropriate than the arithmetic mean because it takes into account the effects of period-to-period compounding that the arithmetic mean ignores. Because of the time-value of money, it is, for example, not correct to say that a deposit of $1000 that earns 4 percent the first year, 8 percent the second year, and 9 percent the third year has earned an average rate of 7 percent over the three-year period. The amount earned is $224.29 on the $1000 principal. The uniform, average annual rate for which $1000 will grow to $1224.29 over three years is not 7 percent but 6.98 percent. For a three-year period, this is not a great difference, but the error of the arithmetic mean over the geometric mean becomes greater the longer the time span covered. For example, if a principal amount can earn 4 percent for ten periods, 8 percent for the next ten periods, and 9 percent for the last ten periods of a 30-year investment life, the geometric mean rate is 6.16 percent, whereas the arithmetic mean is 7 percent.

The *geometric mean rate of return* on an investment, r_g, may be defined by:

$$r_g = \left[\prod_{t=1}^{n} (1 + y_t)\right]^{1/n} - 1 \tag{14.1}$$

where

$$y_t = \frac{E_t - E_{t-1} + R_t}{E_{t-1}} \tag{14.2}$$

with R_t the cash flow at end of period t and the E_t representing the market value of the investment at end of period t. Note that this formulation measures the period-to-period changes in equity value over the life of the investment even though the overall change in equity value is not realized until disposition of the asset at the end of its useful life.

Average Discounted Rate of Return

The *average discounted rate of return*, r_a, may be defined as:

$$r_a = \frac{\sum_{t=1}^{n} y_t(1 + r_a)^{-t}}{\sum_{t=1}^{n} (1 + r_a)^{-t}} \tag{14.3}$$

where y_t is as defined in Eq. (14.2). Since r_a is defined recursively, it would appear difficult and time consuming to compute. However, existing computer programs for finding internal rate of return can be used.

Equation (14.3) is equivalent to:

$$1 - (1 + r_a)^{-n} = \sum_{t=1}^{n} y_t(1 + r_a)^{-t}$$

since

$$\sum_{t=1}^{n} (1 + r_a)^{-t} = \frac{1 - (1 + r_a)^{-n}}{r_a}$$

which is the equation for $a_{\overline{n}|r_a}$, the present value of an annuity of one for n periods at rate r_a.

Rearranging the terms, we obtain:

$$1 = \sum_{t=1}^{n-1} y_t(1 + r_a)^{-t} + (1 + y_n)(1 + r_a)^{-n} \qquad (14.4)$$

To solve for r_a in Eq. (14.4), we need only recognize that this is the equation for an "investment" of \$1, returning $y, \ldots, y_{n-1}$, and a final return of $1 + y_n$ at time n, and apply any computer program for finding IRR. This equation is the same as that for finding yield to maturity for a variable-payment bond that sells for its par value of \$1, and at maturity returns the \$1 with the final payment of interest.

Robert R. Trippi illustrated the application and usefulness of geometric mean return and average-discounted rate of return for measuring the returns on investments that undergo changes in market value over their useful lives.[1] Trippi employed 12 illustrative examples in his exposition. Here we will examine several similar examples to demonstrate the techniques and compare r_g with r_a and the IRR, which is denoted by r_c for "conventional" rate of return in Trippi's notation.

To illustrate the meaning and calculation of r_g and r_a, let us consider the following example, which requires a \$1000 initial investment and returns the net, after-tax cash flows indicated. In addition, the market value of the asset changes from period to period.

EXAMPLE 14-1

	t = 1	t = 2	t = 3	t = 4	t = 5
Cash Flow	\$ 200	200	300	400	200
Market Value	\$1100	1200	1250	1300	1325

[1]Robert R. Trippi, "Conventional and Unconventional Methods for Evaluating Investments," *Financial Management*, Vol. 3 (Autumn 1974), pp. 31–35.

Assuming the asset will be disposed of at the end of year five, the $1325 market value will be realized as a positive salvage value and the total cash flow increased by this amount to $1525. For simplicity we assume that the market values are the after-tax proceeds that would be realized if the asset were to be disposed of at the end of any indicated year. The internal rate of return (here denoted r_c) is 28.5044 percent, on the cash flow series $-\$1000$, \$200, \$200, \$300, \$400, and \$1525.

To calculate r_g we employ Eq. (14.2) $n = 5$ times, substituting into Eq. (14.1). Thus

$$y_1 = \frac{E_1 - E_0 + R_1}{E_0} = \frac{1100 - 1000 + 200}{1000} = .3000$$

$$y_2 = \frac{E_2 - E_1 + R_2}{E_1} = \frac{1200 - 1100 + 200}{1100} = .2727$$

$$\vdots$$

and so on.
And applying Eq. (14.1), we obtain:

$$r_g = [(1.3)(1.27273)(1.29166)(1.36)(1.17308)]^{1/5} - 1$$
$$= 27.8024 \text{ percent}$$

Now, to find r_a we employ Eq. (14.4). This results in the following series to which we apply the procedure for finding the internal rate of return:

$$-1 \quad .3 \quad .27273 \quad .29167 \quad .36 \quad 1.17308$$

Note that this is identical to the series for a hypothetical bond that sells for \$1, yields the various amounts defined by Eq. (14.2), and returns the original investment in a balloon payment of one at $t = 5$. Thus we find that:

$$r_a = 28.6193 \text{ percent}$$

For this example, $r_a > r_c > r_g$. This, however, will not always be the case. In fact, several cases were identified by Trippi. Table 14-1 displays the relationship between r_g, r_a, and r_c for some different patterns of cash flow and market value. It is important to note that the internal rate of return, r_c, depends only on the pattern of *cash flows*, whereas both r_g and r_a depend on the pattern

Table 14-1. Examples of r_g, r_a, and r_c for Various Cases, Each Requiring $1000

Case No.		1	2	3	4	5	r_g %	r_a %	r_c (IRR) %
1	Cash Flow	0	100	200	300	400	19.1956	16.9082	16.9082
	Market Value	1000	1000	1000	1000	1000			
2	Cash Flow	200	200	200	200	200	20.0000	20.0000	20.0000
	Market Value	1000	1000	1000	1000	1000			
3	Cash Flow	400	300	200	100	0	19.1956	24.2573	24.2573
	Market Value	1000	1000	1000	1000	1000			
4	Cash Flow	0	0	0	0	0	14.8698	13.6208	14.8698
	Market Value	1000	1100	1300	1600	2000			
5	Cash Flow	0	0	0	0	0	14.8698	15.5507	14.8698
	Market Value	1000	1400	1600	1800	2000			
6	Cash Flow	0	0	0	0	0	14.8698	19.1003	14.8698
	Market Value	1200	1700	1900	2000	2000			
7	Cash Flow	200	200	200	200	200	−10.7682	−10.5832	0.0000
	Market Value	1000	900	700	400	0			
8	Cash Flow	200	200	200	200	200	0.0000	0.0000	0.0000
	Market Value	800	600	400	200	0			
9	Cash Flow	200	200	200	100	200	9.8561	12.7813	0.0000
	Market Value	800	600	300	200	0			
10	Cash Flow	200	200	200	200	200	25.0228	24.9019	24.8848
	Market Value	1000	1100	1200	1300	1400			
11	Cash Flow	200	200	200	200	200	23.4399	27.0023	24.8848
	Market Value	1000	1400	1400	1400	1400			
12	Cash Flow	200	200	200	200	200	27.1069	24.8848	24.8848
	Market Value	1000	1000	1000	1000	1400			

of changes in market value in addition to cash flows. Thus many projects having the same IRR will have different r_g and still different r_a.

Trippi had proposed the average discounted rate of return as an alternative to the geometric mean rate of return for incorporating the change in equity value and its pattern in measuring the return on investment. This is something that heretofore has received more attention in the area of securities analysis and portfolio management than in capital budgeting. However, the concept is as equally applicable to capital investment projects as it is to investments in securities.

Shortly after the appearance of Trippi's paper, Peter Bacon, Robert Haessler, and Richard Williams[2] found an interesting counterintuitive example in an asset that produces no cash flow prior to its sale, doubles in value in the first year, and then in the second year declines to its original value. To quote Bacon, Haessler, and Williams: "The marginal return in year 1 is 100% and year 2 is −50%. Calculating the geometric mean and the internal rate of return or just relying on intuition all indicate that the true return is zero. . . . However, when . . . r_a is computed, the result is 36%."[3] As they go on to point out, the problem with Trippi's r_a is that it discounts the marginal returns in addition to averaging them. Since percentage increases are weighted the same as percentage decreases, the problem is not readily apparent with those investments that only increase or decrease in market value. However, with assets that first increase and then decrease, or vice versa, the investment return is misrepresented by r_a. The fact that early marginal percentage changes are discounted less than those occurring later further contributes to the problem.

In his reply to Bacon, Haessler, and Williams, Trippi emphasized[4] that his "primary intent . . . was not to advocate universal acceptance of one measure over the others, but rather to demonstrate the general difficulties and frequent lack of conformity of each of the measures. . . . Clearly some nonunity marginal rate of substitution of present for future undistributed wealth is likely

[2]Peter Bacon, Robert Haessler, and Richard Williams, comment on Trippi's "Conventional and Unconventional Methods for Evaluating Investments," *Financial Management*, Vol. 5 (Spring 1975), p. 8.
[3]Ibid.
[4]Robert R. Trippi, "Reply," *Financial Management*, (Spring 1975), pp. 8–9.

to apply . . . this phenomenon being totally lost with the conventional measures."

Thus, although caution must be exercised, the geometric mean rate of return and average discounted rate of return may be considered adjuncts in the process of investment evaluation, particularly where there is unrealized (monotonic) increase or decrease over the life of the investment. The methods yielding r_g and r_a should perhaps not be used at all for investments characterized by nonmonotonically changing market value.

A subsequent chapter takes up the topic of abandonment value in capital budgeting. There it may be seen that an alternative to r_a exists. For now, we shall go on to finish this chapter with the topics of unrecovered investment, duration, and time spread.

TIME-RELATED MEASURES IN INVESTMENT ANALYSIS

Although the literature has generally concentrated on other aspects of the topic of capital budgeting, time-related measures are useful and may provide additional insight. Here we shall consider two time-related measures: Macaulay's *duration* and Boulding's *time spread*. The latter, although identical to the modern actuaries' *equated time*, was proposed in 1936.

Boulding's Time Spread

Kenneth E. Boulding[5] proposed *time spread* (*TS*) as a measure of the average time interval elapsing between sets of capital outlays and returns. For investments having a single initial outlay at time $t = 0$, Boulding's time spread is defined by:

$$\sum_{t=1}^{N} R_t = \sum_{t=1}^{N} R_t(1 + r)^{TS-t} \tag{14.5}$$

Since $(1 + r)^{TS}$ is constant for a given r and TS,

$$\sum_{t=1}^{N} R_t = (1 + r)^{TS} \sum_{t=1}^{N} R_t(1 + r)^{-t} \tag{14.5a}$$

[5]K. E. Boulding, "Time and Investment," *Economica*, Vol. 3 (1936), pp. 196–220.

so that

$$(1 + r)^{TS} = \frac{\sum\limits_{t=1}^{N} R_t}{\sum\limits_{t=1}^{N} R_t(1 + r)^{-t}} \qquad (14.5b)$$

and

$$TS = \log \left\{ \frac{\sum\limits_{t=1}^{N} R_t}{\sum\limits_{t=1}^{N} R_t(1 + r)^{-t}} \right\} \div \log (1 + r) \qquad (14.6)$$

In the case of $r = r°$ (the internal rate of return), it can be shown (as Boulding did) that:

$$TS = \log \left\{ \frac{\sum\limits_{t=1}^{N} R_t}{R_0} \right\} \div \log (1 + r) \qquad (14.7)$$

where R_0 is the initial (and only) capital outlay for the project. The proof of this involves the recognition that for the internal rate of return (IRR) the initial outlay is equal to the sum of the discounted cash flows at discount rate $r°$.

When used with the internal rate of return, time spread shows how long the initial investment remains invested on average at rate $r°$ (the IRR). Time spread provides the point in time at which a *single* amount, equal to the undiscounted sum of cash flows, would be equivalent to the individual cash flows at intervals over the life of the investment, at a given rate of interest. It is a measure of the average time between capital outlays and net cash receipts. In cases in which the only cash outlay is at $t = 0$, time spread therefore measures the average time elapsed to receive the net cash flows over the interval $t = 1$ through $t = N$. The following example will clarify this and set the concept.

Consider case 1 in Table 14-1. This project, costing $1000, yields total cash flows of $2000 over its life, including $1000 realized on disposition of the asset at $t = 5$. Time spread for this project is $TS = 4.4370$ years, and the internal rate of return is

$r_c = 16.9082$ percent. The individual net cash flows could be replaced by a single cash flow of \$2000 (equal to the undiscounted sum of cash inflows) at $t = TS$: the equation

$$R_0 = \sum_{t=1}^{N} R_t(1 + r^\circ)^{-TS} = (1 + r^\circ)^{-TS} \sum_{t=1}^{N} R_t \qquad (14.8)$$

follows directly from Eq. (14.7). Substituting the parameters of case 1, we obtain

$$\$1000 = (1.169082)^{-4.4370}\$2000 = \$1000$$

Thus the entire cash flow series beyond the initial outlay may be replaced by a single amount equal to its sum at $t = TS$. Similarly, rates other than the IRR may be used, with the same interpretation, although for different rates different values for TS will be obtained.

Macaulay's Duration

Following soon after Boulding, Frederick R. Macaulay[6] developed the concept of *duration* as an alternative to the conventional time measure for bonds—the term to maturity. For those investments with a single cash outlay at $t = 0$, duration is a weighted average of repayment times (or dates) with weights equal to the present values of the cash flows at their respective dates. Equation (14.9) defines duration:

$$D = \frac{\sum_{t=1}^{N} tR_t(1 + r)^{-t}}{\sum_{t=1}^{N} R_t(1 + r)^{-t}} \qquad (14.9)$$

For $r = r^\circ$, the internal rate of return, the denominator, by definition of the IRR, is equal to R_0, the initial outlay. Therefore, for r°:

[6]Frederick R. Macaulay, *Some Theoretical Problems Suggested by the Movement of Interest Rates, Bond Yields and Stock Prices in the United States Since 1856* (New York: National Bureau of Economic Research, 1938).

$$D = \frac{\sum\limits_{t=1}^{N} tR_t(1 + r°)^{-t}}{R_0} \qquad (14.10)$$

Calculation of duration is straightforward, even if tedious. As Durand has pointed out,[7] even though different, D converges to the same value as TS when N is finite and the discount rate approaches zero. It might be added that, when the only cash flow is at $t = N$, $D = TS = N$.

The history of development and application of duration has been very well described by Weil, who, among other things, points out that Hick's elasticity of capital with respect to discount factors is equivalent to duration,[8] although apparently developed independently and somewhat later. Weil also mentions Tjalling C. Koopmans' 1942 (unpublished) paper on matching life insurance assets and liabilities to "immunize" the company against effects of interest rate changes. At the time Koopmans was employed by Penn Mutual Life Insurance Company.[9] Credit for the seminal idea on immunization is often awarded to Redington[10] for his later contribution, which appears to be the earliest published paper on the topic although appearing a decade after Koopmans' paper was written.

Like time spread, duration provides a useful adjunct measure to be used in capital budgeting, although it was developed for another purpose, as stated earlier. For case 1 of Table 14-1, $D = 4.3696$. This provides the "average" time that elapses for a dollar of present value to be received from this project. This is somewhat less than the time spread value. It may be shown that $D \leq TS$.

Unrecovered Investment

The *unrecovered investment* of a capital-budgeting project is defined by:

[7]David Durand, "Time as a Dimension of Investment," *Proceedings of the Eastern Finance Association* (April 1973), pp. 200–219.

[8]Roman L. Weil, "Macaulay's Duration: An Appreciation," *Journal of Business,* Vol. 46 (October 1973), p. 590.

[9]Ibid., p. 591.

[10]F. M. Redington, "Review of the Principles of Line-Office Valuations," *Journal of the Institute of Actuaries,* Vol. 78 (1952).

$$U = R_0(1 + r)^T - \sum_{t=1}^{T} R_t(1 + r)^{T-t} \qquad (14.11)$$

With the internal rate of return it is implicitly assumed that the IRR rate, $r°$, is earned on the unrecovered principal as measured at the beginning of each period over the project life. This was made explicit in the treatment of conflicting IRR—net present value rankings in Chapter 8. With $r°$, the unrecovered investment will be exactly zero at $t = N$. For $t < N$ and with $r = r°$, $U > 0$; the unrecovered investment will be positive prior to the end of the project life. For $t < N$ and $r < r°$, U becomes negative prior to $t = N$. Figure 14-1 shows the graphs for U as a function of t and r. Since it is assumed that cash flows occur only at the end of each period, discontinuities occur at these points. For $r = r°$ the unrecovered investment becomes zero after the end of period four. At a higher rate, $r = 30$ percent, for example, the cash flows were not even adequate for paying the "interest" on the unrecovered investment by $t = 5$, so that the investment is not fully recovered by that time. In fact, at $t = 5$ the unrecovered investment is greater than the initial investment at $t = 0$. For rates less than $r°$ the investment is fully recovered prior to $t = 5$.

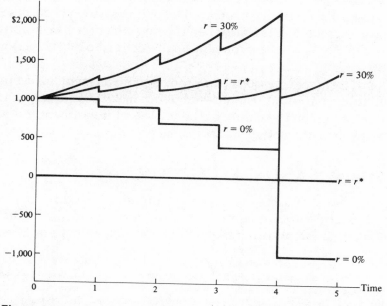

Figure 14-1. Unrecovered Investment at End of Time Period Indicated.

Table 14-2. Component Breakdown of Cash Flows (Amounts Rounded to Nearest Cents) for $r = r^*$

	Beginning Principal	Interest on Beginning Principal	Principal Repayment	Total Payment	Ending Principal
1	$1000.00	169.08	0	0	$1169.08
2	1169.08	197.67	0	100	1266.75
3	1266.75	214.18	0	200	1280.93
4	1280.93	216.58	83.42	300	1197.51
5	1197.51	202.48	1400.00	1400	0

Note: It is assumed that end-of-period payments are composed of interest at $r° = 16.9082$ percent on beginning-of-period principal plus (if there is an excess over the interest) principal repayment.

Table 14-2, which employs the same type component breakdown used in Chapter 8, serves to illustrate the concept of unrecovered investment. The table displays the unrecovered investment under the heading "Ending Principal" for the beginning-of-period points. Table 14-2 treats the investment case 1 of Table 14-1 as though it were a loan, and unrecovered investment is seen to be the "loan principal."

Unrecovered investment, U, is related to payback period P, which was discussed in Chapter 5. The point at which U becomes zero corresponds to the time when the investment has been fully recovered. For $r = 0$, the conventionally defined payback period is obtained.[11]

The concept and measure of unrecovered investment are useful as an adjunct to other capital-budgeting measures. It serves to focus attention on the nature of the process of investment recovery implicit within other measures, as was done in Chapter 8.

SUMMARY AND CONCLUSION

The additional investment measures presented in this chapter provide useful *adjuncts* to other capital-budgeting measures. They illustrate that factors other than cash flow alone may be of inter-

[11]With the conventional calculation of payback, the assumption that cash flows occur only at the end of each period is violated; once the payback period has been bracketed, the end-of-period cash flow at the further time period is treated as if it occurred uniformly over the period. The formula for U does not violate the assumption of end-of-period cash receipts, and to this extent there is a difference with payback calculation.

est; as, for instance, Trippi's average rate of return that, to some extent, incorporates the appreciation in asset value that is not realized until the end of the project life. Used alone they are not especially useful; but used with other measurements of capital-budgeting project characteristics they can provide additional insight, thereby facilitating better decision making.

Perhaps Durand states the case as well as anyone when he says:

From all this I conclude that we need to take a far broader view of capital budgeting than we have in the past. We have squandered altogether too much effort on a futile search for that elusive will-o'-the-wisp the one and only index of profitability; and we have lost valuable perspective thereby.[12]

[12]Durand, p. 191.

15

Project Abandonment Analysis

Up to this point it has been implicitly assumed that capital-budgeting projects, if accepted for investment, would (for better or for worse) be held until $t = N$. This is unduly restrictive. Furthermore, it violates the realities of capital-budgeting practice; capital investments are often abandoned prior to termination of their theoretical useful lives. In this chapter the topic of abandonment analysis is taken up.

THE ROBICHEK-VAN HORNE ANALYSIS

In a paper published in 1969, Alexander A. Robichek and James C. Van Horne (R-VH) presented an algorithm for determining if and when a capital investment project should be abandoned prior to the end of its useful life at $t = N$.[1] The original procedure was modified somewhat[2] after Edward A. Dyl and Hugh W. Long[3] showed that the original algorithm could, in some circumstances, break down.

The R-VH paper has become widely known and cited, perhaps because it was the first paper in a major journal in recent years to have dealt with the subject of abandonment value. It provided an important prod in the process of awakening academics to a problem that in practice has always been a factor to be considered, but for which little mention has been made in the literature.

R-VH assumed, in order to facilitate analysis, that (1) an ade-

[1]Alexander A. Robichek and James C. Van Horne, "Abandonment Value and Capital Budgeting," *The Journal of Finance,* Vol. 22 (December 1967), pp. 577–589.

[2]———. "Abandonment Value and Capital Budgeting: Reply," *The Journal of Finance,* Vol. 24 (March 1969), pp. 96–97.

[3]Edward A. Dyl and Hugh W. Long, "Abandonment Value and Capital Budgeting: Comment," *The Journal of Finance,* Vol. 24 (March 1969), pp. 88–95.

quate estimate of the firm's cost of capital exists; (2) there is no capital rationing; and (3) a unique internal rate of return exists for the projects considered. Assumption (3) may be satisfied by considering only simple investments, in the sense defined in Chapter 10.

The R-VH algorithm (corrected to satisfy the Dyl-Long critique) is stated as:

(a) Compute $PV_{r^\circ a}$ for $a = n$, where

$$PV_{\tau \cdot a} = \sum_{t=\tau+1}^{a} \frac{EC_{t \cdot r}}{(1 + k)^{(t-r)}} + \frac{AV_{a \cdot \tau}}{(1 + k)^{(a-r)}}$$

(b) If $PV_{\tau \cdot n} > AV_r$,
    continue to hold project and evaluate it again at time $r + 1$, based upon expectation at that time.
(c) If $PV_{\tau \cdot n} \leq AV_\tau$,
    compute $PV_{\tau \cdot a}$ for $a = n - 1$.
(d) Compare $PV_{\tau \cdot n-1}$ with AV_r as in (b) and (c) above. Continue procedure until either the decision to hold is reached or $a = \tau + 1$.
(e) If $PV_{\tau \cdot a} \leq AV$ for all $\tau + 1 \leq a \leq n$, then abandon project at time r. . . .
    $EC_{t \cdot \tau}$ = expected cash flow in year t as of year τ.
    AV_t = abandonment value in year t.
    AC_t = "actual" simulated cash flow in year t.[4]

This algorithm as it is stated appears to have been written to deal with the timing of abandonment for a project after it had been accepted. However, R-VH suggested that their rule might be extended to *ex ante* project analysis. This chapter is primarily concerned with such *ex ante* capital investment project analysis. This emphasis, however, should not be construed to imply that continued project review, such as that suggested in the R-VH algorithm, is any less important.

Step (a) of the R-VH algorithm defined the present value *at time reference point* τ as the discounted sum of all cash flows occurring from the period immediately following τ to the end of the project

---

[4]Robichek and Van Horne, "Abandonment Value and Capital Budgeting: Reply," op. cit., p. 96.

life *plus* the present value at τ of the expected salvage value to be received at the end of the project life.

Step (b) states we should keep the project if the present value of continuing to do so as defined in step (a) is greater than the present value of salvage. Note that these present values are *at time* $= \tau$. *Present values are normally calculated for* $t = 0$.

Step (c) requires that we perform additional calculation and analysis before abandoning the project, even though the salvage at time τ is greater than or equal to the present value of expected cash flows from time $\tau + 1$ to the end of the project's maximum useful life at $t = N$. This step is necessary in order to avoid premature abandonment of the project; the NPV may possibly be increased by holding the project for one or more additional time periods even though it will not be held all the way to $t = N$.

Step (d) specifies that the analysis in steps (a) through (c) inclusive be repeated until a period is found for which, in light of the expected returns as of *today*, the decision is to hold on to the project, or else we get to $a = \tau + 1$. In the latter case the decision is to hold on for the current period, then abandon.

Finally, step (e) prescribes that if the salvage value at any point in time τ exceeds the present values that are potentially to be obtained by holding on to the project, it should be abandoned at time τ.

As quoted above, the R-VH algorithm seems particularly designed for ongoing, periodic analysis of capital investments with a view as to whether they should be abandoned or kept in service for another time period. However, although it may not be clear from the wording of the procedure, the R-VH approach is suitable for analyzing capital-budgeting projects *ex ante* (prior to acceptance) as well as the *ex post,* which the R-VH paper appears to stress. In such cases it could be used to help answer these questions. (1) What is the optimal period to keep the project if it is accepted? (2) What is the expected present value if the project were to be accepted and held for the optimal period and no longer?

The R-VH paper was useful in calling attention to the problem of project abandonment. However, it is equivalent to a "dual" formulation of the Terborgh-MAPI method discussed in Chapter 9. Such formulation yields, instead of the MAPI "adverse minimum," a "propitious maximum" NPV, if NPV is the measure of project acceptability or desirability employed. Associated with this maximum is the optimum number of years over which the project, if accepted, would be held. To develop the methodology, we need, in addition to the R-VH assumptions, the assumption that we have or can obtain reliable estimates of salvage values for time periods between the adoption of the project and the end of its useful life at $t = N$. For those fairly standard types of equipment for which there is a well-developed secondary market, this should be a reasonable assumption.[5] On the other hand, for plant and for custom-made equipment this assumption will in general lack the reliability associated with the former category. For a thorough treatment of the problems associated with extraction of such estimates, the reader is referred to Terborgh's *Dynamic Equipment Policy.*[6]

The following two sections illustrate application of the modified MAPI procedure to three capital-budgeting projects and compare results with the R-VH method.

AN ALTERNATE METHOD: A PARABLE[7]

To highlight the points presented an example will be employed.

The capital project committee of Typical Manufacturing Company is considering which of three mutually exclusive production machines it should purchase to perform certain operations on a new product that the company has decided to add to its line. The machines are all of standard design, and hundreds of various vintages are in use across the nation. The following information has been presented to the committee:

	Purchase Price	For the Year Indicated Net After-Tax Cash Benefits						
Machine A	$2,000	$600	$600	$600	$600	$100	$100	$100
Machine B	2,000	700	600	500	400	300	200	100
Machine C	1,000	100	200	300	400	300	200	100
Year		1	2	3	4	5	6	7

[5]For example, we could develop estimates of salvage value deterioration gradients by careful, systematic analysis of trade publications carrying advertisements for used equipment and by consulting with dealers specializing in such equipment.

[6]George Terborgh, *Dynamic Equipment Policy.* Washington: Machinery and Allied Products Institute, 1949.

[7]The following pages are reprinted with permission from *The Engineering Economist*, Vol. 22, No. 1 (Fall 1976). Copyright © American Institute of Industrial Engineers, Inc., 25 Technology Park/Atlanta, Norcross, GA. 30092.

All three machines have useful lives of 7 years. Machine A has an estimated salvage value of $419.43, B $419.43, and C $478.30 at the end of 7 years.

The recommendation provided to the committee is that machine C be purchased since, at the firm's 10 percent cost of capital, it has a net present value of $350.69, while A and B have, respectively NPVs of $286.99 and $346.75. Since most members of the committee are well versed in the traditional finance literature concerned with capital budgeting, C is chosen for purchase with little discussion. Of course, there is some argument over the significance of the slight edge in NPV that C has over B, but A is out of the running from the beginning.

Has the committee selected wisely? No! "But," the reply will be, "by selecting the project with the highest net present value we are assuring the maximum increase in the value of equity." However, there is more to the story. In the approach to project selection that was followed, no attention was paid to salvage value *prior to* the end of each machine's useful life. In the example presented here the salvage values for A and B represent 20 percent per annum declines from the prior year's value, beginning with the purchase price paid for each, while that for C represents a 10 percent per annum decline.

Tables 1-A, 1-B, and 1-C present alternative calculations that might have been performed for machines A, B, and C. Readers familiar with the MAPI method for replacement evaluation presented by Terborgh will note some similarity in that his method also considers intermediate salvage values. However, the MAPI method was developed primarily for replacement decisions, and is based on minimum cost (adverse minima) rather than maximum benefit considerations. The method presented here might be considered the dual to Terborgh's method. Like the MAPI method, that shown in Tables 1-A, 1-B, and 1-C uses the concept of time-adjusted annual averages, or level annuities. However, instead of finding adverse minima, we instead find what might be called "propitious maxima." In this instance these are employed to present matrices representing the continuum of net present value opportunities of each project, assuming that the projects may be abandoned at the end of years 1, 2, 3, . . . , n where "n" represents the last year in the useful life of the project.

Column 6 in the tables gives the level annuity having the same accumulated value at the end of the indicated year as the values in Column 4. Column 7 gives the level annuities for the number of years indicated that are equivalent to the initial outlay. Column 10 gives the uniform annual equivalent to the salvage value in each indicated year. By summing across Columns 6, 7, and 10 and then multiplying by the appropriate factors for the present value of an annuity, the

Table 1-A. Capital-Budgeting Project with Salvage Value at End of Each Year (Initial Outlay = $2000; Estimated Useful Life = 7 Years; Decline in Salvage Value from Beginning of Period Value—20%/Year)

Year	1 Return	2 Present Value Factor— 10%	3 P.V. of Return = (1) × (2)	4 Accum. P.V. = (3) Acc.	5 Capital Recovery Factor— 10%	6 Level Annuity = (4) × (5)	7 Level Annuity = Cost $2000 × (5)
1	$600	.9091	545.46	545.46	1.1000	600.00	−2200.00
2	600	.8264	495.84	1041.30	.5762	600.00	−1152.40
3	600	.7513	450.78	1492.08	.4021	600.00	−804.20
4	600	.6830	409.80	1901.88	.3155	600.00	−631.00
5	100	.6209	62.09	1963.97	.2638	518.10	−527.60
6	100	.5645	56.45	2020.42	.2296	463.89	−459.20
7	100	.5132	51.32	2071.74	.2054	425.54	−410.80

Year	8 Salvage Value at Year End	9 P.V. of Salvage = (2) × (8)	10 Level Annuity = (9) = (5) × (9)	11 (6) + (7) + (10)	12 P.V. of Annuity— 10%	13[a] N.P.V. of (11) = (11) × (12)	14 Internal Rate of Return
1	1600.00	1454.56	1600.00	0.0	.909	0.0	.1000
2	1280.00	1057.79	609.50	57.10	1.736	99.13	.1311
3	1024.00	769.33	309.35	105.15	2.487	261.51	.1609
4	819.20	559.51	176.53	145.53	3.170	461.33	.1881
5	655.36	406.91	107.34	97.84	3.791	370.89	.1680
6	524.28	295.96	67.95	72.64	4.355	316.35	.1565
7	419.43	215.25	44.21	58.95	4.868	286.97	.1502

[a]Column 13 will generally be very slightly different than if NPV were calculated directly, due to rounding.

Table 1-B. Capital-Budgeting Project with Salvage Value at End of Each Year (Initial Outlay = $2000; Estimated Useful Life = 7 Years; Decline in Salvage Value from Beginning of Period Value—20%/Year)

Year	1 Return	2 Present Value Factor— 10%	3 P.V. of Return = (1) × (2)	4 Capital Accum. P.V. = (3) Acc.	5 Level Recovery Factor— 10%	6 Level Annuity = (4) × (5)	7 Level Annuity = Cost $2000 × (5)
1	$700	.9091	636.37	636.37	1.1000	700.00	−2200.00
2	600	.8264	495.84	1132.21	.5762	652.38	−1152.40
3	500	.7513	375.65	1507.86	.4021	606.31	−804.20
4	400	.6830	273.20	1781.06	.3155	561.92	−631.00
5	300	.6209	186.27	1967.33	.2638	518.98	−527.60
6	200	.5645	112.90	2080.23	.2296	477.62	−459.20
7	100	.5132	51.32	2131.55	.2054	437.82	−410.80

Year	8 Salvage Value at Year End	9 P.V. of Salvage = (2) × (8)	10 Level Annuity = (5) × (9)	11 (6) + (7) + (10)	12 P.V. of Annuity Factor— 10%	13[a] N.P.V. of (11) = (11) × (12)	14 Internal Rate of Return
1	1600.00	1454.56	1600.00	100.00	.909	90.90	.1500
2	1280.00	1057.79	609.50	109.48	1.736	190.06	.1602
3	1024.00	769.33	309.35	111.46	2.487	277.20	.1668
4	819.20	559.51	176.53	107.45	3.170	340.62	.1699
5	655.36	406.91	107.34	98.72	3.791	374.25	.1696
6	524.28	295.96	67.95	86.37	4.355	376.14	.1662
7	419.43	215.25	44.21	71.23	4.868	346.75	.1599

[a]Column 13 will generally be very slightly different than if NPV were calculated directly due to rounding.

Table 1-C. Capital-Budgeting Project with Salvage Value at End of Each Year (Initial Outlay = $1000; Estimated Useful Life = 7 Years; Decline in Salvage Value from Beginning of Period Value—10%/Year)

Year	1 Return	2 Present Value Factor—10%	3 P.V. of Return = (1) × (2)	4 Accum. P.V. = (3) Acc.	5 Capital Recovery Factor—10%	6 Level Annuity = (4) × (5)	7 Level Annuity = Cost $1000 × (5)
1	$100	.9091	90.91	90.91	1.1000	100.00	−1100.00
2	200	.8264	165.28	256.19	.5762	147.62	−576.20
3	300	.7513	225.39	481.58	.4021	193.64	−402.10
4	400	.6830	273.20	754.78	.3155	238.13	−315.50
5	300	.6209	186.27	941.05	.2638	248.25	−263.80
6	200	.5645	112.90	1053.95	.2296	241.99	−229.60
7	100	.5132	51.32	1105.27	.2054	227.02	−205.40

Year	8 Salvage Value at Year End	9 P.V. of Salvage = (2) × (8)	10 Level Annuity = (9) = (5) × (9)	11 (6) + (7) + (10)	12 P.V. of Annuity Factor—10%	13[a] N.P.V. of (11) = (11) × (12)	14 Internal Rate of Return
1	900.00	818.19	900.00	−100.00	.909	−90.90	.0000
2	810.00	669.38	385.70	−42.88	1.736	−74.44	.0562
3	729.00	547.70	220.23	11.77	2.487	29.27	.1120
4	656.10	448.12	141.38	64.01	3.170	202.91	.1637
5	590.49	366.64	96.72	55.76	3.791	211.39	.1821
6	531.44	300.00	68.88	81.27	4.355	353.93	.1858
7	478.30	245.46	50.42	72.04	4.868	350.69	.1812

[a]Column 13 will generally be very slightly different than if NPV were calculated directly, due to rounding.

NPVs of Column 13 are obtained. The figures in Column 13 are the NPVs of the projects if they are abandoned and sold for salvage at the end of the year indicated. Column 13 could have been calculated directly, of course, and to a somewhat greater precision in the trailing digits.

Armed with the information contained in Tables 1-A, 1-B, and 1-C the committee probably would have selected project A and not project C. If project A were selected, and then abandoned at the end of the fourth year of service, it would provide an NPV of $461.33. This is higher than that of B, which reaches a peak of $376.14 in the sixth year, and C, which must also be kept for 6 years if its peak NPV of $353.93 is to be realized.

Since the projects reach maximum NPV with different timing, we have a situation tantamount to that of projects with unequal economic lives. Thus, it may appear necessary to adjust the Table 1 figures to reflect the different timing of optimal abandonment for each project. Ordinarily, the easiest means for adjusting for different economic lives is to find the uniform annual equivalent of the NPVs by multiplying them by the corresponding capital recovery factor. However, we already have these results in Column 11.

Over a 12-year time horizon, the least common denominator of 4 and 6 year lives, projects A, B, and C have NPVs of $991.78, $588.46, and $553.71, respectively. These figures may be obtained by multiplying the uniform annual equivalents for optimal abandonment by the present value of annuity factor for twelve periods. Note that since the same present value of annuity factor is used, the comparison could have been directly between the uniform annual equivalents.

Comparison to R-VH[8]

This section is concerned with comparison of the method illustrated in the foregoing section with the revised Robichek-Van Horne algorithm.

Let us begin by applying the R-VH rule to the machines that were considered by TMC. Employing the R-VH procedure with fixed, point estimates of cash returns in each period results in the values displayed in Table 2. The values in row 1 for projects A, B, and C are identical (except for rounding errors in the trailing digits) to the values in column 13 of Table 1.

In row 5 of Table 2-A we see that the first figure is negative. The interpretation of this value is that, if at the end of year 4 project A

[8]Ibid., pp. 63–71.

Table 2-A   Present Value in Row Year I, of Salvage in Column Year J Plus Cumulative Returns Through Column Year J Less Salvage Value at Start of Column Year J

A

	1	2	3	4	5	6	7
1	0.00	99.17	261.46	461.45	370.94	316.41	287.01
2		109.09	287.60	507.59	408.03	348.05	315.71
3			196.36	438.35	328.84	262.86	227.28
4				266.18	145.72	73.14	34.01
5					−132.51	−212.35	−255.39
6						−87.82	−135.17
7							−52.08

B

	1	2	3	4	5	6	7
1	90.91	190.08	277.24	340.62	374.30	376.22	346.82
2		109.09	204.96	274.68	311.73	313.84	281.50
3			105.46	182.15	222.00	225.22	189.65
4				84.36	129.19	131.74	92.62
5					49.31	52.12	9.08
6						3.09	−44.26
7							−52.08

C

	1	2	3	4	5	6	7
1	−90.91	−74.38	29.30	202.92	307.72	353.96	350.73
2		18.18	132.23	323.22	438.50	489.35	485.80
3			125.45	335.54	462.34	518.29	514.38
4				231.09	370.58	432.11	427.82
5					153.44	221.12	216.40
6						74.46	69.26
7							−5.72

is not abandoned, the company will incur an opportunity cost with present value *as of the end of year 4,* of $132.51 during year 5.

The figure of −$212.35 that follows in row 5 is the present value as of the end of year 4, of the cumulative opportunity cost if project A is held through years 5 and 6. The figure of −$255.39 in the last column in row 5 is the present value, as of the end of year 4, of the cumulative opportunity cost that will be suffered if project A is held from the end of year 4 through the end of year 7.

Thus, in terms of the figures of Table 2, each project should be abandoned at the end of the year prior to that corresponding to the row in which the figures become negative. In terms of opportunity cost, the interpretation is that a project should be abandoned when continued retention results in an opportunity cost, from loss in salvage value, greater than revenues in subsequent periods.

The figures in Table 2 could have been generated entirely by the procedure implicit in Table 1, simply by shifting the time reference point forward one period for each new row of figures generated. However, in Table 2, for project A the values in Column 4 are greater than any values in their corresponding rows. Therefore, at $t = 0$ there is no need to generate any more than the first row of values for each project. However, once a particular project has been selected, it may be useful to re-evaluate it at the end of subsequent periods to determine if the optimal time of abandonment has shifted under changing estimates of cash flow and abandonment value. Such a procedure is equivalent to the R-VH approach.

A DYNAMIC PROGRAMMING APPROACH[9]

The solutions shown in Table 15-1 were obtained by using a dynamic programming approach, which provides a useful alternative to that described in the preceding section and also to the R-VH algorithm. Note that this dynamic programming formulation and solution employs the "backward searching" algorithm.[10] This is what James L. Pappas used in his contribution on project abandonment,[11] which was published simultaneously with the paper from which the preceding section was extracted.

Application of dynamic programming to equipment repair and replacement problems is covered by A. O. Converse,[12] who cites the earlier work of R. E. Bellman and S. E. Dreyfus.[13] The problem of abandonment value reduces to a special case of replacement, one in which an existing asset may be replaced by a hypothetical asset that does not exist, and therefore has a value of

[9]The solutions to the preceding examples, which are shown in Table 15-1, were offered by an anonymous referee, who reviewed the paper for *The Engineering Economist.*

[10]This is described in the chapter on dynamic programming by Daniel Teichroew, *An Introduction to Management Science: Deterministic Models* (New York: Wiley, 1964), pp. 610–621.

[11]James L. Pappas, "The Role of Abandonment Value in Capital Asset Management," *The Engineering Economist,* Vol. 22 (Fall 1976), pp. 53–61.

[12]A. O. Converse, *Optimization* (New York: Holt, Rinehart and Winston, 1970), pp. 121–129.

[13]R. E. Bellman and S. E. Dreyfus, *Applied Dynamic Programming* (Princeton, N.J.: Princeton University Press, 1962), p. 116.

Table 15-1. Calculation of Optimal Abandonment Decision and Present Value for Three Example Machines (Dynamic Programming Approach)

Project A (Machine A)

End of Year t	Return R_t	Abandonment Value (AV_t)	Discounted Return $(DR_t) = \max\{AV_t; (.9091) DR_{t+1}\} + R_t$	Decision
7	$100	$ 419.43	$ 519.43	—
6	100	524.28	624.28	Abandon
5	100	655.36	755.36	Abandon
4	600	819.20	1419.20	Abandon
3	600	1024.00	1890.19	Keep
2	600	1280.00	2318.37	Keep
1	600	1600.00	2707.63	Keep
0	—	—	2461.51	—

Project B (Machine B)

End of Year t	Return R_t	Abandonment Value (AV_t)	Discounted Return $(DR_t) = \max\{AV_t; (.9091) DR_{t+1}\} + R_t$	Decision
7	$100	$ 419.43	$ 519.43	—
6	200	524.28	724.28	Abandon
5	300	655.36	958.44	Keep
4	400	819.20	1271.32	Keep
3	500	1024.00	1655.76	Keep
2	600	1280.00	2105.25	Keep
1	700	1600.00	2613.88	Keep
0	—	—	2376.28	Keep

Project C (Machine C)

End of Year t	Return R_t	Abandonment Value (AV_t)	Discounted Return $(DR_t) = \max\{AV_t; (.9091) DR_{t+1}\} + R_t$	Decision
7	$100	$ 478.30	$ 578.30	—
6	200	531.44	731.44	Abandon
5	300	590.49	964.95	Keep
4	400	656.10	1277.24	Keep
3	300	729.00	1461.14	Keep
2	200	810.00	1548.32	Keep
1	100	900.00	1489.40	Keep
0	—	—	1354.00	—

zero for the parameters of cost, cash flows, and so on, associated with it.

Since the methodology may not be familiar to many readers, a few words about Table 15-1 are in order. Starting with the year seven values for project A, the value $519.43 is the sum of that year's return and salvage value. Subsequent returns do not have to be considered since the machine lasts only seven years. For year six, the value $624.28 is obtained by adding the $100 return in year six to $524.28, which is the year six's abandonment value. Since the abandonment value is $524.28, which is a greater amount than the discounted future returns ($519.43 $\times$ .9091 = $472.21), the decision is to abandon. The decision to abandon holds until year three, where the $1024 abandonment value is less than $1290.19 (= $1419.20 $\times$ .9091).

SUMMARY AND CONCLUSION

It has been shown that consideration of abandonment values can change the selection from among alternatives that would otherwise be made if only final salvage values were considered.

The possibility of abandoning a capital investment at a point in time prior to the estimated useful or economic life has important implications for capital budgeting. Although we have not yet considered the effects of risk and uncertainty, the possibility of abandonment expands the options available to management and subsequently reduces the risk associated with decisions based on holding assets to the end of their lives. We must recognize that in a world clouded with great economic and political uncertainties, abandonment analysis synchronizes with the array of techniques that fall under the topic broadly termed *contingency planning*. To neglect the meaning and impact of abandonment and intermediate salvage values would be to refuse a most valuable instrument for gaining additional insight into the process of capital investment evaluation.

The origins of abandonment analysis are implicit in writings going back at least as early as Terborgh's *Dynamic Equipment Policy* published in 1949. Actually, the adverse minimum of the Terborgh-MAPI method does identify the optimal project life. The methods illustrated in this chapter will no doubt be supplemented, modified, argued, and discussed much more over the years to come. Some may prefer the R-VH algorithm, some the tabularized procedure, some the dynamic programming technique. Since the methods presented in this chapter yield equivalent results, the question of which one should be employed is largely a matter of personal preference.

16

Multiple Project Capital Budgeting

Preceding chapters considered various means for measuring the acceptability of individual capital-budgeting projects under conditions of certainty and no risk. Ranking of projects was limited to the problem of choosing which one, and only one, of mutually exclusive projects that should be selected when all the candidates meet at least the minimum criterion for adoption. The problem of capital rationing was not considered, although actually no firm has unlimited capital, and most have funds limitations, at least periodically, that preclude investment in all projects meeting their minimum criteria. Neither, to this point, were the effects of other constraints considered, whether economic, technical, or of management policy.

BUDGET AND OTHER CONSTRAINTS

In this chapter we shall continue to assume a world of certainty in order not to let considerations relating to risk and uncertainty obscure the development of basic principles and methodologies. However, we *shall* deal explicitly with the implications of those factors that constrain management to choose a subset of the total array of projects that would *individually* be acceptable in the absence of restrictions.

To simplify exposition, a single measure of investment worth will be employed here. Throughout this chapter the net present value (NPV) will provide the measure of individual project desirability. The NPV was chosen as the single measure to be used primarily because it relates more directly and unambiguously to the basic valuation model of financial management, which was introduced at the outset of this book, than other measures do. Alternatively, if preferred, the profitability index, internal rate of

Table 16-1.

Project	Cost	NPV
A	$60,000	$30,000
B	30,000	20,000
C	40,000	25,000

Table 16-2.

Budget	Accepted	Total NPV
$\geq$ $130,000	A,B,C,	$75,000
100,000	A,C	55,000
90,000	A,B	50,000
70,000	B,C	45,000
60,000	A	30,000

return, payback, or a composite function of measures could be used.[1]

Consider the three capital investment projects in Table 16-1. If the projects are not mutually exclusive *and* there are no limits on funds that may be invested, all three projects would be undertaken by the firm. However, once we begin to consider capital rationing, it becomes clear that a method is needed for selecting from among the candidate projects. For example, various budget limitations yield differing selections and total NPV for the capital budget (see Table 16-2). Here we have only three projects, and the only constraint is the one on funds available for investments—capital rationing. Other constraints are common and complicate the selection process.

GENERAL LINEAR PROGRAMMING APPROACH

Additional constraints may be of several types. For example, suppose that one project is to construct a new assembly facility a short distance from our existing plant, and another project is to build an overhead conveyer from our existing plant to the new facility. Obviously, we should not even consider building the

---

[1]We would hope, however, that the payback measure would not be adopted as the *sole* criteria by anyone who has read this far.

conveyor unless the construction project has first been accepted. Another type of constraint is that of mutual exclusivity. An example are the two projects: (1) repair the existing facility now and the mutually exclusive alternative being (2) to destroy the existing facility now and replace it with something new. Still another type of constraint is the requirement that if two projects are both accepted, a third project will also be accepted. Depending upon whether our objective is to maximize a value (such as NPV) or minimize a value (such as cost), the general *linear programming* problem may be specified as:

$$
\begin{aligned}
&\text{Maximize} \quad p_1 x_1 + p_2 x_2 + \cdots + p_n x_n && (16.1)\\
&\text{Subject to} \quad a_{11} x_1 + a_{12} x_2 + \cdots + a_{1n} x_n \leq b_1\\
&\hphantom{\text{Subject to} \quad} a_{21} x_1 + a_{22} x_2 + \cdots + a_{2n} x_n \leq b_2\\
&\hphantom{\text{Subject to} \quad} \vdots\\
&\hphantom{\text{Subject to} \quad} a_{m1} x_1 + a_{m2} x_2 + \cdots + a_{mn} x_n \leq b_m\\
&\hphantom{\text{Subject to} \quad} \text{and for all } i \; x_i \geq 0
\end{aligned}
$$

or

$$
\begin{aligned}
&\text{Minimize} \quad b_1 u_1 + b_2 u_2 + \cdots + b_m u_m\\
&\text{Subject to} \quad a_{11} u_1 + a_{21} u_2 + \cdots + a_m u_m \geq p_1\\
&\hphantom{\text{Subject to} \quad} a_{12} u_1 + a_{22} u_2 + \cdots + a_{m2} u_m \geq p_2\\
&\hphantom{\text{Subject to} \quad} \vdots\\
&\hphantom{\text{Subject to} \quad} a_{1n} u_1 + a_{m2} u_2 + \cdots + a_{mn} u_m \geq p_n\\
&\hphantom{\text{Subject to} \quad} \text{and for all } i \; u_i \geq 0
\end{aligned}
$$

which, in matrix algebra notation, becomes:

$$
\begin{aligned}
&\text{Maximize} \quad p \cdot x && \text{Minimize} \quad b'u && (16.2)\\
&\text{Subject to} \quad A \cdot x \leq b \quad or && \text{Subject to} \quad A'u \geq p'\\
&\hphantom{\text{Subject to} \quad} x_i \geq 0 \quad \text{for all } i && \hphantom{\text{Subject to} \quad} u_i \geq 0 \text{ for all } i
\end{aligned}
$$

By adding the requirement that x_i be integer-valued for all i, we have made this into a linear integer programming problem. Further restriction on the x_i, specifically the requirement that they take on only the values zero or one, produces a *zero-one integer programming* problem.

We formally specify the following two frequently encountered and important constraints.

Mutual Exclusivity

A set of n projects, from which at most one may be selected, yields the constraint:

$$\sum_{i=1}^{n} x_i \leq 1 \tag{16.3}$$

Since we already have a nonnegativity constraint on all the xs, this means that only one of the x_i may have a nonzero value, namely a value of one. However, the constraint allows for none being accepted, since zero values for all the x_i satisfy the constraint.

Contingent Projects

Project B is said to be contingent on project A if it can be accepted only if A is accepted. This yields the constraint:

$$x_b \leq x_a \tag{16.4}$$

which is equivalent to:

$$x_b - x_a \leq 0 \tag{16.5}$$

or

$$x_a - x_b \geq 0$$

This last constraint form allows project A to be accepted, yet does not force its acceptance. However, an attempt to accept B with A not accepted produces a value of -1, which is less than zero and violates the constraint. Therefore this constraint accomplishes what we want and no more.

As the number of projects increases, the difficulty of selecting a subset that is in some sense "best" increases. When constraints in addition to budget limitations apply to the selection problem, it quickly becomes unmanageable without a systematic procedure for carrying out the selection process.

We have used the method of linear programming to illustrate how a subset of projects may be selected. Linear programming facilitates the handling of constraints, but its use in capital budgeting is limited. Capital investment projects are not infinitely divisible. We either accept a project or reject it; for example, we do not choose to invest in .763 or 1.917 of a project. This means that we invest in 0, 1, 2, or some other *integer* number of projects of the particular type. In fact, it often will be the case that we have a unique project, so that the relevant values are 0 (reject the project) or 1 (accept the project). For such projects there is no option of accepting a second, a third, and so on, because they do not exist. When there are multiples of a particular project, for example, construction of one warehouse, construction of a second warehouse, and so on, then each may be considered to be a separate project, identical to the others.

Linear programming may be made appropriate to capital-budgeting applications by modifying, for example, the well-known simplex method,[2] to incorporate Gomory's cutting-plane approach.[3] The result of such modification is an *integer linear programming* algorithm. However, because most capital-budgeting proposals involve one or a few projects of a particular type, and because the problem setup and constraint system are similar, the approach that will be taken here is that of 0-1 (zero-one) integer programming. The 0-1 terminology is useful since a project is either selected (1) or it is rejected (0) and thus can be assigned a numerical value of either 0 or 1 as the algorithm proceeds.

ZERO-ONE INTEGER PROGRAMMING

Two similar approaches to 0-1 integer programming are those of Balas[4] and of Lawler and Bell.[5] Both rest on the concept of vector partial ordering as a heuristic for systematically searching out the optimal solution (if one exists) to an array of n projects in m constraints, without the necessity of evaluating each and every one of the 2^n possible combinations of projects.[6] The discussion that follows is patterned on that of Lawler and Bell. Development of new zero-one solution algorithms and refinements on existing methods continues because methods developed so far have their individual idiosyncracies and none is clearly superior to the others for all problems. The Lawler and Bell algorithm, for purposes

---

[2] For applications of the simplex method and a useful FORTRAN implementation, see Hans G. Daellenbach and Earl J. Bell, *User's Guide to Linear Programming* (Englewood Cliffs, N.J.: Prentice-Hall, 1970).

[3] R. E. Gomory, "All-Integer Programming Algorithm," in Muth and Thompson, eds., *Industrial Scheduling* (Englewood Cliffs, N.J.: Prentice-Hall, 1963), chap. 13.

[4] Egon Balas, "An Additive Algorithm for Solving the Linear Programs with Zero-One Variables," *Operations Research,* Vol. 13 (July–August 1965), pp. 517–546.

[5] E. L. Lawler, and M. D. Bell, "A Method for Solving Discrete Optimization Problems," *Operations Research,* Vol. 14 (November–December 1966), pp. 1098–1112.

[6] The number 2^n rapidly becomes very large as n increases. For example, $2^{25} = 33,554,432$, and $2^{35} = 34,359,738,368$.

of illustration, is as useful as any. However, in terms of computational efficiency, there seem to be marked differences between alternative solution algorithms. For instance, Pettway examined the efficiency of several, and found wide differences among them.[7] So has Horvath,[8] who has developed a FORTRAN program for using the algorithm that he found the most efficient and reliable.

A vector x is said to be a binary vector if each element is either 0 or 1. The vector may then be looked upon as a binary number. For two binary vectors, x and y, vector partial ordering means that $x \leq y$ if, *and only if*, $x_i \leq y_i$ for all i. For example, $x \leq y$ for $x = (0\ 0\ 1\ 0\ 1)$ and $y = (0\ 0\ 1\ 1\ 1)$. For a particular vector x, there may or may not exist a vector or vectors x' such that $x \leq x'$.

Lawler and Bell denote by $x°$ the vector following x in numerical (binary number) ordering for which $x \not\leq x°$. The vector $x°$ can be calculated by treating the vector x as a binary number. There are three steps involved. First, subtract 1 from x. Next, apply the logical "or" operation[9] to x and $x - 1$ to obtain $x° - 1$. Finally, add 1 to $x° - 1$. The alert reader will note that these three steps are equivalent to binary addition of "1" to the rightmost "1" in x.

Applying the notion of vector partial ordering to the problem of:

$$\begin{aligned} \text{Minimize} \quad & g_0(x) \\ \text{Subject to} \quad & -g_1(x) \geq 0 \\ & g_2(x) \geq 0 \end{aligned}$$

where $x = (x_1, x_2, \ldots, x_n)$ and $x_1 = 0$ or 1, Lawler and Bell have developed an optimization algorithm containing only three decision rules. The vector $\hat{x}$ denotes the best solution so far obtained.

Rule 1. If $g_0(x) \geq g_0(\hat{x})$, replace x by $x°$.

Rule 2. If x is feasible, replace x by $x°$. Feasibility means that $-g_1(x) \geq 0$ *and* $g_2(x) \geq 0$, or that $g_{i1}(x) - g_{i2}(x) < 0$.

Rule 3. If for any i, $g_{i1}(x° - 1) - g_{i2}(x) \not\geq 0$, replace x by $x°$.

[7] Richard H. Pettway, "Integer Programming in Capital Budgeting: A Note on Computational Experience," *Journal of Financial and Quantitative Analysis* (September 1973), pp. 665–672.

[8] P. A. Horvath, "A High Quality Heuristic for the Resolution of Zero-One Quadratic Programs with Interdependence Constraints," a working paper, 1978.

[9] The logical "or" means here that if *both* the jth element of x and the jth element of $x - 1$ are 0, then the jth element of $x° - 1$ is set to 0, or else it is set to 1.

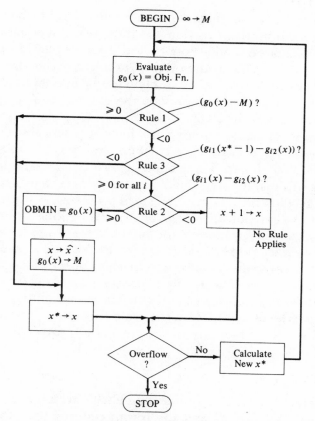

Figure 16-1. Flow Chart for Lawler and Bell 0-1 Integer Algorithm.

If no rule is applicable, replace x by $x + 1$ and continue.[10]

A flow chart for the algorithm with a sample problem and solution is shown in Figure 16-1. In using the algorithm to solve problems, it is suggested, following the experience of Lawler and Bell, that those variables that *a priori* would seem to be least significant be placed so as to occupy the rightmost positions in the solution vector. This should serve to reduce the number of iterations required, and hence the requisite solution time.

This algorithm is minimizing, and is predicated on monotonically nondecreasing functions for the objective equation and the

[10]It is strongly recommended that the reader refer to the original article by Lawler and Bell for a much more detailed explanation of the algorithm, and for examples of how problems involving nonbinary integer coefficients and quadratic objective functions may be handled.

constraints. However, maximization problems can be handled by negating the objective function and the constraint equations and objective function made monotonically nondecreasing by substituting $x' = 1 - x$ in the original problem. After the optimal solution to the minimization problem has been obtained, reverse substitution for the x' will provide the optimal array of projects for the maximum problem.

Since zero-one programming problems of practical scale do not lend themselves to manual calculation, and since computer programs are available for application of zero-one integer programming algorithms, the steps involved in solving a specific problem will not be illustrated here. Even small problems, although easily solvable on a computer, involve too many iterations for the methods to be considered suitable for manual application. The important thing, since problem setup is similar or identical with all the methods, is an understanding and mastery of the *problem setup and constraint specification.* This is vital, because an incorrectly specified constraint will often cause an incorrect problem solution. In practice, it may be useful to have the same problem set up independently by two or more persons or teams to provide a check on results.

EXAMPLE 16-1

To illustrate the type of problem amenable to solution by zero-one integer algorithms and the formulation of the constraints, consider the following problem faced by the management of Tangent Manufacturing Company. Tangent is a small firm engaged in light manufacturing. The company has recently experienced a substantial increase in demand that is expected to continue for several years. The company currently owns a dilapidated warehouse that has 7000 square feet of space, and a small building for assembling its product. The condition of the existing warehouse is such that it cannot be used much longer in its current state of disrepair.

The executive committee has decided that next year the company will require at least 3000 square feet of warehouse floor space and, in the three following years, 7000, 8000, and 11,000 square feet of space. In none of these years, however, do they want more than 20,000 square feet of warehouse space.

The company also wants to expand its assembly operations by either renovating its current plant or by constructing another building for its assembly operations. Outlays for capital improvements are to be limited to $55,000 the first year, and to $45,000, $35,000, and $20,000 in the following three years.

The treasurer of the company has developed information on the present value of returns and on the required outlays for alternatives available to the firm. This information is presented in Table 16-3.

Management will not allow both project 1 and project 2 to be undertaken. Furthermore, adoption of project 7 is dependent on the prior adoption of project 3; project 8 is dependent on the prior adoption of project 4. Lastly, management requires that there be some expansion in assembly capacity, so either project 5, or project 6, or both must be adopted. Table 16-4 contains the system of constraints. Notice that the last constraint may be stated in two alternative ways. Also, constraints 5, 6, 9, and 10 are redundant

Table 16-3.

| | | $ Thousands Required Outlays | | | |
Project	Present Value	Year 1	Year 2	Year 3	Year 4
1. Construct New Warehouse (10,000 sq. ft.) in Year 1	$50	$25	$7	$0	$0
2. Renovate Existing Warehouse (7000 sq. ft.) in Year 1	27	10	5	5	5
3. Lease Warehouse for 2 Years (3000 sq. ft.) in Year 1	15	6	6	0	0
4. Lease Second Warehouse for 2 Years (3000 sq. ft.) in Year 1	15	6	6	0	0
5. Construct New Assembly Plant in Year 1 (3000 unit capacity)	35	20	5	0	0
6. Renovate Existing Plant for Expanded Production (1500 unit increase in capacity)	25	12	3	0	0
7. Lease Warehouse for 2 Years (3000 sq. ft.) in Year 3	13	0	0	6	6
8. Lease Second Warehouse for 2 Years (3000 sq. ft.) in Year 3	13	0	0	6	6
9. Construct New Warehouse (10,000 sq. ft.) in Year 3	40	0	0	25	7
Outlay Constraints		≤ 55	≤ 45	≤ 35	≤ 20
Warehouse Space Constraints (thousands of sq. ft.)		≤ 20	≤ 20	≤ 20	≤ 20
		> 3	> 7	> 8	> 11

Table 16-4.

Constraint			x_1	x_2	x_3	x_4	x_5	x_6	x_7	x_8	x_9	b
Financial Constraints		1.	25	10	6	6	20	12	0	0	0	≤ 55
		2.	7	5	6	6	5	3	0	0	0	≤ 45
		3.	0	5	0	0	0	0	6	6	25	≤ 35
		4.	0	5	0	0	0	0	6	6	7	≤ 20
Warehouse Space		5.	10	7	3	3	0	0	0	0	0	≤ 20
Constraints	Yr. 1											
		6.	10	7	3	3	0	0	0	0	0	> 3
	Yr. 2	7.	10	7	3	3	0	0	0	0	0	≤ 20
		8.	10	7	3	3	0	0	0	0	0	> 7
	Yr. 3	9.	10	7	0	0	0	0	3	3	10	≤ 20
		10.	10	7	0	0	0	0	3	3	10	> 8
	Yr. 4	11.	10	7	0	0	0	0	3	3	10	≤ 20
		12.	10	10	0	0	0	0	3	3	10	> 11
Projects 1 and 2 Mutually Exclusive		13.	1	1	0	0	0	0	0	0	0	≤ 1
Project 7 Dependent on Prior Adoption of Project 3		14.	0	0	1	0	0	0	-1	0	0	≥ 0
Project 8 Dependent on Prior Adoption of Project 4		15.	0	0	0	1	0	0	0	-1	0	≥ 0
Assembly Facilities Must Be Expanded	or	16.	0	0	0	0	3	1.5	0	0	0	≥ 1.5
		16'	0	0	0	0	1	1	0	0	0	≥ 1

in the presence of constraints 7, 8, 11, and 12, respectively, and can be eliminated.

Since the Lawler and Bell algorithm is predicated on monotonically decreasing functions, we must substitute $x' = 1 - x$ for x in the objective function and in the constraints as follows:

Case	Original Constraint	Modified Constraint
I.	$a_i x_i \leq b$	$a_i x_i' \geq +a_i - b$
II.	$a_i x_i \geq b$	$-a_i x_i' \geq -a_i + b$

After substitution, the modified constraint coefficients are ready to be submitted for solution by the program. The modified constraint system is contained in Table 16-5. Note that all constraints are now in the "$\geq$" form.

According to the computer solution to this problem, acceptance of all projects but 1, 5, 7, and 8 yields an objective function value

Table 16-5.

Constraint	x_1	x_2	x_3	x_4	x_5	x_6	x_7	x_8	x_9	$\geq$	b
1.	25	10	6	6	20	12	0	0	0		24
2.	7	5	6	6	5	3	0	0	0		−13
3.	0	5	0	0	0	0	6	6	25		7
4.	0	5	0	0	0	0	6	6	7		4
5.	10	7	3	3	0	0	0	0	0		3
6.	−10	−7	−3	−3	0	0	0	0	0		−20
7.	10	7	0	0	0	0	3	3	10		13
8.	−10	−7	0	0	0	0	−3	−3	−10		−25
9.	1	1	0	0	0	0	0	0	0		1
10.	0	0	−1	0	0	0	1	0	0		0
11.	0	0	0	−1	0	0	0	1	0		0
12.	0	0	0	0	−1	−1	0	0	0		−1

of 122. In other words, the optimum feasible solution to this problem yields a total NPV of $122. The solution is feasible since no constraint is violated. Table 16-6 illustrates the foregoing results.

These results could not have been obtained by ordinary linear programming methods. Integer linear programming could have been used, provided that additional constraints were added to restrict the number of each project accepted to the number available.

GOAL PROGRAMMING

In Chapter 2 the goal of maximization of shareholder wealth was singled out as *the* goal of modern financial management. And use of the NPV criterion for project selection serves to move the firm toward this goal when capital markets are approximately perfect and there is certainty with respect to project parameters. These, however, are abstractions from the reality that typically prevails; capital markets are less than perfect and uncertainty does prevail. Situations are often encountered in which management has more than one objective. In fact, this is probably the norm rather than an exception. Management recognizes that the market takes into account more information than the NPV of accepted capital investment projects could provide. Accounting profits, earnings, and dividend stability and growth, market share, total assets, and so on, affect the value of shareholder wealth.

Table 16-6. Sample Problem to Illustrate Program Usage—9 Variables, 12 Constraints (Objective function maximum equals 122.0000)

Project Number	Decision Value	Decision Action
1	0.	Reject
2	1.	Accept
3	1.	Accept
4	1.	Accept
5	0.	Reject
6	1.	Accept
7	0.	Reject
8	0.	Reject
9	1.	Accept

Constraint Number	Actual Value	Constraint Constants
1	$.54000E\ 02$	≤ 55
2	$.25000E\ 02$	≤ 45
3	$.30000E\ 02$	≤ 35
4	$.12000E\ 02$	≤ 20
5	$.13000E\ 02$	≤ 20
6	$.13000E\ 02$	≤ -3
7	$.17000E\ 02$	≤ 20
8	$.17000E\ 02$	≤ -8
9	$.10000E\ 01$	≤ 1
10	$-.10000E\ 01$	≤ 0
11	$-.10000E\ 01$	≤ 0
12	$-.20000E\ 01$	≤ -1.5

All constraints are satisfied.

Management may have compatible goals, goals for which the achievement of one does not prevent achievement of the others. On the other hand, goals may be incompatible; steps to reach one goal may require moving further from other goals. Ordinary linear programming can lead to less satisfactory results than can be obtained with what is known as *goal programming.* And in cases for which there is no solution when target values are treated as constraints in ordinary linear programming, goal programming can provide feasible solutions.

Goal programming is an extension of ordinary linear programming. In fact, the basic simplex algorithm and its computerized implementations are suitable in those instances in which integer solutions are not required. The general goal programming problem may be specified as:

$$\text{Minimize } f = (M_1 y_1{}^+ + N_1 y_1{}^-) + (M_2 y_2{}^+ + N_2 y_2{}^-) + \cdots \quad (16.6)$$
$$+ (M_n y_n{}^+ + N_n y_n{}^-)$$

$$\text{Subject to} \quad a_{11}x_1 + a_{12}x_2 + \cdots + a_{1n}x_n - y_1{}^+ + y_1{}^- = b_1$$
$$a_{21}x_1 + a_{22}x_2 + \cdots + a_{2n}x_n - y_2{}^+ + y_2{}^- = b_2$$
$$\vdots$$
$$a_{m1}x_1 + a_{m2}x_2 + \cdots + a_{mn}x_n - y_m{}^+ + y_m{}^- = b_m$$
$$\text{and for all } i \; x_i, y_i{}^+, y_i{}^- \geq 0$$

In the more compact form obtained by using matrix notation for the constraint system this becomes:

$$\text{Minimize } f = \sum_{i=1}^{m} (M_i y_i{}^+ + N_i y_i{}^-) \quad (16.7)$$
$$\text{Subject to} \quad A \cdot x - y^+ + y^- = b$$

Several things should be noted about the goal programming model. First, many of the y^+ and y^- will be unimportant; in this case they will not appear in the objective function and may be ignored. Second, the normal linear programming constraints are present. These represent technological, economic, legal, or other requirements that must not be violated. Third, since the $y_i{}^+$ and $y_i{}^-$ represent underachieving or overachieving the same goal, one of them must be zero.

The M_i and N_i provide for different weights to be assigned to under- or over-achieving a goal. If either is zero it means that no importance is attached to that particular deviation from goal. The M_i and N_i also allow priority levels to be established. For instance, if goal i must be achieved before goal j can be considered, this may be specified by defining the *priority level coefficients*. The relationship:

$$M_i > > > M_j$$

denotes M_i to be a very large value in comparison with M_j, so large that goal i will be given *absolute* preference to goal j.

If M_i is to take absolute preference over M_j, but M_j is only twice as important as M_k, this can be stated as:

$$M_i > > > M_j = 2M_k$$

Thus, we can (1) define a hierarchical structure of goals, in which each level is fixed in relation to the others and (2) define *trade-off functions* between goals within a particular hierarchical stratum. When we state that goal j is twice as important as goal k, we are defining a trade-off function. Absolute priority is accomplished by making the trade-off too costly to be considered.

A goal programming problem formulation requires three main items:

1. An objective function. In this function, the weighted deviations from the target or goal levels are minimized according to specified priority rankings. This is in contrast to the ordinary linear programming formulation, in which an aggregate value objective function is maximized or, equivalently, the opportunity costs (shadow prices) are minimized.
2. The normal linear programming constraints reflecting economic, technological, legal, and other constraints.
3. The goal constraints that incorporate one or both of $y_i{}^+$ and $y_i{}^-$, the *deviational variables*.

The objective function must specify (1) the priority level of each goal, (2) the relative weight of each goal, and (3) the appropriate deviational variables. The deviational variables are viewed as penalty costs associated with under- or over-achieving a particular target, or goal.

The specification of deviational variables in the objective function determines whether a particular goal is to be reached as exactly as possible, whether either under- or overachievement is to be avoided, or whether it is desired to move as far from some target level as possible. Specification of these goals is summarized in Table 16-7.

A great advantage of goal programming is that it can handle both complementary and conflicting goals as long as a *trade-off function* is specified that links the conflicting goals. Since management must make decisions in a world of risk and imperfect capital markets, project characteristics beyond NPV may have to be factored into the decision process. Interactions between the value of the firm and capital investments may have to be recognized. For example, large capital projects may require borrowing that could affect the firm's capital structure and its cost of capital for several

Table 16-7. Goal Specification

Reach at Least a Specified Minimum Level:	Minimize y^-
Do Not Exceed a Specified Maximum Level:	Minimize y^+
Approach Specified Target as Closely as Possible:	Minimize $(y^+ + y^-)$
Achieve Specified Minimum Level, Then Move as Far Above as Possible:	Minimize $(-y^+ + y^-)$
Achieve Specified Maximum Level, Then Move as Far Below as Possible:	Minimize $(y^+ - y^-)$

years. Also, accounting profits may be important to the extent they influence the markets for the firm's shares and debt instruments. Goal programming is particularly useful, because it allows management perceptions and policies, and some interrelationships between the firm and the prospective capital investments to be handled simultaneously. It enables management to obtain insight into the implicit costs of its goals and trade-off functions if sensitivity analysis is carried out to show the effects of changing goal and trade-off parameters.

Goal programming allows the objective of maximizing shareholder wealth—enterprise value—to be approached by setting lesser goals that, if reached, contribute to the major objective. In other words, goal programming provides a means for disaggregating a strategic objective into a series of tactical goals that, taken together, move the firm toward that objective. And the tactical goals themselves may be interrelated by trade-off relationships.

Three difficulties affect using goal programming, particularly in capital budgeting. *One,* in capital-budgeting projects indivisibility is the rule rather than the exception. This means that ordinary linear programming computer codes are generally not suitable and one must resort instead to integer programming algorithms that are not as generally available. *Two,* specification of goals is often based on conjecture or "hunches" about empirical questions. Thus, different managers will generally make different subjective assessments of reality, based on individual experience, perception, and bias. This means that solutions obtained will depend on whose goals are achieved in the goal programming formulation. There is nothing necessarily wrong with this. In fact, since goals must be clearly specified, an added benefit may result when managers must articulate goals in a form amenable to programming solution. What goal programming can provide is an objective procedure for systematically and accurately reaching goals—goals that themselves may have been subjectively determined. *Three,* conflicting goals require that trade-off relationships be defined. This often requires that noncommensurables be compared, that exchange rates between "apples and oranges" be defined even though the trade-off function may involve less tangible factors than these. A further difficulty in this vein is that trade-off functions may not be linear, but may change over a range of values. This third difficulty means that one of the strengths of goal programming, its ability to deal with conflicting goals, is also potentially one of its greatest weaknesses if not approached with care.

SUMMARY AND CONCLUSION

Selection of which (if any) capital investments out of an array of candidates should be accepted requires a systematic approach. The indivisible nature of most capital investment projects means that ordinary linear programming may not produce correct results. Integer linear programming may be used, but requires constraints that reflect the number of each project available for adoption. Zero-one integer programming provides a very useful means of selection, and requires fewer explicit constraints.

Several methods of zero-one integer programming have been developed, and likely there will be further refinements and new developments. Experimentation has suggested that some methods are more generally useful than others. However, since problem specification will be identical, or at least very similar, for all existing zero-one integer programming algorithms, and probably for new developments as well, we have concentrated on specification of the problem and constraints.

Programming solution to multiple project selection is particularly useful because many constraints beyond that imposed by capital rationing may be handled easily. Great care must be exercised, however, in specifying all constraints. A seemingly minor error in one constraint may cause an entirely incorrect solution to be obtained.

IV

Capital Budgeting Under Risk—Without Diversification

17

Utility and Risk Aversion

In this chapter, the first one to consider the matter of risk, we examine the concept of utility and how a utility function may be calculated, various ways of estimating risk, and problems associated with the probability of ruin. This last topic is of some importance to the enterprise (perhaps a small firm) for which candidate capital investment projects are large in relation to its financial resources.

The concept of utility is essential if we are to develop a rationale by which a decision may be reached for a capital investment that has a range of possible outcomes, each with an associated probability. Some of the possible outcomes may be large losses, whereas others are large gains.

In a world of certainty we would be able to say whether or not a project was acceptable based on objective criteria, such as the profitability index. Once risk is introduced, however, we must take into account the decision maker's[1] attitude toward risk in order to reach an economically rational decision. Two different persons are likely to disagree about accepting risky projects if they have different attitudes toward risk. One may take risk in stride, whereas the other is considerably bothered by it.

THE CONCEPT OF UTILITY

Economists developed the concept of utility many years ago, and it is the foundation upon which microeconomic analysis rests. Utility is a reflection of personal satisfaction. Something that provides more feeling of pleasure than something else (or, equivalently, less pain) is said to have greater utility.

In this work we measure project traits in currency units—dollars. Because of this our task is much easier than it would be otherwise. We do not have to compare the respective utility of

---

[1] We shall avoid the problem of whose attitude specifically is to be taken into account by using the term "decision maker" or "management."

oranges and that of apples—only that of more dollars versus fewer.

The utility of more dollars is assumed to be greater than the utility of fewer dollars, so that the utility function we will be working with is monotonically nondecreasing in dollars, at least over the range of values we will be considering. A second dollar may have the same utility value of the first (constant marginal utility), greater value (increasing marginal utility), or lesser value (decreasing marginal utility).

When risk is introduced, we recognize that there is a trade-off between possible dollar gain (and thus utility) and risk. Projects promising the greatest return are also normally the riskiest projects. Otherwise others would have snapped them up before now.

The classic article on risk as it relates to utility is that of Tobin.[2] The following section follows his terminology.

Attitudes Toward Risk

Individual attitudes toward risk are revealed in the curvature of utility functions. Before going into the determination of an individual utility function, it will be useful to examine these attitudes toward risk. First, in Figure 17-1 we have a utility function corresponding to a *risk averse* individual, a risk averter. Here the utility function is concave from below. This means that each additional monetary gain, while contributing to increased utility, contributes less than the same amount when the individual has less to begin with. In other words, the function depicts *diminishing marginal utility.* An extra dollar offers less additional utility to given risk averse individuals when they have $100,000 than it does when they have $10,000. Diminishing marginal utility means that the loss of a dollar causes more disutility (negative utility, or loss of utility) than the gain of a dollar offers. For example, consider a person with $10,000 in cash savings, which may have taken many years to accumulate. An extra $1000 would increase utility, but not as much as a loss of $1000 would decrease it. If this person were offered a "fair bet," one with zero expected value based on equal probabilities of gaining or losing a large

[2]James Tobin, "Liquidity Preference as Behavior Towards Risk," *The Review of Economic Studies,* Vol. 67 (February 1958), pp. 65–86.

amount, the bet would be rejected. It would be rejected because the expected utility is negative, even though the expected monetary gain is zero.

For *small* amounts of monetary gain or loss, a risk averse individual may take "fair bets" or even bets where the expected monetary gain is negative. This may be explained on the basis that the negative utility of the small loss is dominated by the utility provided by the entertainment provided, or the utility provided by the hope, however remote, of a large monetary gain (as in a lottery).

Figure 17-2 corresponds to a *risk neutral,* or a risk indifferent individual. Each additional dollar, no matter at what point on the function, offers the same utility.

The utility function of a risk indifferent individual is a straight line. The slope is constant and therefore the marginal utility of monetary gain does not change over the curve. A large loss would

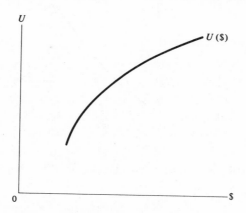

Figure 17-1. Relationship of Money Gain to Utility for a Risk Averter.

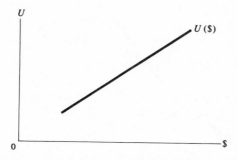

Figure 17-2. Relationship of Money Gain to Utility for a Risk Neutral Person.

reduce this person's utility by the same amount of utility as would be gained by winning an identical dollar amount. A risk indifferent individual could be expected to take fair bets, even those involving large amounts of possible gain or loss.

The final utility curve is that of a *risk lover.* This is illustrated in Figure 17-3. Tobin concluded that there are no 100 percent risk lovers. Such individuals, on reflection, would have to have a self-destructive compulsion to prefer the riskier of any two propositions. The utility curve has the property of increasing marginal utility, suggesting greed. The important thing about such utility function is that most individuals have utility functions that exhibit properties of risk aversion, risk neutrality, or risk seeking for different ranges of monetary values. This is illustrated in Figure 17-4.

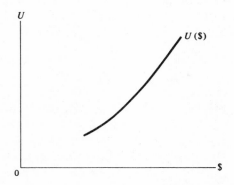

Figure 17-3. Relationship of Money Gain to Utility for a Risk Lover.

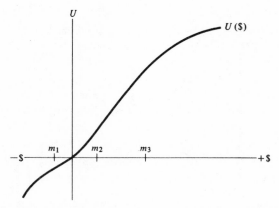

Figure 17-4. Overall Utility of Money for an Individual.

For the individual whose utility function is shown in Figure 17-4 we can observe that the person is risk averse for amounts less than m_1 and greater than m_3. This individual is essentially risk neutral for amounts between m_2 and m_3, and is a risk lover or risk seeker for values between m_1 and m_2. The next section will show you how to estimate your own utility function or that of someone else. Do not be surprised if it is similar to the one in Figure 17-4, nor should you be bothered if it is not. The benefit you derive through plotting points along your utility function is that you gain a better understanding of how you react to risk. Your attitude toward risk influences your performance as a decision maker evaluating capital investments. And it is likely that your attitude toward risk changes as the dollar magnitude of the potential gain or loss changes.

CALCULATING PERSONAL UTILITY

This section presents a method for estimating an individual's utility function. The method could also be used to try to determine a composite utility curve for a group.

The treatment here parallels the presentation contained in Teweles, Harlow, and Stone[3]. Their purpose was to illustrate how the individual commodity futures trader could obtain his or her personal utility function for the risks found in such activity. The principle is applicable here also. However, consider that you are asked to put yourself in the role of manager here, and not one who is risking your own personal funds. That this is a distinction that a sole proprietor cannot make will not be argued. Because most managers in various enterprises do have different attitudes about their own money vis-à-vis that of their employers, try to make this distinction to the extent it is possible.

After assuming the "managerial frame of mind," the next step is to determine the largest dollar gains your capital investment decisions have regularly made and the largest dollar losses that have similarly resulted. This may be impossible for many readers. Thus students and managers who have not made such decisions will have to *imagine* what the amounts would be, and try to be perfectly honest about it. This is not a test, there are no right or

[3]Richard J. Teweles, Charles V. Harlow, and Herbert L. Stone, *The Commodity Futures Game* (New York: McGraw-Hill, 1977).

Table 17-1. Computation of Decision Maker's Utilities for Various Monetary Gains

	Probability of		
(1) Best Result	(2) Worst Result	(3) Computed Utility[a]	(4) Dollar Cash Equivalent	
1.0	0.0	1.0	$2,000,000	Best Result
.9	.1	.9	1,200,000	
.8	.2	.8	950,000	
.7	.3	.7	750,000	
.6	.4	.6	550,000	
.5	.5	.5	400,000	
.4	.6	.4	−100,000	
.3	.7	.3	−300,000	
.2	.8	.2	−400,000	
.1	.9	.1	−450,000	
0.0	1.0	0.0	−500,000	Worst Result

[a]1.0 × column 1 + 0.0 × column 2. The utility of the best result is arbitrarily assigned a value of 1.0, the worst result, a value of 0.0. Other values could be used if desired.

wrong answers. It is not necessary to do any calculations in reaching your answers, although you may if you prefer. Calculation of the reader's personal utility function for monetary gains may be done as an exercise. For now we shall only illustrate the procedure.

Let us begin by developing the utility function for an entrepreneur who tells us that he (individually) has regularly made decisions that have resulted in gains of as much as $2 million and losses of as much as $500,000. We shall not concern ourselves here with whether these are gains and losses over the entire project life, or with other details of the timing of the amounts. The procedure would not be materially different anyway. Having established the largest regular gains and losses, we write them down as shown in Table 17-1, column 4. The value $2 million is associated with utility of 1.0 and the loss of $500,000 with utility 0.0. Other values could have been used for the utilities, such as +1.0 and −1.0, but the scaling is unimportant and by assigning zero utility to the worst outcome the calculations are a little easier.

Having established utilities of 1.0 for a gain of $2 million with probability 1.0, and 0.0 for loss of $500,000 with probability 1.0, we now need to find intermediate values. Suppose now we ask

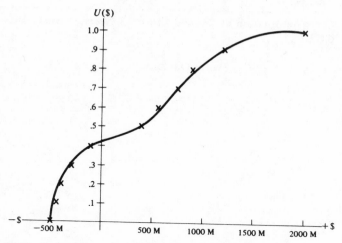

Figure 17-5. Plotted Utility Function of Entrepreneur. From Table 17-1 Dollar Cash Equivalents.

our entrepreneur to tell us if he would accept an investment offering a gain of $2 million with probability .9 and loss of $500,000 with probability .1; in other words, nine chances in ten of gaining $2 million and one chance in ten of losing $500,000. He answers "yes," certainly he would accept such investment. Now we ask if he would pay us $1 million for the opportunity to make such an investment. Yes, he would. $1.5 million? No, not this much. How about $1.2 million? Maybe. At $1.2 million he is not sure. For $50,000 more he will not take the investment, for $50,000 less he will. Thus in Table 17-1 we write in the second row, rightmost column, the amount $1,200,000.

We repeat the process for gain of $2 million with probability .8 and loss of $500,000 with probability .2. Our entrepreneur will pay up to $950,000 but no more for an investment offering these prospects. For each missing value we repeat the process until column 4 is completed. Then we can plot the results obtained, as shown in Figure 17-5, and fit an approximate curve to the points.

In constructing his or her own utility curve for monetary gains and losses, the reader can perform a self-interview or work with someone who will perform the function of interviewer. Further insight into the process is found in Teweles et al., cited earlier.

The curve obtained and plotted in the graph of Figure 17-5 is reasonably satisfactory, except that we do not have enough data points between −$100,000 and +$400,000 to be confident in the

Table 17-2. Computation of Refined Utility of Decision Maker's Monetary Gains

Best Outcome		Worst Outcome		(5) Computed Utility[a]	(6) Dollar Cash Equivalent
(1) Utility	(2) Probability	(3) Utility	(4) Probability		
.5	1.0	.4	0.0	.50	$400,000
.5	.9	.4	.1	.49	360,000
.5	.8	.4	.2	.48	350,000
.5	.7	.4	.3	.47	325,000
.5	.6	.4	.4	.46	280,000
.5	.5	.4	.5	.45	250,000
.5	.4	.4	.6	.44	180,000
.5	.3	.4	.7	.43	160,000
.5	.2	.4	.8	.42	50,000
.5	.1	.4	.9	.41	0
.5	0.0	.4	1.0	.40	−100,000

[a]Computed utility is obtained as best outcome times best outcome probability plus worst outcome times worst outcome probability.

shape of the curve in that range. We can obtain more information by continuing the interview process. Let us begin by constructing Table 17-2 with best result now $400,000 and worst result −$100,000. The associated utilities are, respectively, .5 and .4.

Values between $400,000 gain and $100,000 loss are obtained as before. The decision maker is asked if he would accept an investment project offering $400,000 gain with .9 probability and $100,000 loss with .1 probability. Yes. Would he pay $380,000? No. $370,000? No. $360,000? Maybe. Don't know. $350,000? Yes. We write $360,000 in column 6 of Table 17-2. The process is repeated until column 6 is filled and then the results are plotted. Figure 17-6 contains the graph for the section of utility curve between −$100,000 and +$400,000. The scale is enlarged from that used in Figure 17-5. After combining the information contained in Table 17-2 with that of Table 17-1, and plotting the results, we obtain Figure 17-7. The additional detail for utility between −$100,000 and +$400,000 enables a more refined approximation. The tentative judgment that our entrepreneur is a risk seeker for monetary gains seems to be vindicated by the additional information over the range of about $0 to $400,000. Because of the rather wide spread between utility values for

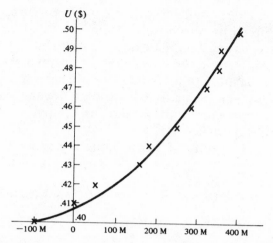

Figure 17-6. Plot of Refined Utility of Decision Maker's Monetary Gains from Table 17-2.

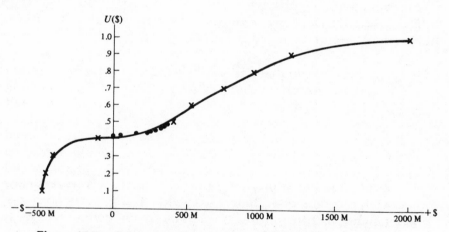

Figure 17-7. Revised Decision Maker's Utility of Monetary Gain.

dollar amounts in the ranges −$300,000 to −$100,000 and $1.2 million to $2 million, we might want to repeat the procedure for obtaining detail over these ranges, if our entrepreneur's patience has not been exhausted. We shall not do this here, however, since the procedure has been illustrated.

The plotted results obtained from our entrepreneur do not deviate very widely from the fitted curve. In fact, they are very close to it, thus indicating a high degree of consistency in evaluating alternatives over the range of values regularly experienced by the decision maker. We should not have been surprised if the points were much more scattered about the fitted curve. What happens if we now attempt to obtain utility values for dollar gains and losses beyond the range of the decision maker's regular experience? If we attempt to do this, we will most likely find that the decision maker becomes increasingly inconsistent as the monetary values become further and further removed from the domain of his experience.

To compute the utility of larger monetary gains, the formula used is:

$$U(\text{Gain}) \times Pr(\text{Gain}) + U(\text{Loss}) \times Pr(\text{Loss}) = U(\text{Cash Equivalent}) \qquad (17.1)$$

which is equivalent to:

$$U(G)p + U(L)(1 - p) = U(C) \qquad (17.2)$$

By rearranging the terms, we obtain formulas for computing the utilities of gains and losses outside the range of the decision maker's experience:

$$U(G) = \frac{U(C) - U(L)(1 - p)}{p} \qquad (17.3)$$

and

$$U(L) = \frac{U(C) - U(G)p}{1 - p} \qquad (17.4)$$

In calculating the utility of gains and losses for extended amounts for commodity traders, Teweles, Harlow, and Stone suggest computing them three times. The reason behind repeating the procedure is to find out how consistent the decision maker is in making decisions outside the range of his or her experience. The reader is referred to the excellent discussion by Teweles et al. for a detailed treatment.

The main reason for concern about the decision maker's consistency for larger gains and losses than he or she has regularly experienced is this: If judgments do become increasingly inconsistent for larger gains and losses, then the decision maker should either exercise greater caution (something the person will probably do anyway) in evaluating such prospects, or else avoid them entirely if possible. Otherwise it is likely that decisions will be made for which the perceived *a priori* and *a posteriori* utilities are different and the decision maker regrets the decision after making it, even before the results are in.

In the next chapter we shall examine capital investments with stochastically determined characteristics. The returns from such projects cannot be known ahead of time with certainty. It will be shown, however, that the probable outcomes can be estimated, and such estimates evaluated by comparison with the decision maker's utility function.

Whose Utility?

In the foregoing discussion of utility it was assumed that the utility function of interest was that of an individual decision maker. An entrepreneur with sole responsibility for capital investment decisions in one's proprietorship provides a clear example. For the entrepreneur it is reasonable to assume that the utility function for monetary gains and losses to the enterprise is none other than that of the entrepreneur.

But what is to be done for a partnership, in which each partner shares personally in the gains and the losses? Can we still obtain a meaningful estimate of the utility of monetary gain? We can certainly repeat the procedures illustrated earlier, and in so doing obtain a curve relating cash equivalents to risky alternatives. This author chooses to dodge the question of whether the curve obtained is really a utility curve or whether an aggregate utility function exists. Instead, let us refer to the curve obtained for all partners in a partnership as the enterprise's *investment curve.*

More complex conceptual considerations enter the scene when we begin to examine the situation for enterprises in which ownership is largely separated from management. For such enterprises (in which we would include public sector undertakings), the utilities of money gain and loss on investments may cover a wide spectrum just among the owners. Those who make the capital investment decisions may (and most likely do) have personal utility curves that are substantially different from their decisions *as managers* would indicate. What managers must do is to surmise the enterprise's *investment curve,* the composite of the aggregated owner's preferences. This may be linked to the personal utilities of individual high-ranking managers inasmuch as their job security, bonuses, reputations, and the like may reflect how well or poorly they serve the owners. Thus, monetary gains and losses to the enterprise may be associated with a manager's personal utility.

To conclude this section, we adopt the operational guideline that the required utility function or investment curve is that of the person or persons who, individually or collectively, are responsible for making investment decisions of the magnitude with which we are concerned. In corporations this may mean the board of directors itself for large projects. Once the individual or the group responsible for decisions on capital investments has been identified it is theoretically possible to derive an investment curve along the lines illustrated for an individual. However, in practice, there may be considerable difficulty in getting a group to cooperate fully over a long enough time to obtain enough data points to be useful.

MEASURES OF RISK

As mentioned earlier, in a risk environment variables are not known with certainty but follow probability distributions. With risk, the outcome of a capital investment decision is a particular value, but the value cannot be known *a priori*. When risk is present, we may be able to predict with statistical confidence the range of values within which the outcome may be expected to occur.

For experiments that may be repeated a number of times we can generally estimate the empirical parameters. However, capital investment projects are usually one-of-a-kind undertakings; we will not have the opportunity to repeat them. Therefore, empirical estimation of the parameters is not possible and we must instead make subjective judgments about the governing probability distributions. Past experience with *similar* projects may be helpful. For example, we may have determined that the useful or economic life of capital investments is, in general, Poisson distributed, or that it is negative-exponentially distributed.

When "risk" is discussed in relation to the overall return on an investment, the word has come to mean the potential variability of the actual return from its expected value. Other things being equal, the investment with the greatest range of possible results is said to be the riskiest. The most widely used measure for risk is the *variance*. Figure 17-8 illustrates the concept. Projects R_A and R_B are both risky; both have a range of possible outcomes associated with them. The possible outcomes are distributed around the most likely values $\overline{V}_A$ and $\overline{V}_B$, which are defined as the expected values of returns on the projects. Project R_B is the riskier project because the range of possible outcomes is much wider than for R_A. If we were able to say with 95 percent (statistical) confidence that project R_A would have a value in the range R_{AL} to R_{AH} and project R_B a value in the range R_{BL} to R_{BH}, then $R_{AH} - R_{AL} < R_{BH} - R_{BL}$. Therefore, R_B is riskier. Since the range of values, for any particular statistical level of confidence, is a function of the distribution's variance (or standard deviation), we can say that for projects whose outcomes follow the same type of probability distribution, the project having the larger variance of outcome is the riskier.

There is a problem with using the variance alone as risk measure, however, although it is easily adjusted for: The variance does not distinguish between projects of different size. A large investment undertaking may have a larger variance than a smaller undertaking simply because it is larger. This problem is readily resolved by substituting for the variance the *coefficient of variation*. The coefficient of variation is a "risk relative" measure defined as the ratio of standard deviation to expected value. The investment

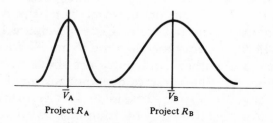

Project R_A Project R_B

Figure 17-8. Comparative Riskiness.

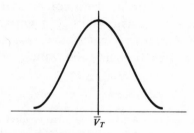

$\overline{V}_T$

Figure 17-9. Risk Perception for Results Better and Worse than Expected Value.

having coefficient of variation 2.3 is relatively riskier than the investment with coefficient 1.9.

Occasionally, we may want to analyze the pattern of net, after-tax cash flows for past projects in order to estimate the cash flows for similar projects under consideration now. Such endeavor is predicated on a stable relationship of the cash flows to one or more variables that presumably can be accurately forecast. If we fit a regression for cash flows to the independent variables, one of the pieces of information obtained is the *standard error of the estimate.* This measures the variability of actual values from predicted values of the regression equation. In other words, the standard error of estimate is analogous to the standard deviation, but is calculated from deviations of actual values around the computed regression line. Estimation of values from a regression equation with large standard error is riskier than from a regression with small standard error.

The question has been raised as to why we use variance to measure risk when people do not feel the same about bad results as they do about better-than-expected results. This asymmetry of attitude toward deviation above and below expected values can be explained in terms of diminishing marginal utility; the increase in utility from a gain above the expected value is less than the utility loss from an outcome with the same dollar amount below the expected value. Consider Figure 17-9.

In Figure 17-9 outcomes less than the Value $\overline{V}_T$ are considered undesirable. On the other hand, outcomes above $\overline{V}_T$ are considered fortuitous. Yet the variance does not distinguish between deviations above the expected value and those below it. Mao[4] and others have suggested that decision makers are sensitive to, and influenced much more by outcomes with values less than the expected value. In other words, when decision makers speak of risk, they mean the distribution of outcomes that are worse than anticipated. This is not measured by the variance but by the *semivariance.* The semivariance is calculated like the variance, but only for values less than the targeted value.[5] For an empirical

---

[4]J. C. T. Mao, "Survey of Capital Budgeting: Theory and Practice," *The Journal of Finance,* Vol. XXV, No. 2 (May 1970), pp. 349–360.

[5]It is necessary to say "targeted value" rather than "expected value" because an arbitrary value may be used in calculating the semivariance. The arbitrary value could be the expected value of the distribution of outcomes, as is the case with the variance, but it may just as well be some critical value established by management policy.

distribution this means summing the squares of the deviations equal to or below the target and dividing by the number of observations. For a theoretical distribution it means integrating or summing the density function up to the target value. Above this value deviations are ignored.[6]

A conceptual problem with the semivariance is that fortuitous outcomes are ignored in risk considerations (although they may enter determination of the target value nevertheless). We might expect that instead of ignoring better-than-expected results, they should to some extent counteract the worse-than-average outcomes that are possible. If we were to use utility weights instead of dollar NPV or other value weights, this problem might be alleviated. Although the variance may leave much to be desired as a risk measure, the semivariance offers a debatable advantage to it, and a generalized utility-based distribution may not be obtainable.

In subsequent chapters the variances and covariances of returns are used to illustrate portfolio selection approaches to investment and the capital asset pricing model. Although the semivariance could, in principle, be substituted, it is not. The reason for this would seem to be that the mathematical calculations are much less tractable for the semivariance. This serves to explain why development of the literature on investments has employed the variance or coefficient of variation almost exclusively. To the extent efforts have been made to use the semivariance, it has been by those who have attempted to modify results obtained originally with variance as the risk measure for a specific application. General substitution of the semivariance has not been successful.

J. C. T. Mao's Survey Results

Mao's survey was based on personal interviews with managers of eight medium and large companies in electronics, aerospace, pe-

---

[6]Mao [Ibid. p. 353] describes the semivariance as follows:

Consider investment return R, as a random variable with known probability distribution. If h stands for a critical value against which the actual values of R are compared, and $(R - h)^-$ stands for $(R - h)$ if $(R - h) \leq 0$ and for zero if $(R - h) > 0$, then S_h (semi-variance with h the reference point) is given by the formula:
$$S_h = E[(R - h)^-]^2$$
where E is the expectation operator.

troleum, household equipment, and office equipment firms. He found that decision makers do indeed think of risk as being related to outcomes that are worse than expected, and that the possibility of a bad outcome significantly influences the capital investment decision. To verify the relevance of semivariance he designed a test in which the decision makers were asked to choose between two (hypothetical) mutually exclusive investments, each costing the same amount and returning after one year the cost plus profit or loss. The probability distributions of the returns were as shown in Figure 17-10.

The reader may readily verify an interesting property of the distributions of projects A and B: They both have expected value of 3 and variance of 4. Since they require the same investment outlay, their coefficients of variation are identical, and therefore their risk as conventionally measured. But are they equally risky? Mao's respondents did not think so. Their answers were consistent with the semivariances (using zero in each as the critical value) that were .2 for project A and 0 for project B. Note also that there is a nonzero probability that project A could actually *lose* money.

To summarize Mao's findings, they are that:

Executives seemed more likely to choose A if their businesses accustomed them to that degree of risk, if they personally preferred risky ventures, and if they could control the loss possibility in A through diversification. When these conditions are absent, the executive is more likely to pick B because the absence of loss possibility makes it a more secure investment. . . .

The previous analysis was concerned with a choice between two individual investments. It is equally important to examine the risk concept from the portfolio viewpoint. The executives were asked to imagine the same alternatives on a larger scale, where X represented the total company investment, and questioned as to which portfolio

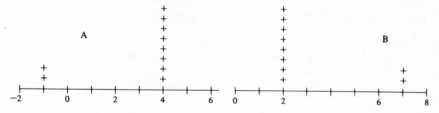

Figure 17-10.   Mao's Test Distributions.

they would select. The answer was unanimously B, and their reasons were most succinctly voiced by the statement of one executive:

"The key is survival. We take a chance on evaluating individual projects rather optimistically, but we will not take a chance on the main company. One of our obligations is to sustain this company in life and every time we put it in a minus position, it dies a little bit if not in total."

This evidence is consistent with semi-variance as a concept of risk. . . .[7]

RISK OF RUIN

If all capital investments were small relative to the enterprise's financial resources, this section would not be necessary. However, capital investments are often large in terms relative to the enterprise's size as well as absolutely. Because of this an adverse investment result may impair the firm's capital; several such adverse investments with one after another destroy the firm. Therefore, in addition to analysis of individual projects, it will be useful to examine the relationship of project size relative to firm size within the context of the risk affecting the probabilities of return on investment.

Risk of ruin, like many useful concepts, has its origins in gambling. It is applicable to other situations in which a series of losses (adverse outcomes) can result in ruin (loss of equity). Teweles, Harlow, and Stone illustrated application of the concept to an individual who undertakes the trading of commodity futures. This is a very risky venture because of the small margin requirements, usually around 10 percent of the commodity contract value. Their discussion is highly recommended to readers who wish to reinforce their understanding of the concept and its application. Here we shall focus attention on risk of ruin as it applies to capital investment decisions.

The probability of eventual ruin (loss of equity, bankruptcy) is given by:

$$R = \left(\frac{1-A}{1+A}\right)^{C} \tag{17.5}$$

[7]Ibid., p. 355.

where A is the investor's advantage in decimal form and C is the number of investment units with which the investor starts.[8] For capital investments we may define the investor's advantage as the probability of a favorable outcome minus the probability of an unfavorable outcome resulting in monetary loss.[9] If P is the probability of a favorable outcome, this means that the advantage is $P - (1 - P)$ or $2P - 1$. To obtain C we divide the required investment outlay into the enterprise's total equity.[10]

To illustrate, let us take the case of a company considering an investment of $40 million in a project that is thought to offer .60 chance of returning 100 percent and a .40 chance of loss of the entire investment. The firm has equity of $160 million. Translating these numbers into risk of ruin, we get:

$$R = \left(\frac{1 - .2}{1 + .2}\right)^4 = .198 \tag{17.6}$$

or about one chance in five of *eventual* ruin.

This one project cannot by itself ruin the firm. However, there is .40 chance that the entire investment will be lost. The significance of the risk of ruin is this: If the firm makes a habit of undertaking investments of similar risk, cost, and return, there is one chance in five that the firm will go bankrupt as a result. Thus, risk of ruin relates to the firm's ongoing policy with respect to investments. Should the firm regularly undertake investments for which the probability of eventual ruin is one-fifth? Is this an exceptional case? If so, how does it relate to the firm's investment policy?

Examination of the formula for risk of ruin yields some principles that may be useful in policy formulation. Of major significance is the fact that by reducing the size of investments that may be considered, the risk of ruin may be greatly reduced, other things being constant. In the example just considered, reducing the size of the investment to $20 million reduces risk of eventual ruin to .039 or four chances in 100. Halving the size of investment outlay in this case reduced the risk of ruin by 80 percent. Al-

---

[8]William Feller, *An Introduction to Probability Theory and Its Applications* (New York: Wiley, 1957).

[9]Ruin, in the sense we are using the word here, rests upon the probability of actual out-of-pocket money losses, if ruin would be considered to result from its loss.

[10]If desired, a lesser amount may be used.

though one chance in five would be considered an unacceptable risk of ruin by many executives, four chances in 100 might well be considered good odds.

Risk of ruin as presented above is somewhat an abstraction. Firms do not have continuing opportunity to undertake a series of identical capital investments over the time continuum. Furthermore, enterprise policy is not immutable; it tends to change to adjust to circumstances. If a firm has a run of losses on its investments, sooner or later it will review its investment policies, objectives, and procedures in order to correct its errors.

Nevertheless, risk of eventual ruin provides a gauge for measuring the enterprise's approach to risky investments. It indicates management's attitude toward the ultimate investment risk—that of financial ruin, bankruptcy. The measure itself could be incorporated into the decision process as a constraint. For instance, a policy could be adopted constraining investments to risk of ruin of X chances in 100 (based on the calculation above, which assumes the same investment outlay and success/failure probabilities to be repeated over time).

SUMMARY

Risk, in the context of this chapter, was considered without regard to portfolio effects. This chapter introduced the subject of risk and the notion that risk cannot be adequately handled without reference to utility. We saw that the utility function governs the investor's attitude toward risky investments, and that diminishing marginal utility of monetary gain leads to risk aversion.

Risk is normally measured by the variance or coefficient of variation of the outcome variable. Professor Mao's interviews with executives who make capital investment decisions yielded attitudes congruent with semivariance as a measure of risk actually representative of management thought.

Even though capital investments are typically one of a kind, the concept of risk of eventual ruin was introduced. By calculating the probability of ruin it is possible to assess more fully than otherwise managements' attitudes toward risky investments. Risk of ruin also ties in well with one of Mao's survey respondents who put survival of the enterprise ahead of any profit aspirations.

18

Single Project Analysis Under Risk

This chapter considers methods that have been used to analyze capital investment projects when one or more project characteristics are random variables. Independence of projects (with respect to the existing assets of the firm as well as one another) is assumed throughout this chapter in order to concentrate on risk considerations without the added complexities introduced by portfolio effects. Project analysis with diversification and project interdependence is covered in the next section.

Chapter 17 considered those factors that influence our attitudes toward risk and the concept of risk of ruin. In this chapter we shall examine means of measuring risk and dealing with it. Among the matters to be covered are the payback as a risk-coping method, the certainty equivalent approach, the risk-adjusted discount rate approach, and computer simulation.

THE PAYBACK METHOD

The payback has been rationalized as a method for coping with risk. If we recognize that considerable importance may be attached to capital preservation, it is understandable that some measure of solace may be gained from the knowledge that a particular investment project promises a quick return of the funds invested in it. The longer the time required to recover a project's investment cost, the more uncertain we are about the recovery. The more time that passes between the present and an anticipated event, the more unanticipated influences can spring up to render our forecast results worthless.

The shortcomings of the payback criterion are well known; an earlier chapter discusses them. As a means of dealing with risk or uncertainty, payback does favor those projects that promise early recovery of investment. It does not make much sense to use the payback as the sole criterion or even major criterion, but, used as an adjunct to the discounted cash flows, it provides an unequivocal, if crude, means of screening projects to eliminate those that take what management considers too long to recover their investment and therefore too likely to fail to help the enterprise's capital preservation efforts.

To an extent, reliance on the payback may be tantamount to an admission of forecasting impotence. That is, if we feel it is not at all possible to make usefully reliable forecasts, then we may adopt the project that exposes our capital to the ravages of time the least. After having gotten back our investment, if the project offers further returns, that is all to the good; if not, we still have our funds to invest in something else. In relatively stable economic times the payback may have little to recommend it. In times like the present, with forecasting made all the more difficult by one crises after another, coupled with chronic inflation, preservation of capital is not a trivial matter, if it ever was. It is understandable that the payback holds a prominent position among the methods of capital asset selection used by those who must make decisions with their firm's resources and be held accountable for results. And if a project selected on the basis of payback does not perform according to expectations, it will be recognized early, within the payback period, and appropriate measures taken—no need to wait years for a return only to find it is a will-o-the-wisp that vanishes as approached.

CERTAINTY EQUIVALENTS: METHOD I

In the previous chapter it was shown how a utility curve could be estimated by determining the (certain) cash amount that was considered equivalent to two different amounts, each with a probability attached. The cash was considered equivalent to the risky investment, which could have yielded either more or less than the cash equivalent. This is the essence of the certainty equivalent approach to capital investment analysis. If amount A may be received with probability $P(A)$ and amount B with probability $P(B) = 1 - P(A)$, and the events are mutually exclusive,[1] then amount C is said to be a certainty equivalent to the invest-

---

[1]Mutually exclusive may be defined in terms of the conditional probabilities as $P(A|B) = 0$ and $P(B|A) = 0$.

ment that could result in outcome A or outcome B, and $P(C) =$ 1.0. This can be generalized to investments with more than two outcome possibilities.

For investments with more than two outcome possibilities, the certainty equivalent, C, may be defined as the (certain) cash amount for which the investor is indifferent to the risky investment for which the dollar returns are described by the probability distribution $P(A)$, where A is a vector. It is important to note that C is *not* the expected value of the investment, $E[A]$. Rather, C is the certain cash amount with utility equivalent to the investment. In other words, if U denotes utility, then:

$$U(C) = E[U(A)] \tag{18.1}$$

Because it is the utility of the returns vector A that determines investor attitudes toward the investment, it is unimportant in determining certainty equivalents whether A is the vector of net present values (NPVs), internal rates of return (IRR), or other measure of investment returns. In this chapter we use the NPV as a matter of convenience only, noting that the certainty equivalent may be based on any measure for which the investor can make consistent choices.

Although utility itself is a personal matter, we may, as suggested in the previous chapter, estimate a composite investment curve for the decision makers of a particular organization.[2] To illustrate the use of certainty equivalents, in Figure 18-1 a risk-return trade-off curve for a given enterprise is illustrated. All points of the curve have equal utility, so we could refer to it as an iso-utility curve. Different organizations may be expected to have different curves. Figure 18-1 is consistent with risk aversion because expected returns must rise more rapidly than risk (however risk is measured) for the utility to remain constant.

EXAMPLE 18-1

The Ajax Company is evaluating a production mixer that costs $25,000. The mixer is expected to produce cash flows of $10,000,

---

[2]Some authors have suggested that the equal market valuation curve be employed in calculating certainty equivalents. Although such an approach may be useful in securities investment analysis, it is questionable within the context of capital investment analysis for an individual firm.

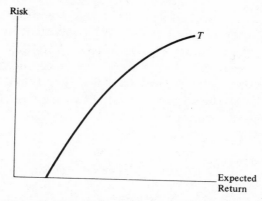

Figure 18-1. Risk-Return Trade-off Curve for the Enterprise.

$15,000, $20,000, and $20,000 at the end of each year of its four-year economic life. The firm's management feels that the cash flows become riskier the further into the future they are expected to occur. Certainty equivalents are calculated at .982, .930, .694, and .422 of the expected cash flows. Since certainty equivalents are used, we discount at the risk-free rate[3] that is assumed to be 8 percent. The NPV of the mixer is:

$$
\begin{aligned}
NPV = {} & -\$25,000 + \frac{(.982)(\$10,000)}{1.08} \\
& + \frac{(.930)(\$15,000)}{(1.08)^2} + \frac{(.694)(\$20,000)}{(1.08)^3} \\
& + \frac{(.422)(\$20,000)}{(1.08)^4} = \\
& - \$25,000 + \$9092.59 + \$11,959.88 \\
& + \$11,018.39 + \$6203.65 = \underline{\$13,274.51}
\end{aligned}
$$

which is positive; thus the project is acceptable under the NPV criterion.

CERTAINTY EQUIVALENTS: METHOD II

The previous section showed one way in which certainty equivalents may be found and used to calculate a project's certainty-equivalent NPV. Another method that is sometimes used is first

---

[3]Here risk free means free of default risk. The rate is generally taken to be the rate on U.S. government securities of the same future maturity as the cash flow's receipt.

to calculate the project's NPV at the risk-free interest rate. The next step is to convert to a "certainty" equivalent by subtracting an allowance for risk, usually taken to be $V[\text{NPV}]$, the variance of NPV. To illustrate, assume the variance of the NPVs of the cash flows in Example 18-1 is $V[\text{NPV}] = \$14,422.07$. First calculate the NPV of the expected cash flows at the risk-free rate (again assumed to be 8 percent):

$$\text{NPV} = -\$25,000 + \frac{\$10,000}{(1.08)^1} + \frac{\$15,000}{(1.08)^2} + \frac{\$20,000}{(1.08)^3} + \frac{\$20,000}{(1.08)^4} =$$
$$\$25,000 + \$9259.26 + \$12,860.08 + \$15,876.64$$
$$+ \ \$14,700.60 = \underline{\$27,696.58}$$

Next, subtract the variance to obtain the certainty equivalent:

$$
\begin{aligned}
\text{NPV} &= \$27,696.58 \\
-V(\text{NPV}) &= \underline{-14,422.07} \\
& \quad \ \$13,274.51 \quad \text{Certainty Equivalent}
\end{aligned}
$$

In this case the certainty equivalent is identical to that obtained with method I; this is because the variance was chosen to make the results identical.

In general, it is unlikely that this method will yield results close to those obtained with method I. Although this is empirically questionable, we can say *a priori* that for this method to yield the same results as method I, it is necessary that the variance measure adequately risk in the same way that calculation of certainty equivalents for the individual period cash flows does. Considering that the certainty equivalents of the individual cash flows are based on utility, and the variance is based on dollars alone, the two methods will not yield comparable results except for investment curves of a most particular type.[4]

Despite the conceptual problems imbedded in method II, it is sometimes used, and it is then necessary to have equations for

[4]The assumption that the distribution of returns is normally distributed means that the distribution is fully described by two parameters: mean and variance. This implies that utility may be maximized by appropriate selection of assets according to a function of mean and variance, provided we know the equation for the investor's utility in terms of these parameters. Certainty equivalent method II, by subtracting the unweighted variance of returns, assumes a very special type of utility function in addition to normally distributed returns.

calculating the expected value of NPV, $E[\text{NPV}]$, and the variance of NPV, $V[\text{NPV}]$. The expected value of NPV is found from:

$$E[\text{NPV}] = \sum_{t=0}^{N} \frac{E[R_t]}{(1 + i)^t} \tag{18.2}$$

where R_0 is the required investment outlay. The variance is found from the relationship:

$$V[\text{NPV}] = \sigma_0{}^2 + \frac{\sigma_1{}^2}{(1 + i)^2} + \frac{\sigma_2{}^2}{(1 + i)^4} + \cdots + \frac{\sigma_N{}^2}{(1 + i)^{2N}} \tag{18.3}$$

if the cash flows are independent of one another (uncorrelated). If the cash flows are perfectly correlated, the variance is defined by:

$$\begin{aligned} V[\text{NPV}] = {} & \sigma_0{}^2 + \frac{\sigma_1{}^2}{(1 + i)^2} + \frac{\sigma_2{}^2}{(1 + i)^4} \\ & + 2\left\{ \frac{\text{Cov } (0, 1)}{(1 + i)^1} + \frac{\text{Cov } (0, 2)}{(1 + i)^2} + \frac{\text{Cov } (1, 2)}{(1 + i)^3} \cdots \right\} \end{aligned} \tag{18.4}$$

For the general case with three cash flows that are random variables, X_0, X_1, X_2 with weights a, b, c, the variance is given by:

$$\begin{aligned} V[\text{NPV}] = {} & V[aX_0 + bX_1 + cX_2] \\ = {} & a^2 V[X_0] + b^2 V[X_1] + c^2 V[X_2] \\ & + 2ab \text{ Cov } [X_0, X_1] + 2ac \text{ Cov } [X_0, X_2] \\ & + 2bc \text{ Cov } [X_1, X_2] \end{aligned} \tag{18.5}$$

where $a = (1 + i)^{-0} = 1$, $b = (1 + i)^{-1}$, $c = (1 + i)^{-2}$. The complexity of this expression suggests why we consider the special cases of zero correlation and perfect correlation, for which the considerably simpler equations apply.

RISK-ADJUSTED DISCOUNT RATE

Another method used for dealing with risky cash flows is that of risk-adjusted discount rate. Although the certainty equivalent method essentially adjusts the cash flows or the NPV of the unadjusted flows, the risk-adjusted discount rate makes the adjustment to the discount rate for each cash flow period prior to calculating the NPV.

In an earlier chapter the NPV method was discussed in the context of a certainty environment. There it was assumed that the enterprise's cost of capital was the appropriate rate of discount,[5] and that this was constant from period to period over the asset's economic lifetime. Now, assuming a risky environment in which the cash flows differ both in futurity and in uncertainty, it is no longer reasonable to assume that a constant discount rate is appropriate. *Ceteris paribus,* the riskier an investment return occurring sometime in the future, the greater the required rate of return— discount rate—that investors will apply to it.

EXAMPLE 18-2

To illustrate the method of risk-adjusted discount rate let us again consider the Ajax Company mixer examined in Example 18-1. The cost of the mixer is $25,000 and the cash flows expected at the end of each year of its four-year economic life are $10,000, $15,000, $20,000, and $20,000.

The NPV, using the risk-adjusted discount rate approach with rates $k = 9.98$ percent, $k_2 = 11.99$ percent, $k_3 = 21.98$ percent, and $k_4 = 34.00$ percent, is:

$$
\begin{aligned}
\text{NPV} = &-\$25,000 + \frac{\$10,000}{(1.0998)^1} + \frac{\$15,000}{(1.1199)^2} \\
&+ \frac{\$20,000}{(1.2198)^3} + \frac{\$20,000}{(1.3400)^4} = \\
&-\$25,000 + \$9092.56 + \$11,960.04 \\
&+ \$11,019.56 + \$6203.68 = \underline{\$13,275.84}
\end{aligned}
$$

which is within 0.01 percent of the certainty equivalent approach result. The difference is due to rounding errors in this case because the risk-adjusted discount rates were chosen to yield identical results.

If α is the constant that relates the certainty equivalent to its

---

[5]Some would argue that the cost of common equity is the appropriate rate since the net, after-tax cash flows accrue to the common shareholders. See, for example, J. C. T. Mao, *Corporate Financial Decisions* (Palo Alto, Cal.: Pavan, 1976), p. 138.

expected value of cash flow, and i the risk-free rate, then the relationship between these variables, as Mao has shown, is:

$$\underbrace{\frac{\alpha E[R_t]}{(1 + i)^t}}_{\text{Certainty Equivalent}} = \underbrace{\frac{E[R_t]}{(1 + k_t)^t}}_{\text{Risk-Adjusted Discount Rate}} \tag{18.6}$$

which, after rearranging terms, yields:

$$k_t = \frac{1 + i}{\alpha^{1/t}} - 1 \tag{18.7}$$

An investor who is perfectly consistent in applying this method and the certainty equivalent method should obtain identical results (except for rounding errors). Whether or not decision makers are consistent in applying the methods is an empirical question, as is the question as to which method is preferred (if either is) by the same decision makers.

COMPUTER SIMULATION

Although the foregoing methods for dealing with risk can be useful, they have some shortcomings. Neither the certainty-equivalent nor the risk-adjusted discount rate provides more than a single, point estimate of the returns on a capital investment. Neither is suited to risky investments for which characteristics other than the cash flows themselves may be random variables. For example, the project life itself may be a random variable, or at least we may wish to examine the implications if it is treated as one. Circumstances may exist that compel us to treat the discount rate itself as a random variable, and we may have reason to want to treat the related cash flows according to a more complex relationship than simple correlation allows for. And we may want to examine the effect of having a particular policy that requires the asset to be abandoned if certain conditions are met; or to examine the effects of random shocks, such as a sudden increase in petroleum price.

Computer simulation (also referred to as Monte Carlo experimentation) enables us to analyze complex investments for which direct mathematical methods either do not exist or are inadequate for our purpose. Because of the speed with which modern digital computers can perform complex, repetitive calculations, we can examine the simulated outcome of hundreds of iterations that taken together provide a profile of the investment. Through analysis of the simulated profile, within the context of management's investment curve (as developed in the previous chapter), a rational decision may be reached to accept or reject the project.

The topic of computer simulation is covered thoroughly in texts devoted exclusively to the subject. For those who desire a detailed development we recommend those works be consulted. It is not our purpose here, however, to become sidetracked into a detailed discussion of computer simulation. For our purposes it should suffice to state that three basic things are required: (1) a computer; (2) a (pseudo-) random number generator; and (3) a mathematical model of the thing we wish to simulate. Since random number generators are often an integral part of the software provided by the computer manufacturer to perform a simulation analysis, we need to specify carefully our model, then translate it into suitable form for the computer. Special simulation "languages" have been developed to facilitate the task such as GPSS, SIMSCRIPT, and DYNAMO, to mention only a few.

It is often recommended that one should use the risk-free rate (i.e., the yield on 90-day U.S. Treasury Bills) in computer simulations because the simulated distribution itself reveals the project's risk. However, the NPV profile obtained with the risk-free rate is difficult to interpret and relate to the NPVs of other projects. Therefore, simulations are in practice often performed using the organization's cost of capital. The following example was analyzed with KAPSIM, a FORTRAN program written by this author to simulate single capital investment projects.

EXAMPLE 18-3

An investment costs $2.5 million and is expected to last nine years. The project life is thought to be Poisson distributed, so the variance is also nine. Management policy: is to dispose of such assets after 20 years; thus if the project should last that long, it would be abandoned then.

The variance of the net, after-tax cash flows is estimated to be ($2 million)^2 every year. The first year cash flow has expected

Table 18-1. Example 18-3 Problem Description (Part 1)

Item	Distribution	Parm 1	Parm 2	Parm 3
Initial Outlay	Constant	$2.50000E + 06$	0	−0.
Period 1 Return	Normal	$-5.00000E + 06$		−0.
Period 2 Return	Normal	$5.00000E + 06$	$2.00000E + 06$	−0.
Period 3 Return	Normal	$6.00000E + 06$	$2.00000E + 06$	−0.
Period 4 Return	Normal	$7.00000E + 06$	$2.00000E + 06$	−0.
Period 5 Return	Normal	$8.00000E + 06$	$2.00000E + 06$	−0.
Period 6 Return	Normal	$9.00000E + 06$	$2.00000E + 06$	−0.
Period 7 Return	Normal	$1.00000E + 07$	$2.00000E + 06$	−0.
Period 8 Return	Normal	$1.10000E + 07$	$2.00000E + 06$	−0.
Period 9 Return	Normal	$1.20000E + 07$	$2.00000E + 06$	−0.
Period 10 Return	Normal	0	$2.00000E + 06$	−0.
Period 11 Return	Normal	0	$2.00000E + 06$	−0.
Period 12 Return	Normal	0	$2.00000E + 06$	−0.
Period 13 Return	Normal	0	$2.00000E + 06$	−0.
Period 14 Return	Normal	0	$2.00000E + 06$	−0.
Period 15 Return	Normal	0	$2.00000E + 06$	−0.
Period 16 Return	Normal	0	$2.00000E + 06$	−0.
Period 17 Return	Normal	0	$2.00000E + 06$	−0.
Period 18 Return	Normal	0	$2.00000E + 06$	−0.
Period 19 Return	Normal	0	$2.00000E + 06$	−0.

Note: Number of iterations equals 1000; expected value of project life is 9 with variance of 9 distribution Poisson; maximum project life is 20.

value of −$5 million; that of the second year is +$5 million; from the third through the ninth year the returns are expected to grow by $1 million each year, starting at $6 million at the end of the third year. The returns in years ten on are zero because the project is expected to last only nine years.

A further complication is that, because of structural changes in the economy, the discount rate is expected to increase over time. The expected rate is 10.1 percent for the first year's cash flow, with variance (1.01 percent).[2] Each subsequent year is expected to be .1 percent higher, and the standard deviation to be 10 percent of expected value.

Finally, because the project may be abandoned prior to the end of its economic lifetime, it is necessary to estimate salvage at the end of each year. Salvage value is assumed to decline from the original investment by 20 percent each year. However, the rate of decline is estimated to be Poisson distributed.

This information is summarized in Tables 18-1 and 18-2,

Table 18-2. Example 18-3 Problem Description (Continued)

Item	Distribution	Parm 1	Parm 2	Parm 3
Period 1 Capital Cost	Normal	.101000	.010100	000000
Period 2 Capital Cost	Normal	.102000	.010200	000000
Period 3 Capital Cost	Normal	.103000	.010300	000000
Period 4 Capital Cost	Normal	.104000	.010400	000000
Period 5 Capital Cost	Normal	.105000	.010500	000000
Period 6 Capital Cost	Normal	.106000	.010600	000000
Period 7 Capital Cost	Normal	.107000	.010700	000000
Period 8 Capital Cost	Normal	.108000	.010800	000000
Period 9 Capital Cost	Normal	.109000	.010900	000000
Period 10 Capital Cost	Normal	.110000	.011000	000000
Period 11 Capital Cost	Normal	.111000	.011100	000000
Period 12 Capital Cost	Normal	.112000	.011200	000000
Period 13 Capital Cost	Normal	.113000	.011300	000000
Period 14 Capital Cost	Normal	.114000	.011400	000000
Period 15 Capital Cost	Normal	.115000	.011500	000000
Period 16 Capital Cost	Normal	.116000	.011600	000000
Period 17 Capital Cost	Normal	.117000	.011700	000000
Period 18 Capital Cost	Normal	.118000	.011800	000000
Period 19 Capital Cost	Normal	.119000	.011900	000000
Period 20 Capital Cost	Normal	.120000	.012000	000000

Note: Salvage assumed to decline from initial outlay by percent per period of: Poison $2.00000E - 01\ 2.00000E - 01\ 0$.

which contain the provided information as part of the computer-printed simulation results. One thousand iterations are employed to obtain a sufficient sample of results, which are measured by the net present value. If too few iterations are used, we cannot draw conclusions from the scattered results, whereas too many iterations would waste some computer time. With the cost of computation being one of the few things that has actually come down in cost (thanks to improved technology), it may be best to err somewhat on the side of too many iterations rather than too few.

Tables 18-1 and 18-2 provide a record of the information we put into the computer simulation of the investment project. All simulations should be accompanied by such "echo" output for two reasons: (1) in order to find mistakes that may have been made in specification of the problems or preparation of the data and (2) in order to provide an organized record to accompany the simulated results. Simulation output for one case may look about the same as output for another. If the input data are attached to the computer printout, one can avoid the frustration and difficulty of trying to reconstruct the assumptions that produced a particular computer run's output.

Table 18-3 contains the frequency interval bounds, and frequency distribution of the simulated NPV results for Example 18-3. The frequency count for an interval is determined by the number of results that are greater than or equal to the lower bound and less than the upper bound.

The decision to accept or reject the investment may be made from the frequency distribution, which is clearly not normally distributed. The first 12 intervals contain only negative NPV results, whereas the thirteenth contains mixed results. If we may assume the distribution within the thirteenth interval to be uniformly spread over that interval, then 87 of the 105 observations

Table 18-3. Example 18-3 NPV Frequency Distribution

Interval	Lower Bound	Upper Bound	Frequency $\geq$ = L.B., < U.B.
1	$-.308229000E + 08$	$-.284193447E + 08$	1.
2	$-.284193447E + 08$	$-.260157834E + 08$	4.
3	$-.260157834E + 08$	$-.236122341E + 08$	2.
4	$-.236122341E + 08$	$-.212086788E + 08$	6.
5	$-.212086788E + 08$	$-.188051235E + 08$	7.
6	$-.188051235E + 08$	$-.164015682E + 08$	20.
7	$-.164015682E + 08$	$-.139980129E + 08$	27.
8	$-.139980129E + 08$	$-.115944576E + 08$	20.
9	$-.115344576E + 08$	$-.919090230E + 07$	35.
10	$-.919090230E + 07$	$-.678734700E + 07$	43.
11	$-.678734700E + 07$	$-.438379170E + 07$	37.
12	$-.438379170E + 07$	$-.198023640E + 07$	74.
13	$-.198023640E + 07$	$.423318900E + 06$	105.
14	$.423318900E + 06$	$.282687420E + 07$	156.
15	$.282887420E + 07$	$.523042950E + 07$	176.
16	$.523042350E + 07$	$.763398480E + 07$	140.
17	$.763398480E + 07$	$.100375401E + 08$	101.
18	$.100375401E + 08$	$.124410354E + 08$	35.
19	$.124410954E + 08$	$.148446507E + 08$	9.
20	$.148446507E + 08$	$.172482060E + 08$	1.

Note: Avg. NPV = $.631806495E + 07$; std. dev. of NPV = $.762450328E + 07$; Low = $-.308229000E + 08$; high = $.172482060E + 08$; range = $.480711060E + 08$

(simulated results) in that interval are negative, and 18 are positive. Therefore, there is probability of 863/1000, or .363 that this project, if accepted, would yield a negative NPV, or better than one chance in three.

Let us say that management will not accept any project for which the odds of losing more than the initial investment (in this case $2.5 million) exceed $\frac{1}{10}$. If we may again assume results to be uniformly distributed over the twelfth interval, 22 of them in the interval are $-$2.5 million or less. This means the odds are $\frac{224}{1000}$, or .224 of losing more than the initial investment (a little less if we were to consider the negative cash flow at the end of the first year as part of the initial investment). This project would be unacceptable to management under this policy, even though the mean NPV is $6,318,065.

A virtually limitless number of management policies may be applied to the frequency distribution. The particular ones applied will depend on the enterprise's investment curve, which reflects the risk attitudes of its management. For instance, management might consider the project acceptable if the odds for an NPV exceeding $10 million were greater than the odds of NPV loss of more than $-$20 million (on the assumption that management could and would intervene to prevent such loss actually occurring; that is, changing the odds during the game). Alternatives are limited only by one's imagination.

This example was not designed to represent necessarily a realistic project, but rather to illustrate how simulation analysis can facilitate the decision-making process for a complex project. No doubt the example may be made more realistic simply by changing some of the parameters. As it stands, this hypothetical project would probably not be very attractive to a risk-averse, capital preservation-oriented management because there are fairly large odds that losses with NPV as large as minus $30 million could result from adopting this project. Unless management believed that the odds could be significantly improved by intervention as time went on, this project would be passed over by most executives if we may extrapolate from Mao's survey findings cited in the previous chapter.

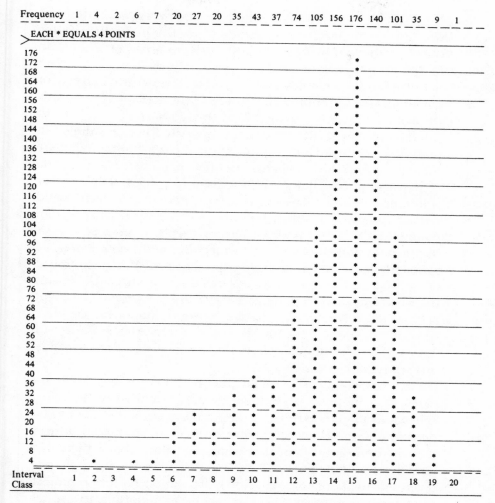

Figure 18-2. Frequency Histogram for Example 18-3 Computer Simulation.

LEWELLEN-LONG CRITICISM

Wilbur G. Lewellen and Michael S. Long, in a very articulate and incisive comparison of simulation results with those obtained from point estimates, draw some thought-provoking conclusions. These should be considered carefully, because of implications that may limit the classes of investment projects that are suitable for Monte Carlo treatment. In summary, the Lewellen-Long conclusions are:

1. If the IRR is used in simulating a capital investment, the relationship between the cash flows and the IRR will cause the mean IRR to be *lower* than the IRR obtained by discounting the means of the respective cash flow distributions. This holds even if the cash flow distributions are symmetrical about their respective means.

2. By using NPV rather than IRR as the measure of a simulated investment, the bias is eliminated because the present value of a future cash flow is a *linear* function of the size of the cash flow, whereas the IRR is not.

3. The discount rate that should be used in present value simulations is the *risk-free* rate (free of default risk, such as federal government securities).

4. Even with the NPV, problems arise when the project lifetime is uncertain. Variable project life will, *ceteris paribus*, cause the mean of the resulting simulated NPV distribution to be slightly less than the NPV obtained by discounting the cash flows over the mean project life.

5. Further disparities can be caused by nonsymmetrical cash flow distributions. This problem is likely to arise when a "most likely," or modal value, is used in place of the mean in specifying the simulation.

6. Since, because of the cost and time required to properly perform a computer simulation, it will be limited to the larger and more important projects, most will be evaluated by other methods, using a point estimate of each cash flow. It is therefore important that expected values rather than modal values be employed.

7. If any elements of the cash flows depend on multiplicative combinations of stochastic variables, it is important to use the cash flows directly in obtaining the expected values. Only if the multiplicative components are completely independent can $E[p \cdot q]$ be treated as equal to $E[p] \cdot E[q]$; otherwise $E[p \cdot q] = E[p] \cdot E[q] + \sigma_{pq}$, where σ_{pq} is the covariance between p and q.

For example, if p represents price and q quantity sold, we should recognize that in all but perfectly elastic or inelastic demand, price and quantity are correlated. Since price and quantity demanded are inversely related, indirect estimation obtained by multiplying $E[p]$ by $E[q]$ will overstate $E[p \cdot q]$. Because the correlation coefficient ρ is defined by:

$$\rho = \frac{\sigma_{pq}}{\sqrt{\sigma_p \sigma_q}}$$

the relationships are:

$$E[p \cdot q] > E[p] \cdot E[q \text{ if } \rho > 0$$
$$E[p \cdot q] < E[p] \cdot E[q] \text{ if } \rho < 0$$

8. All the above problems are either artificial or avoidable, with the exception of the variable project life. Therefore, as an index of investment project worth the point-estimate analysis should serve quite well. While not incorrect in determining a proposal's expected return, simulation is unnecessary.

9. The claim that a major benefit from simulation analysis is that it provides an improved appreciation of the risk the enterprise would assume may be misleading and even dangerous. It is not the riskiness of the individual investment (its "own" risk) which is important, but rather its risk within the context of a collection of assets to which its returns may be related. To quote Lewellen and Long:[6]

> . . . the one irrelevant feature of an asset's prospective returns is its "own risk"—the outcome uncertainties unique to the asset itself. These can, and will, be diversified away by individual investors and by institutions in their securities portfolios, leaving only the degree of correlation between the asset's returns and those of the so-called "market portfolio" as relevant to value, since this connection and its implied risks *cannot* be extinguished via diversification.

And they conclude by stating that:[7]

> Simulated profiles of capital expenditure proposal outcomes are, perforce, chiefly descriptions of "own risk." They do not reveal a project's addition to . . . *total* risk. Having simulated, therefore, the analyst still cannot legitimately compare and choose among alternatives, because nowhere in the information he obtains is the single most important criterion of investment worth—portfolio

[6]Wilbur G. Lewellen and Michael S. Long, "Simulation versus Single-Value Estimates in Capital Expenditure Analysis," *Decision Sciences,* Vol. 3 (1972), pp. 19–33.
[7]Ibid., p. 31.

impact—addressed. However imperfectly, the cost-of-capital/single-point-expected value cash flow forecast approach does get at the issue of portfolio context. For that reason, . . . not only is such an approach less onerous in execution but, paradoxically, also has a higher potential for relevant risk recognition. . . .

Although portfolio effects and diversification are topics that are addressed in the following chapters, the Lewellen-Long criticism of simulation should cause us to reflect carefully on the facts and circumstances surrounding an investment proposal before boldly embarking on a simulation analysis. And there are circumstances under which a simulation analysis may be preferable to using the simplified analysis based on point estimates. These might include the following:

1. The proposal is under consideration by an entrepreneur who will be putting all his or her assets into the project if it is accepted.
2. It is not possible to obtain meaningful estimates of the proposal's correlation with the existing assets of the firm, or the project being considered is estimated to be uncorrelated with them.
3. The project is large in relation to the firm and has a potential for large loss that could threaten the firm's survival.
4. Possible pressure on executives to avoid investments in risky assets that would reduce or leave unchanged the organization's overall risk. If such pressures have been responsible for portfolio managers generally avoiding "second-tier" securities, gold, and commodity futures then we may surmise that similar peer group or external pressures may act to constrain decisions to "own risk" more than portfolio considerations.
5. The cash flows may be governed by complex relationships which preclude analysis of point estimates. (The Lewellen-Long article did not deal with the problem of *simultaneous* variability in cash flows and project life or contingent cash flows, for example.) Although some fairly complex proposals may be analyzed with point estimates, considerable time may pass before the analyst develops the insight and inspiration that may be necessary. Contingent

asset relationships of the type treated in a subsequent chapter, for example, may be impossible to deal with on a point-estimate basis.

6. The matter of risk in the public sector may require a different approach even if the CAPM were unequivocally and universally accepted for firms in the private sector.
7. The CAPM is built upon a set of restrictive assumptions that may not always apply, particularly for smaller firms.

For additional insight into the pros and cons of simulation for the analysis of risky investments, the article by Stewart Myers is recommended. The matter remains controversial and is likely to remain so, at least until some additional questions about the CAPM can be unequivocally answered.

With the conclusion of this chapter we shall leave the domain of risk without diversification and enter that of capital investment in which project proposals are not independent and portfolio aspects must be considered.

19

Multiple Project Selection Under Risk: Computer Simulation and Other Approaches

The previous chapter considered capital investment selection under risk when projects and existing assets are not independent, and projects therefore cannot be evaluated in isolation. It was assumed that all relevant asset characteristics were contained in the expected returns and their variances and covariances. This enabled selecting efficient combinations of investments: those with maximum expected return for a given level of risk or, alternatively, those with minimum risk for a given level of return.

In this chapter we examine further the problem of capital investment selection. Now, however, we shall not require that returns be normally distributed or that the relationship between project returns and existing assets be constant intertemporally. Additionally, we shall consider the problem introduced by sequential, event-contingent decisions over time. Specifically, matters relating to parameters other than the mean and the variance-covariance are considered, as are simultaneous variability of project characteristics.

DECISION TREES

The decision tree approach is a widely employed analytical device for addressing investment projects that contain sequential, event-contingent decisions. Such projects, in other words, have certain chance-determined outcomes during their lifetimes and these outcomes may influence decisions made during the project lifetime and interact with them.

Magee's[1] paper is now a classic on the topic of decision trees, and was responsible for focusing attention on this important technique, which others subsequently built upon. Two years prior to Magee, Massé[2] criticized the view of investments as single-period decisions isolated from future events. He noted that future alternatives are conditioned by present choices. Because of this, investment evaluation cannot be reduced to a single decision, but must be viewed as a sequence of decisions over time.

Decision trees are similar in some respects to Markov chains. They differ in that they include imbedded decisions and not solely probabilistic event nodes. A Markov chain has the properties that (1) the possible outcome set is finite; (2) the probability of any outcome depends only on the immediately preceding outcome,[3] and (3) the outcome probabilities are constant over time. Markov chains are suitable to many types of problems and the mathematics for their analysis is well developed.

Figure 19-1 contains the structure of a generalized decision tree. The letter D denotes a decision and C a chance event. At $D_{1,1}$ the decision maker is faced with two choices.[4] The first subscript number refers to the point in time at which the decision or chance event occurs. Time need not be cardinal. In other words, the actual time between $t = n$ and $t = n + 1$ may be either more or less than the time from $t = n - 1$ to $t = n$. The second subscript refers to the position of the event or decision from top to bottom in the diagram.

The problem illustrated in Figure 19-1 requires two decisions, one at the outset and one after a chance event has occurred. Although they are shown as possibly different events, $C_{2,1}$ and $C_{2,2}$ may refer to the same chance event. The effect on the enterprise, however, is different because of the decision made at $D_{1,1}$. Similarly, $D_{3,1}$, $D_{3,2}$, and so on, could refer to the same decision, tempered by different precedents. Alternatively, the decisions could be quite different.

To find the optimal decisions we examine the payoff utilities

---

[1]John F. Magee, "Decision Trees for Decision Making," *Harvard Business Review,* Vol. 42 (July–August 1964), pp. 126–138.

[2]Pierre Massé, *Optimal Investment Decisions* (Englewood Cliffs, N.J.: Prentice-Hall, 1962).

[3]This is true only for first-order Markov chains. If the chain is second-order, then an outcome may depend on the two prior events, and so on.

[4]In general, there will be n decision choices, where n is a finite number. Our space limitations dictates that for illustrative purposes only two choices be used.

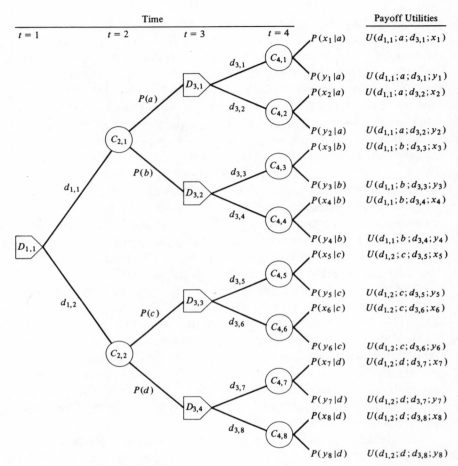

Time

Payoff Utilities

Figure 19-1.   General Structure of a Decision Tree.

associated with a particular sequence of decisions and chance events. The final result, denoted by x and y, is determined by conditional probability of preceding events. The optimal decisions are found by backward induction, by looking at the most distant result, and tracing back from there to the very beginning at $D_{1,1}$. As an alternative to working with the utilities of each separate terminal point, it is possible to find the final monetary outcomes and their associated probabilities for each branch from the final decision nodes, then take the certainty equivalents of the uncertain outcomes.

An example will help clarify how decision trees may be applied to capital investment decisions.

EXAMPLE 19-1

The Northern Lites Manufacturing Company has successfully produced and marketed home heating units for 30 years. The units are designed to use either gas or fuel oil, but not both. The engineers of the firm have now designed a new unit that can use interchangeably either gas, fuel oil, coal, or cord wood; and, with an optional adapter, peanut shells and other waste products. The marketing staff is enthusiastic about the sales prospects for the new multiple-fuel furnace that they are calling the "Hades Hearth Home Heater."

The new heating unit could be produced in the existing factory, but changeover would take at least a year, perhaps longer, and an inventory of replacement parts would have to be built up to meet the owners' needs for repairs of the current models. A new plant could be constructed and in operation within a year, and a nearby facility could be leased and readied for production in the same time span.

Because of shortages and rising fuel oil and natural gas prices, sales are expected to be brisk. However, there is a 30 percent chance of a depression in a year that would be so severe that even though they would like to buy the new furnace, consumers will not have the money. If there is such a depression, the firm will lose $1000 with a new plant facility, $300 with the leased facility, and $100 if it delays its production by deciding to use the existing plant. A deep depression would mean a halt to production until the economy improved.

The new plant will allow maximum production. Delaying production to use the existing plant will allow competitors to take the lead and sales will therefore be less. In two years the engineering staff feels it will have a much improved design that may be required to keep sales up. There is some risk, however, that the improved design may not be as popular as anticipated because of competitive developments and the possibility of meaningful government incentives for fuel conservation.

Figure 19-2 illustrates the tree diagram for this problem. If a new plant is built, if there is no depression, and the design is changed and successfully received in the market, the present value to the firm is $900. If not well received, the present value is $360. The remaining results are similarly interpreted. Note that the expected values shown in Figure 19-2 are expected monetary

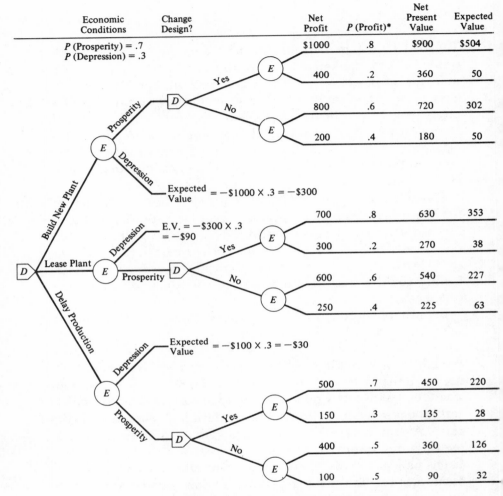

Economic Conditions	Change Design?	Net Profit	P (Profit)*	Net Present Value	Expected Value
P (Prosperity) = .7		$1000	.8	$900	$504
P (Depression) = .3		400	.2	360	50
		800	.6	720	302
		200	.4	180	50
		700	.8	630	353
		300	.2	270	38
		600	.6	540	227
		250	.4	225	63
		500	.7	450	220
		150	.3	135	28
		400	.5	360	126
		100	.5	90	32

Expected Value $= -\$1000 \times .3 = -\$300$

E.V. $= -\$300 \times .3 = -\$90$

Expected Value $= -\$100 \times .3 = -\$30$

* Conditional probability of profit given prosperity

Figure 19-2.   Decision Tree for Example 19-1.

values, not expected utilities or certainty equivalents. Table 19-1 shows the calculations corresponding to the expected monetary values of Figure 19-2 for finding the expected utilities.

Implicit in the approach illustrated in Table 19-1 is the assumption that the expected utility is the proper measure by which the optimum course may be determined. However, we should note that this approach does not take into account the distributions of the outcome utilities but only their expected values. It may well

Table 19-1. Calculation of Payoff Utilities for
Example 19-1

BUILD NEW PLANT

$$.7 \times .8 \times U(\ \ \$900) = .56 \times \ \ .80 = \ \ .448$$
$$.7 \times .2 \times U(\ \ \ \ 360) = .14 \times \ \ .50 = \ \ .070$$
$$.7 \times .6 \times U(\ \ \ \ 720) = .42 \times \ \ .73 = \ \ .307$$
$$.7 \times .4 \times U(\ \ \ \ 180) = .28 \times \ \ .30 = \ \ .084$$
$$.3 \times 1.0 \times U(-1000) = .30 \times -.90 = \underline{-.270}$$
$$.639$$

LEASE PLANT

$$.7 \times .8 \times U(\ \ \$630) = .56 \times \ \ .68 = \ \ .381$$
$$.7 \times .2 \times U(\ \ \ \ 270) = .14 \times \ \ .40 = \ \ .056$$
$$.7 \times .6 \times U(\ \ \ \ 540) = .42 \times \ \ .63 = \ \ .265$$
$$.7 \times .4 \times U(\ \ \ \ 225) = .28 \times \ \ .35 = \ \ .098$$
$$.3 \times 1.0 \times U(\ -300) = .30 \times -.32 = \underline{-.096}$$
$$.703$$

DELAY PRODUCTION

$$.7 \times .7 \times U(\ \ \$450) = .49 \times \ \ .57 = \ \ .279$$
$$.7 \times .3 \times U(\ \ \ \ 135) = .21 \times \ \ .24 = \ \ .048$$
$$.7 \times .5 \times U(\ \ \ \ 360) = .35 \times \ \ .49 = \ \ .172$$
$$.7 \times .5 \times U(\ \ \ \ \ 90) = .35 \times \ \ .18 = \ \ .063$$
$$.3 \times 1.0 \times U(\ -100) = .30 \times -.14 = \underline{-.042}$$
$$.520$$

be the case that certainty equivalents corresponding to the monetary outcomes would yield a different ranking. Therefore, it may be important in practice to have management make its choices on the basis of the certainty equivalents that it assigns to the various choices.

As matters stand, the expected utilities in Table 19-1 favor leasing a plant for production of the multiple fuel furnace to either building a new plant or delaying and using the existing plant. Note that the spread of both dollar and utility outcomes is greater for leasing than for delaying until the current plant can be used, thereby making the lease arrangement more risky. By the same reasoning the building of a new plant would be both more risky and offer a lower expected utility than leasing; it is thus dominated by the leasing alternative.

An alternative to either choosing the path offering the highest expected utility or choosing the path offering the highest certainty equivalent is found in the next chapter. There the capital asset pricing model (CAPM) is discussed and it is shown that the optimal choice may be made by employing the risk/return trade-offs prevailing in the market.

OTHER RISK CONSIDERATIONS

In addition to the types of risk considerations introduced by sequential, event-contingent decisions and intervening stochastic events, there are other situations in which portfolio approaches may not be employed to best advantage. Since portfolio approaches developed by Markowitz and Sharpe assume stable (or at least not suddenly changing) relationships between projects and the enterprise's existing assets, problems in which the relationships may change in response to some future chance event or events do not lend themselves to portfolio selection approaches as they currently exist.

Recognizing the shortcomings pointed out in Chapter 18 for computer simulation of single investment proposals, computer simulation may offer the most suitable approach to the analysis of certain multiple-project problems. One such application arises in the case of problems involving assets with useful lives not only governed by their own unique characteristics but by the life of the aggregate as well. An example will serve to illustrate this type of problem. The following example is rather lengthy because of the nature of the problem and because it illustrates a way of analyzing multiple-project problems by means of computer simulation.

A Comprehensive Simulation Example

EXAMPLE 19-2[5]

In oilfield primary recovery operations equipment deterioration and breakdown create problems over the lifetime of the field. These problems are of a reinvestment/abandonment type for which little theoretical guidance is to be found in texts on capital budgeting, engineering economy, or operations research. For instance: (1) when should a particular well be rehabilitated rather than abandoned? and (2)

[5]Extracted from a paper by Anthony F. Herbst and Sayeed Hasan, "A Simulation Analysis of Primary Recovery Oilfield Reinvestment Management," Proceedings of the American Institute for Decision Sciences, Eighth Annual Meeting, San Francisco, Cal., November 10–12, 1976, pp. 94–96. By permission of the Institute.

when should the entire field be abandoned for continuing primary recovery and secondary recovery operations be undertaken?

Discussion is limited in scope to consideration of decision algorithms for determining:

1. Whether a particular well should be repaired after equipment breakdown, or should instead be shut down.
2. Under what circumstances the entire field should be abandoned as a primary recovery field.

We consider the related problem of replacement of primary recovery with secondary recovery (by means of gas or water injection) before primary recovery in itself becomes economically nonviable, though our emphasis is on the above two problems.

For purposes of classification we distinguish between two cases of primary recovery field abandonment. First, the weak case, in which the primary recovery operation is in itself still economically viable, but inferior to and economically dominated by a change in technology to secondary recovery methods. Second, the strong case, in which primary recovery is in itself economically non-viable regardless of secondary recovery operations.

A difficult but interesting feature of the problems considered in this section is interdependence between the maximum expected economic life of each well and that of the entire field. Abandonment of any given well or set of wells may result in the entire field becoming unprofitable with primary recovery. Adoption of the decision to abandon the entire field, of course, implies abandonment of all individual wells whether or not they are operating profitably at the time.

The decision to abandon the entire field for primary recovery (strong case) is relatively straightforward. The field should be shut down when variable cash revenue contribution of the field no longer exceeds variable cash cost. In other words, in the strong case the field should be abandoned when net cash contribution to fixed cost coverage and profits becomes zero.

The weak case decision to abandon primary recovery and replace it with secondary recovery technology should be made when the expected net present value (NPV) of investment in secondary recovery by gas or water injection exceeds the expected net present value of the remaining cash flows with primary recovery. We will not at this time get into the problem of determining the NPV of secondary recovery investment, as this appears to be amenable to the more standard capital budgeting-engineering economy analysis. We do, however, address the problem of estimating the NPV of the remaining cash flows with primary recovery.

The more difficult question than field abandonment for primary recovery is that of when any particular stripper well should be abandoned. At least two circumstances must be considered. First, under what circumstances should a given well be abandoned prior to equipment failure? Second, given an equipment failure of a particular type, when should repair or replacement be undertaken, and when should the well be shut down and abandoned for primary recovery?

Characteristics of the Problem

The Oilfield

Type of Recovery Process: We adopt the terminology that primary oil and gas recovery is that undertaken by use of pumps and secondary recovery is that undertaken by use of water or gas injection.[6] When pumps are employed to raise the oil to the surface, the wells are called stripper wells. Each stripper well will have its own pump, and therefore there will be a close correspondence between the number of wells and the amount of capital equipment required.

Secondary recovery with water or gas injection is accomplished by drilling wells around the field through which water or gas may be injected to drive out the oil ahead of it. Unlike primary recovery, the number and location of injection wells are not strictly determined by the number of oil wells and there is no one-to-one correspondence between injection sites and oil wells as there is between pumps and stripper wells.

Breakdown of Stripper Wells: Stripper wells are subject to a variety of breakdowns which require the decision be made to either repair the problem or else to abandon that well during primary recovery. Major types of breakdown include pump overhaul, need for condensate wash, broken pump rod, and rupture in production tubing. In addition to the normal costs of repair, a condensate wash involves several days lost production while it is being carried out. Periodic, scheduled maintenance may entail pump overhaul and condensate wash to prevent unscheduled breakdowns which may be more costly than planned preventive maintenance.

The probabilities associated over time with different major breakdowns may not be independent. For instance, a broken pump rod

---

[6]Another classification scheme would relegate to primary recovery the removal of oil by employing the natural subsurface pressure that may exist, secondary recovery to the use of pumps, and tertiary recovery to the water or gas injection methods. Under this alternative classification a field may be taken from primary to tertiary recovery by omitting the use of pumps entirely.

may do other damage to other well equipment, and a condensate wash may sometimes be required after another type of breakdown.

It is not our purpose to become involved in the technical details of the recovery process, but rather to deal with the methodology for determining the optimal reinvestment policy for the oil company. Therefore, after this brief introduction to the technology of recovery, we will move on to the financial, economic, and methodological consideration of our work.

Decision Required

There are three basic decisions which must be made continually over the life of the field:

1. Given a well breakdown, whether to repair or shut down (abandon) the well.
2. Whether to replace all well equipment with new equipment of the same type or switch to another extraction technology and equipment.
3. When to shut down the entire field to recovery with the currently employed technology.

The second decision, we propose, is amenable to more-or-less familiar approaches, such as the MAPI (Machinery and Allied Products Institute) method of replacement analysis.

Financial Measures of Investment Return

Modern financial management heavily favors the use of discounted cash flow (DCF) methods of evaluation, and favors the net present value approach over internal rate of return. While the DCF approach has been favored, the payback criterion has simultaneously been attacked for use in investment decisions. However, DCF methods require certain information and conditions which may not exist.

In the problem we consider, the economic lives of the oilfield and the individual wells are interdependent. We do not know the useful life of any individual well, as that life depends on the nature and frequency of required repairs and especially on the life of the entire field. Similarly, the life of the field depends on the lives of the individual wells. When all wells are shut down, obviously the field life, with the particular technology, has ended. When it has been decided to close the field all wells in it will be closed. It is not known *a priori* how long the useful lives of either the individual wells or the field will be.

Additionally, the DCF methods require that the cash flows for each period be known or estimated. However, in the case of well breakdown the cash flows will be affected by the pattern and types of breakdown experienced, which are stochastically determined. The DCF measures are known to be affected by the pattern of cash flows as well as their magnitudes, and although the expected value of the cash flows could be determined the pattern cannot be on an *a priori* basis.

The absence of *a priori* knowledge of useful lives and cash flow patterns, coupled with the interdependence of the well and field characteristics, negates the usefulness of ordinary DCF methods to the problem we consider.

Methodology

We are interested in determining a policy for repairs that will yield the maximum expected net discounted return, and in the absence of *a priori* information, use the approach of simulation experience with the field under alternative policies. The results of the simulation then provide information that can be converted to the DCF present value measure. In other words, we approach the problem by simulating the cash flows of the field under different repair policies. The cash flows are carried forward with compounding at the firm's cost of capital as *future values*. At abandonment or shutdown of the field the future values are then converted to present value equivalents. Choice of the proper policy will yield results that would be obtainable in ordinary circumstances by a direct DCF approach.

Since the payback criterion is already familiar and widely used in industry we adopt it as our policy variable for repair decisions.[7] If the net cash flow over n periods, where n is the payback policy, is insufficient to recover the repair cost, we shut down the well. If the cash flow is greater than the repair cost, we repair and continue to operate the well. After a representative number of simulations, employing different seed values for the generation of (pseudo-) random numbers, we propose adopting that payback policy that promises the highest net present value for the field.

We also consider as a secondary policy the shut down of the field when the rate of change in the cash revenues becomes less than the rate of change in cash costs (including repair costs) over m periods.

---

[7]We do, however, adjust the payback criterion to include the time-value of funds.

This provides a means for determining when to shut down the entire field before all wells are shut down and before net cash flow becomes negative. We define shutdown under this secondary policy variable as "weak case" shutdown. Treatment of this policy is left to a subsequent paper, as results so far are inconclusive.

The field will be shut down to primary recovery whenever the net cash flow becomes negative. That is, when cash revenues are inadequate to cover cash costs, we will shut down the field. We define shutdown of the field under this condition as "strong case" shutdown.

The Model

I. Net Per Period Cash Revenue for the Field in Period j

$$
\begin{aligned}
NR = {} & \text{Total Cash Revenue} - \text{Variable Cash Cost} \\
& - \text{Fixed Cash Cost}^8 \\
= {} & \text{PCFOIL} \sum_{i=1}^{\text{NWELLS}} \text{OILBBL}_{i,j} \\
& + \text{PCFGAS} \sum_{i=1}^{\text{NWELLS}} \text{GASMCF}_{i,j} \\
& - (\text{ROALTO} + \text{PROCO}) \sum_{i=1}^{\text{NWELL}} \text{OILBBI}_{i,j} \\
& - (\text{ROALTG} + \text{PROCG}) \sum_{i=1}^{\text{NWELLS}} \text{GASMCF}_{i,j} \\
& - \text{CASHFC} \\
& - \sum_{i=1}^{\text{NWELLS}} \text{REPRC}_{i,j}
\end{aligned}
$$

Strong Case Decision: If $NR \leq 0$, shut down the entire field where i denotes individual wells:

PCFOIL and PCFGAS	the price per barrel of oil and MCF of gas, respectively
OILBBL and GASMCF	the barrels of oil output and MCF gas output for the ith well, jth period
ROALTO and ROALTG	the royalty charges levied per barrel of oil and MCF of gas

---

[8]Cash costs that would not exist were the field to be closed.

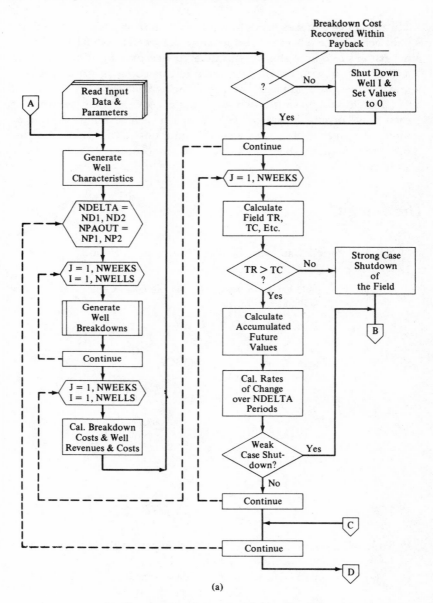

(a)

Figure 19-3(a). Flow Chart of the Model

PROCO and PROCG   processing costs per barrel of oil
                    and MCF of gas
CASHFC   fixed cash expense per period while
                    the field is open

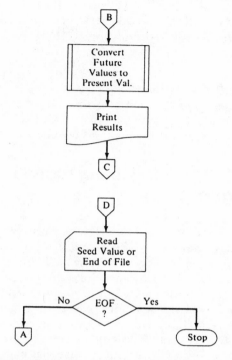

Figure 19-3(b). Continuation of Flow Chart of Model.

REPRC   repair cost for the ith well and jth period if a breakdown occurs and is repaired

II. For a Given Well i:

Let $b_{k,j}$ be the number of breakdowns of type k in period j. Then the reinvestment cost for repairing the breakdown is $C_{i,j}$. Let P_k be the cost of repair for type k breakdown. Then $C_{i,j} = \displaystyle\sum_{k=1}^{\text{NTYPE}} b_{k,j} P_k$ where NTYPE is the total number of major breakdown types. We require recovery of the cost with a payback period of n time periods.

$$\text{If } C_{i,j} < \sum_{l=j+1}^{j+n} \text{OILBBL}_{i,l}(\text{PCFOIL}-\text{ROALTO}-\text{PROCO})/(1 + \text{RATE})^{l-j}$$

$$+ \sum_{l=j+1}^{j+n} \text{GASMCF}_{i,l}(\text{PCFGAS}-\text{ROALTG}-\text{PROCG})/(1 + \text{RATE})^{l-j}$$

where RATE is the firm's per period cost of capital, we repair the well and continue operation. Otherwise we shut down the well.

III. Breakdowns Are Assumed To:
    1. Be Poisson distributed over time, and be
    2. Independent of previous breakdown history of the well.
Figures 19-3(a) and (b) contain a flow chart of the model.[9]

Estimating NPV of Remaining Cash Flows with Primary Recovery

Empirical experience with our model, which provides for application of production deterioration gradients and changes in price, processing costs, and so on, suggests how remaining field NPV may be estimated to any arbitrary point in time. Since the accumulated net future value is calculated for each time period prior to shutdown, the net present value of cash flows over any time span prior to shutdown may be calculated. Thus, if shutdown should occur in period 85, and we are interested in the NPV of flows between period 40 and 85, we can determine this easily with customary financial mathematics.

Analysis of the remaining value of net cash revenues over time will provide information useful in the decision of whether, and when, to switch to other technology for recovery.

Empirical Results

The model was tested with empirical data provided to one of the authors, for a stripper field in Western Canada. Results of a typical simulation run are summarized in Table 19-2. The condition of this field is such that the maximum NPV is obtained with a payback policy of four periods (one week equals one period in this run). Such a short payback meant that after a major breakdown of any type the well involved would be abandoned. This may be attributed to the low oil and gas yields of the wells in a declining old field in relation to the cost of repairs.

Breakdown probabilities were assumed to be independent of prior breakdown history of any well. This assumption may not be warranted, but the authors had no information to the contrary which

---

[9]The paper published in the *Proceedings* did not contain this flow chart because of space limitations.

Table 19-2. Simulation Results

NPAOUT	All Wells Shut Down in Period No.	NPV by Waiting Until All Wells are Shut Down	Strong Case Shut Down in Period No.	NPV with Strong Case Shut Down
4	15	$10,888.50	15	$10,888.50
5	18	−1,756.10	9	8,312.77
6	18	−1,756.10	9	8,312.77
7	18	−2,592.75	5	5,263.98
8	18	−2,592.75	5	5,263.98
9	18	−2,592.75	5	5,263.98
10	26	−18,184.30	5	5,263.98
11	26	−18,184.30	5	5,263.98
12	26	−18,184.30	5	5,263.98
13	26	−18,184.30	5	5,263.98

would enable them to modify the breakdown probabilities for further breakdowns once a well had been repaired. Because of this, breakdowns of the same type could occur within the payback period. This meant that a repair could be carried out only to have the same type of breakdown result in abandonment before the cost of the first repair had been recovered.

CONCLUSION

The aim of this chapter was to illustrate two approaches to capital investment decision-making under risk that may provide useful results when portfolio approaches are not applicable. The first approach shown was that of decision tree analysis. The second was computer simulation of multiple project problems.

In decision tree analysis the problem is characterized by a sequential decision-event-decision event . . . chain over time. Because decisions are contingent on chance events, it may not be possible to specify *a priori* which decision beyond the first will be made. The goal of decision tree analysis is to identify the mixed decision-event sequence that promises the maximum expected utility. By doing so it is possible to identify the superior initial decision because it is determined by all that follows it. Decisions reached through application of the decision tree approach will often be different from those reached through viewing the problem as an isolated, period decision because this latter approach ignores future choices.

Computer simulation of multiple project capital investment problems can be used to reach optimal decisions where the interrelationships between projects are complex. It is difficult to generalize about the type of problem warranting the time and expense of computer simulation. However, problems involving many projects, where their relationships cannot be described by variance-covariance or correlation, will be candidates for simulation, especially if the particular problem represents large resource value to the enterprise. Computer simulation should be viewed not as a replacement for other methods of analysis in normal situations, but rather as a last line of defense when other approaches fail, and a powerful last defense it is. In normal circumstances the extra time, effort, and expense of computer simulation are difficult to rationalize when other, less arcane methods yield correct decisions.

V

Capital Budgeting Under Risk—With Diversification

20

Multiple Project Selection Under Risk: Portfolio Approaches

In Chapter 16 we discussed the matter of investment selection from an array of individually acceptable independent[1] projects. The selection was constrained by conditions of capital rationing (that is, budget constraints), management policy, and technical considerations. Chapter 18 considered the analysis of individual risky projects within a framework of complete project independence. This chapter takes up the problem of capital investment analysis when we recognize stochastic dependence between project proposals themselves and between project proposals and the existing assets of the firm.

INTRODUCTION

When investment projects are statistically related to one another and/or to the currently existing assets of the firm, it is no longer appropriate to treat them as independent for purposes of analysis. When there is dependence, it is not unusual to find that project A is preferable to project B, even though A has a greater variance and coefficient of variation in its returns than B has, and it is therefore more risky as an individual project. The reason that results such as these are obtained is that the covariance of project A makes it more favorable for selection than does the covariance of project B. Up to this point we have assumed that all project

---

[1]We assume here that contingent project relationships do not necessarily reflect stochastic dependence. We shall reserve the term *stochastic dependence* for dependence between the cash flows of projects and not dependencies seen only at the initial accept-reject decision. Contingent relationships are often asymmetrical ("accept B only if A has been accepted," not vice versa), whereas stochastic dependence is generally taken to be symmetrical.

covariances to other projects and to the enterprise's existing assets to be zero—complete independence. We shall now drop the assumption of zero covariances. And because the covariance terms are no longer zero, we shall have to take them explicitly into account; we can no longer base decisions solely on a project's individual characteristics of risk and return as isolated factors.

To illustrate the effect of nonindependence between a project proposal and the firm's existing assets, let us examine the following example.

EXAMPLE 20-1

The owners of Al's Appliance Store are considering a major expansion that, if undertaken, would mean construction of an attached laundromat and an equipment rental shop. The existing building would become one part of a triplex. The owners have investigated the natures of the businesses and have determined the data in Table 20-1 to be representative.

Although the return on investment is higher, the riskiness of the proposed expansion is greater in both absolute and relative terms than those of the firm's existing assets. If we were to treat the proposal as independent of the appliance store, it might well

Table 20-1.   Data for Example 20-1

	Appliance Store (Existing Assets)	Proposed Attached Laundromat and Equipment Rental Shop
Market Value/Cost	$1,000,000	$500,000
Expected Annual Return	$E[R_0] = \$100,000$	$E[R_1] = \$75,000$
Variance of Annual Return	$\sigma_0^2 = (\$10,000)^2$	$\sigma_1^2 = (\$15,000)^2$
Coefficient of Variation	$\sigma_0/E[R_0] = .100$	$\sigma_1/E[R_1] = .200$
Covariance		$\sigma_{0,1}^2 = -(\$12,000)^2$

Table 20-2.   Combined Asset Characteristics, Example 20-1

Value of Combined Assets	$1,500,000
Expected Combined Annual Returns	$E[R_c] = \$175,000$
Variance of Combined Returns	$\sigma_c^2 = (\$2,333)^2$
Coefficient of Variation	$\sigma_c/E[R_c] = .013$

be more risky than the business to which the owners are accustomed. Analysis of the proposed expansion in isolation could be carried out with techniques suggested in previous chapters. *Here we are not interested in the proposal as an entire investment, but as an addition to an investment portfolio that already contains assets.* Therefore, it is not appropriate to analyze the expansion without reference to the combined, or portfolio, effect its acceptance would bring about.

Individually, the proposal is relatively twice as risky as the appliance store. However, the covariance between them is negative because it is expected that the proposal will respond differently to changing status of the economy than will the existing business; in fact, it will respond oppositely. Table 20-2 contains data for the firm assuming the expansion has been undertaken.

Note that the relative riskiness as measured by the coefficient of variation has dropped far below what it was for the appliance store alone, which was less risky than the proposal. The variance of returns on the combined assets[2] is less than on the proposal alone or on the existing assets, so the absolute risk is also less than it would be without the expansion. This highlights the benefits to be gained by diversification among assets whose returns tend to move in opposite directions; the correlation in this case between the appliance store and the laundromat-cum-rental shop is $\rho = -.96$, an almost perfect negative correlation. So perfect is the relationship that 92 percent of the variation in the return on one may be statistically explained by variation in the other $(\rho^2 = .92)$.

Generalizations

In this example the high negative correlation yielded dramatic results. But what if the correlation is not so strongly negative? And, what if, instead of negative correlation, there is positive correlation? Table 20-3 contains comparative figures.

---

[2]The variance of a linear combination of variables, with weights a, b, c, and so on, is given by:

$$\text{Var} (ax + by + cz + \cdots) =$$
$$a^2 \text{ Var} (x) + b^2 \text{ Var} (y) + c^2 \text{ Var} (z) + \cdots$$
$$+ 2ab \text{ Cov} (x,y) + 2ac \text{ Cov} (x,z) + \cdots$$
$$+ 2bc \text{ Cov} (y,z) + \cdots$$

Table 20-3. Risk-Return Relationships For Different
Return Correlations Between Existing Firm and Proposed
Expansion

ρ	Cov (0,1)	σ_c^2	$\sigma_c/E[R_c]$
−1.0	−($12,247)^2	(1,667)^2	.010
− .5	−($ 8,660)^2	(6,009)^2	.034
.0	0	(8,333)^2	.048
+ .5	($ 8,660)^2	(10,138)^2	.058
+1.0	($12,247)^2	(11,667)^2	.067

Comparison of the coefficients of variation for the combined assets with the existing assets reveals the following:

1. As the correlation coefficient changes from perfect negative correlation to perfect positive, the riskiness of the combined enterprise increases.
2. For all correlations acceptance of the proposal will reduce relative risk for the combined enterprise to less than that of the original assets (in this example the appliance store).
3. The case of $\rho = 0.0$ corresponds to covariance of zero and independence of the proposal and the existing firm.
4. Even with perfect positive correlation ($\rho = +1.0$) the relative risk for the combined assets is less than that of the proposed expansion alone.

Project Independence

An important implication of point 3 above is: Even if the proposed business expansion were independent of the existing assets of the firm, proper analysis cannot be done without reference to them. The coefficient of variation for the proposal is .200. Yet, the coefficient for the firm after undertaking the investment is .013, when $\rho = .0$. Thus, although the expansion itself is per se more risky than the existing firm, its acceptance would actually decrease the risk of the firm. The point is that if the expansion is viewed separately, it may be rejected because it is relatively twice as risky as the firm as it exists without the investment. If, on the other hand, the accept/reject decision is based on the *riskiness of the firm before the investment to the firm after the investment* it is apparent that relative risk has decreased measurably. The relevant comparison is not in the terms of the "own" risk of the proposal vis-à-vis the firm without the proposal, but rather the firm without the proposal to the firm with the proposal. This is not to say that techniques of analysis such as computer simulation of individual projects should be rejected, but that their use must be appropriately modified to take the foregoing into account *even when the project is statistically independent* of the existing assets of the enterprise.

Project Indivisibility

In portfolio selection applied to securities it is generally assumed that investments in any particular asset holding are infinitely divisible and, excluding short sales, the percentage of the portfolio committed to a particular asset is between 0 and 100 percent. In the case of securities such an assumption is reasonable because discontinuities are relatively small, amounting to no more than the smallest investment unit. With capital investments, however, the assumption of infinitely divisible investment units is seldom justified. In the foregoing example the question was not what proportion of the proposal should be invested in *between* 0 percent and 100 percent inclusive, but whether the investment would be rejected (0 percent) or accepted (100 percent). Only the extremes were considered because the project was considered indivisible.

Project indivisibilities are much more troublesome in capital budgeting than in (stock and bond) portfolio selection. Therefore, techniques that were originally developed for securities investment portfolio selection must be judiciously modified if correct decisions are to be made. Choices of percentage other than 0 percent (rejection) and 100 percent (acceptance) are generally not possible.

MULTIPLE PROJECT SELECTION

The formal model for optimal choice of risky assets for an investment portfolio is generally credited to Markowitz[3]. What is optimal for one investor will generally be different from what is

[3]Harry M. Markowitz, *Portfolio Selection: Efficient Diversification of Investments* (New York: Wiley, 1962).

optimal for another because of different attitudes toward risk-return relationships. The basic nature of risk and return within the framework of utility was covered in a preceding chapter for individual asset choice decisions. Here we shall extend the treatment of risk-return trade-off to the multiple asset case.

Let us denote the overall return from a portfolio, R, as a weighted average of the returns, R_i, with weights x_i as:

$$R = x_1 R_1 + x_2 R_2 + \cdots + x_n R_n \qquad (20.1)$$

Each x_i is the proportion of the total invested in asset i, and R_i is the expected return from that asset. The R_i are random variables and therefore R, the portfolio return, is also a random variable. If we denote the expected values of the R_i by μ_i, the variance of asset i by σ_{ii}, and the covariance of asset i and asset j as σ_{ij}, we obtain for the portfolio:

$$
\begin{aligned}
E[R] &= X_1\mu_1 + x_2\mu_2 + \cdots + x_n\mu_n \qquad &(20.2)\\
\text{Var}\,[R] &= x_1{}^2\sigma_{11} + x_2{}^2\sigma_{22} + \cdots + x_n{}^2\sigma_{nn} \qquad &(20.3)\\
&\quad + 2x_1 x_2 \sigma_{12} + 2x_1 x_3 \sigma_{13} + \cdots + 2x_1 x_n \sigma_{1n}\\
&\quad + 2x_2 x_3 \sigma_{23} + \cdots + 2x_2 x_n \sigma_{2n}, \cdots =\\
&\quad \sum_{i=1}^{n} \sum_{j=1}^{n} x_i x_j \sigma_{ij}
\end{aligned}
$$

Although the optimum portfolio for any particular individual depends on one's utility function, we can nevertheless narrow considerably the field of choice. We can, for instance, eliminate from consideration those portfolios that will not be selected by anyone regardless of utility function. For this we use the concept of *efficient portfolio.*

An *efficient portfolio* is one for which a higher return cannot be had without incurring higher risk or, equivalently, a portfolio for which one cannot reduce risk without a corresponding loss of return. A portfolio is inefficient if, by changing the proportions of the assets held, we can obtain a higher return with no more risk, or reduce risk without sacrificing some return. Alternatively, an efficient portfolio is the minimum variance portfolio among all portfolios with the same expected return and it is the portfolio with the maximum expected return among all with the same variance of return.

Markowitz suggested two steps in finding an investor's optimum portfolio. First, identify the set of efficient portfolios. Sec-

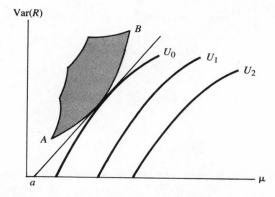

Figure 20-1. Selection of Optimal Portfolio of Risky Assets.

ond, select that efficient portfolio that best matches the investor's risk-return attitude, which maximizes the investor's utility. The exact portfolio will vary from investor to investor, but all of them must be efficient portfolios. Figure 20-1 summarizes the procedure.

Line AB is the efficient set of portfolios. The U_i represents a particular investor's set of utility curves relating risk to returns.[4] The shaded area represents the set of all other portfolios that could be formed from the same assets (assuming infinite divisibility). The point of tangency between the highest indifference curve (U_0) and the efficient set corresponds to the optimum portfolio for this particular investor.

Markowitz considered several different possible forms of utility functions. It was the quadratic form that Farrar[5] employed to determine the coefficients of risk aversion for mutual funds; also the quadratic form of utility function has been widely employed by many other writers, in no small measure due to its consistency with diminishing marginal utility and other generally accepted aspects of preference theory. The discontinuous utility function used by Roy[6] provides a linkage to the notion that survival of the enterprise is an important investment objective.

[4]For investments of the size represented by this portfolio. Chapter 17 suggests that the utility function is related to the size of the required investment and to risk of ruin as well.

[5]Donald E. Farrar, *The Investment Decision Under Uncertainty* (Englewood Cliffs, N.J.: Prentice-Hall, 1962).

[6]A. D. Roy, "Safety First and the Holding of Assets," *Econometrica*, Vol. 20 (July 1952), pp. 431–449.

Roy's utility function was of the form:

$$U(R) = 1 \text{ for } R \geq a$$
$$= 0 \text{ for } R < a$$

which yields expected utility of:

$$E[U] = 1 \cdot Pr(R \geq a) + 0 \cdot Pr(R < a)$$
$$= 1 - Pr(R < a)$$

for which maximization of utility means minimization of the probability that the portfolio return will fall below amount a. Graphically, this corresponds to selecting the portfolio determined by the tangency of a line through point a with the efficient set in Figure 20-1. Roy's model is consistent with the responses elicited in Mao's survey of executives cited in Chapter 17. Together, they suggest that where the survival of the enterprise itself is a factor in the decision process, the decision maker may apply a utility function distinct from that which is used in circumstances in which the enterprise's survival is not in question.

Finding the Efficient Set

Since the first step in the procedure for finding the optimal investment portfolio is to find the set of efficient portfolios, we require a systematic method. This may be formulated as a mathematical programming problem:

$$\text{Maximize} \quad \Phi = E[R] - \lambda \cdot \text{Var}[R] \tag{20.4}$$
$$= x\mu - \lambda\sigma^2 \text{ (in vector notation)}$$

$$\text{Subject to} \quad \sum_i x_i = 1.0 \tag{20.5}$$

$$\text{or} \quad x_i \geq 0$$
$$x_i = 0 \text{ or } 1$$

Lambda (λ) is the coefficient of risk aversion, which we restrict to the range 0 to $+\infty$. To obtain the efficient set we must solve the above problem in Eq. (20.4) for different values of λ until we have enough points on the efficient set to define its curve. It is important to recognize that this model assumes that the investor's risk attitude is adequately reflected by the variance-covariance matrix of all candidate investments. The final constraint restricts us to either accepting a project entirely ($x = 1$) or else rejecting it entirely. This constraint is not necessary (under most circumstances) when we are considering securities portfolio investments. However, most capital investment projects are indivisible; we either accept or reject a particular project; we do not have the option of owning a partial share of it. In securities portfolio selection this constraint is replaced by the restriction that the x_i (the weights) sum to a value of 1.0 (100 percent).

If we measure the return on an investment by its net present value (NPV), then we can formulate the problem of finding a point in the efficient set as:

Maximize $\quad F = p_1x_1 + p_2x_2 + \cdots p_nx_n$ $\qquad\qquad$ (20.6)
$\qquad\qquad - \lambda(x_1{}^2\sigma_{11} + x_1x_2\sigma_{12} + \cdots x_1x_{n1}\sigma_n$
$\qquad\qquad\quad x_2x_1\sigma_{21} + x_2{}^2\sigma_{22} + \cdots x_2x_n\sigma_{2n}$
$\qquad\qquad\quad \vdots$
$\qquad\qquad\quad x_nx_1\sigma_{n1} + x_nx_2\sigma_{n2} + \cdots + x_n{}^2\sigma_{nn})$

Subject to $\quad a_{11}x_1 + a_{12}x_2 + \cdots a_{1n}x_n \leq b_1$ $\qquad\qquad$ (20.7)
$\qquad\qquad a_{21}x_1 + a_{22}x_2 + \cdots a_{2n}x_n \leq b_2$
$\qquad\qquad \vdots$
$\qquad\qquad a_{m1}x_1 + a_{m2}x_2 + \cdots a_{mn}x_n \leq b_m$
$\qquad\qquad$ and for all i $x_i = 0$ or $x_1 = 1$

which, in matrix algebra notation, becomes:

$$\text{Maximize} \quad F = p \cdot x - \lambda(x \cdot V \cdot x) \qquad (20.8)$$
$$\text{Subject to} \quad A \cdot x \leq b \qquad\qquad\qquad (20.9)$$
$$x_i = 0 \text{ or } 1$$

where V is the variance-covariance matrix of returns.

A point regarding problem setup that seems to be often ignored in attempts to transfer this model to capital investments is that existing assets of the enterprise need to be included in the formulation. In other words, we cannot look solely at the proposals under consideration and their interrelationships, but need to include their relationships to the firm as it is now. In the programming framework above this may be done by treating the existing enterprise as a "project" with zero required investment outlay. If divestiture is not to be considered, it will also be necessary to include a constraint that requires the existing enterprise to be included in the optimal solution. It may be interesting, however, to solve again without the constraint to determine if divestiture would be worthwhile.

This formulation may be compared to that of the problem of project selection under certainty in Chapter 16. In fact, certainty means that the elements of the variance-covariance matrix are all zero, and the problem specified in Eqs. (20.6) through (20.9) reduces to Eqs. (16.1) and (16.2).

Mao[7] shows how the Lawler and Bell zero-one integer programming algorithm (discussed in Chapter 16) may be modified to solve problems with objective functions of the form in Eqs. (20.6) and (20.8). However, Baum, Carlson, and Jucker have shown that the Markowitz approach, when applied to problems with indivisible projects, "may result in either (1) a solution set that does not contain all solutions of interest to the decision maker or (2) a requirement that the (implicit) utility function describing the decision maker's preferences be a linear function of the mean and variance of return."[8] By examining all feasible solutions to a problem solved by Mao [pp. 295–296] Baum, Carlson, and Jucker show that no matter what the value of λ, the coefficient of risk aversion, an efficient point is missed by the Markowitz approach. Furthermore, the Markowitz approach to Mao's problem, although missing an efficient point, produced a dominated point[9] "More generally . . . any efficient point which is not located at a corner point of the upper boundary of the convex hull of the complete set of efficient points would also be missed."[10]

The Baum, Carlson, and Jucker article is significant in that it demonstrates that incorrect results may be obtained when the Markowitz approach is employed with problems involving selection of indivisible assets. This is a serious problem and we may expect that researchers will provide suitable modifications to the solution algorithm or offer alternative methods of solution, such as finding only dominant points, for example.

Although problems involving complex constraints of the type illustrated in Chapter 16 do not lend themselves to solution by complete enumerations, an enterprise which has only a few fairly

---

[7]C. T. Mao, *Quantitative Analysis of Financial Decisions* (New York: Macmillan, 1969).

[8]Sanford Baum, Robert C. Carlson, and James V. Jucker, "Some Problems in Applying the Continuous Portfolio Selection Model to the Discrete Capital Budgeting Problem," *Journal of Financial and Quantitative Analysis,* Vol. XIII, No. 2 (June 1978), pp. 333–344.

[9]A *dominated point* is one that is inferior to other asset combinations for all values of λ, the coefficient of risk aversion.

[10]Baum et al., p. 338.

large investment proposals may be able to analyze them quite successfully without relying on the Markowitz approach per se. Baum et al. found the error in the Mao problem solution by evaluating all 32 possible selections of the five candidate projects.[11] Full evaluation can get out of hand quickly, however, as the number of projects considered increases. Nevertheless, with up to ten projects or so ($2^{10} = 1024$) evaluation of all combinations of proposals by modern digital computers is not only possible but not particularly costly. After about ten projects, however, the number of combinations becomes rapidly so great that full enumeration is not possible. In all but the very largest enterprises this should not be an insurmountable problem, particularly if minor projects may be aggregated together.

Another possibly rewarding substitute approach might be found in using a modified zero-one programming algorithm, such as that discussed in Chapter 16 to obtain the partial enumeration combinations that will need to be evaluated in terms of risk in a second step. In other words, if we can eliminate nonfeasible combinations before looking at risk, then the number of combinations to be examined will be reduced, often substantially, particularly where several proposals are mutually exclusive.

The Sharpe Modification

William Sharpe is credited with a modified version of the Markowitz model that has far-reaching implications for the valuation of assets.[12] Sharpe's model is the foundation of the capital asset pricing model (CAPM) discussed in Chapter 21. The Sharpe model is often referred to as the "diagonal model" of portfolio selection. His model assumes that returns on assets are related only through their correlations with some index. Returns are defined as:

$$R_i = A_i + b_i I + u_i \tag{20.10}$$

where I is a random variable denoting an index, and A_i and b_i are constants for asset i. The variable I is assumed to have finite mean

---

[11]The number of possible selections is given by 2^n, where there are n candidate proposals.

[12]William F. Sharpe, "Risk Aversion in the Stock Market: Some Empirical Evidence," *The Journal of Finance*, Vol. 20 (September 1963), pp. 416–422.

and finite variance. The u_i are random errors due to independent, external causes, and satisfy the usual least-squares assumptions of zero expected value, finite variance, and independence (zero covariances).

With these specifications any investment can be split into two parts: (1) an investment in A_i and u_i, the asset's basic, or unique characteristics and (2) an investment in I, the external index. This means that the variance-covariance matrix for n securities plus the external index ($n + 1$ in total) has zero elements *except* on the diagonal containing the covariances between each of the n securities and the external index.

Elimination of the covariances between individual assets makes the Sharpe model much more amenable to computer solution than the original Markowitz formulation, because the computational burden is substantially lessened. It has yet to be determined whether or not the Sharpe model suffers from similar shortcomings to those Baum et al. found for the Markowitz formulation when assets are indivisible.

RELATING TO INVESTOR UTILITY

After determining the set of efficient assets for various[13] coefficients of risk aversion (λ), the actual combination of projects selected will depend on the decision maker's utility function. Graphically, the optimum project selection is that which just touches the indifference curve (that is, constant utility curve) corresponding to the highest utility.

In the case of infinitely divisible assets as depicted in Figure 20-1, the point of tangency equates the marginal rates of substitution of the efficient set curve[14] and the tangent indifference curve. For indivisible assets, the optimum efficient point is the one lying on the highest indifference curve. Figure 20-2 illustrates this.

In practice, it may not be necessary to estimate the family of indifference curves; in fact, most managements will insist on making the final decision on which efficient set of capital investments will be undertaken. There is a marked tendency for executives to resist what they interpret as arrogation of their authority

---

[13]If we knew λ in advance, we could solve directly for the optimal portfolio.
[14]The curve defined by all efficient points is called the "efficient frontier."

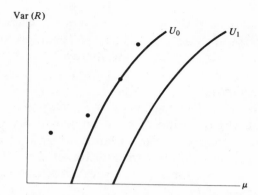

Figure 20-2. Selection of Optimal Portfolio of Risky Indivisible Assets.

and responsibility by technicians armed with computers. It may suffice to present to the executives who have the decision authority those few efficient alternative combinations that are undominated by others. This will generally mean considering which one, two, or few projects will be either removed or entered into the final selection, because alternative efficient collections are often similar over a rather wide range of λ values, differing by only few individual included or excluded projects.

EPILOGUE

Subject to qualifications resulting from the article by Baum, Carlson, and Jucker, the quadratic programming approaches to asset selection used by Markowitz and by Sharpe yield useful insights into the process by which risk averse investors select investment portfolios. Extension from the domain of securities analysis, where individual investments may be considered as finely, if not infinitely, divisible to the domain of indivisible capital project investments, can yield incorrect results. This appears, however, to be more a mechanical problem with implementation of the procedure than it is a problem with the theoretical concepts. As such it is a flaw that should be amenable to correction by modification of the algorithm.

Of a more fundamental nature are questions arising from concerns relating to the choice of measure of return that is used as well as questions about the adequacy of variance-covariance relationship to reflect all relevant risk-return attitudes, although numerous authors have defended this latter factor. Still further unresolved concerns stem from the nature of the trade-off function relating uncertainty and futurity, from considerations of abandonment prior to final project life maturity, and from complex intertemporal contingencies between today's projects and future candidate projects.

Estimation of project variances and covariances is a difficult problem. And the question of solution sensitivity to misspecification or misestimation of the variance-covariance structure and the stability of these parameters over time has not been resolved to everyone's satisfaction for securities investments, not to mention capital expenditure proposals.

These concerns and cautions have not been raised to disparage application of portfolio selection techniques to capital investments, but rather to alert the reader that there are unresolved and controversial matters that tend to be ignored by the more zealous advocates of portfolio selection techniques to capital investment expenditure analysis.

21

The Capital Asset Pricing Model

In Chapter 4 the capital asset pricing model (CAPM) was mentioned in relation to the firm's cost of equity capital. In Chapter 18 it was mentioned again in the discussion of the criticism of computer simulation of individual capital investment proposals. Here we shall examine the capital asset pricing model more closely, to see how it may enable the firm to rationalize the risk-return trade-off and how it may assist in estimating the firm's cost of equity capital and in assessing the interaction between capital investment and cost of capital.

The purpose of this chapter is to present the CAPM as a means for dealing with risk in capital investment. In keeping with this purpose the model is examined critically in terms of how well it facilitates making better decisions, as well as problems that affect application of the model to capital investment projects.

ASSUMPTIONS OF THE CAPM

The CAPM is based on several of the following assumptions, some of which do not conform well to the reality of capital investment projects:

1. Investors are risk-averse maximizers of the expected utility based on wealth at end-of-holding period.
2. Expectations about asset returns are homogeneous: Everyone agrees on the probability distributions governing returns.
3. Assets are fixed in number, marketable, and infinitely divisible.
4. A risk-free asset exists and investors may borrow or lend without limit at the rate of return paid by the risk-free asset.

5. The market is perfect: no taxes, no transactions costs, no restrictions.
6. All investors have the same planning horizon and holding period.
7. Investors do not distinguish between sources of returns. They are indifferent between dividends and interest of equal dollar amount.

THE EFFICIENT SET OF PORTFOLIOS

In Chapter 20 portfolio selection techniques were examined. They required that we first find the set of efficient portfolios, those that cannot be improved upon in this sense: An efficient portfolio is one that has maximum expected return for a given level of risk or, alternatively, has minimum risk for a given expected rate of return. In other words, if a portfolio is efficient, we cannot improve upon it by finding another portfolio that has the same (or greater) return and lower risk or the same (or less) risk and greater return.

Since the investor is assumed to be risk averse and utility maximizing, and since greater utility is associated with greater returns, the only portfolios he or she is interested in are efficient portfolios. In Figure 21-1 the section of curve II' above point 0 is the efficient frontier. Points on II' below point 0 represent nonefficient portfolios because for the same risk each has an alternate providing higher expected return on the segment above.

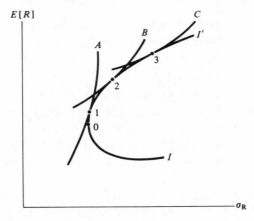

Figure 21-1. The Efficient Set and Investor Portfolio Choices.

The risk-averse, utility maximizing investor we have assumed can be interested only in efficient portfolios: it remains to determine exactly which efficient portfolio is optimum. In Chapter 20 this was found as the point of tangency between the efficiency frontier and the investor's highest indifference curve. These indifference curves contain risk-return combinations which, to the particular investor, offer constant utility along a given curve. In Figure 21-1 the portfolio choices of three investors (A, B, and C) are depicted by points 1, 2, and 3. Investor C may be considered the most aggressive of the three because point 3, although corresponding to higher returns than the others, is also associated with proportionately greater risk. By similar reasoning, investor A may be considered the most conservative of the three. Minimum risk is at point 0, but the return of the portfolio corresponding to that point is also at a minimum.

So far, we have not admitted the existence of a *risk-free* asset into our portfolio considerations. At this point we shall assume such an investment exists, and examine implications.

Enter a Risk-Free Investment

The foregoing assumed that the only assets that existed were risky. Now we shall assume there is a risk-free asset, paying a certain rate of return denoted by R_f. Because federal government securities are risk free in this sense, and they are bonds, we might alternatively use i to denote the fixed, certain rate of return. Those who are totally averse to risk would be expected to purchase only the risk-free asset for its certain return. Others would purchase combinations of the risk-free asset and the market portfolio.

The risk-free assumption, it should be noted, requires several subsidiary assumptions. Although the payment of a fixed, periodic money interest on federal government bonds is reasonable (except possibly in time of war or revolution that may bring to power new government that will repudiate the debt), it raises questions. Is the rate of return in nominal terms or in real terms? What about capital gains or losses brought about by changes in the market rate of interest? If there can be capital gains, then the rate of return is not fixed and certain.

In order for the risk-free return to be in fact risk-free, or certain, we need to require either that (1) we measure nominal returns, unadjusted for inflation or (2) we have constant inflation or know the rate of inflation over the holding period, or (3) the risk-free security is a floating rate bond that pays a certain *real* return, or (4) the holding period is short enough that the effects of inflation can be ignored. If both the risk-free return and the market portfolio return are equally affected by inflation, the problem diminishes and it is not necessary to do more than insure that returns are measured on the same basis in either nominal or real terms.

The problem posed by capital gains may be resolved in either of two ways. We can add the assumption of costless information, which is sometimes listed as one of the required assumptions of the CAPM, or we may instead assume a constant interest rate over the holding period or else a short holding period over which interest-induced capital gains and losses would be minimal, such as with three-month U.S. Treasury bills, for example.

For our purposes we need not be overly concerned about these questions about the risk-free asset. However, because such questions tend to arise from students of the CAPM, this seems an appropriate place to bring them into the open. We shall not dwell on this matter further, but continue, assuming that the risk-free rate is indeed risk free.

A risk-free asset in addition to the efficient set means that now every investor can have a portfolio composed of the risk-free

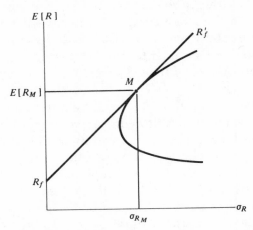

Figure 21-2. Risk-Free Asset, Market Portfolio, and Capital Market Line (CML).

asset plus an efficient portfolio of risky assets. Figure 21-2 illustrates this. Any point on the straight line may be obtained by the appropriate linear combination of the risk-free asset and the efficient portfolio at the point of tangency. If q is the proportion of the investor's wealth invested in the risk-free asset, then $1 - q$ is the proportion invested in the tangent portfolio, and $0 \leq q \leq 1$.

The line from R_f tangent to the efficient set is called the *capital market line* (CML). No longer are investors content to hold only risky assets in efficient portfolios. Now they want to hold some of the risk-free asset in combination with an efficient portfolio. And the one efficient portfolio they will hold in such combination is the *market portfolio*. Every other portfolio is inferior, because now investors can achieve higher returns for a given level of risk. In terms of indifference curves this means that such curves will not be tangent to the efficient set, but rather will be tangent to line R_fR_f' that lies above the efficient set at every point except M, the point of tangency corresponding to the market portfolio.

The market portfolio must include every risky asset; otherwise the prices of some would rise and others fall until all were included, and all assets must be owned by someone. A change in the risk-free return vis-à-vis the return on the market portfolio means that a new point of tangency will exist and risky asset prices will adjust until a new equilibrium is reached and there is a new market portfolio.

The line segment of R_fR_f' above point M corresponds to margin purchases of the market portfolio. In other words, investors who seek a higher return, albeit with higher risk, can borrow at the risk-free rate[1] and invest the proceeds in the market portfolio. Therefore, linear combinations of the risk-free asset and the market portfolio are all that investors will want to hold above point M as well as below it. Again, above point M as well as below it, investors will want to stay on line R_fR_f' because it offers greater utility.

The equation of the capital market line R_fR_f' is:

$$E[R_M] = R_f + \lambda\sigma_M \tag{21.1}$$

[1]By assumption.

or if we can denote $E[R]$ by $\overline{R}$:

$$\overline{R}_M = R_f + \lambda\sigma_M \qquad (21.2)$$

The line slope, λ, is the "price of risk." The risk-free rate and market expectations may change over time and, accordingly, the price of risk may change as a new equilibrium is reached. Equilibrium is assumed to exist now and to reflect expectations over one period into the future. Lambda is defined by:

$$\lambda = \frac{\overline{R}_M - R_f}{\sigma_M} \qquad (21.3)$$

Thus the price of risk is not simply the difference between the price of the risk-free asset and the expected return on the market portfolio, but must be adjusted for the standard deviation of the portfolio return.

THE SECURITY MARKET LINE AND BETA

The equilibrium conditions for efficient holdings of a risk-free asset and the market portfolio are given by the capital market line. But we are also interested in the return on inefficient holdings, whether portfolios or individual assets. Every asset is held in the market portfolio, as we have previously stated; otherwise its price would change until it was included. The capital market line provides a measure of the price of risk for the overall market portfolio. But what is the risk-return trade-off for a given asset or inefficient asset portfolio?

By equating the "price of risk" with the slope of the efficient frontier at point of tangency M (Figure 21-2), we obtain:

$$\frac{\overline{R} - R_f}{\sigma_M} = \frac{E[R_j] - \overline{R}_M}{(\sigma_{jM} - \sigma_M{}^2)/\sigma_M} \qquad (21.4)$$

from which can be obtained the relationship usually called *the capital asset pricing model:*

$$E[R_j] = R_f + \frac{\sigma_{jM}}{\sigma_M{}^2}[\overline{R}_M - R_f] \qquad (21.5)$$

which is usually written in the form:

$$\overline{R}_j = R_f + \beta_j[\overline{R}_M - R_f] \tag{21.6}$$

where β is defined as:

$$\beta_j = \frac{\text{Cov}(R_j, R_M)}{\text{Var}(R_M)} = \frac{\sigma_{jm}}{\sigma_M{}^2} \tag{21.7}$$

Beta can be thought of as the volatility of the jth asset and may be estimated (if data are available) by fitting an ordinary least-squares regression to the equation:

$$R_j = \alpha_j + \beta_j R_M \tag{21.8}$$

Several investment services publish calculated betas for U.S. common stocks. However, because market returns would have to be based on a market portfolio including every asset weighted according to its importance, and because this would be impossible to achieve and prohibitively costly to try to approach, the "market" portfolio is in fact a portfolio of New York Stock Exchange listed common stocks or some more restricted list such as the Standard and Poor's 500.

If we define total risk of any asset as *systematic risk* plus *unsystematic risk,* then the beta is the systematic risk. The actual return on any asset j is given by:

$$R_j = \alpha_j + \beta_j R_M + \mu_j \tag{21.9}$$

with variance

$$\sigma_j{}^2 = \beta_j{}^2 \sigma_M{}^2 + \sigma_\mu{}^2 \tag{21.10}$$

where μ represents an independent random error term, and R_j and R_M are random variables.

Since in (21.10) the variance is the total risk, the right-hand side contains the two component risks. The unsystematic risk is $\sigma_\mu{}^2$, and this can be eliminated by diversification. Because unsystematic risk can thus be eliminated, the market will not pay to avoid it. However, systematic risk is another matter entirely. Investors will pay to avoid systematic risk, and *in equilibrium every asset must fall on the security market line.* Figure 21-3 illustrates the

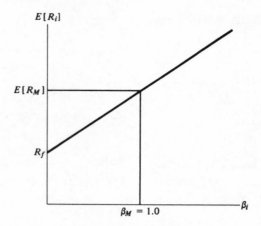

Figure 21-3. The Security Market Line.

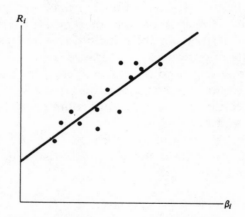

Figure 21-4. Empirical Security Market Line.

security market line. The market portfolio itself has $\beta = 1$, as indicated.

Although *the capital market line related a risk-free asset to the market portfolio, the security market line relates risk and return for individual securities.* These same individual assets are included in the market portfolio. Each has its own systematic, nondiversifiable risk associated with it and therefore its own rate of return that the marketplace will require of it. If the return is higher than necessary, investors will want to add more of it to their holdings, bidding up the price until, in equilibrium, it lies on the security market line. On the other hand, if the return is lower than necessary, holders will want to sell and the price will decline until it rests on the security market line.

If we plot data points for risk (that is, beta) and return on securities, we will obtain a scattergram such as that shown in Figure 21-4, to which an empirical security market line may be fitted by least-squares regression. We shall not address here the question of how well historical data reflect expectations about future performance, the stability of β, and so on. These significant questions have been formally considered by many researchers.

An important property of the CAPM stated here without proof is: The β of a portfolio is a linearly weighted average of the individual constituent assets. If a portfolio is composed of x percent asset A, y percent asset B, and z percent asset C, then the portfolio β is:

$$\beta = x\beta_A + y\beta_B + z\beta_C \tag{21.11}$$

This is *a very important result because it means that the risk of a portfolio may be found without resort to quadratic programming to determine the efficient set.*

THE CAPM AND VALUATION

The CAPM (through the security market line) provides the relationship between risk and required return imposed by the interactions of all investors in the market. Expected return is determined by price paid for an investment. The return is determined as the ratio of earnings return (dividend or interest) plus (or minus) the price change in the asset over the holding period to the price paid for the asset. If we assume a single-period holding, the return is then:

$$R_1 = \frac{D + (P_1 - P_0)}{P_0} \tag{21.12}$$

where D is the income return component and $(P_1 - P_0)$ the capital gain or loss. Combining D with P_1 and calling it P'_1, this becomes:

$$R_1 = \frac{P_1' - P_0}{P_0} \tag{21.13}$$

Equating this to the CAPM of Eq. (21.5) and taking expectations of both sides, we get:

$$\frac{\bar{P}_1' - P_0}{P_0} = R_f + \frac{\sigma_{jm}}{\sigma_M{}^2} [\bar{R}_M - R_f] \tag{21.14}$$

This may be rearranged to obtain P_0:

$$P_0 = \frac{\bar{P}_1'}{1 + R_f + (\sigma_{jM}/\sigma_M{}^2)[R_M - R_f]} \tag{21.15}$$

or

$$P_0 = \frac{\bar{P}_1'}{1 + R_f + (\lambda/\sigma_M)\sigma_{jM}} \tag{21.16}$$

where λ was defined in Eq. (21.3) as the price of risk. Note that this corresponds to the risk-adjusted discount rate discussed in Chapter 18. The certainty equivalent formulation may be obtained from (21.16) by substituting for σ_{jM} the equivalent $(1/P_0)\sigma_{P_1 R_M}$:

$$P_0 = \frac{\bar{P}_1' - (\lambda/\sigma_M)\sigma_{P_1 R_M}}{1 + R_f} \tag{21.17}$$

THE CAPM AND COST OF CAPITAL

Chapter 4 stated that the cost of capital to the firm is the required rate of return. The cost of equity is the rate required by common shareholders, the cost of debt is the rate required by creditors, and so on. That being the case we can write k for $E[R_j]$, where k is the required rate of return. Then Eq. (21.6) becomes:

$$k_e = R_f + \beta_e[\bar{R}_M - R_f] \tag{21.18}$$

for the cost of equity capital, k_e, where β_e is the systematic risk of equity in the particular firm.

The weighted average cost of capital may be found as in Chapter 4 once the component costs have been obtained. Dropping the assumptions used to develop the CAPM, which meant that debt was debt and therefore risk free, how can the cost of debt be found? In principle the CAPM could be used, but how does one estimate beta for a firm's bonds, particularly when the firm has never defaulted? The cost of debt may be observed directly in the market for publicly traded bonds or estimated from market data on those that are. Company debt will always be required to yield more than government debt because the former is not risk free, whereas federal government debt is as close as we can come to approximating a risk-free security.

THE CAPM AND CAPITAL BUDGETING

One of the results yielded by the CAPM is that once we determine an asset's risk we will know the required rate of return it must yield. This being the case, if we can estimate the systematic risk of the capital investment proposal, we can apply the CAPM. Estimation of beta for a capital investment is a formidable task because we normally do not have a foundation of historical data on this or similar projects from which we might comfortably estimate the project's beta. Assuming we have obtained a beta, we could apply the risk-adjusted discount rate or the certainty equivalent method to find the net present value. Or, as illustrated in Figure 21-5, we may employ the security market line to determine whether or not individual capital investment projects should be undertaken.

When we evaluate a capital investment proposal that has the

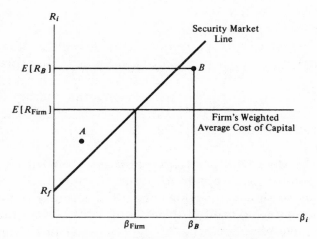

Figure 21-5. The SML and Capital Investment.

same risk as the firm as a whole, we can correctly use the firm's weighted average cost of capital. However, for projects whose risk is either greater or less than that of the firm, it is not appropriate to use the weighted average marginal cost of capital.

In Figure 21-5 proposal B has a higher expected return than the overall firm. Should the project be accepted? No. The return is greater and the risk is greater yet. In fact, because point B lies below the security market line, we can say that its risk is too great in relation to its expected return, or equivalently that its return is too low in relation to its risk. Proposal A has expected return less than the firm. But its risk is also less. In fact, because point A lies above the security market line, its return is greater than it need be for its level of risk or its risk less than it need be for the expected return. For projects having different systematic risk than the firm as a whole, the CAPM provides a rationale for accepting or rejecting them.

COMPARISON WITH PORTFOLIO APPROACHES

Two major theoretical approaches to evaluation of risky, interrelated projects are those of portfolio diversification along the lines pioneered by Markowitz (discussed in Chapter 20) and the approach implied by the CAPM.

The Markowitz approach requires that we solve a programming problem with a quadratic objective function. To do so we need the matrix of the variances and covariances of all assets that may be included in the portfolio. Then, once the quadratic programming problem has been solved, we must either solve again repeatedly until we have the efficient set or efficient frontier and then find a point of tangency with the investor's utility function or, alternatively, we must find the investor's coefficient of risk aversion at the outset, using this in the quadratic program to solve once for the optimum portfolio.

With the Markowitz portfolio approach we must do considerable computation after obtaining a burdensome amount of data. There may be serious questions about the accuracy of variance-covariance data and utility function estimates as well. Assuming that we have obtained accurate data and solved the quadratic programming problem, the result is a selection of proposals that may be unique to the utility function used or the coefficient of risk aversion. Different utility functions may be expected to yield different optimal portfolios.

The CAPM in contrast requires only that we know the security market line and the expected return and the beta for any given investment. Since beta measures the systematic or nondiversifiable risk of an asset, other risk is assumed to be unimportant because (in theory at least) it can be eliminated by suitable diversification. In the case of the CAPM, the market determines, through the security market line, what is an acceptable investment and what is not. In the Markowitz approach, the question of whether or not a particular project is acceptable is internal to the enterprise. It depends on the existing firm, the array of candidate projects, and a utility or investment function. The Markowitz approach assumes there are benefits to be gained through active diversification. The CAPM suggests, however, there is no advantage to diversification by the firm, although it implicitly requires that diversifiable risk is eliminated through appropriate portfolio construction.

SOME CRITICISMS OF THE CAPM

The question we need to be concerned with in a capital investment text is how appropriate a model or technique is to capital investments. The CAPM was developed, and its validity tested, for common stocks. Can it be transferred to capital-budgeting application without loss of validity?

There are some major differences between publicly traded securities and capital investments. Such securities are highly liquid, whereas capital investment projects may not have a secondary market other than for scrap. Securities approach the CAPM assumption of infinite divisibility much more closely than most capital investment proposals. There is usually little information available to the public about capital investment projects, much less a consensus about expected return and risk.

Commodity markets meet the conditions assumed by the CAPM much more closely than capital investments. Yet, in an empirical test of the CAPM, Holthausen and Hughes concluded that the CAPM may not fit commodity markets as well as it does security markets. They also observed that returns on commodities do not seem closely related to the measures of nondiversifiable risk they employed (that is, the betas).[2]

Rendleman points out that although the CAPM provides a basis for valuing securities in a perfect and efficient capital market, there are problems in attempting to use it in capital budgeting. He examines the application of the CAPM under capital rationing, concluding that it is not appropriate "for a firm to use its own beta when computing the expected excess return of a project with risk characteristics identical to the firm itself."[3]

Myers and Turnbull show that under certain circumstances a capital project's beta will be a function of the growth rate of the cash flows and the project life. They suggest it may not be possible to obtain betas that truly represent the systematic risk for the firm's cash flows.[4]

Levy was concerned with the use of the CAPM in public utility regulation. Although his remarks are addressed to utility company securities, they apply also, perhaps more strongly, to use of the CAPM for capital budgeting. His comments are:

1. If a public market for the utility's stock does not exist, the beta cannot be computed. . . .
2. Similarly, if a list of diversified companies were determined (on qualitative grounds) to be equivalent in risk to a particular non-traded utility, the average standard deviation of earnings of firms in the list could probably be used as an estimate of the standard deviation for the utility; but the same inference might not be appropriate regarding the beta. . . .
3. At least two studies . . . find that investors receive some incremental return for incurring diversifiable risk. . . .
4. Unless the independent variable in the regression equation is fully diversified to include bonds, real estate and other investments, the beta coefficient will not properly distinguish between diversifiable and non-diversifiable risk.[4]

[2]Duncan M. Holthausen and John S. Hughes, "Commodity Returns and Capital Asset Pricing," *Financial Management*, Vol. 7, No. 2 (Summer 1978), pp. 37–44.

[3]Richard J. Rendleman, Jr., "Ranking Errors in CAPM Capital Budgeting Applications," *Financial Management*, Vol. 7, No. 4 (Winter 1978), p. 42.

[4]Stewart C. Myers and Stuart W. Turnbull, "Capital Budgeting and the Capital Asset Pricing Model: Good News and Bad News," *The Journal of Finance*, Vol. XXXII, No. 2 (May 1977), pp. 321–332.

5. Large disparities can exist in the beta coefficients for individual stocks when different computational methods are employed [such as time span]. . . .
6. Independent studies reveal marked instability of [calculated] betas over time. . . .
7. [Studies] indicate that returns on high beta stocks were lower than would be expected and returns on low beta stocks higher . . . the expected relationship between betas and individual stock returns prevailed *less than half the time.*
8. . . . tests will show, almost invariably, that the beta coefficients for individual stocks are not significantly different in a statistical sense from the general market beta of 1.00[5]

Fama demonstrated that the future riskless rate, the market price of risk, or the elasticity of a capital project's expected cash flows with respect to the market return must be certain. Otherwise the CAPM cannot be properly employed. The only parameter that can be uncertain through time is that of the cash flows themselves.[6]

THE ARBITRAGE PRICING THEORY (APT)

In recent years the CAPM has yielded to the notion of the arbitrage pricing theory. The CAPM provides a theoretically simple model for measuring and matching risks to expected returns. It affords a way of determining the return that in the view of the overall market is appropriate to the level of risk, and vice-versa.

The CAPM postulates that the relevant, or nondiversifiable risk of an asset is fully measured by its sensitivity to the risk premium on the market portfolio; that is, to $(R_M - R_f)$. That sensitivity is measured by the asset's beta (β). While the CAPM is useful, it fails to explain why there appears to be persistent differences in common stock returns from influences arising from the industry a firm is in, its size, the term structure of interest rates, and so on. And, it has been suggested by Roll[7] that the CAPM cannot be adequately tested empirically.

[5]Robert E. Levy, "Fair Return on Equity for Public Utilities," *Business Economics,* Vol. XIII, No. 4 (September 1978), pp. 46–57.

[6]Eugene F. Fama, "Risk Adjusted Discount Rates and Capital Budgeting Under Uncertainty," *Journal of Financial Economics* (August 1977), pp. 1–24.

[7]Richard Roll, "A Critique of the Asset Pricing Theory's Tests; Part I: On Past and Potential Testability of the Theory," *Journal of Financial Economics,* Vol. 4, No. 2 (March 1977), pp. 129–176.

The fundamental idea behind the APT is that there are *several* influences that together determine the return on a security or other investment, and also the risk. These influences are called *factors* and have a particular statistical meaning and interpretation.

The general awakening of interest in a multiple factor model by financial economists followed Ross,[8] who provided a theoretical foundation that earlier multiple factor models lacked.

Factors—What Are They?

In multivariate statistics there are two closely related techniques called *principal components analysis* and *factor analysis.* Both are based on the notion that observations on real, observable, economic, or other variables can be viewed as being a weighted sum of unobservable variables called *principal components,* or *factors.* Alternatively, the principal components or factors may be viewed as being a weighted sum of the observable variables.

In principal components analysis, if there are j variables then it will require j principal components to account for the total variance.[9] The jth principal component accounts for the jth greatest variance. A small number of principal components may account for *most* of the original variance, but all j of the principal components are required to fully account for the variance. The principal components are linear combinations of the original, observable variables.

In common factor analysis the model is based on the notion that there are fewer factors than the original j variables. However, the factors may not account for as much of the variance as the same number of principal components, since the common factors are linear combinations solely of the common parts of the variables.

Both techniques have been applied to the APT. However, factor analysis is preferred. Factor analysis is directed toward the correlation, or covariance between the original variables. Principal components analysis is directed toward the variance of the variables, not the common influence between variables. Since the APT postulates influences common to many assets in the market,

[8]Stephen A. Ross, "The Arbitrage Theory of Capital Asset Pricing," *Journal of Economic Theory,* Vol. 13 (1976), pp. 341–360.

[9]Mark L. Berenson, David M. Levine, and Matthew Goldstein, *Intermediate Statistical Methods and Applications.* (Englewood Cliffs, N.J.: Prentice-Hall, Inc., 1983).

researchers thus normally should use the technique that better probes for such common influences in preference to one that looks for something that might be unique to each asset.

The idea behind the techniques is perhaps best grasped by seeing how they apply graphically. Consider Figure 21-6, which shows a scatter of points in an axis system with returns to asset A on the vertical and returns to asset B on the horizontal. The two assets have returns that are related, and that is why the scatter of points is elliptical and not circular. Perfect positive correlation would, of course, appear as a straight line rising at a 45-degree angle from the origin; perfective negative correlation would appear as a straight line falling from left to right at a 45-degree angle.

The longer axis fitted to the ellipse containing the returns accounts for the greater proportion of the common variance in returns between the two assets. The shorter axis accounts for the rest of the common variance since there are only two assets. Points on the two axes that correspond to the original pairs of returns, such as pair x, coincide with an "observation" on a factor or principal component. Point q is the value of factor 1, point r the value of factor 2. Because the projection of the first (i.e., principal) axis on the R_B axis is longer than that on the R_A axis, we observe that it is more closely related to asset B's returns. Factor 1 is said to *load* more heavily on asset B.

This graphical model may be extended to three dimensions. Beyond three dimensions the mathematical techniques can deal

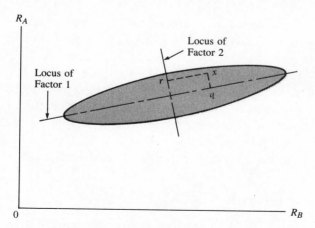

Figure 21-6. Two Assets, Two Factors.

with the calculations even though there may be no meaningful graphical exposition of the hyperellipsoids to which an axis system is being fitted.

Multiple correlations between the original observations and the points on the axes provide what are termed *factor loadings.* The axis system may be *rotated* to obtain factor loadings with the original variables that may facilitate interpretation of the factors. For example, if one were using data for interest rates, a high loading of factor n with the yield on U.S. Treasury bonds, corporate AAA-rated bonds, and mortgages, a promising interpretation would be that factor n is a long-term interest rate factor. When a factor loading is very high on an observable variable, we then may use the observable variable in place of the factor, as a surrogate. In searching for macroeconomic variables that may be called "factors" such high loadings are what one looks for.

Rotation may be *orthogonal* or *nonorthogonal.* That is, rotation may be done with the axes perpendicular to one another, or nonperpendicular. Principal components are always done with orthogonal axes. Factor analysis may be done either way, but the nonorthogonal rotation schemes, despite some subjectivity necessary in their use, provide a richer domain of possible interpretations.

In comparison to other statistical techniques, factor analysis has not had a large variety of tests of significance developed. A traditional rule is that factors (or principal components) having eigenvalues (that is, factor or component variances) greater than 1.0 are likely to be significant. The intuitive interpretation of this is that those factors account for more of the covariance or correlation than any single one of the original variables should be considered important. The lack of powerful statistical tests for determining which, or how many, factors are significant (that is, "priced" in the market) has probably been central to the controversy that continues over how many factors affect the returns of assets, and what interpretations may reasonably be placed upon them. In examining the history of the APT this knowledge will provide a necessary perspective for understanding its evolution.

APT and CAPM

In applying the CAPM we fit a regression equation with return on the jth asset as the dependent variable to one independent variable, return on the market portfolio or index. The APT takes the process a step further, by adding to the market return the macroeconomic variables that are considered to be important in determining the returns on assets. Thus, APT is a multivariate analog to the CAPM and includes the CAPM as a special case.

Development of the APT

APT is considered to offer a testable alternative to the Capital Asset Pricing Model (CAPM) introduced by Sharpe.[10] Ross argued that the APT is an appropriate alternative because it agrees with the intuition behind the CAPM since it is based on a linear return generating process in which risk may be separated into diversifiable and nondiversifiable portions. Unlike the CAPM, however, the APT is claimed to hold in both multiperiod and single period instances, and the "market" portfolio plays no special role in APT.

Perhaps the major differences between APT and Sharpe's model are that (1) APT allows for more than one return generating factor and (2) because no arbitrage profits are possible in a market at equilibrium, every equilibrium may be characterized by a linear relationship between each asset's factors. The easily accepted assumption that no riskless arbitrage profits can exist in equilibrium, given the factor generating model, leads directly to APT.

Bower, Bower, and Logue (BBL) provide an example application of the APT to a sample of companies.[11] Though they had worked with a larger sample, the one for which results were presented in the article cited here was very heavily composed of firms in the broadcasting industry. Nevertheless, the results obtained are worth looking at for the general lesson they contain. The authors used four alleged factors (industrial production, inflation, interest rate term structure, and the spread between low and high grade bonds) in regressions, along with the market index return as a fifth macroeconomic variable. They compared

[10]William F. Sharpe, "Capital Asset Prices: A Theory of Market Equilibrium Under Conditions of Risk," *Journal of Finance,* Vol. 19, No. 4, (September 1964), pp. 425–442.

[11]Dorothy H. Bower, Richard S. Bower, and Dennis E. Logue, "A Primer on Arbitrage Pricing Theory," *Midland Corporate Finance Journal* (a publication of Stern Stewart Management Services, Inc.) Vol. 2, No. 3 (Fall 1984), pp. 31–40. Reprinted in Financial Management Collection, Vol. 2, No. 3 (Autumn 1987), pp. 1, 6–9.

the results with those from regressing the stocks' returns on the market index return, the CAPM model.

BBL found that the R^2 for the APT was 0.36 compared to 0.32 for the CAPM. Taking the regression coefficients they had obtained, they applied them to estimate the required rate of return on each firm's stock. For the sample they found the APT yielded a lower required rate of return than the CAPM, an average of 18.8 percent versus 23.0 percent. However, the standard deviation of the required returns was 6.05 percent with the APT, compared to 4.43 percent for the CAPM.

Since BBL did not state whether or not they used the R^2 adjusted for degrees of freedom, it is not possible to determine from the article if the four additional macroeconomic variables made a genuine contribution or not. For each additional independent variable used in a regression there is generally an increase in the R^2 due to loss of degrees of freedom. Use of $\overline{R}^2$ (called "r-bar-squared") takes this into account.

Close examination of BBL's regression coefficients reveals that with the consistent exception of the return on the market index, most of them are very close to zero, even though some of them are statistically significant. The reason for mentioning this is to bring to attention the difference between statistical significance and economic or practical significance. For example, for Cook International, BBL calculated a coefficient of 0.05 (one of the *larger* such coefficients), with a *t*-value of 3.32 indicating high significance, for the third macroeconomic variable (interest rate term structure). The coefficient for the market return in contrast was 0.90 with a *t*-value of 3.12. Thus, the statistical significance of interest rate term structure is greater than that of the market, but its impact on the required return only $\frac{1}{18}$th as great!

If indeed there are only 4 or 5 factors one might be forgiven if he or she looks for somewhat greater economic significance from each.

VI

Appendix: Financial Mathematics Tables and Formulas

Formulas for Interest and Discount

For:

P = Principal or Present Value
F = Future Value
R = Annuity Periodic Receipt or Payment
i = Annual Rate of Interest (in decimal)
N = Number of Annual Periods

Table A-1. Single Payment Compound Amount Factor. To find F for a given P, $F = P(1 + i)^N$

Table A-2. Single Payment Present Worth Factor. To find P for a given F, $P = F(1 + i)^{-N}$
°Ordinary† Annuity Sinking Fund Factor. To find R for a given F, $R = F[i/((1 + i)^N - 1)]$
°Ordinary† Annuity Capital Recovery Factor. To find R for a given P, $R = P[i/(1 - (1 + i)^{-N})]$

Table A-3. Ordinary† Annuity Compound Amount Factor. To find F for a given R received at the end of each period,

$$F = R \left\{ \frac{(1 + i)^N - 1)}{i} \right\}$$

Table A-4. Ordinary† Annuity Present Worth Factor. To find P for a given R received at the end of each period

$$F = R \left\{ \frac{(1 - (1 + i)^{-N})}{i} \right\}$$

°These factors are not tabulated.
†Ordinary annuities normally apply to capital investment problems. With them the periodic payments, R, occur at the end of each period. With "annuities due" they would occur at the beginning.

°To convert a *nominal* annual rate j, compounded M times per year, to its *effective* annual counterpart, i, use the relationship, $(1 + i) = (1 + j/M)^M$

°At *continuous* interest rate i, $F = Pe^{iN}$, where e is the base of natural logarithms, 2.71828.

Table A-1. Single Payment Compound Amount Factor. To Find F for a Given P. $F = P(1 + i)^N$

N/i	1	2	3	4	5	6	7	8	9	10
1	1.010000	1.020000	1.030000	1.040000	1.050000	1.060000	1.070000	1.080000	1.090000	1.100000
2	1.020100	1.040400	1.060900	1.081600	1.102500	1.123600	1.144900	1.166400	1.188100	1.210000
3	1.030301	1.061208	1.092727	1.124864	1.157625	1.191016	1.225043	1.259712	1.295029	1.331000
4	1.040604	1.082432	1.125509	1.169859	1.215506	1.262477	1.310796	1.360489	1.411582	1.464100
5	1.051010	1.104081	1.159274	1.216653	1.276282	1.338226	1.402552	1.469328	1.538624	1.610510
6	1.061520	1.126162	1.194052	1.265319	1.340096	1.418519	1.500730	1.586874	1.677100	1.771561
7	1.072135	1.148686	1.229874	1.315932	1.407100	1.503630	1.605781	1.713824	1.828039	1.948717
8	1.082857	1.171659	1.266770	1.368569	1.477455	1.593848	1.718186	1.850930	1.992563	2.143589
9	1.093685	1.195093	1.304773	1.423312	1.551328	1.689479	1.838459	1.999005	2.171893	2.357948
10	1.104622	1.218994	1.343916	1.480244	1.628895	1.790848	1.967151	2.158925	2.367364	2.593742
11	1.115668	1.243374	1.384234	1.539454	1.710339	1.898299	2.104852	2.331639	2.580426	2.853117
12	1.126825	1.266242	1.425761	1.601032	1.795856	2.012196	2.252192	2.518170	2.812665	3.138428
13	1.138093	1.293607	1.468534	1.665074	1.885649	2.132928	2.409845	2.719624	3.065805	3.452271
14	1.149474	1.319479	1.512590	1.731676	1.979932	2.260904	2.578534	2.937194	3.341727	3.797498
15	1.160969	1.345868	1.557967	1.800944	2.078928	2.396558	2.759032	3.172169	3.642482	4.177248
16	1.172579	1.372786	1.604706	1.872981	2.182875	2.540352	2.952164	3.425943	3.970306	4.594973
17	1.184304	1.400241	1.652848	1.947900	2.292018	2.692773	3.158815	3.700018	4.327633	5.054470
18	1.196147	1.428246	1.702433	2.025817	2.406619	2.854339	3.379932	3.996019	4.717120	5.559917
19	1.208109	1.456811	1.753506	2.106849	2.526950	3.025600	3.616528	4.315701	5.141661	6.115909
20	1.220190	1.485947	1.806111	2.191123	2.653298	3.207135	3.869684	4.660957	5.604411	6.727500

Table A-1. Single Payment Compound Amount Factor. To Find F for a Given P. $F = P(1 + i)^N$

N/i	1	2	3	4	5	6	7	8	9	10
21	1.232392	1.515666	1.860295	2.278768	2.785963	3.399564	4.140562	5.033834	6.108808	7.400250
22	1.244716	1.545980	1.916103	2.369919	2.925261	3.603537	4.430402	5.436540	6.658600	8.140275
23	1.257163	1.576899	1.973587	2.464716	3.071524	3.819750	4.740530	5.871464	7.257874	8.954302
24	1.269735	1.608437	2.032794	2.563304	3.225100	4.048935	5.072367	6.341181	7.911083	9.849733
25	1.282432	1.640606	2.093778	2.665836	3.386355	4.291871	5.427433	6.848475	8.623081	10.83471
26	1.295256	1.673418	2.156591	2.772470	3.555673	4.549383	5.807353	7.396353	9.399158	11.91818
27	1.308209	1.706886	2.221289	2.883369	3.733456	4.822346	6.213868	7.988061	10.24508	13.10999
28	1.321291	1.741024	2.287928	2.998703	3.920129	5.111687	6.648838	8.627106	11.16714	14.42099
29	1.334504	1.775845	2.356566	3.116651	4.116136	5.418388	7.114257	9.317275	12.17218	15.86309
30	1.347849	1.811362	2.427262	3.243398	4.321942	5.743491	7.612255	10.06266	13.26768	17.44940
31	1.361327	1.847589	2.500080	3.373133	4.538039	6.088101	8.145113	10.86767	14.46177	19.19434
32	1.374941	1.884541	2.575083	3.508059	4.764941	6.453387	8.715271	11.73708	15.76333	21.11378
33	1.388690	1.922231	2.652335	3.648381	5.003189	6.840590	9.325340	12.67605	17.18203	23.22515
34	1.402577	1.960676	2.731905	3.794416	5.253348	7.251025	9.978114	13.69013	18.72841	25.54767
35	1.416603	1.999890	2.813862	3.946089	5.516015	7.686087	10.67658	14.78534	20.41397	28.10244
36	1.430769	2.039887	2.898278	4.103933	5.791816	8.147252	11.42394	15.96817	22.25123	30.91268
37	1.445076	2.080685	2.985227	4.266090	6.081407	8.636087	12.22362	17.24563	24.25384	34.00395
38	1.459527	2.122299	3.074783	4.438813	6.385477	9.154252	13.07927	18.62528	26.43668	37.40434
39	1.474123	2.164745	3.167027	4.616366	6.70751	9.703507	13.99482	20.11530	28.81598	41.14478
40	1.488864	2.208040	3.262038	4.801021	7.039989	10.28572	14.97446	21.72452	31.40942	45.25926

Table A-1. Single Payment Compound Amount Factor. To Find F for a Given P. $F = P(1 + i)^N$

N/i	1	2	3	4	5	6	7	8	9	10
41	1.503752	2.252200	3.359899	4.993061	7.391988	10.90286	16.02267	23.46248	34.23627	49.78518
42	1.518790	2.297244	3.460696	5.192784	7.761588	11.55703	17.14426	25.33948	37.31753	54.76370
43	1.533378	2.343189	3.564517	5.400495	8.149667	12.25045	18.34435	27.36664	40.67611	60.24007
44	1.549318	2.390053	3.671452	5.616515	8.557150	12.98548	19.62846	29.55597	44.33696	66.26408
45	1.564811	2.437854	3.781596	5.841176	8.985008	13.76461	21.00245	31.92045	48.32729	72.89048
46	1.580459	2.486611	3.895044	6.074823	9.434258	14.59049	22.47262	34.47409	52.67674	80.17953
47	1.596263	2.536344	4.011895	6.317816	9.905971	15.46592	24.04571	37.23201	57.41765	88.19749
48	1.612226	2.587070	4.132252	6.570528	10.40127	16.39387	25.72891	40.21057	62.58524	97.01723
49	1.628348	2.638812	4.256219	6.833349	10.92133	17.37750	27.52993	43.42742	68.21791	106.7190
50	1.644632	2.691588	4.383906	7.106683	11.46740	18.42015	29.45703	46.90161	74.35752	117.3909
51	1.661078	2.745420	4.515423	7.390951	12.04077	19.52536	31.51902	50.65374	81.04970	129.1299
52	1.677689	2.800328	4.650886	7.686589	12.64281	20.69689	33.72535	54.70604	88.34417	142.0429
53	1.694466	2.856335	4.790412	7.994052	13.27495	21.93870	36.08612	59.08252	96.29514	156.2472
54	1.711410	2.913461	4.934125	8.313814	13.93870	23.25502	38.61215	63.80913	104.9617	171.8719
55	1.728525	2.971731	5.082149	8.646367	14.63563	24.65032	41.31500	68.91386	114.4083	189.0591
56	1.745810	3.031165	5.234613	8.992222	15.36741	26.12934	44.20705	74.42696	124.7050	207.9651
57	1.763268	3.091789	5.391651	9.351910	16.13578	27.69710	47.30155	80.38112	135.9285	228.7616
58	1.780901	3.153624	5.553401	9.725987	16.94257	29.33893	50.61265	86.81161	148.1620	251.6377
59	1.798710	3.216697	5.720003	10.11503	17.78970	31.12046	54.15554	93.75654	161.4966	276.8015
60	1.816697	3.281031	5.891603	10.51963	18.67919	32.98769	57.94643	101.2571	176.0313	304.4816

Table A-1. Single Payment Compound Amount Factor. To Find F for a Given P. $F = P(1 + i)^N$

N/i	1	2	3	4	5	6	7	8	9	10
61	1.834864	3.346651	6.068351	10.94041	19.61315	34.96695	62.00268	109.3576	191.8741	334.9298
62	1.853212	3.413584	6.250402	11.37803	20.59380	37.06497	66.34286	118.1062	209.1428	368.4228
63	1.871744	3.481856	6.437914	11.83315	21.62349	39.28887	70.98686	127.5547	227.9656	405.2651
64	1.890462	3.551493	6.631051	12.30648	22.70467	41.64620	75.95595	137.7591	248.4825	445.7916
65	1.909366	3.622523	6.829983	12.79874	23.83990	44.14497	81.27286	148.7798	270.8460	490.3707
66	1.928460	3.694974	7.034882	13.31068	25.03190	46.79367	86.96196	160.6822	295.2221	539.4078
67	1.947745	3.768873	7.245929	13.84311	26.28349	49.60129	93.04930	173.5368	321.7921	593.3486
68	1.967222	3.844251	7.463307	14.39684	27.59766	52.57737	99.56275	187.4198	350.7534	652.6634
69	1.986894	3.921136	7.687206	14.97271	28.97755	55.73201	106.5321	202.4133	382.3212	717.9518
70	2.006763	3.999558	7.917822	15.57162	30.42643	59.07593	113.9894	218.6064	416.7301	789.7470
71	2.026831	4.079549	8.155357	16.19448	31.94775	62.62049	121.9686	236.0949	454.2358	868.7217
72	2.047099	4.161140	8.400017	16.84226	33.54513	66.37772	130.5065	254.9825	495.1170	955.5938
73	2.067570	4.244363	8.652018	17.51595	35.22239	70.36038	139.6419	275.3811	539.6775	1051.153
74	2.088246	4.329250	8.911578	18.21659	36.98351	74.58200	149.4168	297.4116	588.2485	1156.269
75	2.109128	4.415835	9.178926	18.94525	38.83269	79.05692	159.8760	321.2045	641.1909	1271.895
76	2.130220	4.504152	9.454293	19.70306	40.77432	83.80034	171.0673	346.9009	698.8981	1399.085
77	2.151522	4.594235	9.737922	20.49119	42.81304	88.82836	183.0421	374.6530	761.7989	1538.993
78	2.173037	4.686120	10.03006	21.31083	44.95369	94.15806	195.8550	404.6252	830.3608	1692.893
79	2.194768	4.779842	10.33096	22.16327	47.20137	99.80754	209.5648	436.9952	905.0933	1862.182
80	2.216715	4.875439	10.64089	23.04980	49.56144	105.7960	224.2344	471.9548	986.5517	2048.400

Table A-1.   Single Payment Compound Amount Factor. To Find F for a Given P. $F = P(1 + i)^N$

N/i	1	2	3	4	5	6	7	8	9	10
81	2.238882	4.972948	10.96012	23.97179	52.03951	112.1438	239.9308	509.7112	1075.341	2253.240
82	2.261271	5.072407	11.28892	24.93066	54.64149	118.8724	256.7260	550.4881	1172.122	2478.564
83	2.283884	5.173855	11.62759	25.92789	57.37356	126.0047	274.6968	594.5272	1277.613	2726.421
84	2.306723	5.277332	11.97642	26.96500	60.24224	133.5650	293.9255	642.0893	1392.598	2999.063
85	2.329790	5.382879	12.33571	28.04360	63.25435	141.5789	314.5003	693.4565	1517.932	3298.969
86	2.353088	5.490536	12.70578	29.16535	66.41707	150.0736	336.5154	748.9330	1654.546	3628.866
87	2.376619	5.600347	13.08695	30.33196	69.73792	159.0781	360.0714	808.8476	1803.455	3991.753
88	2.400385	5.712354	13.47956	31.54524	73.22482	168.6227	385.2764	873.5555	1965.766	4390.928
89	2.424389	5.826601	13.88395	32.80705	76.88606	178.7401	412.2458	943.4399	2142.685	4830.021
90	2.448633	5.943133	14.30047	34.11933	80.73037	189.4645	441.1030	1018.915	2335.527	5313.023
91	2.473119	6.061996	14.72948	35.48411	84.76688	200.8324	471.9802	1100.428	2545.724	5844.325
92	2.497850	6.183236	15.17137	36.90347	89.00523	212.8823	505.0188	1188.463	2774.839	6428.757
93	2.522829	6.306900	15.62651	38.37961	93.45549	225.6553	540.3701	1283.540	3024.575	7071.633
94	2.548057	6.433038	16.09530	39.91479	98.12826	239.1946	578.1960	1386.223	3296.786	7778.796
95	2.573538	6.561699	16.57816	41.51139	103.0347	253.5463	618.6697	1497.121	3593.497	8556.676
96	2.599273	6.692933	17.07551	43.17184	108.1864	268.7590	661.9766	1616.890	3916.912	9412.344
97	2.625266	6.826792	17.58777	44.89872	113.5957	284.8846	708.3150	1746.241	4269.434	10353.58
98	2.651518	6.963328	18.11540	46.69466	119.2755	301.9776	757.8970	1885.941	4653.683	11388.94
99	2.678033	7.102594	18.65887	48.56245	125.2393	320.0963	810.9498	2036.816	5072.514	12527.83
100	2.704814	7.244646	19.21863	50.50495	131.5013	339.3021	867.7163	2199.761	5529.041	13780.61

Table A-1. Single Payment Compound Amount Factor. To Find F for a Given P. $F = P(1 + i)^N$

N/i	11	12	13	14	15	16	17	18	19	20
1	1.1100000	1.1200000	1.1300000	1.1400000	1.1500000	1.1600000	1.1700000	1.1800000	1.1900000	1.2000000
2	1.2321000	1.2544000	1.2769000	1.2996000	1.3225000	1.3456000	1.3689000	1.3924000	1.4161000	1.4400000
3	1.3676310	1.4049280	1.4428970	1.4815440	1.5208750	1.5608960	1.6016130	1.6430320	1.6851590	1.7280000
4	1.5180704	1.5735194	1.6304736	1.6889602	1.7490062	1.8106394	1.8738872	1.9387778	2.0053392	2.0736000
5	1.6850582	1.7623417	1.8424352	1.9254146	2.0113572	2.1003417	2.1924480	2.2877578	2.3863537	2.4883200
6	1.8704146	1.9738227	2.0819518	2.1949726	2.3130608	2.4363963	2.5651642	2.6995542	2.8397609	2.9859840
7	2.0761602	2.2106814	2.3526055	2.5022688	2.6600199	2.8262197	3.0012421	3.1854739	3.3793154	3.5831808
8	2.3045378	2.4759632	2.6584442	2.8525864	3.0590229	3.2784149	3.5114533	3.7588592	4.0213853	4.2998170
9	2.5580369	2.7730788	3.0040419	3.2519485	3.5178763	3.8029613	4.1084003	4.4354539	4.7854486	5.1597804
10	2.8394210	3.1058482	3.3945674	3.7072213	4.0455577	4.4114351	4.8068284	5.2338356	5.6946838	6.1917364
11	3.1517573	3.4785500	3.8358612	4.2262323	4.6523914	5.1172647	5.6239892	6.1759260	6.7766737	7.4300837
12	3.4984506	3.8959760	4.3345231	4.8179048	5.3502501	5.9360270	6.5800674	7.2875926	8.0642417	8.9161004
13	3.8832802	4.3634931	4.8980111	5.4924115	6.1527876	6.8857914	7.6986788	8.5993593	9.5964476	10.6993205
14	4.3104410	4.8871123	5.5347525	6.2613491	7.0757058	7.9875180	9.0074542	10.1472440	11.4197727	12.8391846
15	4.7845895	5.4735658	6.2542704	7.1379380	8.1370616	9.2655209	10.5387215	11.9737479	13.5895295	15.4070216
16	5.3108943	6.1303937	7.0673255	8.1372493	9.3576209	10.7480042	12.3303041	14.1290225	16.1715401	18.4884259
17	5.8950927	6.8660409	7.9860778	9.2764642	10.7612640	12.4676849	14.426458	16.6722466	19.2441327	22.1861111
18	6.5435529	7.6899658	9.0242680	10.5751692	12.3754536	14.4625145	16.8789533	19.6732509	22.9005180	26.6233333
19	7.2633437	8.6127617	10.1974228	12.0556929	14.2317716	16.7765168	19.7483754	23.2144361	27.2516164	31.9479999
20	8.0623115	9.6462931	11.5230878	13.7434899	16.3665374	19.4607595	23.1055392	27.3330346	32.4294235	38.3375999

Table A-1.   Single Payment Compound Amount Factor. To Find F for a Given P. $F = P(1 + i)^N$

N/i	11	12	13	14	15	16	17	18	19	20
21	8.9491658	10.8038483	13.0210892	15.6675785	18.8215180	22.5744810	27.0335510	32.3237808	38.5910139	46.0051199
22	9.9335740	12.1003101	14.7138308	17.8610394	21.6447457	26.1863979	31.6292547	38.1420614	45.923066	55.2061439
23	11.0262672	13.5523473	16.6266288	20.3615850	24.8914576	30.376216	37.0062280	45.0076324	54.6487348	66.2473727
24	12.2391566	15.1786289	18.7880905	23.2122069	28.6251762	35.2364170	43.2972868	53.1090063	65.0319944	79.4968472
25	13.5854638	17.0000644	21.2305423	26.4619158	32.9189526	40.8742438	50.6578255	62.6686274	77.3880734	95.3962166
26	15.0798648	19.0400721	23.9905128	30.1665840	37.8567955	47.4141228	59.2696558	73.9449803	92.0918073	114.4754600
27	16.7386500	21.3248808	27.1092794	34.3399058	43.5353148	55.0003824	69.345497	87.2597968	109.5892507	137.3705520
28	18.5799014	23.8838665	30.633485	39.2044926	50.0656121	63.8004436	81.1342319	102.9665602	130.4112084	164.8446624
29	20.6236906	26.7499305	34.6158389	44.6931216	57.5754539	74.0085146	94.9270513	121.5005410	155.1893379	197.8135948
30	22.8922966	29.9559221	39.1158980	50.9501586	66.2117720	85.8498769	111.0645500	143.3706384	184.6753122	237.3763138
31	25.4104492	33.5551128	44.2009847	58.0831808	76.1435378	99.5885572	129.9456405	169.1773534	219.7636215	284.8515766
32	28.2055986	37.5817263	49.9470901	66.2148261	87.5650684	115.5195944	152.0363994	199.6292770	261.5187095	341.8218919
33	31.3082145	42.0915335	56.4402118	75.4849017	100.6998287	134.0027295	177.8825873	235.5625468	311.2072644	410.1862702
34	34.7521180	47.1425175	63.7774394	86.0527880	115.8048030	155.4431662	208.1226271	277.9638052	370.3356446	492.2235243
35	38.5748510	52.7996196	72.0685065	98.1001783	133.1755234	180.3140728	243.5034738	327.9972902	440.7006071	590.6682292
36	42.8180846	59.1355739	81.4374123	111.8342033	153.1518519	209.1643244	284.8990643	387.0368024	524.4337224	708.8018750
37	47.5280740	66.2318428	92.0242759	127.4909917	176.1246297	242.6306163	333.3319052	456.7034269	624.0761296	850.5622500
38	52.7561621	74.1796639	103.9874318	145.3397306	202.5433242	281.4515149	389.9983291	538.9100437	742.6505943	1.021E+03
39	58.5593399	83.0812236	117.5057979	165.6872929	232.9248228	326.4837573	456.2980451	635.9138515	883.7542072	1.225E+03
40	65.0008673	93.0509704	132.7815516	188.8835139	267.8635462	378.7211585	533.867127	750.3783448	1.052E+03	1.470E+03

Table A-1. Single Payment Compound Amount Factor. To Find F for a Given P. $F = P(1 + i)^N$

N/i	11	12	13	14	15	16	17	18	19	20
41	72.1509627	104.2170869	150.0431533	215.3272058	308.0430782	439.3165439	624.6263939	885.446469	1.251E+03	1.764E+03
42	80.0875666	116.7231373	169.5487633	245.4730146	354.2495399	509.6071909	730.8128808	1.045E+03	1.489E+03	2.116E+03
43	88.8972012	130.7299138	191.5901025	279.8392367	407.3869709	591.1443414	855.0510706	1.233E+03	1.772E+03	2.540E+03
44	98.6758933	146.4175035	216.4968158	319.0167298	468.4950165	685.7274360	1.000E+03	1.455E+03	2.109E+03	3.048E+03
45	109.5302415	163.9876039	244.6414019	363.6790720	538.7692690	795.4438258	1.170E+03	1.717E+03	2.510E+03	3.657E+03
46	121.5785681	183.6661163	276.4447841	414.5941420	619.5846593	922.7148379	1.369E+03	2.026E+03	2.986E+03	4.389E+03
47	134.9522106	205.7060503	312.3826061	472.6373219	712.5223582	1.070E+03	1.602E+03	2.390E+03	3.554E+03	5.266E+03
48	149.7969538	230.3907763	352.9923449	538.8065470	819.4007120	1.242E+03	1.875E+03	2.821E+03	4.229E+03	6.320E+03
49	166.2746187	258.0376695	398.8813497	614.2394636	942.3108188	1.440E+03	2.193E+03	3.328E+03	5.033E+03	7.584E+03
50	184.5648267	289.0021898	450.7359252	700.2329885	1.084E+03	1.671E+03	2.566E+03	3.927E+03	5.989E+03	9.100E+03
51	204.8669577	323.6824526	509.3315954	798.2656068	1.246E+03	1.938E+03	3.002E+03	4.634E+03	7.127E+03	1.092E+04
52	227.4023230	362.5243469	575.5447028	910.0227918	1.435E+03	2.248E+03	3.513E+03	5.468E+03	8.481E+03	1.310E+04
53	252.4165786	406.0272686	650.3655142	1.037E+03	1.648E+03	2.608E+03	4.110E+03	6.453E+03	1.009E+04	1.573E+04
54	280.1824022	454.7505408	734.9130310	1.183E+03	1.895E+03	3.025E+03	4.809E+03	7.614E+03	1.201E+04	1.887E+04
55	311.0024664	509.3206057	830.4517251	1.348E+03	2.180E+03	3.509E+03	5.626E+03	8.985E+03	1.429E+04	2.264E+04
56	345.2127378	570.4390784	938.4104493	1.537E+03	2.507E+03	4.070E+03	6.583E+03	1.060E+04	1.701E+04	2.717E+04
57	383.1861389	638.8917678	1.060E+03	1.752E+03	2.883E+03	4.722E+03	7.702E+03	1.251E+04	2.024E+04	3.261E+04
58	425.3366142	715.5587799	1.198E+03	1.997E+03	3.315E+03	5.477E+03	9.011E+03	1.476E+04	2.408E+04	3.913E+04
59	472.1236417	801.4258335	1.354E+03	2.277E+03	3.812E+03	6.354E+03	1.054E+04	1.742E+04	2.866E+04	4.696E+04
60	524.0572423	897.5969335	1.530E+03	2.596E+03	4.384E+03	7.370E+03	1.234E+04	2.056E+04	3.410E+04	5.635E+04

Table A-1. Single Payment Compound Amount Factor. To Find F for a Given P. $F = P(1 + i)^N$

N/i	11	12	13	14	15	16	17	18	19	20
61	581.7035390	1.005E+03	1.729E+03	2.959E+03	5.042E+03	8.549E+03	1.445E+04	2.426E+04	4.058E+04	6.762E+04
62	645.6909283	1.126E+03	1.954E+03	3.374E+03	5.798E+03	9.917E+03	1.689E+04	2.862E+04	4.830E+04	8.114E+04
63	716.7169304	1.261E+03	2.208E+03	3.846E+03	6.668E+03	1.150E+04	1.976E+04	3.377E+04	5.747E+04	9.737E+04
64	795.5557927	1.412E+03	2.495E+03	4.384E+03	7.668E+03	1.334E+04	2.312E+04	3.985E+04	6.839E+04	1.168E+05
65	883.0669299	1.582E+03	2.819E+03	4.998E+03	8.818E+03	1.548E+04	2.704E+04	4.703E+04	8.139E+04	1.402E+05
66	980.2042922	1.772E+03	3.185E+03	5.698E+03	1.014E+04	1.796E+04	3.164E+04	5.549E+04	9.685E+04	1.683E+05
67	1.088E+03	1.984E+03	3.600E+03	6.496E+03	1.166E+04	2.083E+04	3.702E+04	6.548E+04	1.153E+05	2.019E+05
68	1.208E+03	2.222E+03	4.068E+03	7.405E+03	1.341E+04	2.416E+04	4.332E+04	7.726E+04	1.371E+05	2.423E+05
69	1.341E+03	2.489E+03	4.596E+03	8.442E+03	1.542E+04	2.803E+04	5.068E+04	9.117E+04	1.632E+05	2.907E+05
70	1.488E+03	2.788E+03	5.194E+03	9.624E+03	1.774E+04	3.251E+04	5.929E+04	1.076E+05	1.942E+05	3.489E+05
71	1.652E+03	3.122E+03	5.869E+03	1.097E+04	2.040E+04	3.772E+04	6.937E+04	1.269E+05	2.311E+05	4.187E+05
72	1.833E+03	3.497E+03	6.632E+03	1.251E+04	2.346E+04	4.375E+04	8.117E+04	1.498E+05	2.750E+05	5.024E+05
73	2.035E+03	3.917E+03	7.494E+03	1.426E+04	2.697E+04	5.075E+04	9.497E+04	1.768E+05	3.273E+05	6.029E+05
74	2.259E+03	4.387E+03	8.468E+03	1.625E+04	3.102E+04	5.887E+04	1.111E+05	2.086E+05	3.895E+05	7.235E+05
75	2.507E+03	4.913E+03	9.569E+03	1.853E+04	3.567E+04	6.829E+04	1.300E+05	2.461E+05	4.635E+05	8.681E+05
76	2.783E+03	5.503E+03	1.081E+04	2.112E+04	4.102E+04	7.921E+04	1.521E+05	2.904E+05	5.515E+05	1.042E+06
77	3.089E+03	6.163E+03	1.222E+04	2.408E+04	4.718E+04	9.189E+04	1.780E+05	3.427E+05	6.563E+05	1.250E+06
78	3.429E+03	6.902E+03	1.381E+04	2.745E+04	5.425E+04	1.066E+05	2.082E+05	4.044E+05	7.810E+05	1.500E+06
79	3.806E+03	7.731E+03	1.560E+04	3.130E+04	6.239E+04	1.236E+05	2.436E+05	4.772E+05	9.294E+05	1.800E+06
80	4.225E+03	8.656E+03	1.763E+04	3.568E+04	7.175E+04	1.434E+05	2.850E+05	5.631E+05	1.106E+06	2.160E+06

Table A-1. Single Payment Compound Amount Factor. To Find F for a Given P. $F = P(1 + i)^N$

N/i	11	12	13	14	15	16	17	18	19	20
81	4.690E+03	9.698E+03	1.992E+04	4.067E+04	8.251E+04	1.664E+05	3.335E+05	6.644E+05	1.316E+06	2.592E+06
82	5.206E+03	1.086E+04	2.251E+04	4.637E+04	9.489E+04	1.930E+05	3.902E+05	7.840E+05	1.566E+06	3.111E+06
83	5.778E+03	1.216E+04	2.544E+04	5.286E+04	1.091E+05	2.239E+05	4.565E+05	9.251E+05	1.864E+06	3.733E+06
84	6.414E+03	1.362E+04	2.875E+04	6.026E+04	1.255E+05	2.597E+05	5.341E+05	1.092E+06	2.218E+06	4.479E+06
85	7.120E+03	1.526E+04	3.248E+04	6.869E+04	1.443E+05	3.013E+05	6.249E+05	1.288E+06	2.639E+06	5.375E+06
86	7.903E+03	1.709E+04	3.671E+04	7.831E+04	1.660E+05	3.495E+05	7.311E+05	1.520E+06	3.141E+06	6.450E+06
87	8.772E+03	1.914E+04	4.148E+04	8.927E+04	1.909E+05	4.054E+05	8.554E+05	1.794E+06	3.738E+06	7.740E+06
88	9.737E+03	2.144E+04	4.687E+04	1.018E+05	2.195E+05	4.702E+05	1.001E+06	2.116E+06	4.448E+06	9.289E+06
89	1.081E+04	2.401E+04	5.296E+04	1.160E+05	2.524E+05	5.455E+05	1.171E+06	2.497E+06	5.293E+06	1.115E+07
90	1.200E+04	2.689E+04	5.985E+04	1.323E+05	2.903E+05	6.327E+05	1.370E+06	2.947E+06	6.298E+06	1.338E+07
91	1.332E+04	3.012E+04	6.763E+04	1.508E+05	3.338E+05	7.340E+05	1.603E+06	3.477E+06	7.495E+06	1.605E+07
92	1.478E+04	3.373E+04	7.642E+04	1.719E+05	3.839E+05	8.514E+05	1.875E+06	4.103E+06	8.919E+06	1.926E+07
93	1.641E+04	3.778E+04	8.636E+04	1.960E+05	4.415E+05	9.876E+05	2.194E+06	4.842E+06	1.061E+07	2.311E+07
94	1.821E+04	4.231E+04	9.758E+04	2.234E+05	5.077E+05	1.146E+06	2.567E+06	5.714E+06	1.263E+07	2.774E+07
95	2.022E+04	4.739E+04	1.103E+05	2.547E+05	5.838E+05	1.329E+06	3.004E+06	6.742E+06	1.503E+07	3.328E+07
96	2.244E+04	5.308E+04	1.246E+05	2.903E+05	6.714E+05	1.542E+06	3.514E+06	7.956E+06	1.789E+07	3.994E+07
97	2.491E+04	5.945E+04	1.408E+05	3.310E+05	7.721E+05	1.788E+06	4.112E+06	9.388E+06	2.128E+07	4.793E+07
98	2.765E+04	6.658E+04	1.591E+05	3.773E+05	8.879E+05	2.074E+06	4.811E+06	1.108E+07	2.533E+07	5.751E+07
99	3.069E+04	7.457E+04	1.798E+05	4.301E+05	1.021E+06	2.406E+06	5.629E+06	1.307E+07	3.014E+07	6.901E+07
100	3.406E+04	8.352E+04	2.032E+05	4.903E+05	1.174E+06	2.791E+06	6.585E+06	1.542E+07	3.587E+07	8.282E+07

Table A-1. Single Payment Compound Amount Factor. To Find F for a Given P. $F = P(1 + i)^N$

N/i	21	22	23	24	25	26	27	28	29	30
1	1.2100000	1.2200000	1.2300000	1.2400000	1.2500000	1.2600000	1.2700000	1.2800000	1.2900000	1.3000000
2	1.4641000	1.4884000	1.5129000	1.5376000	1.5625000	1.5876000	1.6129000	1.6384000	1.6641000	1.6900000
3	1.7715610	1.8158480	1.8608670	1.9066240	1.9531250	2.0003760	2.0483830	2.0971520	2.1466890	2.1970000
4	2.1435888	2.2153346	2.2886640	2.3642138	2.4414062	2.5204738	2.6014464	2.6843546	2.7692288	2.8561000
5	2.5937425	2.7027082	2.8153057	2.9316251	3.0517578	3.1757969	3.3038369	3.4359738	3.5723052	3.7129300
6	3.1384284	3.2973040	3.4628260	3.6352151	3.8146973	4.0015041	4.1958729	4.3980465	4.6082737	4.8268090
7	3.7974983	4.0227108	4.2592760	4.5076667	4.7683716	5.0418952	5.3287586	5.6294995	5.9446730	6.2748517
8	4.5949730	4.9077072	5.2388094	5.5895067	5.9604645	6.3527880	6.7675234	7.2057594	7.6688282	8.1573072
9	5.5599173	5.9874028	6.4436586	6.9309883	7.4505806	8.0045128	8.5947547	9.2233720	9.8925304	10.6044994
10	6.7274999	7.3046314	7.9259461	8.5944255	9.3132257	10.0856862	10.9153385	11.8059162	12.7613642	13.7858492
11	8.1402749	8.9116503	9.7489137	10.6570876	11.6415322	12.7079646	13.8624799	15.1115727	16.4621598	17.921639
12	9.849327	10.8722134	11.9911638	13.2147087	14.5519152	16.0120354	17.6053495	19.3428131	21.2361862	23.2980851
13	11.9181765	13.2641003	14.7491315	16.3863379	18.1898940	20.1751646	22.3587939	24.7588008	27.3346801	30.2875107
14	14.4209936	16.1822024	18.1414318	20.3190590	22.7373675	25.4207074	28.3956682	31.6912650	35.3391374	39.3737639
15	17.4494023	19.7422870	22.3139611	25.1956632	28.4217094	32.0300913	36.0624987	40.5648192	45.5874872	51.1858930
16	21.1137767	24.0855901	27.4461722	31.2425852	35.5271368	40.3579151	45.7993733	51.9229686	58.8078585	66.5416609
17	25.5476699	29.3844199	33.7587917	38.7408056	44.4089210	50.8509730	58.1652041	66.4613998	75.8621375	86.5041592
18	30.9126805	35.8489233	41.5233138	48.0385990	55.5111512	64.0722259	73.8698092	85.0705917	97.8621573	112.4554070
19	37.4043434	43.7357706	51.0736760	59.5678627	69.3889330	80.7310047	93.8146577	108.8903574	126.2421830	146.1920290
20	45.2592556	53.3576401	62.8206215	73.8641498	86.7361738	101.7210659	119.1446152	139.3796575	162.8524160	190.0496377

Table A-1. Single Payment Compound Amount Factor. To Find F for a Given P. $F = P(1 + i)^N$

N\i	21	22	23	24	25	26	27	28	29	30
21	54.7636992	65.0963209	77.2693645	91.5915457	108.4202172	128.1685430	151.3136614	178.4059616	210.0796167	247.0645291
22	66.2640761	79.4175115	95.0413183	113.5735167	135.5252716	161.4923642	192.1683499	228.3596308	271.0027055	321.1838878
23	80.1795321	96.8893641	116.9008215	140.8311607	169.4065895	203.4803789	244.0538044	292.3003275	349.5934901	417.5390541
24	97.0172338	118.2050242	143.7880104	174.6306393	211.7582368	256.385274	309.9483316	374.1444192	450.9756022	542.8007704
25	117.3308529	144.2101295	176.8592528	216.5419927	264.6977960	323.0454496	393.6343811	478.9048565	581.7585289	705.6410015
26	142.0429320	175.9363580	217.5368810	268.5120710	330.8722450	407.0372665	499.9156640	612.9982163	750.468997	917.3333019
27	171.8719477	214.6423568	267.5703636	332.9549680	413.5903063	512.8669557	634.8928933	784.6377169	968.1043646	1.193E+03
28	207.9650567	261.8636752	329.1115473	412.8641603	516.9878828	646.2123642	806.3139745	1.004E+03	1.249E+03	1.550E+03
29	251.6377186	319.4736838	404.8072031	511.9515588	646.2348536	814.275789	1.024E+03	1.286E+03	1.611E+03	2.015E+03
30	304.4816395	389.7578942	497.9128599	634.8199329	807.7935669	1.026E+03	1.301E+03	1.646E+03	2.078E+03	2.620E+03
31	368.4227838	475.5046310	612.4328176	787.1787168	1.010E+03	1.293E+03	1.652E+03	2.106E+03	2.681E+03	3.40E+03
32	445.7915685	580.1156498	753.2923657	976.0991289	1.262E+03	1.629E+03	2.098E+03	2.696E+03	3.458E+03	4.428E+03
33	539.4077978	707.7410927	926.5496098	1.210E+03	1.578E+03	2.052E+03	2.664E+03	3.451E+03	4.461E+03	5.756E+03
34	652.6834354	863.4441331	1.140E+03	1.501E+03	1.972E+03	2.586E+03	3.383E+03	4.417E+03	5.755E+03	7.483E+03
35	789.7469568	1.053E+03	1.402E+03	1.861E+03	2.465E+03	3.258E+03	4.297E+03	5.654E+03	7.424E+03	9.728E+03
36	955.5938177	1.285E+03	1.724E+03	2.308E+03	3.081E+03	4.105E+03	5.457E+03	7.237E+03	9.577E+03	1.265E+04
37	1.156E+03	1.568E+03	2.121E+03	2.862E+03	3.852E+03	5.173E+03	6.930E+03	9.263E+03	1.235E+04	1.644E+04
38	1.399E+03	1.913E+03	2.609E+03	3.548E+03	4.815E+03	6.517E+03	8.801E+03	1.186E+04	1.594E+04	2.137E+04
39	1.693E+03	2.334E+03	3.208E+03	4.400E+03	6.019E+03	8.212E+03	1.118E+04	1.518E+04	2.056E+04	2.778E+04
40	2.048E+03	2.847E+03	3.946E+03	5.456E+03	7.523E+03	1.035E+04	1.420E+04	1.943E+04	2.652E+04	3.612E+04

Table A-1. Single Payment Compound Amount Factor. To Find F for a Given P. $F = P(1 + i)^N$

N/i	21	22	23	24	25	26	27	28	29	30
41	2.479E+03	3.473E+03	4.854E+03	6.765E+03	9.404E+03	1.304E+04	1.803E+04	2.487E+04	3.421E+04	4.695E+04
42	2.999E+03	4.238E+03	5.971E+03	8.399E+03	1.175E+04	1.643E+04	2.290E+04	3.183E+04	4.413E+04	6.104E+04
43	3.629E+03	5.170E+03	7.344E+03	1.040E+04	1.469E+04	2.070E+04	2.908E+04	4.074E+04	5.693E+04	7.935E+04
44	4.391E+03	6.307E+03	9.033E+03	1.290E+04	1.837E+04	2.608E+04	3.693E+04	5.215E+04	7.344E+04	1.032E+05
45	5.313E+03	7.695E+03	1.111E+04	1.599E+04	2.296E+04	3.286E+04	4.690E+04	6.675E+04	9.474E+04	1.341E+05
46	6.429E+03	9.388E+03	1.367E+04	1.983E+04	2.870E+04	4.140E+04	5.956E+04	8.544E+04	1.222E+05	1.743E+05
47	7.779E+03	1.145E+04	1.681E+04	2.459E+04	3.587E+04	5.217E+04	7.564E+04	1.094E+05	1.577E+05	2.266E+05
48	9.412E+03	1.397E+04	2.067E+04	3.050E+04	4.484E+04	6.573E+04	9.607E+04	1.400E+05	2.034E+05	2.946E+05
49	1.139E+04	1.705E+04	2.543E+04	3.781E+04	5.605E+04	8.282E+04	1.220E+05	1.792E+05	2.624E+05	3.830E+05
50	1.378E+04	2.080E+04	3.128E+04	4.689E+04	7.006E+04	1.044E+05	1.549E+05	2.293E+05	3.384E+05	4.979E+05

Table A-2. Single Payment Present Worth Factor. To Find P for a Given t. $P = F(1 + i)^{-N}$

N/i	1	2	3	4	5	6	7	8	9	10
1	0.9900990	0.9803922	0.9708738	0.9615385	0.9523810	0.9433962	0.9345794	0.9259259	0.9174312	0.9090909
2	0.9802960	0.9611688	0.9425959	0.9245562	0.9070295	0.8899964	0.8734387	0.8573388	0.8416800	0.8264463
3	0.9705901	0.9423223	0.9151417	0.8889964	0.8638376	0.8396193	0.8162979	0.7938322	0.7721835	0.7513148
4	0.9609803	0.9238454	0.8884870	0.8548042	0.8227025	0.7920937	0.7628952	0.7350299	0.7084252	0.6830135
5	0.9514657	0.9057308	0.8626088	0.8219271	0.7835262	0.7472582	0.7129862	0.6805832	0.6499314	0.6209213
6	0.9420452	0.8879714	0.8374843	0.7903145	0.7462154	0.7049605	0.6663422	0.6301696	0.5962673	0.5644739
7	0.9327181	0.8705602	0.8130915	0.7599178	0.7106813	0.6650571	0.6227497	0.5834904	0.5470342	0.5131581
8	0.9234832	0.8534904	0.7894092	0.7306902	0.6768394	0.6274124	0.5820091	0.5402689	0.5018663	0.4665074
9	0.9143398	0.8367553	0.7664167	0.7025867	0.6446089	0.5918985	0.5439337	0.5002490	0.4604278	0.4240976
10	0.9052870	0.8203483	0.7440939	0.6755642	0.6139133	0.5583948	0.5083493	0.4631935	0.4224108	0.3855433
11	0.8963237	0.8042630	0.7224213	0.6495809	0.5846793	0.5267875	0.4750928	0.4288829	0.3875329	0.3504939
12	0.8874492	0.7884932	0.7013799	0.6245970	0.5568374	0.4969694	0.4440120	0.3971138	0.3555347	0.3186308
13	0.8786626	0.7730325	0.6809513	0.6005741	0.5303214	0.4688390	0.4149644	0.3676979	0.3261786	0.2896644
14	0.8699630	0.7578750	0.6611178	0.5774751	0.5050680	0.4423010	0.3878172	0.3404610	0.2992465	0.2633313
15	0.8613495	0.7430147	0.6418619	0.5552645	0.4810171	0.4172651	0.3624460	0.3152417	0.2745380	0.2393920
16	0.8528213	0.7284458	0.6231669	0.5339082	0.4581115	0.3936463	0.3387346	0.2918905	0.2518698	0.2176291
17	0.8443775	0.7141626	0.6050164	0.5133732	0.4362967	0.3713644	0.3165744	0.2702690	0.2310732	0.1978447
18	0.8360173	0.7001594	0.5873946	0.4936281	0.4155207	0.3503438	0.2958639	0.2502490	0.2119937	0.1798588
19	0.8277399	0.6864308	0.5702860	0.4746424	0.3957340	0.3305130	0.2765083	0.2317121	0.1944897	0.1635080
20	0.8195445	0.6729713	0.5536758	0.4563869	0.3768895	0.3118047	0.2584190	0.2145482	0.1784309	0.1486436

Table A-2.   Single Payment Present Worth Factor. To Find P for a Given t. $P = F(1 + i)^{-N}$

N/i	1	2	3	4	5	6	7	8	9	10
21	0.8114302	0.6597758	0.5375493	0.4388336	0.3589424	0.2941554	0.2415131	0.1986557	0.1639981	0.1351306
22	0.8033962	0.6466390	0.5219925	0.4219554	0.3418499	0.2775051	0.2257132	0.1839405	0.1501817	0.1228460
23	0.7954418	0.6341559	0.5066917	0.4057263	0.3255713	0.2617973	0.2109469	0.1703153	0.1377814	0.1116782
24	0.7875661	0.6217215	0.4919337	0.3901215	0.3100679	0.2469785	0.1971466	0.1576993	0.1264049	0.1015256
25	0.7797684	0.6095309	0.4776056	0.3751168	0.2953028	0.2329986	0.1842492	0.1460179	0.1159678	0.0922960
26	0.7720480	0.5975793	0.4636947	0.3606892	0.2812407	0.2198100	0.1721955	0.1352018	0.1063925	0.0839055
27	0.7644039	0.5858620	0.4501891	0.3468166	0.2678483	0.2073680	0.1609304	0.1251868	0.0976078	0.0762777
28	0.7568356	0.5743746	0.4370768	0.3334775	0.2550936	0.1956301	0.1504022	0.1159137	0.0895484	0.0693433
29	0.7493421	0.5631123	0.4243464	0.3206514	0.2429463	0.1845567	0.1405628	0.1073275	0.0821545	0.0630394
30	0.7419229	0.5520709	0.4119868	0.3083187	0.2313774	0.1741101	0.1313671	0.0993773	0.0753711	0.0573086
31	0.7345771	0.5412460	0.3999871	0.2964603	0.2203595	0.1642548	0.1227730	0.0920160	0.0691478	0.0520987
32	0.7273041	0.5306333	0.3883370	0.2850379	0.2098662	0.1549574	0.1147411	0.0852000	0.0634384	0.0473624
33	0.7201031	0.5202287	0.3770262	0.2740942	0.1998725	0.1461862	0.1072347	0.0788889	0.0582003	0.0430568
34	0.7129733	0.5100282	0.3660449	0.2635521	0.1903548	0.1379115	0.1002193	0.0730453	0.0533948	0.0391425
35	0.7059142	0.5000276	0.3553834	0.2534155	0.1812903	0.1301052	0.0936629	0.0676345	0.0489861	0.0355841
36	0.6989249	0.4902232	0.3450324	0.2436687	0.1726574	0.1227408	0.0875355	0.0626246	0.0449413	0.0323492
37	0.6920049	0.4806109	0.3349829	0.2342968	0.1644356	0.1157932	0.0818088	0.0579857	0.0412306	0.0294083
38	0.6851534	0.4711872	0.3252262	0.2252854	0.1566054	0.1092389	0.0764569	0.0536905	0.0378262	0.0267349
39	0.6783697	0.4619482	0.3157535	0.2166206	0.1491480	0.1030555	0.0714550	0.0497134	0.0347030	0.0243044
40	0.6716531	0.4528904	0.3065568	0.2082890	0.1420457	0.0972222	0.0667804	0.0460309	0.0318376	0.0220949

Table A-2. Single Payment Present Worth Factor. To Find P for a Given t. $P = F(1 + i)^{-N}$

N/i	1	2	3	4	5	6	7	8	9	10
51	0.6020186	0.3642430	0.2214632	0.1353006	0.0830512	0.0512154	0.0317269	0.0197419	0.0123381	0.0077441
52	0.5960581	0.3571010	0.2150128	0.1300967	0.0790964	0.0483164	0.0296513	0.0182795	0.0113194	0.0070401
53	0.5901565	0.3500990	0.2087503	0.1250930	0.0753299	0.0455816	0.0277115	0.0169255	0.0103847	0.0064001
54	0.5843134	0.3432343	0.2026702	0.1202817	0.0717427	0.0430015	0.0258986	0.0156717	0.0095273	0.0058183
55	0.5785281	0.3365042	0.1967672	0.1156555	0.0683264	0.0405674	0.0242043	0.0145109	0.0087406	0.0052894
56	0.5728001	0.3299061	0.1910361	0.1112072	0.0650728	0.0382712	0.0226208	0.0134360	0.0080189	0.0048085
57	0.5671288	0.3234374	0.1854719	0.1069300	0.0619741	0.0361049	0.0211410	0.0124407	0.0073568	0.0043714
58	0.5615137	0.3170955	0.1800698	0.1028173	0.0590229	0.0340612	0.0197579	0.0115192	0.0067494	0.0039740
59	0.5559541	0.3108779	0.1748251	0.0988628	0.0562123	0.0321332	0.0184653	0.0106659	0.0061921	0.0036127
60	0.5504496	0.3047823	0.1697331	0.0950604	0.0535355	0.0303143	0.0172573	0.0098759	0.0056808	0.0032843
41	0.6650031	0.4440102	0.2976280	0.2002779	0.1352816	0.0917190	0.0624116	0.0426212	0.0292088	0.0200863
42	0.6584189	0.4353041	0.2889592	0.1925749	0.1288396	0.0865274	0.0583286	0.0394641	0.0267971	0.0182603
43	0.6518999	0.4267688	0.2805429	0.1851682	0.1227044	0.0816296	0.0545127	0.0365408	0.0245845	0.0166002
44	0.6454455	0.4184007	0.2723718	0.1780463	0.1168613	0.0770091	0.0509464	0.0338341	0.0225545	0.0150911
45	0.6390549	0.4101968	0.2644386	0.1711984	0.1112965	0.0726501	0.0476135	0.0313279	0.0206922	0.0137192
46	0.6327276	0.4021537	0.2567365	0.1646139	0.1059967	0.0685378	0.0444996	0.0290073	0.0189937	0.0124720
47	0.6264630	0.3942688	0.2492588	0.1582826	0.1009492	0.0646583	0.0415875	0.0268586	0.0174162	0.0113382
48	0.6202604	0.3865376	0.2419988	0.1521948	0.0961421	0.0609984	0.0388668	0.0248691	0.0159782	0.0103074
49	0.6141192	0.3789584	0.2349503	0.1463411	0.0915639	0.0575457	0.0363241	0.0230269	0.0146589	0.0093704
50	0.6080388	0.3715279	0.2281071	0.1407126	0.0872037	0.0542884	0.0339478	0.0213212	0.0134485	0.0085186

Table A-2.   Single Payment Present Worth Factor. To Find P for a Given t. $P = F(1 + i)^{-N}$

N/i	1	2	3	4	5	6	7	8	9	10
61	0.5449996	0.2988061	0.1647894	0.0914042	0.0509862	0.0285984	0.0161283	0.0091443	0.0052118	0.0029857
62	0.5396036	0.2929472	0.1599897	0.0878887	0.0485583	0.0269797	0.0150732	0.0084670	0.0047814	0.0027143
63	0.5342610	0.2872031	0.1553298	0.0845084	0.0462460	0.0254525	0.0140871	0.0078398	0.0043866	0.0024675
64	0.5289713	0.2815717	0.1508057	0.0812580	0.0440438	0.0240118	0.0131655	0.0072590	0.0040244	0.0022432
65	0.5237339	0.2760507	0.1464133	0.0781327	0.0419465	0.0226526	0.0123042	0.0067213	0.0036921	0.0020393
66	0.5185484	0.2706379	0.1421488	0.0751276	0.0399490	0.0213704	0.0114993	0.0062235	0.0033873	0.0018539
67	0.5134143	0.2653313	0.1380085	0.0722381	0.0380467	0.0201608	0.0107470	0.0057625	0.0031076	0.0016853
68	0.5083310	0.2601287	0.1339889	0.0694597	0.0362349	0.0190196	0.0100439	0.0053356	0.0028510	0.0015321
69	0.5032980	0.2550282	0.1300863	0.0667882	0.0345095	0.0179430	0.0093868	0.0049404	0.0026156	0.0013929
70	0.4983149	0.2500276	0.1262974	0.0642194	0.0328662	0.0169274	0.0087727	0.0045744	0.0023996	0.0012662
71	0.4933810	0.2451251	0.1226188	0.0617494	0.0313011	0.0159692	0.0081988	0.0042356	0.0022015	0.0011511
72	0.4884961	0.2403187	0.1190474	0.0593744	0.0298106	0.0150653	0.0076625	0.0039218	0.0020197	0.0010465
73	0.4836595	0.2356066	0.1155800	0.0570908	0.0283910	0.0142125	0.0071612	0.0036313	0.0018530	9.513E-04
74	0.4788708	0.2309969	0.1122136	0.0548950	0.0270391	0.0134081	0.0066927	0.0033623	0.0017000	8.649E-04
75	0.4741295	0.2264577	0.1089452	0.0527837	0.0257515	0.0126491	0.0062548	0.0031133	0.0015596	7.862E-04
76	0.4694351	0.2220174	0.1057721	0.0507535	0.0245252	0.0119331	0.0058457	0.0028827	0.0014308	7.148E-04
77	0.4647873	0.2176641	0.1026913	0.0488015	0.0233574	0.0112577	0.0054632	0.0026691	0.0013127	6.498E-04
78	0.4601854	0.2133962	0.0997003	0.0469245	0.0222451	0.0106204	0.0051058	0.0024714	0.0012043	5.907E-04
79	0.4556291	0.2092119	0.0967964	0.0451197	0.0211858	0.0100193	0.0047718	0.0022884	0.0011049	5.370E-04
80	0.4511179	0.2051097	0.0939771	0.0433843	0.0201770	0.0094522	0.0044596	0.0021188	0.0010136	4.882E-04

Table A-2. Single Payment Present Worth Factor. To Find P for a Given t. $P = F(1 + i)^{-N}$

N/i	1	2	3	4	5	6	7	8	9	10
81	0.4466514	0.2010880	0.0912399	0.0417157	0.0192162	0.0089171	0.0041679	0.0019619	9.299E-04	4.438E-04
82	0.4422291	0.1971451	0.0885824	0.0401112	0.0183011	0.0084124	0.0038952	0.0018166	8.532E-04	4.035E-04
83	0.4378506	0.1932795	0.0860024	0.0385685.	0.0174296	0.0079362	0.0036404	0.0016820	7.827E-04	3.668E-04
84	0.4335155	0.1894497	0.0834974	0.0370851	0.0165996	0.0074870	0.0034022	0.0015574	7.181E-04	3.334E-04
85	0.4292232	0.1857742	0.0810655	0.0356588	0.0158092	0.0070632	0.0031796	0.0014421	6.588E-04	3.031E-04
86	0.4249735	0.1821316	0.0787043	0.0342873	0.0150564	0.0066634	0.0029716	0.0013352	6.044E-04	2.756E-04
87	0.4207658	0.1785604	0.0764120	0.0329685	0.0143394	0.0062862	0.0027772	0.0012363	5.545E-04	2.505E-04
88	0.4165998	0.1750592	0.0741864	0.0317005	0.0136566	0.0059304	0.0025955	0.0011447	5.087E-04	2.277E-04
89	0.4124751	0.1716266	0.0720256	0.0304813	0.0130063	0.0055947	0.0024257	0.0010600	4.667E-04	2.070E-04
90	0.4083912	0.1682614	0.0699278	0.0293089	0.0123869	0.0052780	0.0022670	9.814E-04	4.282E-04	1.882E-04
91	0.4043477	0.1649622	0.0678911	0.0281816	0.0117971	0.0049793	0.0021187	9.087E-04	3.928E-04	1.711E-04
92	0.4003443	0.1617276	0.0659136	0.0270977	0.0112353	0.0046974	0.0019801	8.414E-04	3.604E-04	1.556E-04
93	0.3963805	0.1585565	0.0639938	0.0260555	0.0107003	0.0044315	0.0018506	7.791E-04	3.306E-04	1.414E-04
94	0.3924559	0.1554475	0.0621299	0.0250534	0.0101907	0.0041807	0.0017295	7.214E-04	3.033E-04	1.286E-04
95	0.3885702	0.1523995	0.0603203	0.0240898	0.0097055	0.0039441	0.0016164	6.679E-04	2.783E-04	1.169E-04
96	0.3847230	0.1494113	0.0585634	0.0231632	0.0092433	0.0037208	0.0015106	6.185E-04	2.553E-04	1.062E-04
97	0.3809138	0.1464817	0.0568577	0.0222724	0.0088031	0.0035102	0.0014118	5.727E-04	2.342E-04	9.658E-05
98	0.3771424	0.1436095	0.0552016	0.0214157	0.0083840	0.0033115	0.0013194	5.302E-04	2.149E-04	8.780E-05
99	0.3734083	0.1407936	0.0535938	0.0205920	0.0079847	0.0031241	0.0012331	4.910E-04	1.971E-04	7.982E-05
100	0.3697112	0.1380330	0.0520328	0.0198000	0.0076045	0.0029472	0.0011525	4.546E-04	1.809E-04	7.257E-05

Table A-2. Single Payment Present Worth Factor. To Find P for a Given t. $P = F(1 + i)^{-N}$

N/i	11	12	13	14	15	16	17	18	19	20
1	0.9009009	0.8928571	0.8849558	0.8771930	0.8695652	0.8620690	0.8547009	0.8474576	0.8403361	0.8333333
2	0.8116224	0.7971939	0.7831467	0.7694675	0.7561437	0.7431629	0.7305136	0.7181844	0.7061648	0.6944444
3	0.7311914	0.7117802	0.6930502	0.6749715	0.6575162	0.6406577	0.6243706	0.6086309	0.5934158	0.5787037
4	0.6587310	0.6355181	0.6133187	0.5920803	0.5717532	0.5522911	0.5336500	0.5157889	0.4986668	0.4822531
5	0.5934513	0.5674269	0.5427599	0.5193687	0.4971767	0.4761130	0.4561112	0.4371092	0.4190494	0.4018776
6	0.5346408	0.5066311	0.4803185	0.4555865	0.4323276	0.4104423	0.3898386	0.3704315	0.3521423	0.3348980
7	0.4816584	0.4523492	0.4250606	0.3996373	0.3759370	0.3538295	0.3331954	0.3139250	0.2959179	0.2790816
8	0.4339265	0.4038832	0.3761599	0.3505591	0.3269018	0.3050255	0.2847824	0.2660382	0.2486705	0.2325680
9	0.3909248	0.3606100	0.3328848	0.3075079	0.2842624	0.2629530	0.2434037	0.2254561	0.2089668	0.1938067
10	0.3521845	0.3219732	0.2945883	0.2697438	0.2471847	0.2266836	0.2080374	0.1910645	0.1756024	0.1615056
11	0.3172833	0.2874761	0.2606977	0.2366174	0.2149432	0.1954169	0.1778097	0.1619190	0.1475650	0.1345880
12	0.2858408	0.2566751	0.2307059	0.2075591	0.1869072	0.1684628	0.1519741	0.1372195	0.1240042	0.1121567
13	0.2575143	0.2291742	0.2041645	0.1820694	0.1625280	0.1452266	0.1298924	0.1162877	0.1042052	0.0934639
14	0.2319948	0.2046198	0.1806766	0.1597100	0.1413287	0.1251953	0.1110192	0.0985489	0.0875674	0.0778866
15	0.2090043	0.1826963	0.1598908	0.1400965	0.1228945	0.1079270	0.0948882	0.0835160	0.0735861	0.0649055
16	0.1882922	0.1631217	0.1414962	0.1228917	0.1066848	0.0930405	0.0811010	0.0707763	0.0618370	0.0540879
17	0.1696326	0.1456443	0.1252179	0.1077997	0.0929259	0.0802074	0.0693171	0.0599799	0.0519639	0.0450732
18	0.1528222	0.1300396	0.1108123	0.0945611	0.0808051	0.0691443	0.0592454	0.0508304	0.0436671	0.0375610
19	0.1376776	0.1161068	0.0980640	0.0829484	0.0702653	0.0596071	0.0506371	0.0430766	0.0366951	0.0313009
20	0.1240339	0.1036668	0.0867823	0.0727617	0.0611003	0.0513855	0.0432796	0.0365056	0.0308362	0.0260841

Table A-2.   Single Payment Present Worth Factor. To Find P for a Given t. $P = F(1 + i)^{-N}$

N/i	11	12	13	14	15	16	17	18	19	20
21	0.1117423	0.0925596	0.0767985	0.0638261	0.0531307	0.0442978	0.0369911	0.0309370	0.0259128	0.0217367
22	0.1006687	0.0826425	0.0679633	0.0559878	0.0462006	0.0381878	0.0316163	0.0262178	0.0217754	0.0181139
23	0.0906925	0.0737880	0.0601445	0.0491121	0.0401744	0.0329205	0.0270225	0.0222185	0.0182987	0.0150949
24	0.0817050	0.0658821	0.0532252	0.0430808	0.0349343	0.0283797	0.0230961	0.0188292	0.0153770	0.0125791
25	0.0736081	0.0588233	0.0471020	0.0377902	0.0303776	0.0244653	0.0197403	0.0159569	0.0129219	0.0104826
26	0.0663136	0.0525208	0.0416831	0.0331493	0.0264153	0.0210908	0.0168720	0.0135228	0.0108587	0.0087355
27	0.0597420	0.0468936	0.0368877	0.0290783	0.0229699	0.0181817	0.0144205	0.0114600	0.0091250	0.0072796
28	0.0538216	0.0418693	0.0326440	0.0255073	0.0199738	0.0156739	0.0123253	0.0097119	0.0076681	0.0060663
29	0.0484879	0.0373833	0.0288885	0.0223748	0.0173685	0.0135120	0.0105344	0.0082304	0.0064437	0.0050553
30	0.0436828	0.0333779	0.0255651	0.0196270	0.0151031	0.0116482	0.0090038	0.0069749	0.0054149	0.0042127
31	0.0393539	0.0298017	0.0226239	0.0172167	0.0131331	0.0100416	0.0076955	0.0059110	0.0045503	0.0035106
32	0.0354540	0.0266087	0.0200212	0.0151024	0.0114201	0.0086565	0.0065774	0.0050093	0.0038238	0.0029255
33	0.0319405	0.0237577	0.0177179	0.0132477	0.0099305	0.0074625	0.0056217	0.0042452	0.0032133	0.0024379
34	0.0287752	0.0212123	0.0156795	0.0116208	0.0086352	0.0064332	0.0048049	0.0035976	0.0027002	0.0020316
35	0.0259236	0.0189395	0.0138757	0.0101937	0.0075089	0.0055459	0.0041067	0.0030488	0.0022691	0.0016930
36	0.0233546	0.0169103	0.0122794	0.0089418	0.0065295	0.0047809	0.0035100	0.0025837	0.0019068	0.0014108
37	0.0210402	0.0150985	0.0108667	0.0078437	0.0056778	0.0041215	0.0030000	0.0021896	0.0016024	0.0011757
38	0.0189551	0.0134808	0.0096165	0.0066804	0.0049372	0.0035530	0.0025641	0.0018556	0.0013465	9.797E-04
39	0.0170767	0.0120364	0.0085102	0.0060355	0.0042932	0.0030629	0.0021916	0.0015725	0.0011315	8.165E-04
40	0.0153844	0.0107468	0.0075312	0.0052943	0.0037332	0.0026405	0.0018731	0.0013327	9.509E-04	6.804E-04

Table A-2. Single Payment Present Worth Factor. To Find P for a Given t. $P = F(1 + i)^{-N}$

N/i	11	12	13	14	15	16	17	18	19	20
41	0.0138598	0.0095954	0.0066647	0.0046441	0.0032463	0.0022763	0.0016010	0.0011294	7.991E-04	5.670E-04
42	0.0124863	0.0085673	0.0058980	0.0040738	0.0028229	0.0019623	0.0013683	9.571E-04	6.715E-04	4.725E-04
43	0.0112489	0.0076494	0.0052195	0.0035735	0.0024547	0.0016916	0.0011695	8.111E-04	5.643E-04	3.937E-04
44	0.0101342	0.0068298	0.0046190	0.0031346	0.0021345	0.0014583	9.996E-04	6.874E-04	4.742E-04	3.281E-04
45	0.0091299	0.0060980	0.0040876	0.0027497	0.0018561	0.0012572	8.544E-04	5.825E-04	3.985E-04	2.734E-04
46	0.0062251	0.0054447	0.0036174	0.0024120	0.0016140	0.0010838	7.302E-04	4.937E-04	3.349E-04	2.279E-04
47	0.0074100	0.0048613	0.0032012	0.0021158	0.0014035	9.343E-04	6.241E-04	4.184E-04	2.814E-04	1.899E-04
48	0.0066757	0.0043405	0.0028329	0.0018560	0.0012204	8.054E-04	5.334E-04	3.545E-04	2.365E-04	1.582E-04
49	0.0060141	0.0038754	0.0025070	0.0016280	0.0010612	6.943E-04	4.559E-04	3.005E-04	1.987E-04	1.319E-04
50	0.0054182	0.0034602	0.0022186	0.0014281	9.228E-04	5.986E-04	3.897E-04	2.546E-04	1.670E-04	1.099E-04
51	0.0048812	0.0030894	0.0019634	0.0012527	8.024E-04	5.160E-04	3.331E-04	2.158E-04	1.403E-04	9.157E-05
52	0.0043975	0.0027584	0.0017375	0.0010989	6.978E-04	4.448E-04	2.847E-04	1.829E-04	1.179E-04	7.631E-05
53	0.0039617	0.0024629	0.0015376	9.639E-04	6.068E-04	3.835E-04	2.433E-04	1.550E-04	9.909E-05	6.359E-05
54	0.0035691	0.0021990	0.0013607	8.455E-04	5.276E-04	3.306E-04	2.080E-04	1.313E-04	8.327E-05	5.299E-05
55	0.0032154	0.0019634	0.0012042	7.417E-04	4.588E-04	2.850E-04	1.777E-04	1.113E-04	6.997E-05	4.416E-05
56	0.0028968	0.0017530	0.0010656	6.506E-04	3.990E-04	2.457E-04	1.519E-04	9.432E-05	5.880E-05	3.680E-05
57	0.0026097	0.0015652	9.430E-04	5.707E-04	3.469E-04	2.118E-04	1.298E-04	7.993E-05	4.941E-05	3.067E-05
58	0.0023511	0.0013975	8.345E-04	5.006E-04	3.017E-04	1.826E-04	1.110E-04	6.774E-05	4.152E-05	2.556E-05
59	0.0021181	0.0012478	7.385E-04	4.392E-04	2.623E-04	1.574E-04	9.465E-05	5.741E-05	3.489E-05	2.130E-05
60	0.0019082	0.0011141	6.536E-04	3.852E-04	2.281E-04	1.357E-04	8.107E-05	4.865E-05	2.932E-05	1.775E-05

Table A-2. Single Payment Present Worth Factor. To Find P for a Given t. $P = F(1 + i)^{-N}$

N/i	11	12	13	14	15	16	17	18	19	20
61	0.0017191	9.947E-04	5.784E-04	3.379E-04	1.983E-04	1.170E-04	6.929E-05	4.123E-05	2.464E-05	1.479E-05
62	0.0015487	8.881E-04	5.118E-04	2.964E-04	1.725E-04	1.008E-04	5.922E-05	3.494E-05	2.071E-05	1.232E-05
63	0.0013953	7.930E-04	4.530E-04	2.600E-04	1.500E-04	8.693E-05	5.062E-05	2.961E-05	1.740E-05	1.027E-05
64	0.0012570	7.080E-04	4.008E-04	2.281E-04	1.304E-04	7.494E-05	4.326E-05	2.509E-05	1.462E-05	8.559E-06
65	0.0011324	6.322E-04	3.547E-04	2.001E-04	1.134E-04	6.460E-05	3.698E-05	2.127E-05	1.229E-05	7.132E-06
66	0.0010202	5.644E-04	3.139E-04	1.755E-04	9.861E-05	5.569E-05	3.160E-05	1.802E-05	1.033E-05	5.943E-06
67	9.191E-04	5.040E-04	2.778E-04	1.539E-04	8.575E-05	4.801E-05	2.701E-05	1.527E-05	8.677E-06	4.953E-06
68	8.280E-04	4.500E-04	2.458E-04	1.350E-04	7.457E-05	4.139E-05	2.309E-05	1.294E-05	7.291E-06	4.127E-06
69	7.460E-04	4.018E-04	2.176E-04	1.185E-04	6.484E-05	3.568E-05	1.973E-05	1.097E-05	6.127E-06	3.439E-06
70	6.720E-04	3.587E-04	1.925E-04	1.039E-04	5.638E-05	3.076E-05	1.687E-05	9.295E-06	5.149E-06	2.866E-06
71	6.054E-04	3.203E-04	1.704E-04	9.115E-05	4.903E-05	2.651E-05	1.441E-05	7.877E-06	4.327E-06	2.389E-06
72	5.454E-04	2.860E-04	1.508E-04	7.996E-05	4.263E-05	2.286E-05	1.232E-05	6.676E-06	3.636E-06	1.990E-06
73	4.914E-04	2.553E-04	1.334E-04	7.014E-05	3.707E-05	1.970E-05	1.053E-05	5.657E-06	3.055E-06	1.659E-06
74	4.427E-04	2.280E-04	1.181E-04	6.152E-05	3.224E-05	1.699E-05	9.000E-06	4.794E-06	2.568E-06	1.382E-06
75	3.988E-04	2.035E-04	1.045E-04	5.397E-05	2.803E-05	1.464E-05	7.692E-06	4.063E-06	2.158E-06	1.152E-06
76	3.593E-04	1.817E-04	9.248E-05	4.734E-05	2.438E-05	1.262E-05	6.575E-06	3.443E-06	1.813E-06	9.599E-07
77	3.237E-04	1.623E-04	8.184E-05	4.153E-05	2.120E-05	1.088E-05	5.619E-06	2.918E-06	1.524E-06	7.999E-07
78	2.916E-04	1.449E-04	7.242E-05	3.643E-05	1.843E-05	9.382E-06	4.803E-06	2.473E-06	1.280E-06	6.666E-07
79	2.627E-04	1.294E-04	6.409E-05	3.195E-05	1.603E-05	8.088E-06	4.105E-06	2.096E-06	1.076E-06	5.555E-07
80	2.367E-04	1.155E-04	5.672E-05	2.803E-05	1.394E-05	6.972E-06	3.509E-06	1.776E-06	9.042E-07	4.629E-07

Table A-2. Single Payment Present Worth Factor. To Find *P* for a Given *t*. $P = F(1 + i)^{-N}$

N/i	11	12	13	14	15	16	17	18	19	20
81	2.132E-04	1.031E-04	5.019E-05	2.459E-05	1.212E-05	6.010E-06	2.999E-06	1.505E-06	7.598E-07	3.858E-07
82	1.921E-04	9.207E-05	4.442E-05	2.157E-05	1.054E-05	5.181E-06	2.563E-06	1.275E-06	6.385E-07	3.215E-07
83	1.731E-04	8.221E-05	3.931E-05	1.892E-05	9.164E-06	4.467E-06	2.191E-06	1.081E-06	5.365E-07	2.679E-07
84	1.559E-04	7.340E-05	3.479E-05	1.660E-05	7.969E-06	3.851E-06	1.872E-06	9.160E-07	4.509E-07	2.232E-07
85	1.405E-04	6.553E-05	3.078E-05	1.456E-05	6.929E-06	3.319E-06	1.600E-06	7.763E-07	3.789E-07	1.860E-07
86	1.265E-04	5.851E-05	2.724E-05	1.277E-05	6.025E-06	2.862E-06	1.368E-06	6.579E-07	3.184E-07	1.550E-07
87	1.140E-04	5.224E-05	2.411E-05	1.120E-05	5.239E-06	2.467E-06	1.169E-06	5.575E-07	2.676E-07	1.292E-07
88	1.027E-04	4.665E-05	2.134E-05	9.826E-06	4.556E-06	2.127E-06	9.992E-07	4.725E-07	2.248E-07	1.077E-07
89	9.252E-05	4.165E-05	1.888E-05	8.619E-06	3.962E-06	1.833E-06	8.540E-07	4.004E-07	1.889E-07	8.972E-08
90	8.336E-05	3.719E-05	1.671E-05	7.561E-06	3.445E-06	1.580E-06	7.299E-07	3.393E-07	1.588E-07	7.476E-08
91	7.509E-05	3.320E-05	1.479E-05	6.632E-06	2.996E-06	1.362E-06	6.239E-07	2.876E-07	1.334E-07	6.230E-08
92	6.765E-05	2.964E-05	1.309E-05	5.818E-06	2.605E-06	1.175E-06	5.332E-07	2.437E-07	1.121E-07	5.192E-08
93	6.095E-05	2.647E-05	1.158E-05	5.103E-06	2.265E-06	1.013E-06	4.557E-07	2.065E-07	9.422E-08	4.327E-08
94	5.491E-05	2.363E-05	1.025E-05	4.477E-06	1.970E-06	8.729E-07	3.895E-07	1.750E-07	7.917E-08	3.605E-08
95	4.947E-05	2.110E-05	9.069E-06	3.927E-06	1.713E-06	7.525E-07	3.329E-07	1.483E-07	6.653E-08	3.005E-08
96	4.457E-05	1.884E-05	8.025E-06	3.445E-06	1.489E-06	6.487E-07	2.845E-07	1.257E-07	5.591E-08	2.504E-08
97	4.015E-05	1.682E-05	7.102E-06	3.022E-06	1.295E-06	5.592E-07	2.432E-07	1.065E-07	4.698E-08	2.087E-08
98	3.617E-05	1.502E-05	6.285E-06	2.650E-06	1.126E-06	4.821E-07	2.079E-07	9.027E-08	3.948E-08	1.739E-08
99	3.259E-05	1.341E-05	5.562E-06	2.325E-06	9.793E-07	4.156E-07	1.777E-07	7.650E-08	3.318E-08	1.449E-08
100	2.936E-05	1.197E-05	4.922E-06	2.039E-06	8.516E-07	3.583E-07	1.518E-07	6.483E-08	2.788E-08	1.207E-08

Table A-2. Single Payment Present Worth Factor. To Find P for a Given t. $P = F(1 + i)^{-N}$

N/i	21	22	23	24	25	26	27	28	29	30
1	0.8264463	0.8196721	0.8130081	0.8064516	0.8000000	0.7936508	0.7874016	0.7812500	0.7751938	0.7692308
2	0.6830135	0.6718624	0.6609822	0.6503642	0.6400000	0.6298816	0.6200012	0.6103516	0.6009254	0.5917160
3	0.5644739	0.5507069	0.5373839	0.5244873	0.5120000	0.4999060	0.4881900	0.4768372	0.4658337	0.4551661
4	0.4665074	0.4513991	0.4368975	0.4229736	0.4096000	0.3967508	0.3844015	0.3725290	0.3611114	0.3501278
5	0.3855433	0.3699993	0.3552012	0.3411077	0.3276800	0.3148816	0.3026784	0.2910383	0.2799313	0.2693291
6	0.3186308	0.3032781	0.2887815	0.2750869	0.2621440	0.2499060	0.2383294	0.2273737	0.2170010	0.2071762
7	0.2633313	0.2485886	0.2347817	0.2218443	0.2097152	0.1983381	0.1876610	0.1776357	0.1682178	0.1593663
8	0.2176291	0.2037611	0.1908794	0.1789067	0.1677722	0.1574112	0.1477645	0.1387779	0.1304014	0.1225895
9	0.1798588	0.1670173	0.1551865	0.1442796	0.1342177	0.1249295	0.1163500	0.1084202	0.1010864	0.0942996
10	0.1486436	0.1368994	0.1261679	0.1163545	0.1073742	0.0991504	0.0916142	0.0847033	0.0783615	0.0725382
11	0.1228460	0.1122127	0.1025755	0.0938343	0.0858993	0.0786908	0.0721372	0.0661744	0.0607454	0.0557986
12	0.1015256	0.0919776	0.0833947	0.0756728	0.0687195	0.0624530	0.0568009	0.0516988	0.0470894	0.0429220
13	0.0839055	0.0753915	0.0678006	0.0610264	0.0549756	0.0495659	0.0447251	0.0403897	0.0365034	0.0330169
14	0.0693433	0.0617963	0.0551224	0.0492149	0.0439805	0.0393380	0.0352166	0.0315544	0.0282972	0.0253376
15	0.0573086	0.0506527	0.0448150	0.0396894	0.0351844	0.0312206	0.0277296	0.0246519	0.0219358	0.0195366
16	0.0473624	0.0415186	0.0364350	0.0320076	0.0281475	0.0247783	0.0218344	0.0192593	0.0170045	0.0150282
17	0.0391425	0.0340316	0.0296219	0.0258126	0.0225180	0.0196653	0.0171924	0.0150463	0.0131818	0.0115601
18	0.0323492	0.0278948	0.0240829	0.0208166	0.0180144	0.0156074	0.0135373	0.0117549	0.0102185	0.0088924
19	0.0267349	0.0228646	0.0195796	0.0167876	0.0144115	0.0123868	0.0106593	0.0091835	0.0079213	0.0068403
20	0.0220949	0.0187415	0.0159183	0.0135384	0.0115292	0.0098308	0.0083932	0.0071746	0.0061405	0.0052618

Table A-2. Single Payment Present Worth Factor. To Find P for a Given t. $P = F(1 + i)^{-N}$

N/i	21	22	23	24	25	26	27	28	29	30
21	0.0182603	0.0153619	0.0129417	0.0109180	0.0092234	0.0070022	0.0066088	0.0056052	0.0047601	0.0040475
22	0.0150911	0.0125917	0.0105217	0.0088049	0.0073787	0.0061922	0.0052038	0.0043791	0.0036900	0.0031135
23	0.0124720	0.0103211	0.0085543	0.0071007	0.0059030	0.0049145	0.0040975	0.0034211	0.0028605	0.0023950
24	0.0103074	0.0084599	0.0069547	0.0057264	0.0047224	0.0039004	0.0032263	0.0026728	0.0022174	0.0018423
25	0.0085186	0.0069343	0.0056542	0.0046180	0.0037779	0.0030955	0.0025404	0.0020881	0.0017189	0.0014172
26	0.0070401	0.0056839	0.0045969	0.0037242	0.0030223	0.0024568	0.0020003	0.0016313	0.0013325	0.0010901
27	0.0058183	0.0046589	0.0037373	0.0030034	0.0024179	0.0019498	0.0015751	0.0012745	0.0010329	8.386E-04
28	0.0048085	0.0038188	0.0030385	0.0024221	0.0019343	0.0015475	0.0012402	9.957E-04	8.007E-04	6.450E-04
29	0.0039740	0.0031301	0.0024703	0.0019533	0.0015474	0.0012282	9.765E-04	7.779E-04	6.207E-04	4.962E-04
30	0.0032843	0.0025657	0.0020084	0.0015752	0.0012379	9.747E-04	7.689E-04	6.077E-04	4.812E-04	3.817E-04
31	0.0027143	0.0021030	0.0016328	0.0012704	9.904E-04	7.736E-04	6.055E-04	4.748E-04	3.730E-04	2.936E-04
32	0.0022432	0.0017238	0.0013275	0.0010245	7.923E-04	6.140E-04	4.767E-04	3.709E-04	2.892E-04	2.258E-04
33	0.0018539	0.0014129	0.0010793	8.262E-04	6.338E-04	4.873E-04	3.754E-04	2.898E-04	2.242E-04	1.737E-04
34	0.0015321	0.0011582	8.775E-04	6.663E-04	5.071E-04	3.867E-04	2.956E-04	2.264E-04	1.738E-04	1.336E-04
35	0.0012662	9.493E-04	7.134E-04	5.373E-04	4.056E-04	3.069E-04	2.327E-04	1.769E-04	1.347E-04	1.028E-04
36	0.0010465	7.781E-04	5.800E-04	4.333E-04	3.245E-04	2.436E-04	1.833E-04	1.382E-04	1.044E-04	7.908E-05
37	8.649E-04	6.378E-04	4.715E-04	3.495E-04	2.596E-04	1.933E-04	1.443E-04	1.080E-04	8.094E-05	6.083E-05
38	7.148E-04	5.228E-04	3.834E-04	2.818E-04	2.077E-04	1.534E-04	1.136E-04	8.434E-05	6.275E-05	4.679E-05
39	5.907E-04	4.285E-04	3.117E-04	2.273E-04	1.662E-04	1.218E-04	8.947E-05	6.589E-05	4.864E-05	3.599E-05
40	4.882E-04	3.512E-04	2.534E-04	1.833E-04	1.329E-04	9.664E-05	7.045E-05	5.148E-05	3.771E-05	2.769E-05

Table A-2. Single Payment Present Worth Factor. To Find P for a Given t. $P = F(1 + i)^{-N}$

N/i	21	22	23	24	25	26	27	28	29	30
41	4.035E-04	2.879E-04	2.060E-04	1.478E-04	1.063E-04	7.670E-05	5.547E-05	4.022E-05	2.923E-05	2.130E-05
42	3.334E-04	2.360E-04	1.675E-04	1.192E-04	8.507E-05	6.087E-05	4.368E-05	3.142E-05	2.266E-05	1.638E-05
43	2.756E-04	1.934E-04	1.362E-04	9.613E-05	6.806E-05	4.831E-05	3.439E-05	2.455E-05	1.756E-05	1.260E-05
44	2.277E-04	1.586E-04	1.107E-04	7.753E-05	5.445E-05	3.834E-05	2.708E-05	1.918E-05	1.362E-05	9.694E-06
45	1.882E-04	1.300E-04	9.001E-05	6.252E-05	4.356E-05	3.043E-05	2.132E-05	1.498E-05	1.056E-05	7.457E-06
46	1.556E-04	1.065E-04	7.318E-05	5.042E-05	3.484E-05	2.415E-05	1.679E-05	1.170E-05	8.182E-06	5.736E-06
47	1.286E-04	8.731E-05	5.949E-05	4.066E-05	2.788E-05	1.917E-05	1.322E-05	9.144E-06	6.343E-06	4.412E-06
48	1.062E-04	7.157E-05	4.837E-05	3.279E-05	2.230E-05	1.521E-05	1.041E-05	7.144E-06	4.917E-06	3.394E-06
49	8.780E-05	5.866E-05	3.932E-05	2.644E-05	1.784E-05	1.207E-05	8.196E-06	5.581E-06	3.812E-06	2.611E-06
50	7.257E-05	4.808E-05	3.197E-05	2.133E-05	1.427E-05	9.582E-06	6.454E-06	4.360E-06	2.955E-06	2.008E-06

N/i	31	32	33	34	35	36	37	38	39	40
1	0.7633588	0.7575758	0.7518797	0.7462687	0.7407407	0.7352941	0.7299270	0.7246377	0.7194245	0.7142857
2	0.5827166	0.5739210	0.5653231	0.5569169	0.5486968	0.5406574	0.5327934	0.5250998	0.5175716	0.5102041
3	0.4448219	0.4347887	0.4250549	0.4156096	0.4064421	0.3975422	0.3889003	0.3805071	0.3723536	0.3644315
4	0.3395587	0.3293853	0.3195902	0.3101564	0.3010682	0.2923105	0.2838688	0.2757298	0.2678803	0.2603082
5	0.2592051	0.2495344	0.2402934	0.2314600	0.2230135	0.2149342	0.2072035	0.1998042	0.1927197	0.1859344
6	0.1978665	0.1890412	0.1806717	0.1727314	0.1651952	0.1580398	0.1512435	0.1447856	0.1386472	0.1328103
7	0.1510431	0.1432130	0.1358434	0.1289040	0.1223668	0.1162058	0.1103367	0.1049171	0.0997462	0.0948645
8	0.1153001	0.1084947	0.1021379	0.0961970	0.0906421	0.0854454	0.0805815	0.0760269	0.0717599	0.0677604
9	0.0880153	0.0821930	0.0767954	0.0717888	0.0671423	0.0628275	0.0588186	0.0550920	0.0516258	0.0484003
10	0.0671873	0.0622674	0.0577409	0.0535737	0.0497350	0.0461967	0.0429333	0.0399217	0.0371409	0.0345716

Table A-2.   Single Payment Present Worth Factor. To Find P for a Given t. $P = F(1 + i)^{-N}$

N/i	31	32	33	34	35	36	37	38	39	40
31	2.315E-04	1.829E-04	1.447E-04	1.147E-04	9.113E-05	7.249E-05	5.776E-05	4.611E-05	3.686E-05	2.951E-05
32	1.767E-04	1.386E-04	1.088E-04	8.563E-05	6.750E-05	5.330E-05	4.216E-05	3.341E-05	2.652E-05	2.108E-05
33	1.349E-04	1.050E-04	8.183E-05	6.391E-05	5.000E-05	3.919E-05	3.078E-05	2.421E-05	1.908E-05	1.506E-05
34	1.030E-04	7.952E-05	6.152E-05	4.769E-05	3.704E-05	2.882E-05	2.246E-05	1.754E-05	1.372E-05	1.076E-05
35	7.861E-05	6.024E-05	4.626E-05	3.559E-05	2.744E-05	2.119E-05	1.640E-05	1.271E-05	9.874E-06	7.683E-06
36	6.001E-05	4.564E-05	3.478E-05	2.656E-05	2.032E-05	1.558E-05	1.197E-05	9.212E-06	7.103E-06	5.488E-06
37	4.581E-05	3.458E-05	2.615E-05	1.982E-05	1.505E-05	1.146E-05	8.737E-06	6.675E-06	5.110E-06	3.920E-06
38	3.497E-05	2.619E-05	1.966E-05	1.479E-05	1.115E-05	8.424E-06	6.377E-06	4.837E-06	3.677E-06	2.800E-06
39	2.669E-05	1.984E-05	1.478E-05	1.104E-05	8.260E-06	6.194E-06	4.655E-06	3.505E-06	2.645E-06	2.000E-06
40	2.038E-05	1.503E-05	1.112E-05	8.238E-06	6.119E-06	4.555E-06	3.398E-06	2.540E-06	1.903E-06	1.428E-06
41	1.556E-05	1.139E-05	8.358E-06	6.148E-06	4.532E-06	3.349E-06	2.480E-06	1.841E-06	1.369E-06	1.020E-06
42	1.187E-05	8.628E-06	6.284E-06	4.588E-06	3.357E-06	2.462E-06	1.810E-06	1.334E-06	9.849E-07	7.288E-07
43	9.064E-06	6.536E-06	4.725E-06	3.424E-06	2.487E-06	1.811E-06	1.321E-06	9.665E-07	7.085E-07	5.206E-07
44	6.919E-06	4.952E-06	3.552E-06	2.555E-06	1.842E-06	1.331E-06	9.645E-07	7.004E-07	5.097E-07	3.718E-07
45	5.282E-06	3.751E-06	2.671E-06	1.907E-06	1.365E-06	9.789E-07	7.040E-07	5.075E-07	3.667E-07	2.656E-07
46	4.032E-06	2.842E-06	2.008E-06	1.423E-06	1.011E-06	7.198E-07	5.139E-07	3.678E-07	2.638E-07	1.897E-07
47	3.078E-06	2.153E-06	1.510E-06	1.062E-06	7.497E-07	5.293E-07	3.751E-07	2.665E-07	1.898E-07	1.355E-07
48	2.350E-06	1.631E-06	1.135E-06	7.924E-07	5.546E-07	3.892E-07	2.738E-07	1.931E-07	1.365E-07	9.680E-08
49	1.794E-06	1.236E-06	8.536E-07	5.914E-07	4.108E-07	2.861E-07	1.998E-07	1.399E-07	9.824E-08	6.914E-08
50	1.369E-06	9.361E-07	6.418E-07	4.413E-07	3.043E-07	2.104E-07	1.459E-07	1.014E-07	7.067E-08	4.935E-08

Table A-2. Single Payment Present Worth Factor. To Find P for a Given t. $P = F(1 + i)^{-N}$

N/i	31	32	33	34	35	36	37	38	39	40
11	0.0512880	0.0471723	0.0434142	0.0399804	0.0368408	0.0333682	0.0313382	0.0289288	0.0267200	0.0246940
12	0.0391511	0.0357366	0.0326423	0.0298361	0.0272894	0.0249766	0.0228746	0.0209629	0.0192231	0.0176386
13	0.0298864	0.0270732	0.0245431	0.0222658	0.0202144	0.0183651	0.0166968	0.0151905	0.0138295	0.0125990
14	0.0228140	0.0205100	0.0184534	0.0166162	0.0149736	0.0135038	0.0121874	0.0110076	0.0099493	0.0089993
15	0.0174153	0.0155379	0.0138748	0.0124002	0.0110916	0.0099292	0.0089959	0.0079765	0.0071578	0.0064281
16	0.0132941	0.0117711	0.0104321	0.0092539	0.0082160	0.0073009	0.0064934	0.0057801	0.0051495	0.0045915
17	0.0101482	0.0089175	0.0078437	0.0069059	0.0060859	0.0053683	0.0047397	0.0041885	0.0037047	0.0032796
18	0.0077467	0.0067557	0.0058975	0.0051536	0.0045081	0.0039473	0.0034596	0.0030351	0.0026652	0.0023426
19	0.0059135	0.0051179	0.0044342	0.0038460	0.0033393	0.0029024	0.0025253	0.0021994	0.0019174	0.0016733
20	0.0045141	0.0038772	0.0033340	0.0028701	0.0024736	0.0021341	0.0018433	0.0015937	0.0013794	0.0011952
21	0.0034459	0.0029373	0.0025068	0.0021419	0.0018323	0.0015692	0.0013455	0.0011549	9.924E-04	8.537E-04
22	0.0026305	0.0022252	0.0018848	0.0015984	0.0013572	0.0011538	9.821E-04	8.369E-04	7.140E-04	6.098E-04
23	0.0020080	0.0016858	0.0014171	0.0011929	0.0010054	8.484E-04	7.168E-04	6.064E-04	5.136E-04	4.356E-04
24	0.0015328	0.0012771	0.0010655	8.902E-04	7.447E-04	6.238E-04	5.232E-04	4.394E-04	3.695E-04	3.111E-04
25	0.0011701	9.675E-04	8.011E-04	6.643E-04	5.516E-04	4.587E-04	3.819E-04	3.184E-04	2.658E-04	2.222E-04
26	8.932E-04	7.330E-04	6.024E-04	4.958E-04	4.086E-04	3.373E-04	2.788E-04	2.308E-04	1.913E-04	1.587E-04
27	6.818E-04	5.553E-04	4.529E-04	3.700E-04	3.027E-04	2.480E-04	2.035E-04	1.672E-04	1.376E-04	1.134E-04
28	5.205E-04	4.207E-04	3.405E-04	2.761E-04	2.242E-04	1.824E-04	1.485E-04	1.212E-04	9.899E-05	8.099E-05
29	3.973E-04	3.187E-04	2.560E-04	2.060E-04	1.661E-04	1.341E-04	1.084E-04	8.780E-05	7.121E-05	5.785E-05
30	3.033E-04	2.414E-04	1.925E-04	1.538E-04	1.230E-04	9.859E-05	7.914E-05	6.362E-05	5.123E-05	4.132E-05

Table A-3. Ordinary Annuity Compound Amount Factor. To Find F for a Given R Received at the End of Each Period.

$$F = R \frac{(1+i)^N - 1}{i}$$

N/i	1	2	3	4	5	6	7	8	9	10
1	1.0000000	1.0000000	1.0000000	1.0000000	1.0000000	1.0000000	1.0000000	1.0000000	1.0000000	1.0000000
2	2.0100000	2.0200000	2.0300000	2.0400000	2.0500000	2.0600000	2.0700000	2.0800000	2.0900000	2.1000000
3	3.0301000	3.0604000	3.0909000	3.1216000	3.1525000	3.1836000	3.2149000	3.2464000	3.2781000	3.3100000
4	4.0604010	4.1216080	4.1836270	4.2464640	4.3101250	4.3746160	4.4399430	4.5061120	4.5731290	4.6410000
5	5.1010050	5.2040402	5.3091358	5.4163226	5.5256313	5.6370930	5.7507390	5.8666010	5.9847106	6.1051000
6	6.1520151	6.3081210	6.4684099	6.6329755	6.8019128	6.9753185	7.1532907	7.3359290	7.5233346	7.7156100
7	7.2135352	7.4342834	7.6624622	7.8982945	8.1420085	8.3938376	8.6540211	8.9228034	9.2004347	9.4871710
8	8.2856706	8.5829691	8.8923360	9.2142263	9.5491089	9.8974679	10.259026	10.636276	11.0284738	11.4358881
9	9.3685273	9.7546284	10.1591061	10.5827953	11.0265643	11.4913160	11.9779887	12.4875578	13.0210364	13.5794769
10	10.4622125	10.9497210	11.4638793	12.0061071	12.5778925	13.1807949	13.816480	14.4865625	15.1929297	15.9374246
11	11.5668347	12.1687154	12.8077957	13.4863514	14.2067872	14.9716426	15.7835993	16.6454875	17.5602934	18.5311671
12	12.6825030	13.4120897	14.1920296	15.0258055	15.9171265	16.8699412	17.8884513	18.9771265	20.1407198	21.3842838
13	13.8093280	14.6803315	15.6177904	16.6268377	17.7129828	18.8821377	20.1406429	21.4952966	22.9533846	24.5227121
14	14.9474213	15.9739382	17.0863242	18.2919112	19.5986320	21.0150659	22.5504879	24.2149203	26.0191892	27.9749834
15	16.0968955	17.2934169	18.5989139	20.0235876	21.5785636	23.2759699	25.1290220	27.1521139	29.3609162	31.7724817
16	17.2578645	18.6392853	20.1568813	21.8245311	23.6574918	25.6725281	27.8880536	30.3242830	33.0033987	35.9497299
17	18.4304431	20.0120710	21.7615877	23.6975124	25.8403664	28.2128798	30.8402173	33.7502257	36.9737046	40.5447028
18	19.6147476	21.4123124	23.4144354	25.6454129	28.1323847	30.9056525	33.9990325	37.4502437	41.3013380	45.5991731
19	20.8108950	22.8405586	25.1168684	27.6712294	30.5390039	33.7599917	37.3789648	41.4462632	46.0184584	51.1590904
20	22.0190040	24.2973698	26.8703745	29.7780786	33.0659541	36.7855912	40.9954923	45.7619643	51.1601196	57.2749995

Table A-3. Ordinary Annuity Compound Amount Factor. To Find F for a Given R Received at the End of Each Period.

$$F = R \frac{(1+i)^N - 1}{i}$$

N/i	1	2	3	4	5	6	7	8	9	10
21	23.2391940	25.7833172	28.6764857	31.9692017	35.7192518	39.9927267	44.8651768	50.4229214	56.7645304	64.0024994
22	24.4715860	27.2989835	30.5367803	34.2479698	38.5052144	43.3922903	49.0057392	55.4567552	62.8733381	71.4027494
23	25.7163018	28.8449632	32.4528837	36.6178886	41.4304751	46.9958277	53.4361409	60.8932956	69.5319386	79.5430243
24	26.9734649	30.4218625	34.4264702	39.0826041	44.5019989	50.8155774	58.1766708	66.7647592	76.7898131	88.4973268
25	28.2431995	32.0302997	36.4592643	41.6459083	47.7270988	54.8645120	63.2490377	73.1059400	84.7008962	98.3470594
26	29.5256315	33.6709057	38.5530423	44.3117446	51.1134538	59.1563827	68.6764704	79.9544151	93.3239769	109.1817654
27	30.8208878	35.3443238	40.7096335	47.0842144	54.6691264	63.7057657	74.4838233	87.3507684	102.7231348	121.0999419
28	32.1290967	37.0512103	42.9309225	49.9675830	58.4025828	68.5281116	80.6976909	95.3388298	112.9682169	134.2099361
29	33.4503877	38.7922345	45.2188502	52.9662863	62.3227119	73.6397983	87.3465293	103.9659362	124.1353565	148.6309297
30	34.7848915	40.5680792	47.5754157	56.0849378	66.4388475	79.0581862	94.4607863	113.2832111	136.3075385	164.4940227
31	36.1327404	42.3794408	50.0026782	59.3283353	70.7607899	84.8016774	102.0730414	123.3458680	149.5752170	181.9434250
32	37.4940679	44.2270296	52.5027585	62.7014687	75.2988294	90.8897780	110.2181543	134.2135374	164.0369865	201.1377675
33	38.8690085	46.1115702	55.0778413	66.2095274	80.0637708	97.3431647	118.9334251	145.9506204	179.8003153	222.2515442
34	40.2576986	48.0338016	57.7301765	69.8579085	85.0669594	104.1837546	128.2587648	158.6266701	196.9823437	245.4766986
35	41.6602756	49.9944776	60.4620818	73.6522249	90.3203074	111.4347799	138.2368784	172.3168037	215.7107547	271.0243685
36	43.0768784	51.9943672	63.2759443	77.5983138	95.8363227	119.1208667	148.9134598	187.1021480	236.1247226	299.1268053
37	44.5076471	54.0342545	66.1742226	81.7022464	101.6281389	127.2681187	160.3374026	203.0703198	258.3759476	330.0394859
38	45.9527236	56.1149396	69.1594493	85.9703363	107.7095458	135.9042058	172.5610202	220.3159454	282.6297829	364.0434344
39	47.4122509	58.2372384	72.2342328	90.4091497	114.0950231	145.0584581	185.6402916	238.9412210	309.0664633	401.4477779
40	48.8863734	60.4019832	75.4012597	95.0255157	120.7997742	154.7619656	199.6351120	259.0565187	337.8824450	442.5255557

Table A-3. Ordinary Annuity Compound Amount Factor. To Find F for a Given R Received at the End of Each Period.

$$F = R\frac{(1+i)^N - 1}{i}$$

N/i	1	2	3	4	5	6	7	8	9	10
41	50.3752371	62.6100228	78.6632975	99.8265363	127.8397630	165.0476836	214.6095698	280.7810402	369.2918651	487.8518112
42	51.8789895	64.8622233	82.0231965	104.8195978	135.2317511	175.9505446	230.6322397	304.2435234	403.5281330	537.6369924
43	53.3977794	67.1594678	85.4838923	110.0123817	142.9933387	187.5075772	247.7764965	329.5830053	440.8456649	592.4006916
44	54.9317572	69.5026571	89.0484091	115.4128770	151.1430056	199.7580319	266.1208513	356.9496457	481.5217748	652.6407608
45	56.4810747	71.8927103	92.7198614	121.0293920	159.7001559	212.7435138	285.7493108	386.5056174	525.8587345	718.9048369
46	58.0458855	74.3305645	96.5014572	126.8705677	168.6851637	226.5081246	306.7517626	418.4260668	574.1860206	791.7953205
47	59.6263443	76.8171758	100.3965009	132.9453904	178.1194218	241.0986121	329.2243860	452.9001521	626.8627625	871.9748826
48	61.2226078	79.3535193	104.4083960	139.2632060	188.0253929	256.5645288	353.2700330	490.1321643	684.2804111	960.1723378
49	62.8348338	81.9405897	108.5406479	145.8337343	198.4266626	272.9584006	378.9989995	530.3427374	746.8656481	1.057E+03
50	64.4631822	84.5794015	112.7966873	152.6670837	209.3479957	290.3359046	406.5289295	573.7701564	815.0835564	1.164E+03
51	66.1078140	87.2709895	117.1807733	159.7737670	220.8153955	308.7560589	435.9859545	620.6717689	889.4410765	1.281E+03
52	67.768921	90.0164093	121.6961965	167.1647177	232.8561653	328.2814224	467.5049714	671.3255104	970.4907734	1.410E+03
53	69.466581	92.8167375	126.3470824	174.8513064	245.4989735	348.9783077	501.2303193	726.0315513	1.059E+03	1.552E+03
54	71.1410469	95.6730722	131.1374949	182.8453586	258.7739222	370.9170062	537.3164417	785.1140754	1.155E+03	1.709E+03
55	72.8524573	98.5865337	136.0716197	191.1591730	272.7126183	394.1720266	575.9285926	848.9232014	1.260E+03	1.881E+03
56	74.5809819	101.5582643	141.1537683	199.8055399	287.3482492	418.8223482	617.2435941	917.8370575	1.375E+03	2.070E+03
57	76.3267917	104.5894296	146.3883814	208.7977615	302.7156617	444.9516891	661.4506457	992.2640221	1.499E+03	2.278E+03
58	78.0900597	107.6812182	151.7800328	218.1496720	318.8514448	472.6487904	708.7521909	1.073E+03	1.635E+03	2.506E+03
59	79.8709603	110.8348426	157.3334338	227.8756588	335.7940170	502.0077178	759.3648443	1.159E+03	1.783E+03	2.758E+03
60	81.6696699	114.0515394	163.0534368	237.9906852	353.5837179	533.1281809	813.5203834	1.253E+03	1.945E+03	3.035E+03

Table A-3.   Ordinary Annuity Compound Amount Factor. To Find F for a Given R Received at the End of Each Period.

$$F = R \frac{(1 + i)^N - 1}{i}$$

N/i	1	2	3	4	5	6	7	8	9	10
61	83.4865366	117.3325702	168.9450399	248.5103126	372.262938	566.1158717	871.466102	1.354E+03	2.121E+03	3.339E+03
62	85.3212302	120.6792216	175.0133911	259.4507251	391.8760490	601.0828240	933.4694869	1.464E+03	2.313E+03	3.674E+03
63	87.1744425	124.0928060	181.2637928	270.8287541	412.4698514	638.1477935	9.998E+02	1.582E+03	2.522E+03	4.045E+03
64	89.0461869	127.5746622	187.7017066	282.6619043	434.0933440	677.436611	1.071E+03	1.709E+03	2.750E+03	4.448E+03
65	90.9366488	131.1261554	194.3327578	294.9683805	456.7980112	719.0928608	1.147E+03	1.847E+03	2.998E+03	4.894E+03
66	92.8460153	134.7486785	201.1627406	307.7671157	480.6379117	763.2278324	1.228E+03	1.996E+03	3.269E+03	5.384E+03
67	94.7744755	138.4436521	208.1976228	321.0778003	505.6698073	810.0215024	1.315E+03	2.157E+03	3.564E+03	5.923E+03
68	96.7222202	142.2125251	215.4435515	334.9209123	531.9532977	859.6227925	1.408E+03	2.330E+03	3.886E+03	6.517E+03
69	98.6894424	146.0567756	222.9068580	349.3177488	559.5509626	912.2001600	1.508E+03	2.518E+03	4.237E+03	7.170E+03
70	100.6763368	149.9779111	230.5940637	364.2904588	588.5285107	967.9321696	1.614E+03	2.720E+03	4.619E+03	7.887E+03
71	102.6831002	153.9774694	238.5118856	379.8620771	618.9549362	1.027E+03	1.728E+03	2.939E+03	5.036E+03	8.677E+03
72	104.7099312	158.0570188	246.6672422	396.0565602	650.902631	1.090E+03	1.850E+03	3.175E+03	5.490E+03	9.546E+03
73	106.7570305	162.2181591	255.0672595	412.8998226	684.4478172	1.156E+03	1.981E+03	3.430E+03	5.995E+03	1.050E+04
74	108.8246008	166.4625223	263.7192773	430.4147755	719.6702081	1.226E+03	2.120E+03	3.705E+03	6.525E+03	1.155E+04
75	110.9128468	170.7917728	272.6308556	448.6313665	756.6537185	1.301E+03	2.270E+03	4.003E+03	7.113E+03	1.271E+04
76	113.0219753	175.2076082	281.8097813	467.5766212	795.464044	1.380E+03	2.430E+03	4.324E+03	7.754E+03	1.398E+04
77	115.1521951	179.7117604	291.2640747	487.2796860	836.2607246	1.464E+03	2.601E+03	4.671E+03	8.453E+03	1.538E+04
78	117.3037170	184.3059956	301.0019969	507.7708735	879.0737608	1.553E+03	2.784E+03	5.045E+03	9.215E+03	1.692E+04
79	119.4767542	188.9921155	311.0320568	529.0817084	924.0274489	1.647E+03	2.979E+03	5.450E+03	1.005E+04	1.861E+04
80	121.6715217	193.7719578	321.3630185	551.2449767	971.2288213	1.747E+03	3.189E+03	5.887E+03	1.095E+04	2.047E+04

Table A-3. Ordinary Annuity Compound Amount Factor. To Find *F* for a Given *R* Received at the End of Each Period.

$$F = R \frac{(1 + i)^N - 1}{i}$$

N/i	1	2	3	4	5	6	7	8	9	10
81	123.8882369	198.6473970	332.0039091	574.2947758	1.021E+03	1.852E+03	3.413E+03	6.359E+03	1.194E+04	2.252E+04
82	126.1271193	203.6203449	342.9640264	598.2665668	1.073E+03	1.965E+03	3.653E+03	6.869E+03	1.301E+04	2.478E+04
83	128.3883905	208.6927518	354.2529472	623.1972295	1.127E+03	2.083E+03	3.910E+03	7.419E+03	1.418E+04	2.725E+04
84	130.6722744	213.866068	365.8805356	649.1251187	1.185E+03	2.209E+03	4.185E+03	8.014E+03	1.546E+04	2.998E+04
85	132.9789971	219.1439390	377.8569517	676.0901235	1.245E+03	2.343E+03	4.479E+03	8.656E+03	1.685E+04	3.298E+04
86	135.3087871	224.5268178	390.1926602	704.1337284	1.308E+03	2.485E+03	4.793E+03	9.349E+03	1.837E+04	3.628E+04
87	137.6618750	230.0173541	402.8984400	733.2990775	1.375E+03	2.635E+03	5.130E+03	1.010E+04	2.003E+04	3.991E+04
88	140.0384937	235.6177012	415.9853932	763.6310406	1.444E+03	2.794E+03	5.490E+03	1.091E+04	2.183E+04	4.390E+04
89	142.4388787	241.3300552	429.4649550	795.1762823	1.518E+03	2.962E+03	5.875E+03	1.178E+04	2.380E+04	4.829E+04
90	144.8632675	247.1566563	443.3489037	827.9833335	1.595E+03	3.141E+03	6.287E+03	1.272E+04	2.594E+04	5.312E+04
91	147.3119001	253.0997894	457.6493708	862.1026669	1.675E+03	3.331E+03	6.728E+03	1.374E+04	2.827E+04	5.843E+04
92	149.7850191	259.1617852	472.3788519	897.5867736	1.760E+03	3.531E+03	7.200E+03	1.484E+04	3.082E+04	6.428E+04
93	152.2828693	265.3450209	487.5502174	934.4902445	1.849E+03	3.744E+03	7.705E+03	1.603E+04	3.360E+04	7.071E+04
94	154.8056980	271.6519214	503.1767240	972.8698543	1.943E+03	3.970E+03	8.246E+03	1.732E+04	3.662E+04	7.778E+04
95	157.3537550	278.0849598	519.2720257	1.013E+03	2.041E+03	4.209E+03	8.824E+03	1.870E+04	3.992E+04	8.556E+04
96	159.9272926	284.6466590	535.8501865	1.054E+03	2.144E+03	4.463E+03	9.443E+03	2.020E+04	4.351E+04	9.411E+04
97	162.5265655	291.3395922	552.9256920	1.097E+03	2.252E+03	4.731E+03	1.010E+04	2.182E+04	4.743E+04	1.035E+05
98	165.1518311	298.1663840	570.5134628	1.142E+03	2.366E+03	5.016E+03	1.081E+04	2.356E+04	5.170E+04	1.139E+05
99	167.8033494	305.1297117	588.6288667	1.189E+03	2.485E+03	5.318E+03	1.157E+04	2.545E+04	5.635E+04	1.253E+05
100	170.4813829	312.2323059	607.2877327	1.238E+03	2.610E+03	5.638E+03	1.238E+04	2.748E+04	6.142E+04	1.378E+05

Table A-3. Ordinary Annuity Compound Amount Factor. To Find F for a Given R Received at the End of Each Period.

$$F = R \frac{(1+i)^N - 1}{i}$$

N/i	11	12	13	14	15	16	17	18	19	20
1	1.0000000	1.0000000	1.000000	1.000000	1.000000	1.000000	1.000000	1.000000	1.000000	1.000000
2	2.1100000	2.1200000	2.1300000	2.1400000	2.1500000	2.1600000	2.1700000	2.1800000	2.1900000	2.2000000
3	3.3421000	3.3744000	3.4069000	3.4396000	3.4725000	3.5056000	3.5389000	3.5724000	3.6061000	3.6400000
4	4.7097310	4.7793280	4.8497970	4.9211440	4.9933750	5.0664960	5.1405130	5.2154320	5.2912590	5.3680000
5	6.2278014	6.3528474	6.4802706	6.6101042	6.7423812	6.8771354	7.0144002	7.1542098	7.2965982	7.4416000
6	7.9128596	8.1151890	8.3227058	8.5355187	8.7537384	8.9774770	9.2068482	9.4419675	9.6829519	9.9299200
7	9.7832741	10.0890117	10.4046575	10.7304914	11.0667992	11.4138733	11.7720124	12.1415217	12.5227127	12.9159040
8	11.8594343	12.2996931	12.7572630	13.2327602	13.7268191	14.2400931	14.7732546	15.3269956	15.9020281	16.4990848
9	14.1639720	14.7756563	15.4157072	16.0853466	16.7858419	17.5185080	18.2847078	19.0858548	19.9234135	20.7989018
10	16.7220090	17.5487351	18.4197492	19.3372951	20.3037182	21.3214692	22.3931082	23.5213086	24.7088621	25.9586821
11	19.5614300	20.6545833	21.8143165	23.0445164	24.3492760	25.7329043	27.1999366	28.7551442	30.4035458	32.1504185
12	22.7131872	24.1331333	25.6501777	27.2707487	29.0016674	30.8501690	32.8239258	34.9310701	37.1802196	39.5805022
13	26.2116378	28.0291093	29.9847008	32.0886535	34.3519175	36.7861961	39.4039932	42.2186628	45.2444613	48.4966027
14	30.0949180	32.3926024	34.8827119	37.5810650	40.5047051	43.6719874	47.1026720	50.8180221	54.8409089	59.1959232
15	34.4053590	37.2797147	40.4174644	43.8424141	47.5804109	51.6595054	56.1101262	60.9652660	66.2606816	72.0351079
16	39.1899485	42.7532804	46.6717348	50.9803521	55.7174725	60.9250263	66.6488477	72.9390139	79.8502111	87.4421294
17	44.5008428	48.8836741	53.7390603	59.1176014	65.0750934	71.6730305	78.9791518	87.0680364	96.0217512	105.9305553
18	50.3959355	55.7497150	61.7251382	68.3940656	75.8365574	84.1407154	93.4056076	103.7402830	115.2658839	128.1166664
19	56.9394884	63.4396808	70.7494062	78.9692348	88.2118110	98.6032298	110.2845609	123.4135339	138.1664019	154.7399997
20	64.2028321	72.0524424	80.9468290	91.0249277	102.4435826	115.3797466	130.0329363	146.6279700	165.4180183	186.6879996

Table A-3. Ordinary Annuity Compound Amount Factor. To Find F for a Given R Received at the End of Each Period.

$$F = R \frac{(1+i)^N - 1}{i}$$

N/i	11	12	13	14	15	16	17	18	19	20
21	72.2651437	81.6987355	92.4699167	104.7684175	118.8101200	134.8405060	153.1385354	174.0210046	197.8474417	225.0255995
22	81.2143095	92.5025838	105.4910059	120.4359960	137.6316380	157.4149870	180.1720864	206.3447855	236.4384557	271.0307195
23	91.147835	104.6028939	120.2048367	138.2970354	159.2763837	183.6013849	211.8013411	244.4868468	282.3617622	326.2368633
24	102.1741507	118.1552411	136.8314654	158.6586204	184.1678413	213.9776065	248.8075691	289.4944793	337.0104971	392.4842360
25	114.4133073	133.3338701	155.6195559	181.8708272	212.7930175	249.2140235	292.1048559	342.6034855	402.0424915	471.9810832
26	127.9987711	150.3339345	176.8500982	208.3327430	245.7119701	290.0882673	342.7826814	405.2721129	479.4305649	567.3772999
27	143.0786359	169.3740066	200.8406110	238.4993271	283.5687656	337.5023901	402.0323372	479.2210933	571.5223722	681.8527598
28	159.8172859	190.6988874	227.9498904	272.8892329	327.1040804	392.5027725	471.3778345	566.4808901	681.1116229	819.2233118
29	178.3971873	214.5827539	258.5833762	312.0937255	377.1698925	456.3032161	552.5120664	669.4474503	811.5228313	984.0679742
30	199.0208779	241.3326843	293.1992151	356.7886470	434.7451464	530.311307	647.4391177	790.9479913	966.7121692	1.182E+03
31	221.9131745	271.2926065	332.3151130	407.7370056	500.9569183	616.1616076	758.5037677	934.3186298	1.151E+03	1.419E+03
32	247.3236237	304.8477192	376.5160777	465.8201864	577.1004561	715.7474648	888.494082	1.103E+03	1.371E+03	1.704E+03
33	275.5292223	342.4294455	426.4631678	532.0350125	664.6655245	831.2670592	1.040E+03	1.305E+03	1.633E+03	2.046E+03
34	306.8374368	384.5209790	482.9033796	607.5199142	765.3653532	965.2697886	1.218E+03	1.539E+03	1.944E+03	2.456E+03
35	341.5895548	431.6663965	546.6808190	693.5727022	881.1701561	1.121E+03	1.426E+03	1.817E+03	2.314E+03	2.948E+03
36	380.1644058	484.4631161	618.7493254	791.6728805	1.014E+03	1.301E+03	1.670E+03	2.145E+03	2.755E+03	3.539E+03
37	422.9824905	543.5986900	700.1867377	903.5070838	1.167E+03	1.510E+03	1.955E+03	2.532E+03	3.279E+03	4.248E+03
38	470.5105644	609.8305328	792.2110137	1.031E+03	1.344E+03	1.753E+03	2.288E+03	2.988E+03	3.905E+03	5.098E+03
39	523.2667265	684.0101967	896.1984454	1.176E+03	1.546E+03	2.034E+03	2.678E+03	3.527E+03	4.646E+03	6.119E+03
40	581.8260664	767.0914203	1.014E+03	1.342E+03	1.779E+03	2.361E+03	3.135E+03	4.163E+03	5.530E+03	7.344E+03

Table A-3. Ordinary Annuity Compound Amount Factor. To Find F for a Given R Received at the End of Each Period.

$$F = R \frac{(1 + i)^N - 1}{i}$$

N/i	11	12	13	14	15	16	17	18	19	20
41	646.8269337	860.1423908	1.146E+03	1.531E+03	2.047E+03	2.739E+03	3.668E+03	4.914E+03	6.581E+03	8.814E+03
42	718.9778964	964.3594777	1.297E+03	1.746E+03	2.355E+03	3.179E+03	4.293E+03	5.799E+03	7.833E+03	1.058E+04
43	799.0654650	1.081E+03	1.466E+03	1.992E+03	2.709E+03	3.688E+03	5.024E+03	6.844E+03	9.322E+03	1.269E+04
44	887.9626662	1.212E+03	1.658E+03	2.272E+03	3.117E+03	4.280E+03	5.879E+03	8.077E+03	1.109E+04	1.523E+04
45	986.6385595	1.358E+03	1.874E+03	2.591E+03	3.585E+03	4.965E+03	6.879E+03	9.532E+03	1.320E+04	1.828E+04
46	1.096E+03	1.522E+03	2.119E+03	2.954E+03	4.124E+03	5.761E+03	8.050E+03	1.125E+04	1.571E+04	2.194E+04
47	1.218E+03	1.706E+03	2.395E+03	3.369E+03	4.743E+03	6.683E+03	9.419E+03	1.327E+04	1.870E+04	2.633E+04
48	1.353E+03	1.912E+03	2.708E+03	3.841E+03	5.456E+03	7.754E+03	1.102E+04	1.566E+04	2.225E+04	3.159E+04
49	1.502E+03	2.142E+03	3.061E+03	4.380E+03	6.275E+03	8.995E+03	1.290E+04	1.848E+04	2.648E+04	3.791E+04
50	1.669E+03	2.400E+03	3.460E+03	4.995E+03	7.218E+03	1.044E+04	1.509E+04	2.181E+04	3.152E+04	4.550E+04

N/i	21	22	23	24	25	26	27	28	29	30
1	1.000000	1.000000	1.000000	1.0000000	1.0000000	1.0000000	1.0000000	1.0000000	1.0000000	1.0000000
2	2.2100000	2.2200000	2.2300000	2.2400000	2.2500000	2.2600000	2.2700000	2.2800000	2.2900000	2.3000000
3	3.6741000	3.7084000	3.7429000	3.7776000	3.8125000	3.8476000	3.8829000	3.9184000	3.9541000	3.9900000
4	5.4456610	5.5242480	5.6037670	5.6842240	5.7656250	5.8479760	5.9312830	6.0155520	6.1007890	6.1870000
5	7.5892498	7.7395826	7.8926334	8.0484378	8.2070312	8.3684498	8.5327294	8.6999066	8.8700178	9.0431000
6	10.1829923	10.4422907	10.7079391	10.9800628	11.2587891	11.5442467	11.8365664	12.1358804	12.4423230	12.7560300
7	13.3214206	13.7395947	14.1707651	14.6152779	15.0734863	15.5457508	16.0324393	16.5339269	17.0505966	17.5828390
8	17.1189190	17.7623055	18.4300411	19.1229446	19.8418579	20.5876461	21.3611979	22.1634264	22.9952697	23.8576907
9	21.7138920	22.6700127	23.6689505	24.7124513	25.8023224	26.9404340	28.1287213	29.3691858	30.6638979	32.0149979
10	27.2738093	28.6574155	30.1128091	31.6434396	33.2529030	34.949469	36.7234760	38.5925579	40.5564282	42.6194973

Table A-3. Ordinary Annuity Compound Amount Factor. To Find F for a Given R Received at the End of Each Period.

$$F = R\frac{(1+i)^N - 1}{i}$$

N/i	21	22	23	24	25	26	27	28	29	30
11	34.0013092	35.9620469	38.0387552	40.2378651	42.5661287	45.0306331	47.6388146	50.3984741	53.3177924	56.4053465
12	42.1415842	44.8736973	47.7876689	50.8945527	54.2076609	57.7385977	61.5012945	65.5100468	69.7799522	74.3269504
13	51.9913168	55.7459107	59.7788328	64.1097414	68.7595761	73.7506331	79.1066440	84.8528599	91.0161384	97.6250355
14	63.9094934	69.0100110	74.5279643	80.4960793	86.9494702	93.9257977	101.4654379	109.6116607	118.4108185	127.9125462
15	78.3304870	85.1922134	92.6693961	100.8151384	109.6863377	119.3465050	129.8611061	141.3029257	153.7499559	167.2863100
16	95.7798893	104.9345004	114.9833572	126.0107716	138.1085472	151.3765964	165.9326048	181.8677449	199.3374431	218.4722031
17	116.8936660	129.0200905	142.4295293	157.2533568	173.6356639	191.7345114	211.7229781	233.7907135	258.1453016	285.0138640
18	142.4413359	158.4045104	176.1883211	195.9941624	218.0446049	242.5854844	269.8881822	300.2521133	334.0074391	371.5180232
19	173.3540164	194.2535027	217.7116349	244.0327614	273.5557562	306.6577103	343.7579914	385.3227051	431.8695964	483.9734301
20	210.7583598	237.9892733	268.7853109	303.6006241	342.9446952	387.3887150	437.5726490	494.2130625	558.1117794	630.1654592
21	256.0176154	291.3469134	331.6059325	377.4647739	429.6808690	489.1097009	556.7172643	633.5927200	720.9641954	820.2150969
22	310.7813147	356.4432343	408.8752969	469.0563196	538.1010862	617.2783239	708.0309256	811.9986815	931.0438121	1.067E+03
23	377.0453907	435.8607459	503.9166152	582.6298363	673.6263578	778.7706882	900.1992756	1.040E+03	1.202E+03	1.388E+03
24	457.2249228	532.7501099	620.8174367	723.4609971	843.0329473	982.510671	1.144E+03	1.335E+03	1.552E+03	1.806E+03
25	554.2421566	650.9551341	764.6054472	898.0916364	1.055E+03	1.239E+03	1.454E+03	1.707E+03	2.003E+03	2.349E+03
26	671.6330094	795.1652636	941.4647000	1.115E+03	1.319E+03	1.562E+03	1.848E+03	2.186E+03	2.584E+03	3.054E+03
27	813.6759414	971.1016216	1.159E+03	1.383E+03	1.650E+03	1.969E+03	2.348E+03	2.799E+03	3.335E+03	3.972E+03
28	985.5478891	1.186E+03	1.427E+03	1.718E+03	2.064E+03	2.482E+03	2.983E+03	3.583E+03	4.303E+03	5.164E+03
29	1.194E+03	1.448E+03	1.756E+03	2.129E+03	2.581E+03	3.128E+03	3.789E+03	4.588E+03	5.552E+03	6.715E+03
30	1.445E+03	1.767E+03	2.160E+03	2.641E+03	3.227E+03	3.942E+03	4.813E+03	5.873E+03	7.163E+03	8.730E+03

Table A-3.   Ordinary Annuity Compound Amount Factor. To Find F for a Given R Received at the End of Each Period.

$$F = R\frac{(1 + i)^N - 1}{i}$$

N/i	21	22	23	24	25	26	27	28	29	30
31	1.750E+03	2.157E+03	2.658E+03	3.276E+03	4.035E+03	4.968E+03	6.113E+03	7.519E+03	9.241E+03	1.135E+04
32	2.118E+03	2.632E+03	3.271E+03	4.063E+03	5.045E+03	6.261E+03	7.765E+03	9.625E+03	1.192E+04	1.476E+04
33	2.564E+03	3.212E+03	4.024E+03	5.039E+03	6.307E+03	7.889E+03	9.863E+03	1.232E+04	1.538E+04	1.918E+04
34	3.103E+03	3.920E+03	4.951E+03	6.249E+03	7.885E+03	9.942E+03	1.253E+04	1.577E+04	1.984E+04	2.494E+04
35	3.756E+03	4.784E+03	6.090E+03	7.750E+03	9.857E+03	1.253E+04	1.591E+04	2.019E+04	2.560E+04	3.242E+04
36	4.546E+03	5.837E+03	7.492E+03	9.611E+03	1.232E+04	1.579E+04	2.021E+04	2.584E+04	3.302E+04	4.215E+04
37	5.501E+03	7.122E+03	9.216E+03	1.192E+04	1.540E+04	1.989E+04	2.566E+04	3.308E+04	4.260E+04	5.480E+04
38	6.658E+03	8.690E+03	1.134E+04	1.478E+04	1.926E+04	2.506E+04	3.259E+04	4.234E+04	5.495E+04	7.124E+04
39	8.057E+03	1.060E+04	1.395E+04	1.833E+04	2.407E+04	3.158E+04	4.139E+04	5.420E+04	7.089E+04	9.261E+04
40	9.750E+03	1.294E+04	1.715E+04	2.273E+04	3.009E+04	3.979E+04	5.257E+04	6.938E+04	9.145E+04	1.204E+05
41	1.180E+04	1.578E+04	2.110E+04	2.818E+04	3.761E+04	5.014E+04	6.677E+04	8.880E+04	1.180E+05	1.565E+05
42	1.428E+04	1.926E+04	2.595E+04	3.495E+04	4.702E+04	6.318E+04	8.480E+04	1.137E+05	1.522E+05	2.035E+05
43	1.728E+04	2.349E+04	3.193E+04	4.334E+04	5.877E+04	7.960E+04	1.077E+05	1.455E+05	1.963E+05	2.645E+05
44	2.090E+04	2.866E+04	3.927E+04	5.374E+04	7.346E+04	1.003E+05	1.368E+05	1.862E+05	2.532E+05	3.439E+05
45	2.530E+04	3.497E+04	4.830E+04	6.664E+04	9.183E+04	1.264E+05	1.737E+05	2.384E+05	3.267E+05	4.470E+05
46	3.061E+04	4.267E+04	5.941E+04	8.264E+04	1.148E+05	1.592E+05	2.206E+05	3.051E+05	4.214E+05	5.811E+05
47	3.704E+04	5.205E+04	7.308E+04	1.025E+05	1.435E+05	2.006E+05	2.802E+05	3.906E+05	5.436E+05	7.555E+05
48	4.482E+04	6.351E+04	8.989E+04	1.271E+05	1.794E+05	2.528E+05	3.558E+05	4.999E+05	7.013E+05	9.821E+05
49	5.423E+04	7.748E+04	1.106E+05	1.576E+05	2.242E+05	3.186E+05	4.519E+05	6.399E+05	9.047E+05	1.277E+06
50	6.562E+04	9.453E+04	1.360E+05	1.954E+05	2.803E+05	4.014E+05	5.739E+05	8.191E+05	1.167E+06	1.660E+06

Table A-3.   Ordinary Annuity Compound Amount Factor. To Find F for a Given R Received at the End of Each Period.

$$F = R\frac{(1 + i)^N - 1}{i}$$

N/i	31	32	33	34	35	36	37	38	39	40
1	1.0000000	1.0000000	1.0000000	1.0000000	1.0000000	1.0000000	1.0000000	1.000000	1.000000	1.000000
2	2.3100000	2.3200000	2.3300000	2.3400000	2.3500000	2.3600000	2.3700000	2.3800000	2.3900000	2.4000000
3	4.0261000	4.0624000	4.0989000	4.1356000	4.1725000	4.2096000	4.2469000	4.2844000	4.3221000	4.3600000
4	6.2741910	6.3623680	6.4515370	6.5417040	6.6328750	6.7250560	6.8182530	6.9124720	7.0077190	7.1040000
5	9.2191902	9.3983258	9.5805442	9.7658834	9.9543813	10.1460762	10.3410066	10.5392114	10.7407294	10.9456000
6	13.0771392	13.4057900	13.7421238	14.0862837	14.4384147	14.7986636	15.1671791	15.5441117	15.9296139	16.3238400
7	18.1310523	18.6956428	19.2770247	19.8756202	20.4918598	21.1261825	21.7790353	22.4508741	23.1421633	23.8533760
8	24.7516785	25.6782485	26.6384428	27.6333310	28.6640108	29.7316082	30.8372784	31.9822063	33.1676070	34.3947264
9	33.4246989	34.8952880	36.4291289	38.0286636	39.6964145	41.4349871	43.2470714	45.1354447	47.1029737	49.1526170
10	44.7863555	47.0617802	49.4507414	51.9564092	54.5901596	57.3515824	60.2484878	63.2869136	66.4731334	69.8136637
11	59.6701258	63.1215498	66.7694861	70.6242683	74.6967155	78.9981521	83.5404282	88.3359408	93.3976555	98.7391292
12	79.1678647	84.3204458	89.8034165	95.6365195	101.8405659	108.4374869	115.4503867	122.9035983	130.8227411	139.2347809
13	104.7099028	112.3029885	120.4385440	129.1529361	138.4847640	148.4749822	159.1670298	170.6069657	182.8436102	195.9286933
14	138.1699727	149.2399448	161.1832635	174.0649344	187.9544314	202.9259757	219.0588308	236.4376127	255.1526181	275.3001706
15	182.0026642	197.9967271	215.3737405	234.2470121	254.7384824	276.9793270	301.1105982	327.2839055	355.6621392	386.4202389
16	239.4234901	262.3556798	287.4470749	314.8909963	344.8969512	377.691847	413.5215195	452.6517895	495.3703735	541.9883345
17	314.6447721	347.3094973	383.3046096	422.9539350	466.6108841	514.6609632	567.524817	625.6594696	689.5648191	759.7836682
18	413.1846514	459.4485364	510.7951307	567.7582729	630.9246935	700.9389100	778.5085400	864.4100680	959.4950986	1.065E+03
19	542.2718933	607.4720681	680.3575239	761.7960857	852.7483363	954.2769176	1.068E+03	1.194E+03	1.335E+03	1.492E+03
20	711.3761803	802.8631298	905.8755067	1.022E+03	1.152E+03	1.299E+03	1.464E+03	1.649E+03	1.856E+03	2.089E+03

Table A-3.   Ordinary Annuity Compound Amount Factor. To Find F for a Given R Received at the End of Each Period.

$$F = R \frac{(1+i)^N - 1}{i}$$

N/i	31	32	33	34	35	36	37	38	39	40
21	932.9027961	1.061E+03	1.206E+03	1.370E+03	1.556E+03	1.767E+03	2.006E+03	2.276E+03	2.581E+03	2.926E+03
22	1.223E+03	1.401E+03	1.605E+03	1.837E+03	2.102E+03	2.405E+03	2.749E+03	3.142E+03	3.589E+03	4.097E+03
23	1.603E+03	1.851E+03	2.135E+03	2.463E+03	2.839E+03	3.271E+03	3.768E+03	4.337E+03	4.989E+03	5.737E+03
24	2.101E+03	2.444E+03	2.841E+03	3.301E+03	3.834E+03	4.450E+03	5.163E+03	5.986E+03	6.936E+03	8.033E+03
25	2.754E+03	3.227E+03	3.779E+03	4.424E+03	5.177E+03	6.053E+03	7.074E+03	8.261E+03	9.643E+03	1.125E+04
26	3.608E+03	4.260E+03	5.028E+03	5.930E+03	6.989E+03	8.233E+03	9.692E+03	1.140E+04	1.340E+04	1.575E+04
27	4.728E+03	5.625E+03	6.688E+03	7.947E+03	9.437E+03	1.120E+04	1.328E+04	1.574E+04	1.863E+04	2.205E+04
28	6.195E+03	7.426E+03	8.896E+03	1.065E+04	1.274E+04	1.523E+04	1.819E+04	2.172E+04	2.590E+04	3.087E+04
29	8.116E+03	9.803E+03	1.183E+04	1.427E+04	1.720E+04	2.071E+04	2.493E+04	2.997E+04	3.600E+04	4.321E+04
30	1.063E+04	1.294E+04	1.574E+04	1.912E+04	2.322E+04	2.817E+04	3.415E+04	4.136E+04	5.004E+04	6.050E+04
31	1.393E+04	1.708E+04	2.093E+04	2.563E+04	3.135E+04	3.832E+04	4.679E+04	5.708E+04	6.956E+04	8.470E+04
32	1.825E+04	2.255E+04	2.784E+04	3.434E+04	4.232E+04	5.211E+04	6.410E+04	7.876E+04	9.669E+04	1.186E+05
33	2.391E+04	2.977E+04	3.703E+04	4.602E+04	5.714E+04	7.087E+04	8.781E+04	1.087E+05	1.344E+05	1.660E+05
34	3.132E+04	3.929E+04	4.925E+04	6.167E+04	7.714E+04	9.638E+04	1.203E+05	1.500E+05	1.868E+05	2.324E+05
35	4.103E+04	5.187E+04	6.550E+04	8.264E+04	1.041E+05	1.311E+05	1.648E+05	2.070E+05	2.597E+05	3.254E+05
36	5.375E+04	6.847E+04	8.712E+04	1.107E+05	1.406E+05	1.783E+05	2.258E+05	2.857E+05	3.610E+05	4.556E+05
37	7.041E+04	9.038E+04	1.159E+05	1.484E+05	1.898E+05	2.425E+05	3.094E+05	3.942E+05	5.017E+05	6.378E+05
38	9.224E+04	1.193E+05	1.541E+05	1.988E+05	2.562E+05	3.297E+05	4.238E+05	5.440E+05	6.974E+05	8.929E+05
39	1.208E+05	1.575E+05	2.050E+05	2.664E+05	3.459E+05	4.484E+05	5.806E+05	7.508E+05	9.694E+05	1.250E+06
40	1.583E+05	2.079E+05	2.726E+05	3.570E+05	4.670E+05	6.099E+05	7.955E+05	1.036E+06	1.347E+06	1.750E+06

Table A-3. Ordinary Annuity Compound Amount Factor. To Find F for a Given R Received at the End of Each Period.

$$F = R \frac{(1 + i)^N - 1}{i}$$

N/i	31	32	33	34	35	36	37	38	39	40
41	2.074E+05	2.744E+05	3.626E+05	4.784E+05	6.304E+05	8.295E+05	1.090E+06	1.430E+06	1.873E+06	2.450E+06
42	2.717E+05	3.622E+05	4.822E+05	6.411E+05	8.510E+05	1.128E+06	1.493E+06	1.973E+06	2.603E+06	3.430E+06
43	3.559E+05	4.781E+05	6.414E+05	8.591E+05	1.149E+06	1.534E+06	2.045E+06	2.723E+06	3.619E+06	4.802E+06
44	4.662E+05	6.311E+05	8.530E+05	1.151E+06	1.551E+06	2.086E+06	2.802E+06	3.757E+06	5.030E+06	6.723E+06
45	6.107E+05	8.331E+05	1.135E+06	1.543E+06	2.094E+06	2.838E+06	3.839E+06	5.185E+06	6.992E+06	9.412E+06
46	8.000E+05	1.100E+06	1.509E+06	2.067E+06	2.827E+06	3.859E+06	5.259E+06	7.156E+06	9.719E+06	1.318E+07
47	1.048E+06	1.452E+06	2.007E+06	2.770E+06	3.816E+06	5.248E+06	7.206E+06	9.875E+06	1.351E+07	1.845E+07
48	1.373E+06	1.916E+06	2.669E+06	3.712E+06	5.152E+06	7.138E+06	9.872E+06	1.363E+07	1.878E+07	2.583E+07
49	1.799E+06	2.529E+06	3.550E+06	4.973E+06	6.955E+06	9.707E+06	1.352E+07	1.881E+07	2.610E+07	3.616E+07
50	2.356E+06	3.338E+06	4.721E+06	6.664E+06	9.389E+06	1.320E+07	1.853E+07	2.595E+07	3.628E+07	5.062E+07

Table A-4 Ordinary Annuity Present Worth Factor. To Find P for a Given R Received at the End of Each Period.

$$P = R \frac{1 - (1 + i)^{-N}}{i}$$

N/i	1	2	3	4	5	6	7	8	9	10
1	0.9900990	0.9803922	0.9708738	0.9615385	0.9523810	0.9433962	0.9345794	0.9259259	0.9174312	0.9090909
2	1.9703951	1.9415609	1.9134697	1.8860947	1.8594104	1.8333927	1.8080182	1.7832647	1.7591112	1.7355372
3	2.9409852	2.8838833	2.8286114	2.7750910	2.7232480	2.6730119	2.6243160	2.5770970	2.5312947	2.4868520
4	3.9019656	3.8077287	3.7170984	3.6298952	3.5459505	3.4651056	3.3872113	3.3121268	3.2397199	3.1698654
5	4.8534312	4.7134595	4.5797072	4.4518223	4.3294767	4.2123638	4.1001974	3.9927100	3.8896513	3.7907868
6	5.7954765	5.6014309	5.4171914	5.2421369	5.0756921	4.9173243	4.7665397	4.6228797	4.4859186	4.3552607
7	6.7281945	6.4719911	6.2302830	6.0020547	5.7863734	5.5823814	5.3892894	5.2063701	5.0329528	4.8684188
8	7.6516778	7.3254814	7.0196922	6.7327449	6.4632128	6.2097938	5.9712985	5.7466389	5.5348191	5.3349262
9	8.5660176	8.1622367	7.7861089	7.4353316	7.1078217	6.8016923	6.5152322	6.2468879	5.9952469	5.7590238
10	9.4713045	8.9825850	8.5302028	8.1108958	7.7217349	7.3600871	7.0235815	6.7100814	6.4176577	6.1445671
11	10.3676282	9.7868480	9.2526241	8.7604767	8.3064142	7.8868746	7.4986743	7.1389643	6.8051906	6.4950610
12	11.2550775	10.5753412	9.9540040	9.3850738	8.8632516	8.3838439	7.9426863	7.5360780	7.1607253	6.8136918
13	12.1337401	11.3483737	10.6349553	9.9856478	9.3935730	8.8526830	8.3576507	7.9037759	7.4869039	7.1033562
14	13.0037030	12.1062488	11.2960731	10.5631229	9.8986409	9.2949839	8.7454680	8.2442370	7.7861504	7.3666875
15	13.8650525	12.8492635	11.9379351	11.1183874	10.3796580	9.7122490	9.1079140	8.5594787	8.0606884	7.6060795
16	14.7178738	13.5777093	12.5611020	11.6522956	10.8377696	10.1058953	9.4466486	8.8513692	8.3125582	7.8237086
17	15.5622513	14.2918719	13.1661185	12.1656689	11.2740662	10.4772597	9.7632230	9.1216381	8.5436314	8.0215533
18	16.3982686	14.9920313	13.7535131	12.6592970	11.6895869	10.8276035	10.0590869	9.3718871	8.7556251	8.2014121
19	17.2260085	15.6784620	14.3237991	13.1339394	12.0853209	11.1581165	10.3355952	9.6035992	8.9501148	8.3649201
20	18.0455530	16.3514333	14.8774749	13.5903263	12.4622103	11.4699212	10.5940142	9.8181474	9.1285457	8.5135637

Table A-4 Ordinary Annuity Present Worth Factor. To Find P for a Given R Received at the End of Each Period.

$$P = R\frac{1 - (1 + i)^{-N}}{i}$$

N/i	1	2	3	4	5	6	7	8	9	10
21	18.8569831	17.0112092	15.4150241	14.0291599	12.8211527	11.7640766	10.8355273	10.0168032	9.2922437	8.6646943
22	19.6603793	17.6580482	15.9369166	14.4511153	13.1630026	12.0415817	11.0612405	10.2007437	9.4422454	8.7715403
23	20.4558211	18.2922041	16.4436084	14.8568417	13.4885739	12.3033790	11.2721874	10.3710589	9.5802068	8.8832184
24	21.2433873	18.9139256	16.9355421	15.2469631	13.7986418	12.5503575	11.4693340	10.5287583	9.7066118	8.9847440
25	22.0231557	19.5234565	17.4131477	15.6220799	14.0939446	12.7833562	11.6535832	10.6747762	9.8225796	9.0770400
26	22.7952037	20.1210358	17.8768424	15.9827692	14.3751853	13.0031662	11.8257787	10.8099780	9.9289721	9.1609455
27	23.5596076	20.7068978	18.3270315	16.3295857	14.6430336	13.2105341	11.9867090	10.9351648	10.0265799	9.2372232
28	24.3164432	21.2812724	18.7641082	16.6630632	14.8981273	13.4061643	12.1371113	11.0510785	10.1161284	9.3065665
29	25.0657853	21.8443847	19.1884546	16.9837146	15.1410736	13.5907210	12.2776741	11.1584060	10.1982829	9.3696059
30	25.8077082	22.3964556	19.6004413	17.2920333	15.3724510	13.7648312	12.4090412	11.2577833	10.2736540	9.4269145
31	26.5422854	22.9377015	20.0004285	17.5884936	15.5928105	13.9290860	12.5318142	11.3497994	10.3428019	9.4790132
32	27.2695895	23.4683348	20.3887655	17.8735515	15.8026767	14.0840434	12.6465553	11.4349994	10.4062403	9.5263756
33	27.9996925	23.9885636	20.7657918	18.1476457	16.0025492	14.2302296	12.7537900	11.5138884	10.4644406	9.5694324
34	28.7026659	24.4995917	21.1318367	18.4111978	16.1929040	14.3681411	12.8540094	11.5869337	10.5178354	9.6085749
35	29.4085801	24.9986193	21.4872201	18.6646132	16.3741943	14.4982464	12.9476723	11.6545682	10.5666215	9.6441590
36	30.1075050	25.4888425	21.8322525	18.9082820	16.5468517	14.6209871	13.0352078	11.7171928	10.6117628	9.6765082
37	30.7995099	25.9694534	22.1672354	19.1425788	16.7112873	14.7367803	13.1170166	11.7751785	10.6529934	9.7059165
38	31.4846633	26.4406406	22.4924616	19.3678642	16.8678927	14.8460192	13.1934735	11.8288690	10.6908196	9.7326514
39	32.1630330	26.9025888	22.8082151	19.5844848	17.0170407	14.9490747	13.2649285	11.8785824	10.7255226	9.7569558
40	32.8346861	27.3554792	23.1147720	19.7927739	17.1590864	15.0462969	13.3317088	11.9246133	10.7573602	9.7790507

Table A-4.   Ordinary Annuity Present Worth Factor. To Find P for a Given R Received at the End of Each Period.

$$P = R \frac{1 - (1 + i)^{-N}}{i}$$

N/i	1	2	3	4	5	6	7	8	9	10
41	33.4996892	27.7994895	23.4124000	19.9930518	17.2943680	15.1380159	13.3941204	11.9672346	10.7865690	9.7991370
42	34.1581081	28.2347936	23.7013592	20.1856267	17.4232076	15.2245433	13.4524490	12.0066987	10.8133660	9.8173973
43	34.8100081	28.6615623	23.9819021	20.3707949	17.5459120	15.3061729	13.5069617	12.0432395	10.8379505	9.8339975
44	35.4554535	29.0799631	24.2542739	20.5488413	17.6627733	15.3831820	13.5579081	12.0770736	10.8605050	9.8490887
45	36.0945084	29.4901599	24.5187125	20.7200397	17.7740698	15.4558321	13.6055216	12.1084015	10.8811973	9.8628079
46	36.7272361	29.8923136	24.7754491	20.8846536	17.8800665	15.5243699	13.6500202	12.1374088	10.9001810	9.8752799
47	37.3536991	30.2865820	25.0247078	21.0429361	17.9810157	15.5890282	13.6916076	12.1642674	10.9175972	9.8866181
48	37.9739595	30.6731196	25.2667066	21.1951309	18.0771578	15.6500266	13.7304744	12.1891365	10.9335755	9.8969255
49	38.5880787	31.0520780	25.5016569	21.3414720	18.1687217	15.7075723	13.7667985	12.2121634	10.9482344	9.9062959
50	39.1961175	31.4236059	25.7297640	21.4821846	18.2559255	15.7618606	13.8007463	12.2334846	10.9616829	9.9148145
51	39.7981382	31.7878489	25.9512272	21.6174852	18.3389766	15.8130761	13.8324732	12.2532265	10.9740210	9.9225556
52	40.3941942	32.1449499	26.1662400	21.7475819	18.4180730	15.8613925	13.8621245	12.2715060	10.9853404	9.9295987
53	40.9843507	32.4950489	26.3749903	21.8726749	18.4934028	15.9069741	13.8898359	12.2884315	10.9957251	9.9359999
54	41.5686641	32.8382833	26.5776605	21.9929567	18.5561456	15.9499755	13.9157345	12.3041033	11.0052524	9.9418171
55	42.1471922	33.1747875	26.7744276	22.1086122	18.6334720	15.9905430	13.9399388	12.3186141	11.0139930	9.9471065
56	42.7199922	33.5046936	26.9654637	22.2198194	18.6985447	16.0288141	13.9625596	12.3320501	11.0220120	9.9519150
57	43.2871210	33.8281310	27.1509357	22.3267494	18.7605188	16.0649190	13.9837006	12.3444908	11.0293688	9.9562864
58	43.8486347	34.1452265	27.3310055	22.4295668	18.8195417	16.0989802	14.0034585	12.3560100	11.0361181	9.9602603
59	44.4045888	34.4561044	27.5056306	22.5284296	18.8757540	16.1311134	14.0219238	12.3666760	11.0423102	9.9638730
60	44.9550384	34.7608867	27.6755637	22.6234900	18.9292895	16.1614277	14.0391812	12.3765518	11.0479910	9.9671573

Table A-4. Ordinary Annuity Present Worth Factor. To Find P for a Given R Received at the End of Each Period.

$$P = R\frac{1-(1+i)^{-N}}{i}$$

N/i	1	2	3	4	5	6	7	8	9	10
61	45.5000380	35.0596928	27.8403531	22.7148942	18.9902757	16.1900261	14.0553095	12.3856961	11.0532028	9.9701430
62	46.0396416	35.3526400	28.0003428	22.8027829	19.0288340	16.2170058	14.0703827	12.3941631	11.0579842	9.9728573
63	46.5739026	35.6398432	28.1556726	22.8872912	19.0750800	16.2424583	14.0844698	12.4020029	11.0623708	9.9753248
64	47.1028738	35.9214149	28.3064783	22.9685493	19.1191238	16.2664701	14.0976353	12.4092619	11.0663952	9.9775680
65	47.626078	36.1974655	28.4528915	23.0466820	19.1610703	16.2891227	14.1099396	12.4159832	11.0700874	9.9796073
66	48.1451552	36.4681035	28.5950403	23.1218096	19.2010194	16.3104931	14.1214388	12.422067	11.0734747	9.9814612
67	48.6585705	36.7334348	28.7330488	23.1940477	19.2390661	16.3306539	14.1321858	12.4279692	11.0765823	9.9831465
68	49.1669015	36.9935635	28.8670377	23.2635074	19.2753010	16.3496735	14.142298	12.4333048	11.0794333	9.9846786
69	49.6701995	37.2485917	28.9971240	23.3302956	19.3098105	16.3676165	14.1516166	12.4382452	11.0820489	9.9860715
70	50.1685143	37.4986193	29.1234214	23.3945150	19.3426766	16.3845439	14.1603893	12.4428196	11.0844485	9.9873377
71	50.6619954	37.7437444	29.2460401	23.4562644	19.3739778	16.4005131	14.1685882	12.4470552	11.0866500	9.9884888
72	51.1503915	37.9840631	29.3650875	23.5156388	19.4037883	16.4155784	14.1762506	12.4509770	11.0886697	9.9895353
73	51.6340510	38.2196697	29.4806675	23.5727297	19.4321794	16.4297909	14.1834118	12.4546084	11.0905227	9.9904866
74	52.1129218	38.4506566	29.5928811	23.6276247	19.4592185	16.4431990	14.1901045	12.4579707	11.0922226	9.9913515
75	52.5870512	38.6771143	29.7018263	23.6804083	19.4849700	16.4558481	14.1963593	12.4610840	11.0937822	9.9921377
76	53.0564864	38.8991317	29.8075983	23.7311619	19.5094952	16.4677812	14.2022050	12.4639667	11.0952131	9.9928525
77	53.5212736	39.1167958	29.9102896	23.7799633	19.5328526	16.4790389	14.2076682	12.4666358	11.0965258	9.9935022
78	53.9814590	39.3301919	30.0099899	23.8268878	19.5550977	16.4896593	14.2127740	12.4691072	11.0977300	9.9940930
79	54.4370882	39.539039	30.1067863	23.8720075	19.5762835	16.496786	14.2175458	12.4713956	11.0988349	9.9946300
80	54.8882061	39.745136	30.2007634	23.9153918	19.5964605	16.5091308	14.2220054	12.4735144	11.0999485	9.9951181

Table A-4.   Ordinary Annuity Present Worth Factor. To Find P for a Given R Received at the End of Each Period.

$$P = R\frac{1-(1+i)^{-N}}{i}$$

N/i	1	2	3	4	5	6	7	8	9	10
81	55.3348575	39.9456016	30.2920033	23.9571075	19.6156767	16.5180479	14.2261733	12.4754763	11.1007785	9.9955619
82	55.7770867	40.1427466	30.3305858	23.9972188	19.6339778	16.5266003	14.2300685	12.4772929	11.1016316	9.9959654
83	56.2149373	40.3360261	30.4665881	24.0357873	19.6514074	16.5343965	14.2337089	12.4789749	11.1024143	9.9963322
84	56.6484528	40.5255158	30.5500856	24.0728724	19.6680070	16.5418835	14.2371111	12.4805323	11.1031324	9.9966656
85	57.0776760	40.7112900	30.6311510	24.1085312	19.6838162	16.5489467	14.2402908	12.4819744	11.1037912	9.9969687
86	57.5026495	40.8934216	30.7098554	24.1428184	19.6998726	16.5556101	14.2432624	12.4833096	11.1043956	9.9972443
87	57.9234154	41.0719819	30.7862673	24.1757869	19.7132120	16.5619863	14.2460396	12.4845459	11.1049501	9.9974948
88	58.3400152	41.2470411	30.8604537	24.2074874	19.7266686	16.5678267	14.2486352	12.4856907	11.1054588	9.9977226
89	58.7524903	41.4186677	30.9243794	24.2379687	19.7398748	16.5734214	14.2510609	12.4867506	11.1059255	9.9979296
90	59.1608815	41.5869292	31.0024071	24.2672776	19.7522617	16.5786994	14.2533279	12.4877320	11.1063537	9.9981178
91	59.5652292	41.7518913	31.0702992	24.2954592	19.7640588	16.5836787	14.2554467	12.4886408	11.1067465	9.9982889
92	59.9655735	41.9136190	31.1362118	24.3225569	19.7752941	16.5883762	14.2574268	12.4894822	11.1071069	9.9984445
93	60.3619539	42.0721754	31.2002057	24.3486124	19.7859944	16.5928077	14.2592774	12.4902613	11.1074375	9.9985859
94	60.7544098	42.2276230	31.2623356	24.3736658	19.7961851	16.5969984	14.2610069	12.4909827	11.1077408	9.9987145
95	61.1429800	42.3800225	31.3226559	24.3977556	19.8058906	16.6009324	14.2626233	12.4916506	11.1080191	9.9988313
96	61.5277030	42.5294339	31.3812193	24.4209188	19.8151339	16.6046532	14.2641339	12.4922691	11.1082744	9.9989376
97	61.9086168	42.6759155	31.4380770	24.4431912	19.8239370	16.6081634	14.2655457	12.4928418	11.1085086	9.9990342
98	62.2857592	42.8195250	31.4932787	24.4646069	19.8323210	16.6114749	14.2668651	12.4933720	11.1087235	9.9991220
99	62.6591676	42.9603187	31.5468725	24.4851990	19.8403057	16.6145990	14.2680983	12.4938630	11.1089207	9.9992018
100	63.0288788	43.0983516	31.5989053	24.5049990	19.8479102	16.6175462	14.2692507	12.4943176	11.1091015	9.9992743

Table A-4. Ordinary Annuity Present Worth Factor. To Find *P* for a Given *R* Received at the End of Each Period.

$$P = R \frac{1 - (1+i)^{-N}}{i}$$

N/i	11	12	13	14	15	16	17	18	19	20
1	0.9009009	0.8928571	0.8849558	0.8771930	0.8695652	0.8620690	0.8547009	0.8474576	0.8403361	0.8333333
2	1.7125233	1.6900510	1.6681024	1.6466605	1.6257089	1.6052319	1.5852144	1.5656421	1.5465010	1.5277778
3	2.4437147	2.4018313	2.3611526	2.3216320	2.2832251	2.2458895	2.2095850	2.1742729	2.1399168	2.1064815
4	3.1024457	3.0373493	2.9744713	2.9137123	2.8549784	2.7981806	2.7432350	2.6900618	2.6385855	2.5887346
5	3.6958970	3.6047762	3.5172313	3.4330810	3.3521551	3.2742937	3.1993462	3.1271710	3.0576349	2.9906121
6	4.2305379	4.1114073	3.9975498	3.8886675	3.7844827	3.6847359	3.5891848	3.4976026	3.4097772	3.3255101
7	4.7121963	4.5637565	4.4226104	4.2883048	4.1604197	4.0385654	3.9223801	3.8115276	3.7056951	3.6045918
8	5.1461228	4.9676398	4.7987703	4.6388639	4.4873215	4.3435909	4.2071625	4.0775658	3.9543657	3.8371598
9	5.5370475	5.3282498	5.1316551	4.9463718	4.7715839	4.6065439	4.4505662	4.3030218	4.1633325	4.0309665
10	5.8892320	5.6502230	5.4262435	5.2161156	5.0187686	4.8332275	4.6586036	4.4940863	4.3389349	4.1924721
11	6.2065153	5.9376991	5.6869411	5.4527330	5.2337118	5.0286444	4.8364134	4.6560053	4.4864999	4.3270601
12	6.4923561	6.1943742	5.9176470	5.6602921	5.4206190	5.1971072	4.9883875	4.7932249	4.6105041	4.4392167
13	6.7498704	6.4235494	6.1218115	5.8423615	5.5831470	5.3423338	5.1182799	4.9095126	4.7147093	4.5326806
14	6.9818652	6.6281682	6.3024881	6.0020715	5.7244756	5.4675291	5.2292991	5.0080615	4.8022768	4.6105672
15	7.1908696	6.8108645	6.4623788	6.1421680	5.8473701	5.5754562	5.3241872	5.0915776	4.8758628	4.6754726
16	7.3791618	6.9739862	6.6038751	6.2650596	5.9542349	5.6684967	5.4052882	5.1623539	4.9376998	4.7295605
17	7.5487944	7.1196305	6.7290930	6.3728593	6.0471608	5.7487040	5.4746053	5.2223338	4.9896637	4.7746338
18	7.7016166	7.2496701	6.8399053	6.4674205	6.1279659	5.8178483	5.5338507	5.2731642	5.0333309	4.8121948
19	7.8392942	7.3657769	6.9379693	6.5503688	6.1982312	5.8774554	5.5844878	5.3162409	5.0700259	4.8434957
20	7.9633281	7.4694436	7.0247516	6.6231306	6.2593315	5.9288409	5.6277673	5.3557465	5.1008621	4.8695797

Table A-4. Ordinary Annuity Present Worth Factor. To Find P for a Given R Received at the End of Each Period.

$$P = R\frac{1 - (1 + i)^{-N}}{i}$$

N/i	11	12	13	14	15	16	17	18	19	20
21	8.0750704	7.5620032	7.1015501	6.6865566	6.3124622	5.9731387	5.6647584	5.3836835	5.1267749	4.8913164
22	8.1757391	7.6446457	7.1695133	6.7429444	6.3586627	6.0113265	5.6963747	5.4099012	5.1485503	4.9094304
23	8.2664316	7.7184337	7.2296578	6.7920565	6.3988372	6.0442470	5.7233972	5.4321197	5.1668490	4.9245253
24	8.3481366	7.7843158	7.2828830	6.8351373	6.4337714	6.0726267	5.7464933	5.4509489	5.1822261	4.9371044
25	8.4217447	7.8431391	7.3299850	6.8729274	6.4641491	6.0970920	5.7662336	5.4669058	5.1951480	4.9475870
26	8.4880583	7.8956599	7.3716681	6.9060767	6.4905644	6.1181827	5.7831056	5.4804287	5.2060067	4.9563225
27	8.5478002	7.9425535	7.4085559	6.9351550	6.5135343	6.1363644	5.7975262	5.4918887	5.2151317	4.9636021
28	8.6016218	7.9944228	7.4411999	6.9606623	6.5335081	6.1520383	5.8098514	5.5016006	5.2227997	4.9696684
29	8.6501098	8.0218060	7.4700884	6.9830371	6.5508766	6.1655503	5.8203859	5.5098310	5.2292445	4.9747237
30	8.6937926	8.0551840	7.4956534	7.0026641	6.5659796	6.1771985	5.8293896	5.5160060	5.2346684	4.9789364
31	8.7331465	8.0849857	7.5182774	7.0198808	6.5791127	6.1872401	5.8370851	5.5227169	5.2392087	4.9824470
32	8.7688004	8.1115944	7.5382986	7.0349832	6.5905328	6.1958966	5.8436625	5.5277262	5.2430325	4.9853725
33	8.8005409	8.1353521	7.5560164	7.0482308	6.6004633	6.2033592	5.8492842	5.5319713	5.2462458	4.9878104
34	8.8293161	8.1565644	7.5716960	7.0598516	6.6090995	6.2097924	5.8540891	5.5355689	5.2489461	4.9898420
35	8.8552398	8.1755039	7.5855716	7.0700453	6.6166074	6.2153383	5.8581958	5.5386177	5.2512152	4.9915350
36	8.8785944	8.1924142	7.5978510	7.0789871	6.6231369	6.2201192	5.8617058	5.5412015	5.2531220	4.9929458
37	8.8996346	8.2075127	7.6087177	7.0866308	6.6288147	6.2242407	5.8647058	5.5433911	5.2547244	4.9941215
38	8.9185897	8.2209935	7.6183343	7.0937112	6.6337519	6.2277937	5.8672699	5.5452467	5.2560709	4.9951013
39	8.9356664	8.2330299	7.6266445	7.0997467	6.6380451	6.2308566	5.8694615	5.5468192	5.2572024	4.9959177
40	8.9510508	8.2437767	7.6343756	7.1050409	6.6417784	6.2334971	5.8713346	5.5481519	5.2581533	4.9965981

Table A-4. Ordinary Annuity Present Worth Factor. To Find P for a Given R Received at the End of Each Period.

$$P = R \frac{1 - (1+i)^{-N}}{i}$$

N/i	11	12	13	14	15	16	17	18	19	20
41	8.9649106	8.2533720	7.6410404	7.1096850	6.6450247	6.2357734	5.8729355	5.5492813	5.2589524	4.9971651
42	8.9773970	8.2619393	7.6469384	7.1137588	6.6478475	6.2377357	5.8743039	5.5502384	5.2596238	4.9976376
43	8.9986459	8.2695887	7.6521579	7.1173323	6.6503022	6.2394273	5.8754734	5.5510495	5.2601881	4.9980313
44	8.9987801	8.2764185	7.6567769	7.1204669	6.6524367	6.2408856	5.8764730	5.5517368	5.2606623	4.9983594
45	9.0079100	8.2825165	7.6608645	7.1232166	6.6542928	6.2421428	5.8773273	5.5523193	5.2610607	4.9986329
46	9.0161351	8.2879611	7.6644819	7.1256286	6.6559068	6.2432265	5.8780576	5.5528130	5.2613956	4.9988607
47	9.0235452	8.2928225	7.6676831	7.1277444	6.6573102	6.2441608	5.8786817	5.5532314	5.2616769	4.9990506
48	9.0302209	8.2971629	7.6705160	7.1296003	6.6585306	6.2449962	5.8792151	5.5535859	5.2619134	4.9992088
49	9.0362350	8.3010383	7.6730230	7.1312284	6.6595919	6.2456605	5.8796710	5.5538864	5.2621121	4.9993407
50	9.0416532	8.3044985	7.6752416	7.1326565	6.6605147	6.2462591	5.8800607	5.5541410	5.2622791	4.9994506

N/i	21	22	23	24	25	26	27	28	29	30
1	0.8264463	0.8196721	0.8130081	0.8064516	0.8000000	0.7936508	0.7874016	0.7812500	0.7751938	0.7692308
2	1.5094597	1.4915345	1.4739903	1.4568158	1.4400000	1.4235324	1.4074028	1.3916016	1.3761192	1.3609467
3	2.0739337	2.0422414	2.0113743	1.9813031	1.9520000	1.9234484	1.8955928	1.8684387	1.8419529	1.8116129
4	2.5404410	2.4936405	2.4482718	2.4042767	2.3616000	2.3201892	2.2799943	2.2409678	2.2030643	2.1662407
5	2.9259843	2.8636398	2.8034730	2.7453844	2.6892800	2.6350708	2.5826727	2.5320061	2.4829955	2.4355698
6	3.2446152	3.1669178	3.0922545	3.0204713	2.9514240	2.8849768	2.8210021	2.7593797	2.6999965	2.6427460
7	3.5079464	3.4155064	3.3270361	3.2423156	3.1611392	3.0833149	3.0086631	2.9370154	2.8682144	2.8021123
8	3.7255755	3.6192676	3.5179156	3.4212222	3.3289114	3.2407261	3.1564276	3.0757933	2.9996158	2.9247018
9	3.9054343	3.7862849	3.6731021	3.5655018	3.4631291	3.3656557	3.2727777	3.1842135	3.0997022	3.0190013
10	4.0540780	3.9231843	3.7992700	3.6818563	3.5705033	3.4640061	3.3643919	3.2689168	3.1780637	3.0915395

Table A-4   Ordinary Annuity Present Worth Factor. To Find P for a Given R Received at the End of Each Period.

$$P = R\frac{1 - (1 + i)^{-N}}{i}$$

N/i	21	22	23	24	25	26	27	28	29	30
11	4.1769239	4.0355970	3.9018455	3.7756906	3.656026	3.5434969	3.4365290	3.3350913	3.238091	3.1473381
12	4.2784495	4.1273746	3.9852403	3.8513634	3.7251221	3.6059499	3.4933299	3.3867900	3.2858885	3.1902601
13	4.3623550	4.2027661	4.0530409	3.9123898	3.7800977	3.6555158	3.5380551	3.4271797	3.3224019	3.2232770
14	4.4316983	4.2645623	4.1081633	3.9616047	3.8240781	3.6948538	3.5732717	3.4587342	3.3506992	3.2486746
15	4.4890069	4.3152150	4.1529783	4.0012941	3.8592625	3.7260745	3.6010013	3.4833861	3.3726350	3.2682112
16	4.5363693	4.3567336	4.1894132	4.0333017	3.8874100	3.7508527	3.6228357	3.5026454	3.3896396	3.2832394
17	4.5755118	4.3907653	4.2190352	4.0591143	3.9099280	3.7705180	3.6400281	3.5176917	3.4028214	3.2947995
18	4.6078610	4.4186601	4.2431180	4.0799309	3.9279424	3.7861254	3.6535654	3.5294466	3.4130398	3.3036920
19	4.6345959	4.4415546	4.2626976	4.0967184	3.9423539	3.7985123	3.6642248	3.5386302	3.4209611	3.3105323
20	4.6556908	4.4602661	4.2786159	4.1102568	3.9538831	3.8083431	3.6726179	3.5458048	3.4271016	3.3157941
21	4.6749511	4.4756279	4.2915577	4.1211748	3.9631065	3.8161453	3.6792267	3.5514100	3.4318617	3.3198416
22	4.6900422	4.4882196	4.3020794	4.1299797	3.9704952	3.8223375	3.6844305	3.5557891	3.4355517	3.3229551
23	4.7025142	4.4985407	4.3106337	4.1370804	3.9763882	3.8272520	3.6885279	3.5592102	3.4384122	3.3253500
24	4.7128217	4.5070006	4.3175883	4.1428068	3.9811105	3.8311524	3.6917543	3.5618830	3.4406296	3.3271923
25	4.7213402	4.5139349	4.3232425	4.1474248	3.9848884	3.8342479	3.6942947	3.5639711	3.4423485	3.3286095
26	4.7283804	4.5196188	4.3278395	4.1511491	3.9879107	3.8367047	3.6962950	3.5655024	3.4436810	3.3296996
27	4.7341986	4.5242777	4.3315768	4.1541525	3.9903286	3.8386545	3.6978701	3.5668769	3.4447140	3.3305382
28	4.7390071	4.5280965	4.3346153	4.1565746	3.9922629	3.8402020	3.6991103	3.5678726	3.4455147	3.3311832
29	4.7429811	4.5312266	4.3370856	4.1585279	3.9938103	3.8414302	3.7000869	3.5686504	3.4461354	3.3316794
30	4.7462654	4.5337923	4.3390940	4.1601031	3.9950482	3.8424049	3.7008558	3.5692582	3.4466166	3.3320611

Table A-4 Ordinary Annuity Present Worth Factor. To Find P for a Given R Received at the End of Each Period.

$$P = R\frac{1 - (1 + i)^{-N}}{i}$$

N/i	21	22	23	24	25	26	27	28	29	30
31	4.7489797	4.5358953	4.3407268	4.1613735	3.9960386	3.8431785	3.7014613	3.5697329	3.4469896	3.3323547
32	4.7512229	4.5376191	4.3420543	4.1623980	3.9968309	3.8437924	3.7019380	3.5701039	3.4472788	3.3325805
33	4.7530767	4.5390321	4.3431336	4.1632242	3.9974647	3.8442797	3.7023134	3.5703936	3.4475029	3.3327542
34	4.7546089	4.5401902	4.3440111	4.1638905	3.9979718	3.8446664	3.7026090	3.5706200	3.4476767	3.3328879
35	4.7558751	4.5411395	4.3447244	4.1644278	3.9983774	3.8449734	3.7028417	3.5707969	3.4478114	3.3329907
36	4.7569216	4.5419176	4.3453044	4.1648611	3.9987019	3.8452170	3.7030250	3.5709351	3.4479158	3.3330697
37	4.7577864	4.5425554	4.3457759	4.1652106	3.9989615	3.8454103	3.7031693	3.5710430	3.4479967	3.3331306
38	4.7585012	4.5430782	4.3461593	4.1654924	3.9991692	3.8455637	3.7032829	3.5711274	3.4480595	3.3331774
39	4.7590919	4.5435067	4.3464710	4.1657197	3.9993354	3.8456855	3.7033724	3.5711933	3.4481081	3.3332134
40	4.7595801	4.5438580	4.3467244	4.1659030	3.9994683	3.8457821	3.7034428	3.5712447	3.4481458	3.3332410
41	4.7599835	4.5441459	4.3469304	4.1660508	3.9995746	3.8458588	3.7034983	3.5712849	3.4481751	3.3332623
42	4.7603170	4.5443819	4.3470979	4.1661700	3.9996597	3.8459197	3.7035419	3.5713164	3.4481977	3.3332787
43	4.7605925	4.5445753	4.3472340	4.1662661	3.9997278	3.8459680	3.7035763	3.5713409	3.4482153	3.3332913
44	4.7608203	4.5447339	4.3473448	4.1663436	3.9997822	3.8460064	3.7036034	3.5713601	3.4482289	3.3333010
45	4.7610085	4.5448638	4.3474348	4.1664062	3.9998258	3.8460368	3.7036247	3.5713751	3.4482395	3.3333085
46	4.7611640	4.5449703	4.3475079	4.1664566	3.9998606	3.8460610	3.7036415	3.5713868	3.4482476	3.3333142
47	4.7612926	4.5450577	4.3475674	4.1664972	3.9998885	3.8460801	3.7036547	3.5713959	3.4482540	3.3333186
48	4.7613988	4.5451292	4.3476158	4.1665300	3.9999108	3.8460953	3.7036652	3.5714031	3.4482589	3.3333220
49	4.7614866	4.5451879	4.3476551	4.1665565	3.9999286	3.8461074	3.7036733	3.5714086	3.4482627	3.3333246
50	4.7615592	4.5452360	4.3476871	4.1665778	3.9999429	3.8461170	3.7036798	3.5714130	3.4482657	3.3333266

Table A-4.   Ordinary Annuity Present Worth Factor. To Find P for a Given R Received at the End of Each Period.

$$P = R \frac{1 - (1+i)^{-N}}{i}$$

N/i	31	32	33	34	35	36	37	38	39	40
1	0.7633588	0.7575758	0.7518797	0.7462687	0.7407407	0.7352941	0.7299270	0.7246377	0.7194245	0.7142857
2	1.3460754	1.3314968	1.3172028	1.3031856	1.2894376	1.2759516	1.2627204	1.2497375	1.2369960	1.2244898
3	1.7908973	1.7662854	1.7422577	1.7187952	1.6958797	1.6734938	1.6516208	1.6302445	1.6093497	1.5889213
4	2.1304559	2.0956708	2.0618479	2.0289516	1.9969479	1.9658043	1.9354896	1.9059743	1.8772300	1.8492295
5	2.3896610	2.3452051	2.3021413	2.2604117	2.2199614	2.1807384	2.1426931	2.1057785	2.0699496	2.0351639
6	2.5875275	2.5342463	2.4828130	2.4331430	2.3851566	2.3387783	2.2993366	2.2505541	2.2085968	2.1679742
7	2.7385706	2.6774593	2.6186564	2.5620470	2.5075234	2.4549840	2.4043333	2.3554812	2.3083431	2.2628387
8	2.8538707	2.7859540	2.7207943	2.6582441	2.5981655	2.5404294	2.4849148	2.4315081	2.3801029	2.3305991
9	2.9418860	2.8681470	2.7975897	2.7300329	2.6653078	2.6032569	2.5437334	2.4866001	2.4317287	2.3789994
10	3.0090733	2.9304144	2.8553306	2.7836066	2.7150428	2.6494536	2.5866667	2.5265218	2.4688696	2.4135710
11	3.0603613	2.9775867	2.8997448	2.8235870	2.7518836	2.6834218	2.6180049	2.5554506	2.4955896	2.4382650
12	3.0995124	3.0133232	2.9313871	2.8534232	2.7791730	2.7083984	2.6408795	2.5764135	2.5148127	2.4559036
13	3.1293988	3.0403964	2.9559301	2.8756889	2.7993874	2.7267635	2.6575763	2.5916040	2.5286422	2.4685025
14	3.1522128	3.0609064	2.9743836	2.8923052	2.8143610	2.7402673	2.6697637	2.6026116	2.5385915	2.4775018
15	3.1696281	3.0764442	2.9882583	2.9047053	2.8254526	2.7501965	2.6786596	2.6105881	2.5457493	2.4839299
16	3.1829922	3.0882153	2.9996905	2.9139592	2.8336686	2.7574975	2.6851530	2.6163682	2.5508988	2.4885213
17	3.1930704	3.0971328	3.0065342	2.9208651	2.8397545	2.7628658	2.6899927	2.6205567	2.5546034	2.4918010
18	3.2008171	3.1038885	3.0124317	2.9260187	2.8442626	2.7668131	2.6933523	2.6235918	2.5572687	2.4941435
19	3.2067306	3.1090064	3.0168660	2.9298647	2.8476019	2.7697155	2.6958776	2.6257911	2.5591861	2.4958168
20	3.2112447	3.1128837	3.0202000	2.9327349	2.8500755	2.7718496	2.6977209	2.6273849	2.5605655	2.4970120

Table A-4. Ordinary Annuity Present Worth Factor. To Find *P* for a Given *R* Received at the End of Each Period.

$$P = R \frac{1 - (1 + i)^{-N}}{i}$$

N/i	31	32	33	34	35	36	37	38	39	40
21	3.2146906	3.1158210	3.0227067	2.9348768	2.8519078	2.7734188	2.6990663	2.6285398	2.5615579	2.4978657
22	3.2173211	3.1180462	3.0245915	2.9364752	2.8532650	2.7745727	2.7000484	2.6293766	2.5622719	2.4984755
23	3.2193291	3.1197320	3.0260087	2.9376681	2.8542704	2.7754211	2.7007653	2.6299831	2.5627855	2.4989111
24	3.2208619	3.1210091	3.0270742	2.9385583	2.8550151	2.7760449	2.7012885	2.6304225	2.5631551	2.4992222
25	3.2220320	3.1219766	3.0278753	2.9392226	2.8555667	2.7765036	2.7016705	2.6307410	2.5634209	2.4994444
26	3.2229252	3.1227095	3.0284777	2.9397183	2.8559754	2.7768409	2.7019492	2.6309717	2.5636122	2.4996032
27	3.2236070	3.1232648	3.0289306	2.9400883	2.8562780	2.7770889	2.7021527	2.6311389	2.5637498	2.4997165
28	3.2241275	3.1236854	3.0292711	2.9403644	2.8565023	2.7772712	2.7023013	2.6312601	2.5638487	2.4997975
29	3.2245248	3.1240041	3.0295272	2.9405705	2.8566683	2.7774053	2.7024097	2.6313479	2.5639200	2.4998554
30	3.2248281	3.1242455	3.0297197	2.9407242	2.8567914	2.7775039	2.7024888	2.6314115	2.5639712	2.4998967
31	3.2250596	3.1244284	3.0298644	2.9408390	2.8568825	2.7775764	2.7025466	2.6314576	2.5640081	2.4999262
32	3.2252363	3.1245670	3.0299732	2.9409246	2.8569500	2.7776297	2.7025887	2.6314910	2.5640346	2.4999473
33	3.2253713	3.1246720	3.0300551	2.9409885	2.8570000	2.7776689	2.7026195	2.6315152	2.5640536	2.4999624
34	3.2254742	3.1247515	3.0301166	2.9410362	2.8570370	2.7776977	2.7026420	2.6315328	2.5640674	2.4999731
35	3.2255529	3.1248117	3.0301629	2.9410718	2.8570645	2.7777189	2.7026584	2.6315455	2.5640772	2.4999808
36	3.2256129	3.1248574	3.0301976	2.9410984	2.8570848	2.7777345	2.7026704	2.6315547	2.5640844	2.4999863
37	3.2256587	3.1248920	3.0302238	2.9411182	2.8570998	2.7777460	2.7026791	2.6315614	2.5640895	2.4999902
38	3.2256936	3.1249181	3.0302434	2.9411330	2.8571110	2.7777544	2.7026855	2.6315662	2.5640931	2.4999930
39	3.2257203	3.1249380	3.0302582	2.9411440	2.8571193	2.7777606	2.7026901	2.6315697	2.5640958	2.4999950
40	3.2257407	3.1249530	3.0302693	2.9411522	2.8571254	2.7777651	2.7026935	2.6315723	2.5640977	2.4999964

Table A-4. Ordinary Annuity Present Worth Factor. To Find P for a Given R Received at the End of Each Period.

$$P = R \frac{1 - (1 + i)^{-N}}{i}$$

N/i	31	32	33	34	35	36	37	38	39	40
41	3.2257563	3.1249644	3.0302777	2.9411584	2.8571299	2.7777685	2.7026960	2.6315741	2.5640991	2.4999974
42	3.2257681	3.1249730	3.0302840	2.9411630	2.8571333	2.7777709	2.7026978	2.6315754	2.5641000	2.4999982
43	3.2257772	3.1249796	3.0302887	2.9411664	2.8571358	2.7777727	2.7026991	2.6315764	2.5641007	2.4999987
44	3.2257841	3.1249845	3.0302923	2.9411690	2.8571376	2.7777741	2.7027001	2.6315771	2.5641013	2.4999991
45	3.2257894	3.1249883	3.0302949	2.9411709	2.8571390	2.7777751	2.7027008	2.6315776	2.5641016	2.4999993
46	3.2257934	3.1249911	3.0302969	2.9411723	2.8571400	2.7777758	2.7027013	2.6315780	2.5641019	2.4999995
47	3.2257965	3.1249933	3.0302985	2.9411733	2.8571407	2.7777763	2.7027017	2.6315782	2.5641021	2.4999997
48	3.2257989	3.1249949	3.0302996	2.9411741	2.8571413	2.7777767	2.7027020	2.6315784	2.5641022	2.4999998
49	3.2258007	3.1249961	3.0303004	2.9411747	2.8571417	2.7777770	2.7027022	2.6315786	2.5641023	2.4999998
50	3.2258020	3.1249971	3.0303011	2.9411752	2.8571420	2.7777772	2.7027023	2.6315787	2.5641024	2.4999999

Index